Crisis and Decline

THE FRENCH SOCIALIST PARTY
IN THE POPULAR FRONT ERA

Léon Blum. (Courtesy of French Embassy Press and Information Division.)

Crisis and Decline

THE FRENCH SOCIALIST PARTY
IN THE POPULAR FRONT ERA

Nathanael Greene

CORNELL UNIVERSITY PRESS

Ithaca, New York

Library of Congress Catalog Card Number: 68–31072

PRINTED IN THE UNITED STATES OF AMERICA
BY KINGSPORT PRESS, INC.

For Phyllis

Preface

On June 4, 1936, as the result of the Popular Front's electoral triumph and at the call of a very apprehensive President of the Republic, Léon Blum assumed power at the head of the first government under Socialist direction in the history of the Third Republic. In an atmosphere of crisis and euphoria, created largely by the intoxicating optimism and impatient expectation of much of France's working class, Blum inaugurated an "experiment" which he believed to be unique in the history of his nation. Armed with an apparent popular mandate and an expression of confidence and trust from his party, but pledged to respect "Republican legality," the veteran Socialist leader undertook his mission to "restore France's confidence in herself" and to revive faith in democracy in a continent darkened by fascism. Recent scholarship has revealed how dim were his chances of real achievement: his principal political partners, the Radicals and the Communists, shared few of his aims, even fewer of his ideals; his opposition, within the parliament and without, momentarily on the defensive, possessed an ample arsenal of counter-weapons—and the will to employ them ruthlessly. But what was the condition of the Socialist party, itself, at the hub of the Popular Front, albeit reluctantly, and for the first time at the helm of government? Was it prepared to "exercise power" with a united will, and was it capable of responding to Blum's call to participate in the task of "rejuvenating the old historic nation"[1] by a massive infusion of its energy and its aspirations into the life of the nation?

Surely the response must be an unequivocal no: the Socialist

[1] These are Blum's words, taken from a speech to the National Congress of the Socialist Party in 1936. Léon Blum, *L'Exercice du pouvoir* (Paris, 1937), 65; Léon Blum, *L'Oeuvre, 1934–1937* (Paris, 1964), 269.

party was neither ready nor able to fulfill the tasks required of it. Its energy was to be dissipated by internal conflicts, themselves a consequence of contradictory aspirations; by 1938 the party's pronouncements were to be marked by a purposeful ambiguity. Even in 1936, on the eve of Blum's assumption of power, any attempt to define a specifically "Socialist" international policy and —to a lesser degree—domestic policy, is futile. Examination of the party's leaders, the groupings within its so-called Center majority, and its extraordinary regional diversification, betrays its fragility. Its unity was superficial, even at the pinnacle of leadership, where its two major figures spoke with contrasting voices but declined to perceive the contrast; even its left wing was sharply divided. The policies of its leaders do not wholly defy rational analysis, but the obvious prerequisite to an understanding of the dreary evolution of the Socialist party during the years 1936–1939 must be the recognition that all of these leaders were addicted to certain fixed notions about the nature and role of socialism. Caught in a web of conflicting beliefs, the party was progressively reduced to impotence and finally to humiliation. Thus the history of the party in this period cannot be explained simply in terms of a conflict between belief and reality; it is comprehensible only as a conflict among many beliefs, a conflict intensified first by increasing international tension and second by disappointments on the domestic scene. In 1936, the fragility of this party was effectively masked by its expression of confidence in its leader; awareness of the challenge and of the opportunity presented by the "exercise of power," as well as by a vague and lofty sentiment of common purpose, momentarily provided the essential cement of unity. A fragile party was not a fragmented party, but if fragmentation finally came in 1938 and 1939, its origins are to be found in the years prior to 1936.

In 1936 the philosopher Gabriel Marcel thought that he detected a "spirit of surrender . . . concealed . . . by an antifascist rhetoric in which no clear intelligence could place any trust."[2] Perhaps he had the S.F.I.O. in mind. Political habits, once entrenched, may acquire a life and an inertia of their own; in the

[2] H. Stuart Hughes, *The Obstructed Path: French Social Thought in the Years of Desperation, 1930–1960* (New York, 1968), 86.

case of the S.F.I.O. such habits may have reinforced older ideological inclinations, even in the face of the apparent threat of fascism. The intertwining of political habits and ideological inclinations may well have predetermined the response of the S.F.I.O. to the "exercise of power," but the crises of those months of power, especially the international crisis generated by the war in Spain, made it certain that the party, in its majority, could not sustain the antifascist reflex that had carried it to power. I propose, then, to follow two distinct but inseparable lines of inquiry: the first, the ideological diversity of the party, both obvious and hidden, and the subsequent sharpening of ideological divides during the year of power and thereafter; the second, the political posture of the party, with attention to the behavior of Socialist elites, especially deputies, in determining the attitudes of the rank and file. In attempting this dual analysis I am persuaded that the major factor in the decline of the S.F.I.O. as a viable political unit was not the accumulated disappointments—the "poisoned fruits," as a militant of the Left put it—of the "exercise of power," or the apparent impossibility of carrying out a democratization of French society within the existing constitutional framework, or the fact that, as a veteran opposition party, Socialists were ill prepared to become a government party, but rather the impact of international crisis, indeed the specter of general war, upon the party. My emphasis, then, falls upon foreign affairs as a catalyst to the decomposition of the S.F.I.O., a decomposition which became public knowledge after the Munich conference in 1938. Finally, I hope to demonstrate that the S.F.I.O. reacted to events; only rarely did it act to control them.

I wish to express my gratitude to Professor H. Stuart Hughes of Harvard University for his guidance and patient counsel, and to Professors Jean-Baptiste Duroselle of the Sorbonne and René Rémond of the Institut d'Etudes Politiques for their advice and interest in this study. The following persons were very generous in their assistance: Robert Blum, André Blumel, Jean Castagnez, Gaston Cusin, Lucien Laurat, Daniel Mayer, Jules Moch, Alexandre Rauzy, Fernand Roucayrol, Etienne Weill-Raynal, and Jean Zyromski. Special mention should be made of the kindness given to the author by the late Oreste Rosenfeld. Generous also were the anonymous authorities who selected the author to receive a Fulbright grant, and the trustees of Wesleyan University, who furnished a research grant. To all of these persons I owe my appreciation.

N. G.

Middletown, Connecticut
January, 1968

Contents

Illustrations

Tables

Crisis and Decline

THE FRENCH SOCIALIST PARTY
IN THE POPULAR FRONT ERA

1

An Introduction to the French Socialist Party in the 1930's

FROM SCHISM TO "EXERCISE OF POWER"

The schism of the French Socialist party at the Congress of Tours in 1920 was the product of irreconcilable differences within its ranks over the question of adherence to the Communist Third International. The success of the Bolshevik Revolution in Russia had generated a powerful wave of enthusiasm in French socialist circles, and—thanks to working-class effervescence, chargin over the electoral victory of the Right in 1919, and the potent legacy of syndicalism—the appeal of Moscow was simply too attractive to be denied for the great majority of the delegates.[1] The badly defeated minority, refusing to accept the decision of its comrades, launched a new Socialist party, but retained the name of the old party: *Section Française de l'Internationale Ouvrière* (S.F.I.O.). Essentially the S.F.I.O. was a union of two minorities of the congress, the *Reconstructeurs* and the *Résistance*. The *Reconstructeurs,* led by Jean Longuet, a grandson of Karl Marx, and Paul Faure, a young and articulate spokesman of the pacifist wing of the party during the World War, had supported adherence with "reservations," but had recognized fully that these "reservations" stood no chance of being adopted, and thus had intended them to serve as a justification for an inevitable schism rather than as serious proposals. The *Résistance,* led by Léon Blum, an

---

[1] Parti Socialiste S.F.I.O., *XVIIIᵉ Congrès National, Compte rendu sténographique* (Paris, 1921), 478; Annie Kriegel, *Le Congrès de Tours* (Paris, 1964), 241.

1

intimate of Jaurès although he had entered active politics only in 1919, had been resolutely hostile to adherence, and his vigorous speech to the congress in defense of the principles of the "old house" was to become the gospel of the new Socialist party. Blum denounced Bolshevism as a narrow creed based upon its own peculiar experience and characterized it as a brutal departure from the traditions of European socialism. Its errors, he declared, were staggering: it wrongly equated the seizure of political power with social revolution, its concept of party organization was a thorough perversion of the democratic process, it threatened the independence of the trade unions from party control, and it denied that the workers could fight to defend their nation. Since the majority of the congress, by voting to join the Third International, signaled that it subscribed to these heresies, Blum asserted that there could be no solution other than schism in order to ensure the continued existence of a Socialist party committed to the preservation of traditional socialist doctrines.[2]

The rebuilding of the S.F.I.O. was begun immediately after the conclusion of the congress with the appointment of Paul Faure as General Secretary—a position of critical importance in the development of party cadres—and the designation of Léon Blum as leader of the Socialist parliamentarians (known as the parliamentary group), whose precongress strength of sixty-eight was reduced by only thirteen defections to the Communist party. Serious dislocation at the local level was avoided by the fidelity of many Socialist officeholders and leaders of important *fédérations* (the unit of party organization in each department) to the S.F.I.O.[3] Deprived of *L'Humanité,* the newspaper founded by Jean Jaurès, the party's central organ became Longuet's relatively insignificant journal *Le Populaire,* but the S.F.I.O. was able to maintain control of several influential provincial dailies, among them *Le Midi Socialiste* of Toulouse and *Le Populaire du Centre* of Limoges. The democratic structure of the old party was retained, thus affording

---

[2] *XVIIIe Congrès National,* 243–275, *passim.*

[3] Daniel Ligou, *Histoire du socialisme en France, 1871–1961* (Paris, 1962), 333; Marcel Prélot, *L'Evolution politique du socialisme en France, 1789–1934* (Paris, 1939), 234; Georges Lefranc, *Le Mouvement socialiste sous la Troisième République (1875–1940)* (Paris, 1963), 241–264, *passim.*

representation to all *tendances* (factions) [4] on the executive bodies proportionate to their strength at the most recent National Congress, which was the party's highest authority.[5] The policies decreed by the National Congress were executed ordinarily by the Permanent Administrative Committee (C.A.P.) and exceptionally by the National Council, which was convoked twice a year and in emergencies; technically, neither body was empowered to make policy, but the executive powers of both organs were sufficiently elastic to provide for effective action in most contingencies.

During the first interwar decade the S.F.I.O. augmented its membership steadily, increasing from 35,000 in 1921 to 50,000 in 1923, and to 119,000 in 1929.[6] It profited also from the return to its ranks of many prominent figures who either became disenchanted with, or were expelled by, the Communist Party, notably L.-O. Frossard, Maurice Paz, Amedée Dunois, and Charles Lussy. The party fared well at the ballot box: after agonizing debate, it participated in the *Cartel des Gauches* in 1924, winning 104 seats in the Chamber of Deputies; in 1928, it received 1,698,000 votes and 101 Socialist deputies were returned. The latter election revealed the decline of the Socialist appeal in areas heavily populated with workers to the benefit of the Communists—Léon Blum himself was defeated in Paris by the ex-pastry chef Jacques Duclos, although he later secured a seat in a by-election in the Aude. On the other hand, the Socialists increased their vote handsomely in the essentially rural and semirural areas of the Massif Central,

[4] *Tendance* is difficult to translate properly; literally it translates "tendency" or "leaning"; faction implies a degree of organization often not associated with these groupings. The party defined a *tendance* as a group which offered a motion at a congress and received enough support to merit representation on the executive organs.

[5] The National Congress was composed of delegates from the *fédérations*, with each *fédération* possessing a bloc of votes proportionate to the number of members in it; one or two delegates might hold several hundred *mandats*. A congress was a gathering of several hundred delegates at most, and not "three or four thousand" as one commentator has claimed. See John T. Marcus, *French Socialism in the Crisis Years, 1933–1936: Fascism and the French Left* (New York, 1958), 16.

[6] Paul Faure et Jean-Baptiste Séverac, *Le Parti Socialiste, ses principes, son organisation, son action* (Paris, 1936), 20. D. Ligou, *op. cit.*, 337, believes these figures to be in excess of the actual number of members.

the Loire valley, Languedoc, and Provence, areas which were formerly strongholds of the Radical party.

Electoral success, however, threatened to renew the old quarrel over the question of participation in power with a "bourgeois" party. Prior to Blum's formulation of a theory called the "exercise of power" in 1925, a majority of the party, believing in the necessity to conquer power by all means—including legal ones—in order to carry out a socialist revolution, coexisted uneasily with a minority which preferred the "reformist" tactic of participation in order to ameliorate working-class conditions. Designed to placate both camps and to provide a solution more suited to the realities of French politics, Blum's theory sanctioned Socialist acceptance of governmental responsibility within the existing political system as long as Socialists were assured of direction of the government by their "bourgeois" partners. The Socialists would reciprocate by adhering strictly to "Republican legality," and the capitalist economic structure would remain essentially untouched while measures favorable to the working class would be enacted. In other words, Socialists would permit Radicals to sit in a Socialist-dominated cabinet, but would not themselves participate in a cabinet led by a Radical. Instead of appeasing the intraparty conflict, Blum's theory may have only clarified the division within the party. An amorphous majority, known as the Center or Blum-Faure majority, maintained a keen opposition to participation under Radical tutelage, but affirmed that the achievement of reforms was a necessary stage on the road to socialism.[7] Its leaders confessed that their immediate proposals were tame indeed: suppression of the Senate, advocacy of female suffrage and proportional representation, and defense of the secular school system; these were buttressed by demands for the nationalization of insur-

[7] Thus the party refused to participate in the Heriot government in 1924. Concerning the concept of the "exercise of power," Blum declared: "I am not a legalist when it is a question of the conquest of power, but I declare categorically that I am concerning the exercise of power." See Daniel Ligou, *op. cit.*, 378; Joel Colton, "Léon Blum and the French Socialists as a Government Party," in *Journal of Politics*, XV (November, 1953), 517–543; Boris Mirkine-Guetzévitch, "La République parlementaire dans la pensée politique de Léon Blum," in *La Revue Socialiste*, XLIII (January, 1951), 10–24; and Léon Blum, "Notes sur la doctrine," in *La Revue Socialiste*, III (July, 1946), 257–261.

ance and petroleum companies, mines, and public utilities. The Left, guided by Bracke and Zyromski, was adamant in its hostility toward the Radicals, and insisted upon preparation for a revolutionary eventuality that would occur either as the result of the verdict of universal suffrage or from an ill-defined "movement of the masses." In substance, the Left postulated that antagonisms between the proletariat and bourgeoisie would inevitably increase, and hence the party must pursue a strict "class policy" and exclude the possibility of any alliance with "bourgeois" parties. The Right, among whose ranks figured the future President of the Fourth Republic, Vincent Auriol, and Pierre Renaudel, Joseph Paul-Boncour, and Marx Dormoy, supported a policy of permanent collaboration with the Radicals in the belief that socialism would be the product of a long evolutionary process of reform. This threefold division over the question of participation in power was to be a nagging source of disarray within the S.F.I.O. throughout the interwar decades.

In the 1920's Socialists were in general agreement that their international policy should support Franco-German *rapprochement,* revision of the treaties of 1919, general and complete disarmament, and the League of Nations, and they were united in their opposition to actions prejudicial to the Soviet Union. Most Socialists shared the conviction that a genuine international *détente* was dependent upon the eradication of the "iniquities" of the Treaty of Versailles and upon the achievement of general disarmament, itself the only real guarantee of peace in a nonsocialist Europe. A party resolution vehemently condemned Poincaré's occupation of the Ruhr as an act of "blindness and brutality," and Blum decried the "loss of France's moral credit." The foreign policy of the Herriot government enjoyed the approbation of the S.F.I.O., as did the policies of Aristide Briand in succeeding governments, notably in regard to his actions in support of the League. The party demonstrated its approval by consenting to the appointment of Paul-Boncour to the post of permanent French representative at Geneva, although subsequently it directed him to resign. The S.F.I.O. fully recognized the moral value of the Kellogg-Briand Pact: speaking in its behalf in the Chamber, Faure and Renaudel urged that its application begin with the evacuation of the Rhineland. Blum incorporated a similar appeal

into his approval of the Young Plan, and pleaded that it constitute the initial stage of an energetic effort for general disarmament. Socialist opposition to the conservative governments of Tardieu and Laval did not preclude approval of Briand's conduct of
foreign affairs, and the party systematically sustained "the man of
peace."

The question of national defense had been one of the determining factors in the rupture of 1920, and although the S.F.I.O.
demonstrated its opposition to "militarism" by continuous agitation in favor of reducing the term of military service, it did not
contemplate outright rejection of military credits until
1930–1931.[8] The issue was posed at the National Congress of
Bordeaux in 1930, and in the following year the congress, meeting
at Tours, adopted a resolution sponsored by Faure and Zyromski
affirming that socialism alone could give to national defense "its
full and historic meaning." Respect for national independence, it
declared, must not be confused with the "chauvinistic patriotism"
of the "ruling class," and the Socialist parliamentary group was
warned not to vote for military credits: "not a *sou*, not a man for
the military machine of the bourgeoisie."[9] Despite Blum's belated
effort to conciliate the party's right wing with the dubious assertion that "the vote for military credits is not linked to the question of national defense" the followers of Renaudel attacked the
decision of the congress as "grave," declaring that the Socialist
party "must affirm its will to safeguard the national independence
of France."[10] A schism was averted—temporarily—by the proximity of national elections.

The elections of 1932 were a considerable success for the non-
Communist Left: the Radicals emerged as the principal victors
with 157 seats, but the Socialists increased their number in the
Chamber to 130 and garnered approximately two million votes.
This achievement, however, sharpened the conflict within the
S.F.I.O. over the critical problems of participation and national

---

[8] An excellent discussion of the Socialist party's attitude toward national
defense will be found in P. Fourchy, "Les Doctrines du Parti Socialiste
Français (S.F.I.O.)" (Thesis, University of Nancy, 1929), 79–87, and in Joseph
Paul-Boncour, *Entre deux guerres: Souvenirs sur la Troisième République*,
Vol. II: *Les Lendemains de la Victoire, 1919–1934* (Paris, 1945), 236–271.

[9] *Le Populaire*, May 29, 1931.   [10] *Le Populaire*, May 25, June 6, 1931.

defense, and a special congress was asked to stipulate the minimal conditions for participation with the Radicals. This congress adopted the so-called Cahiers de Huyghens, heavily weighted toward the position of the Left, which effectively prevented any participation in the Herriot government.[11] Open strife within the S.F.I.O. erupted again in March, 1933, when a majority of the parliamentary group, disregarding the counsel of Blum, followed Renaudel in voting for a budget which contained appropriations for military expenditure. This defiance of Socialist policy necessitated the convocation of yet another special congress, which met in April at Avignon, where the issue was debated with an intensity bordering upon rancor. In the eyes of the majority the question was basically one of fidelity to the party's decisions; for most of the Right, it was a matter of defending the nation against the threat posed by Hitler's accession to power. The majority resolution spoke ambiguously about the need to defend democracy but stated plainly that "no concern about parliamentary majorities may prevail against the fundamental principles of the party on such matters as military appropriations, funds for colonial conquests, or the rejections of the entire budget."[12] It concluded with a blunt threat of a "strict accounting" should the parliamentary group persist in its insubordination.

The accounting was soon forthcoming: on May 26, a majority of the Socialist deputies again voted for the budget on a new reading, and incurred a public censure by the C.A.P. The congress, held in Paris in July, was confronted with a very real threat of a schism. Despite the presentation of a bland "unity resolution" by Auriol, which asserted that "there is no reason for a rupture of unity," the majority disavowed and condemned the action of the deputies. Renaudel announced that he was unable to accept the decision, and the speech by Adrien Marquet, Mayor of Bordeaux,

[11] The "Cahiers de Huyghens" were named after the meeting hall, the Salle Huyghens. The minimum conditions for participation were stiff: reduction of the term of military service, interdiction of private commerce in armaments, a ban on a deflationary policy, a capital levy, control of banks by the state, creation of a "Wheat Office" to regulate the sale and distribution of wheat, a program of social security measures, and enactment of legislation fixing forty hours as the maximum work week. See Daniel Ligou, *op. cit.,* 389.
[12] *La Vie Socialiste,* April 29, 1933.

revealed that a split was unavoidable and perhaps desirable. Elaborating upon ideas previously expounded by Marcel Déat,[13] Marquet told a stunned audience that "order and authority are, I believe, the new foundations of the actions we must undertake to win over the masses"; the party, he declared, must discard its "antiquated ideas" such as internationalism and democracy, and adapt itself to the "new reality" of an authoritarian nation-state. Léon Blum expressed the deep shock of the majority: "We Socialists are not a party . . . of authority and order; we are a party of liberty and justice." Although Marquet's assault upon venerable Socialist principles did not lead immediately to a schism of the party—the schism was not officially recognized as such until November—the delegates left the congress with the knowledge that the continued coexistence within the same party of groups so fundamentally opposed to each other was impossible.[14]

This schism has been interpreted as a split that carried away only "a few members," and also as "a sharp, if temporary swing in the Socialist party's center of gravity toward the revolutionary left."[15] Each view contains a certain degree of truth: if the party lost thirty deputies and one-sixth of its adherents, it retained many prominent Renaudelians, notably Marx Dormoy and Salomon Grumbach. Thus the S.F.I.O. had not lost all of its "reformists," but had rid itself of the "Neo-Socialists" Déat and Marquet, whose departure was all but inevitable given their new ideological posture. The Center majority considered Renaudel's case to be a matter of discipline; he had twice disobeyed the orders of his party. The "Neo-Socialists," however, were doctrinally unpalatable. If the Center condemned the crude attempt of the Right to form an alliance with the Radicals, and was supported vigorously by the Left, it did not adopt any of the demands

---

[13] Marcel Déat, *Perspectives socialistes* (Paris, 1930) ; see also B. Montagnon, A. Marquet, and M. Déat, *Néo-socialisme* (Paris, 1933). The doctrines and activities of the so-called Neo-Socialists lie outside the scope of this study; see A. Spire, "Le Déclin du marxisme dans les tendances socialistes de la France contemporaine" (Thesis, University of Nancy, 1937).

[14] *La Vie Socialiste,* July 29, 1933. Parti Socialiste S.F.I.O., *XXXᵉ Congrès National, compte rendu sténographique* (Paris, 1933), 369–370.

[15] Louise Elliott Dalby, *Léon Blum: Evolution of a Socialist* (New York, 1963), 282; John T. Marcus, *French Socialism in the Crisis Years, 1933–1936,* 37.

of the Left, for example, the constitution of an antiwar front with the Communists or the renunciation, in advance, of Socialist participation in a war of national defense. Perhaps the party's "center of gravity" shifted leftward by means of a simple process of elimination, but the Center shifted much less perceptibly, if at all. Paradoxically, an alliance with both Communists and Radicals was to be realized within three years, but this alliance was to be in a form quite different from that envisaged by either the Socialist Left or Right in 1933.

The Popular Front alignment, formed gradually and laboriously in 1934 and 1935 and effectuated politically in 1936 by the acceptance of a common program by the Communists, Socialists, Radicals, and splinter parties of the Left, has been the subject of considerable discussion.[16] Hence a detailed narrative account of its formation is unnecessary here. Our purpose will be to examine, in broad outline, the stages of its development by concentrating upon the role of the Socialist party.

The events of February 6, 1934, were undoubtedly at the origins of this alignment, agreed to in the "unity of action" pact between Communists and Socialists in July, 1934. Convinced that the threat of a fascist-inspired coup was very much a reality, these two parties cooperated, unwillingly and unofficially, in the general strike of February 12, but resumed their bitter mutual polemic immediately thereafter. Any Communist desire for unity was scarcely evident, especially in view of the invective that *L'Humanité* increasingly poured upon the Socialist Left, whose leaders had seized the initiative for unity of action in the Paris region immediately after the riots of February 6. The Socialist Congress, held in May at Toulouse, was devoted entirely to the problems created by a possible "fascist" threat to Republican institutions. After interminable discussion, a general, if wary,

[16] See James Joll, "The Making of the Popular Front," in James Joll, ed., *The Decline of the Third Republic* (New York, 1959), 36–66; Georges Dupeux, *Le Front Populaire et les élections de 1936* (Paris, 1959), 23–95; L. Bodin and J. Touchard, *Front Populaire 1936* (Paris, 1961), 15–26; Georges Lefranc, *Histoire du Front Populaire* (Paris, 1965); Maurice Thorez, *France Today and the People's Front* (New York, n.d.); Jacques Chambaz, *Le Front Populaire pour le pain, la liberté et la paix* (Paris, 1961); Peter J. Larmour, *The French Radical Party in the 1930's* (Stanford, 1964).

consensus was reached: the majority of the delegates acknowledged that working-class unity would represent a formidable
weapon against the "fascists," but indicated—with obvious relief
—that, owing to Communist intransigence, unity was impossible
to attain at present. Nonetheless the congress did adopt, unanimously, a resolution inviting the Socialist International (I.O.S.)
to engage in discussion with the Third International on the possi-
bilities of joint action against fascism. The very adoption of such
a resolution, however, indicated that the Center majority, faced
with what it believed to be a real challenge from fascism, was
beginning to consider actions which a year before it had deemed
scandalous. Yet without a series of concessions granted suddenly
by the Communist party, the unity of action pact would not have
been achieved. At a party conference in June, Maurice Thorez,
the Communist leader, indicated his willingness to undertake
negotiations with the Socialist leadership; this represented a significant departure from the habitual Communist policy of "unity
from below." Discussion between representatives of the two parties began shortly thereafter and resulted in a general agreement
on July 14, thanks to Communist acceptance of all the conditions
posed by the S.F.I.O. In particular the Communists agreed to
cease all polemic against the S.F.I.O., promised that they would
no longer address appeals to Socialist militants, rejected "systematic recourse to violence," acknowledged that the essential task
was to preserve democratic liberties, and agreed to the establishment of a joint committee of coordination to supervise common
action. At a hastily convoked National Council, the Socialists
overwhelmingly approved of the agreement, although certain
leaders were frankly disturbed by it.[17] But in the atmosphere
created by the events of February 6, by Hitler's consolidation of
power, and since the Communists gave way to all Socialist demands, a refusal would have been inconceivable. The unity of
action agreement, signed on July 27, consisted of four major
provisions: (1) joint action by the two parties against the "fascist"
leagues, (2) joint meetings, (3) common opposition to the decree

---

[17] *Le Populaire,* July 16, 1934. Dormoy declared: "I believe in unity, but an
honest unity, and not unity directed from Moscow—Moscow, which, under
the mask of Bolshevism, pursues a tsarist policy." On the attitude of Paul
Faure, see below, pp. 38–39.

laws and "war preparation," and (4) pledges by each party to discipline any of its adherents who violated the pact, and retention by each party in turn of its freedom to propagandize and recruit. Thus, out of fear of "fascism," the Socialist party had no choice but to respond favorably to the Communist initiative, but the fact that it was the Communist party which took the lead and made all the concessions was to contribute in no small measure toward giving that party the appearance of being the dynamic leader in the struggle against fascism.

Similarly, it was the Communist party which took the initiative in the formation of the Popular Front, and once again Socialists seemed to be hesitant followers. In October, 1934, Thorez launched a public appeal for a "Popular Front of Labor, Liberty, and Peace," which he described as an invitation to "the millions of proletarians and little people of the middle classes [who remain] outside of the great current of unity."[18] At the outset this overture was not directed to the Radical party, but to the *Confédération Générale du Travail* (C.G.T.) and to professional and corporate groups, such as organizations of peasants, artisans, and veterans. The appeal was characterized by the creation of "action committees" charged with "recruitment at the base," a euphemism for an effort to foster a groundswell of enthusiasm which the leaders of these organizations could resist only at their peril.

To have any coherence, a common front required a common program, and a "Committee of Coordination" of the Socialist and Communist parties was designated to fulfill this task, but it failed to reach agreement. The Communist proposal was simple and direct: immediate amelioration of economic distress by a reduction in the hours of labor plus a rise in wages, thereby stopping the deflationary policy of the government; the proposal failed, however, to make mention of basic reforms in the structure of economy. The Socialists, on the contrary, insisted upon a vigorous program of "structural reform"—nationalization of banks and key industries—and thus appeared in the eyes of the public to be doctrinaires who stubbornly refused to abandon cherished dogma. Without agreement on a common program, the first attempt to build a "common front" met with no success.

[18] Georges Dupeux, *op. cit.*, 82.

The Communists, however, persisted in their appeal, and after the success of the Left in the municipal elections of May, 1935, they directed their attentions to the Radical party, which became suddenly aware of the value of an electoral alliance with the Socialists and Communists in the national election, scheduled for the spring of 1936. The details of the evolution of the Radicals in 1934 and 1935, which culminated in the acceptance of a common program with the Socialists and Communists need not be repeated here;[19] it should suffice to observe that knowledge of advantages to be won at the ballot box was perhaps the most important factor in their decision. As for the Socialists, despite the fact that "unity of action" had been evident only in a handful of common demonstrations, owing largely to the suspicion generated by Stalin's startling approval of French rearmament, the National Congress of 1935 adopted a motion signifying the party's enthusiasm for "a great popular movement [which will] defend democratic liberties against the political, economic, and social efforts of the capitalist class."[20] Endorsement of the principle, however, did not mean that the S.F.I.O. would acquiesce to the immediate formation of a Popular Front; extensive discussion—lasting almost six months—was to be required before agreement on a common program was attained. And once again the Socialist insistence on specific commitments suggested that the S.F.I.O. was in fact reluctant to enter a common front. Actually such was not the case: after the emotional demonstration of solidarity on July 14, 1935, climaxed by a parade headed by Radical, Socialist, and Communist leaders, the Socialist party moved steadily toward agreement with its future partners, and a joint program was promulgated on January 10, 1936.

Thus the Popular front was formed. The leadership of the S.F.I.O., as well as the leaders of the party's left wing, had arrived, by 1936, at a favorable estimation of the value of a common front, but all of these leaders had come to a similar conclusion for quite different reasons and with varying degrees of enthusiasm. More-

[19] See James Joll, "The Making of the Popular Front," 53; Daniel Ligou, *op. cit.*, 407; Peter J. Larmour, *op. cit.*, ch. vi; Georges Lefranc, *Histoire du Front Populaire*, chs. i–iii.

[20] Parti Socialiste S.F.I.O., *XXXIIᵉ Congrès National, compte rendu sténographique* (Paris, 1936), 570.

over, each conceived of the Popular Front essentially as a vehicle for the realization of his particular beliefs about the nature of socialism and its role in internal and international affairs. To comprehend the position of the Socialist party and its policies from 1936 through 1939, one must understand the fundamental beliefs, especially on questions of international affairs, of its four major personalities: Léon Blum, Paul Faure, Jean Zyromski, and Marceau Pivert.

LEADER OF THE PARTY: LEON BLUM

The name Léon Blum was synonymous with French socialism during the interwar decades: as leader of the S.F.I.O.'s parliamentary contingent and political director of *Le Populaire,* he stood as the acknowledged head of his party, although his leadership did not go unchallenged. In large measure he owed his pre-eminence less to political astuteness than to the sheer force of his intelligence and his unimpeachable integrity. Born in Paris in 1872, the son of a Jewish ribbon manufacturer, he attended the École Normale Supériéure and the Institut des Sciences Politiques. In 1895 he began a brilliant career at the Conseil d'Etat, advancing rapidly to the rank of Auditeur première classe in 1900, and to the position of Commissaire du Gouvernement in 1910. In addition to his legal profession, he enjoyed a reputation as a literary critic and author. But upon his election to the Chamber of Deputies in 1919 he virtually abandoned both his legal and literary careers, and devoted his energies to political activities.

Blum's socialist beliefs have been the subject of much analysis,[21] but commentators have tended to agree that they represented, as in the case of his mentor Jaurès, an attempt to synthesize much of the French democratic tradition with selected aspects of Marxism. The product, primarily the result of an avowedly moral impulse,

[21] Consult especially: Louise E. Dalby, *Léon Blum: Evolution of a Socialist;* James Joll, *Intellectuals in Politics* (London, 1960); Paul Ramadier, *Le Socialisme de Léon Blum* (Paris, 1951); Colette Audry, *Léon Blum ou la politique du juste* (Paris, 1955); Gilbert Ziebura, *Léon Blum: Theorie und Praxis einer sozialistischen Politik* (Berlin, 1963); Milorad M. Drachkovitch, *De Karl Marx à Léon Blum* (Geneva, 1954); Joel Colton, *Léon Blum: Humanist in Politics* (New York, 1966). For a list of secondary works on Blum, consult the bibliography.

was cast in a humanist mold. Blum consistently expressed his conviction that political and social democracy were inseparable terms: socialism would simply implement "the great ideals defined in '89 . . . [and] infuse the economic and social order with political, civil, and personal liberty." And thus "by a revolution similar to that accomplished by our fathers, we will install reason and justice." His intellect persuaded him that socialism was necessary; his emotions told him that it was morally just:

Of what is socialism born? Of the revolt of all the senses wounded by life and disowned by society. Socialism is born of the consciousness of human equality, whereas the society in which we live is based entirely upon privilege. It is born of the compassion and anger which is raised in any honest heart at the intolerable spectacles of poverty, cold, unemployment, hunger. . . . It is not, as has been said so often, the product of envy, which is the basest of human motives, but of justice and pity, which are the most noble.[22]

Blum was equally persuaded that all men, if shown by rational demonstration, would recognize socialism to be the only logical human community.[23] He was certain that socialism's victory would be mankind's victory; hence the essence of his socialism was neither class hatred nor dogmatic arrogance, but humanism and democracy. Finally, the role of human will could not be excluded in the determination of the nature and purpose of socialist revolution.

How then would the ideal society be attained? Blum firmly rejected the idea that it could be brought about merely by the gradual reform of capitalist society, since this would fail to eliminate totally the evil of capitalism; nonetheless, he did not deny the desirability of reforms as palliatives and as stimulants to the revolutionary appetite of the working class. The ultimate triumph would be the task of this class alone, but only after it had conquered political power, either by violent action, or as he preferred, by legal means—that is, by the general recognition by the

[22] Léon Blum, *L'Oeuvre, 1940–1945: Mémoires; La Prison et le procès; A l'échelle humaine* (Paris, 1955), 472; Léon Blum, *Pour être Socialiste* (Paris, 1919), 12, 14. [23] Léon Blum, *L'Oeuvre, 1940–1945*, 495.

majority of the population that socialism was necessary.[24] Blum
warned, however, that the proletariat could not take political
power until it was fully prepared to carry out the social revolution, and preparation for this endeavor was sure to be slow and
laborious. Since the workers were disunited and uninstructed, a
lengthy period of "revolutionary preparation" was obligatory; in
this period the maximum benefits and the best preparation for
revolution could be gained by utilizing the institutions of the
Republic. Hence the necessity to formulate the theory of the
"exercise of power."

Blum's criticism of communism derived from his conviction
that the seizure of political power must not be equated with
revolution, which, by definition, was the social transformation
which would follow the political take-over. He asserted that the
purposeful confusion of the means with the end explained the
failure of the Bolsheviks to accomplish this transformation, and
he accused the French Section of the Communist International of
committing the identical blunder. Without careful revolutionary
preparation, a premature seizure of power could result only in
tyrannical dictatorship in the event of success, and in cruel repression should it fail. Blum believed that the Communist party's
intransigent hostility to any meaningful reform of the condition
of the working class was a baneful consequence of a faith in the
primacy of political revolution. The Socialist leader attacked
what he considered the Communist deviation from the venerable
tradition of French socialism by contrasting the aims and organization of the S.F.I.O. with those of the S.F.I.C.

For the Bolsheviks as for us, the system of party organization corre-
sponds to our conception of the revolution. . . . The Socialist party is
therefore a party freely and largely open, which aspires to identify
itself with all of the working class, and, when its victory will have
made class antagonisms disappear, with all humanity. The Communist
party seeks not to enroll the proletarian masses, which it scorns, but to

---

[24] Paul Ramadier, *op. cit.*, 27. Even in this eventuality there would be a
temporary *vacances de légalité* until the revolution was consummated. See
Léon Blum, *Radicalisme et Socialisme,* 5th ed. (Paris, 1938) , 19.

select shock troops from its midst, always mobilized, a kind of professional arm of insurrection.

The Socialist party regulates the education of its followers according to the revolutionary mission that it attributes to the proletariat. It seeks to raise them to a consciousness of their role, to adapt them in advance to the work of the most formidable transformation that history has probably ever known, to make each of them a cell of the future society within present society. Communism aspires only to maintain among its men a spirit of audacity and attack. . . . Its propaganda does not elevate, does not instruct: it exalts, overexcites, overheats. It tends to create suspicion and hatred as a drunkenness, as a fanaticism of violence.[25]

In substance, communism's doctrine of "democratic centralism" and its apparent addiction to violence were entirely alien to a man whose conscience demanded allegiance to party democracy, to freedom of thought and action, and to the dignity of the working class.

Yet there was another aspect of Bolshevism which was more repugnant to Blum, at least until 1934: he suspected that the Bolsheviks were perfectly willing to accept war in order to achieve their ambitions. Generalizing from their own peculiar experience, as they had done in so many other respects, they might seek to provoke a world catastrophe so as to provide an opportunity for revolution. He pointed to the Communist party's denial of national defense and its exploitation of national and religious hatreds as evidence that its propaganda militated in favor of war.[26]

Nevertheless, Blum always believed that the split between the working-class parties was only temporary, and that their unity was an essential prerequisite to the accomplishment of revolution. Bolshevism was simply a socialist heresy, and the heretics would

[25] Léon Blum, *Bolchevisme et Socialisme,* 2nd ed. (Paris, 1927), 7–8, 16–18. It should be noted that this brochure was written in 1925, and although Blum may have de-emphasized its content during the Popular Front era, it was reissued by the party secretariat in 1938.

[26] *Ibid.,* 23–24. This particular aspect of Blum's critique was intended to combat Communist doctrine in the 1920's. It succeeded only too well in becoming an indelible credo for many members of the S.F.I.O., much to Blum's anguish, in the late 1930's.

be welcomed back into the "old house" once they recanted their errors.[27] But Blum fully recognized that the act of contrition depended, for the time being, on the will of the Soviet rulers: only if Russia should break her own "tyranny" and return to the principles of social democracy could reunion be effectuated. No compromise or doctrinal synthesis of Bolshevism and democratic socialism was possible; yet Blum was the first to admit that the Communist party and its partisans could not be excluded from any effort to safeguard the Republic against its enemies on the Right.[28] After February 6, 1934, Blum argued that the inclusion of the Communists among the ranks of the Republic's defenders was both essential and desirable, although his assurances that this represented no compromise of Socialist principles were to leave many Socialists unconvinced.

Blum conceded readily that there were aspirations common to the Radical and Socialist parties, particularly in the area of political liberties and the achievement of social reforms.[29] The fundamental divergence between them derived from the Socialist belief that these aspirations were but a means to accelerate the transition to the future society, while for the Radicals they were ends in themselves. Socialists, he declared, would lend their complete support to the Radicals in an effort to achieve the goals of the latter, but the intrinsic difference in aims precluded any lengthy Radical-S.F.I.O. collaboration or Socialist participation in Radical-led governments. Blum's stern opposition to participation was firmly rooted: he feared that the working masses would be deceived into believing that power was being conquered, and thus would revolt prematurely; furthermore, the example of Renaudel illustrated the very real threat that the party could be transformed into a noisy but nonrevolutionary appendage of the Radicals.

The author of a recent study has observed that "the basic points of Blum's political theories had been spelled out by 1932"[30] but surely it must be emphasized that the application of his theories changed perceptibly after the events of February 6, 1934. To the end of his life Blum was genuinely convinced that the attempt of the rioters to invade the Palais-Bourbon was a fascist-inspired

[27] *Ibid.*, 1; Parti Socialiste S.F.I.O., *XVIII° Congrès National*, 275.
[28] Léon Blum, *L'Oeuvre, 1940–1945*, 323.
[29] Léon Blum, *Radicalisme et Socialisme*, 19.   [30] L. E. Dalby, *op. cit.*, 273.

insurrection designed to topple the Republic.[31] His immediate response to the threat posed by the demonstrations was to plead with Daladier to remain in office, and more significantly, to offer, purely on his own authority, Socialist participation in a government resolved to defend the Republic with every conceivable means. This indeed was a striking departure from the position that he had upheld tenaciously against the Renaudelians, who had been excluded from the Socialist fold over the lesser issue of supporting Radical governments. Blum's initial impulse, in a moment of extreme crisis, was to appeal for active collaboration with the "bourgeois" Left, and subsequently to accept cooperation with the Communist party. On this occasion at least, Blum demonstrated that he could act swiftly and decisively.

Radical participation in subsequent governments of the Center-Right served to prevent common action by Radicals and Socialists until the formation of the Popular Front, but the abrupt shift in Communist policy opened the way for the "unity of action" agreement of July, 1934. Blum greeted the Communist transformation with a restrained expression of "hope and anxiety," observing that while unity would be "the best guarantee against a fascist victory," Socialism would retain its freedom of judgment concerning the intentions and future activities of its newly acquired partners. But if his acquiescence was reticent and negative in tone, he admitted that the pact was both necessary and inevitable, and that the working class would fail to comprehend a refusal by the S.F.I.O.[32] Very simply, he was keenly aware that Socialist party's prestige would suffer an incalculable loss to the

[31] Assemblée Nationale, Première Legislature, session de 1947, *Rapport fait au nom de la Commission chargée d'enquêter sur les événements survenus en France de 1933 à 1945*, I, 123 (hereafter referred to as *Les Evénements survenus en France*). Blum told the parliamentary commission in 1947 that "the sixth of February was a terrible crime against the Republic, and, even now, I continue to ask myself why it failed, for logically it should have succeeded." Recent investigation has shown Blum's fears to have been exaggerated. See Max Beloff, "The Sixth of February," in James Joll, ed., *The Decline of the Third Republic*, 9–35.

[32] *Le Populaire*, February 25, 1935. In an interview with me on July 29, 1962, the late Oreste Rosenfeld, former editor of *Le Populaire* and a close friend and political associate of Blum, emphasized strongly that Blum believed that unity of action was absolutely essential.

benefit of its rivals on the Left. Moreover, Blum reasoned that any defense of the Republic, to be effective, required the cessation of polemics between the two major organizations claiming to represent the workers. Yet if Blum's acceptance of the unity pact was motivated basically by considerations of domestic policy, his decision was undoubtedly influenced by his increasing awareness of the menace of Nazi Germany.

Blum's international outlook, complex in its structure and occasionally confusing in its subtleties, was extremely simple in its substance: socialism was necessary for peace, and conversely, peace was necessary for socialism. War would be inevitable or necessary only when men began to believe it inevitable or necessary; peace could be created by the determined free will of men.[33] Peace was the supreme virtue, for it was the condition of advance to socialist society; war was the major impediment to its realization. Definitive peace would be guaranteed only when the incipient cause of conflict, capitalist society, had been suppressed, and then the Socialist International would be the guarantor of security. In the prerevolutionary period, socialism would support international agreements designed to mitigate the peril of war. Finally, Blum urged that pressure be applied on existing governments to carry out a policy of disarmament, to erect a system of international arbitration of disputes, and to subscribe to a genuine concept of collective security.

Blum's profession of an international faith was largely a declaration of intention: in a prerevolutionary period most of socialism's activities had to be undertaken within the framework of existing national states. This was a position which was extremely congenial to his own very real consciousness of nationality; on numerous occasions he took care to emphasize his devotion to France (e.g., "I am a Frenchman—for I am French—proud of his country, proud of its history, nourished as much as anyone, in spite of my race, in its tradition"[34]) . Blum vigorously affirmed the duty of Socialists to defend the nation should it be the victim of unprovoked attack, but he asserted with equal vigor that France's security could not be found in force of arms. Such a policy was

[33] Léon Blum, *Les Problèmes de la paix* (Paris, 1931) , 8.
[34] Léon Blum, *L'Exercice du pouvoir* (Paris, 1937) , 187. From a speech delivered to members of the Seine Socialist *fédération* on September 6, 1936.

both odious and self-defeating; odious because it enriched capitalist magnates and burdened all economies, self-defeating because it encouraged a mounting arms race. Thus in 1930 he attributed the successful appeal of Nazism and other nationalist and authoritarian movements primarily to Europe's failure to disarm, and secondarily to the "iniquities" of the Treaty of Versailles and economic distress. Territorial revision and economic recovery could be achieved only in a Europe free from tension and mutual suspicion:

To want to organize Europe economically on a basis of collective security before having disarmed, before having excluded the idea of a possible war, is to build without foundations, is to build on sand.

One nation, he declared, could take a daring initiative of integral disarmament without prior consultation and agreement with other nations—and that nation was France:

I say France because she is militarily the strongest, because she is at the head of the victorious powers, and also from national *amour-propre,* because, as a Frenchman, I want this glory for her. In disarming would we not break the force of the nationalists, militarists, parties of revenge, and without doubt the dictators in other countries? What government would be capable of resisting this current of enthusiasm, the imperious will of all peoples?[35]

Blum confessed willingly that his preference for unilateral disarmament was a personal opinion at variance with the official position of the S.F.I.O., which favored progressive and simultaneous disarmament by all nations, guaranteed by some form of international control. He conceded that this policy was "less adventurous and probably less chimerical" than his own, and acknowledged that general and complete disarmament would be achieved only by stages. But he believed it imperative that France seize the initiative: the most efficacious means to curb European rearmament—that of Germany in particular—would be for France to reduce her military forces in agreement with other powers and to consent to a system of arbitration and real collective security.

[35] Léon Blum, *Les Problèmes de la paix,* 92, 153–154.

The belief that security must be a collective endeavor was central to Blum's international outlook throughout the interwar years, but the terms "security" and "collective" underwent several alterations in definition, especially after Hitler's accession to power. Prior to 1933, Blum was adamant in his conviction that "security" could best be achieved by a progressive reduction of armaments culminating in complete disarmament, and he never abandoned this basic premise: nonetheless, until all powers were sufficiently disarmed so as to be incapable of an aggressive act, "security" also denoted the necessity of the "pacific powers" to render assistance to any nation victim of wanton aggression. In this respect, Blum emphasized the guarantees of Locarno and of the Pact of the League of Nations, but essentially he envisioned assistance as a policy of quarantine involving the application of sanctions against the disturbers of peace; hence it would be a "collective" effort. But Blum went a step further: since the obvious candidates for the role of aggressor were the "dictatorial states," which, by their very existence constituted a threat of war, the "pacific" or "democratic" states should undertake to destroy them by *peaceful* means. Thus "collective" action was restricted, by Blum's definition, to action by the "democracies":

All the dictatorships are the enemies of free states. We by no means intend to make war on them, but in order to establish peace in the world we refuse systematically any kind of sympathy, aid, or cooperation. . . . In the name of peace, we will put them outside the international solidarity.[36]

The "peaceful destruction" of the dictatorships could be accomplished only if the "democratic states" were to regain the initiative from their adversaries on the matter of disarmament. Blum insisted that the appeal of the "Fascist states" (he was wont to use the terms "fascist" and "dictatorship" interchangeably) was essentially attributable to their cynical "double game" of posing as champions of peace and disarmament, thus appealing to the deepest sentiments of all mankind. The "democracies" should unmask

[36] Léon Blum, *Les Problèmes de la paix,* 193–194. At this time Blum was referring to Italy, Poland, Yugoslavia, Hungary, and Rumania. He was especially antagonized by France's alliances with dictatorships.

and dishonor the dictators by proposing an equitable disarmament treaty to them: should they refuse, "their rebellion against
the spirit of peace will be demonstrated as will their duplicity,
and no government of liberty and integrity could refuse to sur-
round them with the indispensable cordon sanitaire."[37] Should
they acquiesce, their own position in their respective countries
would be jeopardized seriously, since any treaty would inevitably
necessitate a limitation of national sovereignty, and their doctrine
—and their existence—rested upon the incessant exaltation of the
nation. Blum recognized that his proposal involved considerable
risk, but the alternative, an increase in armaments, would be a
more serious risk.

Thus Blum's international policy, before January, 1933, was
predicated upon the belief that progress toward socialism was
dependent upon the preservation of peace; it was axiomatic for
him that complete disarmament must be the ultimate objective of
Socialist policy. Since a socialist society alone could and would be
the definitive guarantee of peace, admittedly imperfect means
must be utilized to alleviate tensions and eliminate potential
sources of conflict in a prerevolutionary Europe. Socialist objectives, for the time being, must therefore be limited to the attainment of a progressive reduction of armaments and the eradication
of the threat to peace represented by the dictators. Blum sought to
achieve these objectives in two ways: on the one hand, he addressed moving appeals to men's consciences and to world opinion; on the other hand, he saw the need for some sort of compulsion, and the vehicle of compulsion, in the early 1930's, was
"collective action" by a loosely defined group of "democratic
powers" against the malefactors. This "action" would accomplish
either a reduction in arms by all powers, thereby undermining the
dictators, or it would lead to the imposition of sanctions against
the recalcitrant powers. As the decade progressed, however,
Blum's conception of "collective action" was to become the basis
of his international policy, and the term was to undergo a metamorphosis in both its scope and meaning.

Although Blum long had predicted an extreme nationalist reaction in Germany as a consequence of the policies pursued by the

[37] *Ibid.,* 197.

victorious powers of the world war, he was incapable of conceiving that National Socialism actually could come to power. In *Les Problèmes de la paix* he asserted blandly that "Hitler's star has already reached its zenith," and ten days after Hitler's installation as Chancellor, he argued that the Nazi leader was simply the head of a coalition government, dependent upon feudal and reactionary capitalist interests. Events soon persuaded Blum that he had erred grossly, and thoroughly appalled by the brutality and racist overtones of the new German regime, he expressed his fear that Hitler's intention was to rearm as rapidly as possible. The surest obstacle that Europe could place in the path of this rearmament, said Blum, was general agreement on a disarmament convention which would be so equitable that Germany could reject it only at the risk of "denouncing and accusing herself before the conscience of the world." The Socialist leader exhorted European nations to agree upon a disarmament program with or without Germany's participation; should Germany reject the disarmament convention, the other powers should envisage the possibility of erecting an economic blockade against her, thus forcing her to accept it. Blum appealed for

a resolute determined, unbreakable pressure of the European collectivity on German Hitlerism, *but a pressure which is not war and does not imply war.* . . . German Hitlerism could not contemplate resistance against the will of the European collectivity, provided that this will is demonstrated with enough vigor, with enough persistence, and especially with enough cohesion.[38]

Blum's initial reaction to the menace of an authoritarian and rearmed Germany followed essentially the same pattern as his policy of 1930–1931: an entreaty to conscience was combined with an appeal for collective action to constrain the newly installed dictator to disarm under the threat of punitive measures by the community of nations. In 1934 Blum continued to plead that Germany not be permitted to rearm, and that France must exhibit a willingness to disarm in order to facilitate the happy conclusion of an international accord. Fearing that the French government would utilize German rearmament as a convenient

[38] *Le Populaire,* February 9, March 16, August 31, 1933.

vindication for an increase in France's armaments, he declared that such a course could lead only to moral isolation. Blum refused absolutely to countenance the use of military force against Germany, either for the purpose of liberation—German liberation, he argued, would be achieved solely by the revolt of the German conscience—or to remove the Nazi regime by virtue of its threat to peace. "Preventive war is an absurd solution" became a habitual preface to his articles concerning international affairs.[39]

Equally absurd to Blum was the reconstitution of alliances: instead of providing even a temporary security, this step, he said, would divide Europe "into armed leagues, into rival camps inevitably seeking an equilibrium or superiority of forces to their own profit." Rather than preparing for peace, Europe would be preparing for war. Disarmament remained the sole road to peace, and the effort demanded that France participate in the "organization of peace" by negotiating even with those whose hands "were soiled by blood."[40] A treaty should be proposed to and, if necessary, imposed upon Germany, but Blum's immediate objective was to eliminate the possibility of war, not to destroy a despicable regime.

Blum was adamant in his belief that any arrangements concluded with the dictators must be the product of collective action, and he chastised those who thought that amity or confidence was conceivable with regimes founded upon "brutality and duplic-

[39] *Ibid.*, March 10, April 21, 1934. In the number of March 16, 1934, Blum declared that "we persist in our appeal to international conscience." In 1947, speaking before the parliamentary commission, Blum confessed that he had erred: "In my opinion, there existed perhaps only one way to have prevented the war [which erupted] in 1939. This was, at the moment that Hitler took power, to have carried out a preventive operation." *Les Evénements survenus en France,* I: *Dépositions,* 121. Shortly before his death in 1960, Blum's former comrade, Paul Faure, lamented that "this is the most sensational public confession to come from one of the men who held a post of responsibility in the prewar period: it is a recognition that he was mistaken, that his party was mistaken with him; it is the most categorical condemnation of twenty years of activity, of electoral campaigns, of congresses, of parliamentary and governmental activities. . . . It is the frightening confession that their [*sic*] pacifism, as ardent and as sincere as it was, should paradoxically be counted among the causes of the conflict among nations." See Paul Faure, "Les Intrus du Capitole" (unpublished ms.) , 41.

[40] *Le Populaire,* June 7, December 2, 1934.

ity." Although he conceded that Franco-German understanding was a crucial prerequisite to European peace, he warned that France must not contemplate direct negotiations with Hitler, nor should she offer any unilateral concessions, because Nazi Germany merited none.[41] But by 1934 Blum's concept of "collective action" had begun to evolve quickly, particularly after the failure of the major powers to secure a disarmament treaty.

The keystone of this evolution was Blum's new attitude toward the Soviet Union, whose dictatorship he had castigated since 1918 and as recently as 1931 had put in the same category as that of Fascist Italy.[42] With Hitler securely in power, Blum was unable to believe that Stalin could fail to comprehend that the U.S.S.R. was the most likely target of Nazi aggression. Should awareness of this prospect lead the Soviet government to conclude alliances with "bourgeois" governments, it might also militate in favor of the union of Socialist and Communist parties. Blum attributed the sudden willingness of the Communist party to agree to unity of action to Moscow's concern for the security of the Soviet homeland. Impressed by the restraint exhibited by the U.S.S.R. in its dispute with Japan, he asserted that Stalin's desire for peace was unquestionable, and in 1934 he hailed the entrance of the Soviets into the League of Nations as an act motivated by a sincere will "to serve peace."[43]

But it was the German denunciation of the disarmament clauses of the Versailles Treaty and the reintroduction of conscription on March 16, 1935, that fundamentally changed the character of Blum's concept of "collective security." His objective, to be sure, remained the same: to oblige Hitler to subscribe to a universal convention of controlled disarmament. But "collective action" now was understood to mean the concerted and determined action of France, Great Britain, and the Soviet Union, linked by pacts of mutual assistance if necessary, to impose a

[41] *Ibid.,* June 14, October 27, 1933; December 7, 1934.

[42] Léon Blum, *Les Problèmes de la paix,* 186.

[43] *Le Populaire,* March 11, November 18, 1933; October 1, 1934. In the number of April 10, 1935, Blum wrote: "We consider that at the present moment, the essential guarantee of peace resides in the unity of action of the western 'democracies' and Soviet Russia. England wants peace; Soviet Russia wants peace—she has proven it with magnificence and courage."

treaty upon Germany. "Pacific powers" now implied three powers
—not all of them democracies—and pacts of assistance, so forcefully condemned a few months before, now were regarded as
elements of security. Blum ridiculed those who persisted in "the
obstinate illusion of negotiation and of a direct *entente* with
Hitler."[44] The Führer must be convinced that Europe was resolved to halt German rearmament, even if this temporarily
should require the use of pacts of mutual assistance.

Although in April, 1935, Blum was as yet unaware of the
contents of the accord that Laval was negotiating with the Soviet
government, he supported the Soviet view that assistance pacts
were the only means immediately available to deter aggression.[45]
France's duty was to persuade the U.S.S.R. that such pacts could
not constitute a permanent substitute for real collective security,
that is, common action by all nations to prevent and punish
aggression; more importantly, she must persuade England that
special pacts of assistance were not incompatible with the ideal of
collective security. As an added justification—or rationalization
—of his new position, Blum recommended that such special pacts
be invested with the approval of the League of Nations, and be
open to the signature of all nations.

Stalin's declaration of May 15, 1935, approving the national
defense policy of the French government, was an anguishing, if
temporary, shock to Blum inasmuch as it appeared to constitute a
categoric, if not brutal, denial of the objective of his international
policy, that is, disarmament. It sanctioned a policy against which
the S.F.I.O. had mounted an attack of unprecedented vehemence
in the early months of 1935; Blum had accused the Flandin
government of "playing Hitler's game when it increased armaments and . . . [of preferring] superarmament [*surarmement*] of
France to the disarmament of Germany." Although the Socialist
leader had reiterated strongly that his party would defend the
patrie against any aggression, his onslaught against the government's proposal to increase the term of military service had become the focal point of a campaign in favor of disarmament.
When one considers that only a month prior to Stalin's astound-
ing pronouncement Blum had urged a joint effort by England,

[44] *Ibid.,* April 11, 1935.   [45] *Ibid.,* April 12, 1935.

France, and the Soviet Union to *secure* disarmament, and had fully approved of the Franco-Soviet Pact in advance, his initial consternation is readily comprehensible.

We have always denied that the security of a nation was dependent upon the strength of its armed forces. Now Stalin recognizes that the security of France depends upon an increase in her military strength. . . . Stalin approves, against us, of the government which we have fought.[46]

Significantly, however, Blum's depression gave way rapidly to renewed optimism on the question of unity of the Socialist and Communist parties. On May 18 he asserted that Stalin's declaration should not hinder the achievement of unity, and at the Socialist congress in June he went a step further: ignoring the elementary fact that whatever Stalin decided for at one moment he could decide against at the next, Blum told his comrades that the Soviet leader's action was not an impediment to unity, but that it could make unity possible because it had forced the Communists to accept the principle of national defense.

Do you not see today that Vaillant-Couturier [the editor of *L'Humanité*] is using practically the same formula that I employed at Tours?[47] I think that we should greet the explanations given by the Communists as . . . a fact which will facilitate organic unity. A common position is possible. The problem [of national defense] no longer constitutes a preliminary obstacle to the rebuilding of unity. Moreover, a free and united party will fix our doctrine on the subject.[48]

Thus the major barrier to unity had been smashed by the Soviet fiat; yet Blum seemed to believe that once organic unity had been accomplished, the Communists would shrug off foreign tutelage, and a free party would establish, by a democratic process, the definitive doctrine of the party! Blum was soon to discover that his optimism rested upon very fragile foundations.

The prospect of imminent aggression by Italy against Ethiopia in the summer of 1935 prompted Blum to repeat his appeal for a

[46] *Ibid.*, January 23, May 17, 1935.
[47] Concerning the coexistence of the proletariat's national and international duty in the event of war.   [48] *Le Populaire*, June 11, 1935.

resolute coordination of the efforts of France, Great Britain, and the Soviet Union, with participation by the latter "indispensable." Despite the Stresa agreement, Blum entertained no illusions about the aspirations of the Italian dictator: "The power that bases its security on Mussolini's word is lost." Convinced that Europe finally realized that "fascism is war," he called for swift action by the international community to prevent the subjugation of Ethiopia, and with the actual outbreak of hostilities and the official designation of Italy as the aggressor by the League, he demanded that economic sanctions be applied rigorously.[49] By the end of the year, however, it was painfully evident that the irresolute application of sanctions had ensured Mussolini's success in his African adventure; this was shockingly apparent after the public disclosure of the abortive Hoare-Laval agreement. For Blum the real tragedy of the Ethiopian affair was that the failure of the French government to fulfill its obligations had seriously compromised the principle of collective security. In an impassioned speech to the Chamber of Deputies on December 27, 1935, Blum advanced a hypothesis that reflected the evolution of his international policy since 1933, was implicit in his concept of "collective security" as "unity of action for peace," and was inescapable from the moment that he admitted to the risk of war in imposing sanctions; in a Europe in which nations remained armed, security required the assurance of *military* assistance, and logically the principal sources of assistance for France could be only Great Britain and the U.S.S.R. Blum stressed that Laval's intrigues and lack of fidelity to the Pact of the League had isolated France from these powers, for at the very moment when England had attempted to fulfill her obligations under the Covenant, France had sought to scuttle Ethiopia.

All the pacific powers are discouraged. . . . M. Laval has destroyed the confidence that the Soviets placed in him. . . . If, unhappily, war should erupt . . . the elementary condition of our security would be the unreserved assistance of Soviet Russia and of Great Britain.

Security lies in the assurance of mutual assistance in case of peril. How can a nation refuse this guarantee and assistance to others yet invoke them itself when the need arises?[50]

[49] *Ibid.,* June 23, August 20, 23, October 8, 1935.
[50] Léon Blum, *L'Histoire jugera* (Paris, 1945), 121–122.

The truth behind this blunt warning received a startling confirmation in March, 1936, when France discovered that the British government had no enthusiasm for challenging Hitler's military reoccupation of the Rhineland.[51] Blum was absent from Paris, convalescing from injuries suffered at the hands of the *Camelots du Roi,* and his views were not known until March 12, a week after the event, when he lauded the "vigorous terms" with which the party spokesmen, Faure and Rosenfeld, had condemned Hitler's *coup de force* as "inadmissible and unacceptable."[52] Actually Faure had said nothing of the sort, and in fact had said quite the contrary. Although Blum urged the League to condemn this flagrant violation of the Locarno Pact, he recognized that the effectiveness of the world organization had been sapped catastrophically by the Ethiopian affair. Accordingly he suggested that the Rhineland problem be envisaged as an integral part of the larger European problem created by the twin dangers to peace, Hitler and Mussolini. For the Socialist leader collective security must be recast along lines that he had been suggesting for over a year: France, Great Britain, and the Soviet Union must act in concert, so as to prevent a recurrence of aggression and to establish a reliable system of mutual assistance in the present. But the long-range goal must be complete disarmament. Blum repeated his suggestion that a disarmament treaty be proposed to or imposed upon the dictators—how their acceptance would be secured was not specified, but war was excluded as a means.[53]

Thus Blum's international policy immediately prior to his "exercise of power" in 1936 was rooted in the belief that the inherently aggressive character of the German and Italian regimes constituted an imminent danger to the peace of Europe. As a consequence of this belief his policy had apparently changed since 1933—which raises questions concerning the extent of the change

[51] See in this connection the testimony of Albert Sarraut in *Les Evénements survenus in France,* III, 559–624, 643–673; W. F. Knapp, "The Rhineland Crisis of March 1936," in James Joll, *The Decline of the Third Republic,* 67–85; République Française, Ministère des Affaires Etrangères, *Documents diplomatiques françaises, 1932–1939,* 2nd series (1936–1939), Vol. I (Jan. 1–Mar. 31, 1936) (Paris, 1963); and Jean-Baptiste Duroselle, "France and the Crisis of March 1936," trans. Nancy L. Roelker, in Evelyn Acomb and Marvin Brown, eds., *French Society and Culture Since the Old Regime* (New York, 1966), 243–268.   [52] *Le Populaire,* March 12, 1936.

[53] *Le Populaire,* March 19, April 16, 1936.

and, more important, poses the problem of consistency. Was the change in his outlook as perceptible to his contemporaries as it appears to have been in retrospect, especially when he never abandoned the rhetoric of pacifist idealism?

Certainly universal disarmament and the preservation of peace remained Blum's fixed objectives—he could not speak of the horrors of war without intense emotion and he dismissed preventive war as immoral—but it is obvious that an *entente* of three powers, linked in part by a special pact of assistance and resolved to impose a disarmament treaty, even at the risk of war, was somewhat different from a loosely defined group of "pacific democracies" who would simply exclude those who refused to disarm from the community of nations. Was it not inconsistent to continue to condemn alliances and yet to approve of the Franco-Soviet Pact and urge close cooperation with England; to claim endlessly that war was possible only if men admitted it to be possible and yet to admit that one's policy contained a risk of war; to appeal to international conscience and also to selfish interests; to attack French rearmament but also to advocate the obligation of mutual assistance, which presupposed a posture of strength; to depend upon the Soviet Union as a force for peace but to condemn dictatorships as the principal cause of the danger of war; to condemn the injustices of the Treaty of Versailles but to refuse any concessions to Germany; and to acknowledge that a Franco-German understanding was necessary to European peace and yet to refuse any direct Franco-German negotiation?

Perhaps the many inconsistencies in Blum's international policy ought to be ascribed to a basic dualism in his outlook, a dualism resulting from a confrontation of ideals with necessity. Blum was much too honest intellectually to mask his intentions with ideals in which he had no faith; both ideals and the harsh demands of necessity coexisted uneasily in his policy, making for massive confusion and opening him to misinterpretation. It is clear that Blum thought that whatever concessions he had made to necessity in no sense betrayed his socialist beliefs. He would argue that necessity had forced him to accept temporary and unpalatable arrangements in order to ensure final success, but first principles remained steadfast. He had always warned that dictatorships, by their very nature, represented the major threat to peace, and had asserted unceasingly that only collective action could force the dictators to disarm. In response to a more powerful and brutal dictatorship, was it not logical and natural that a more cohesive coalition, persuasive because of its unity, should be required to prevent aggression and secure disarmament? Collective security, after 1933, necessitated the assurance of mutual assistance or it would have no deterrent value; hence special pacts were required. Since Blum maintained that collective action should employ peaceful means to attain peaceful objectives and should utilize force only in response to force, he could claim with considerable justification that his international policy was a faithful application of his ideals to the harsh realities of 1936.

But this explanation does not touch upon the problem of the dual character of his policy, for if he believed necessity to be the determining factor in an increasingly ominous European situation, why did he continue to proclaim his ideals as absolutes and as realistic responses to the threat of war? Should he not have recognized that if the bellicosity of the dictators should increase, the logical implication of his new concept of collective action would be support of an armed alliance resolved to use sheer force to crush aggression, thereby requiring that France increase her armaments immediately in prudent preparation for this eventuality? Was he not confusing or misleading his party by persisting in his appeal to international conscience and for disarmament, as if the former truly existed and the latter was attainable, and by continuing to declare passionately that war was not possible as long as men believed it to be impossible?

Blum's international policy as head of the government in 1936 and 1937 was to be weakened to the point of paralysis by the dualism at the heart of his outlook; stubbornly refusing to renounce his pacifist catechism, yet fully conscious of the terrible threat of Nazi Germany, he was to attempt to fuse his aspirations with requirements born of necessity, and was to meet with dismal failure. When the events of 1938 persuaded him that there was no alternative to a policy of armed alliances, his decision was to precipitate the collapse of the Socialist party. And then his supporters could claim that his decision was perfectly consistent with all that he had said and believed since 1920; his opponents could argue that it was a shameful betrayal of his socialist and pacifist ideals. In a sense both were right and both were wrong; just as all Christians find support for their own brand of Christianity in the Bible, all French Socialists could utilize Blum's own words as a vindication of their positions.

The Popular Front has often been described as a loose and tenuous political alignment whose existence was attributable solely to fear of fascism, and whose creed, in consequence, was essentially negative and defensive. Surely there is ample evidence to sustain such an assessment, but it would be erroneous to assume that Blum's conception of the Popular Front was wholly defensive or even negative; he considered it to be an entirely new phenomenon in French history, a "current and an organization of forces which, until this moment, did not exist."[54] He believed its task to be threefold. First, it must render France immune to the disease of fascism by a vigorous assertion of the "republican spirit" via the defense and development of democratic liberties. Second, France, by her example, would reanimate Europe's confidence in herself, thus facilitating the construction of a real system of collective security. Third, the economic distress created by "the absurdities and iniquities" of the capitalist regime would be met with a series of measures applying state intervention to "the nerve center of the economic body."[55] In essence, a government of the *Front Populaire* would be a government of the "public good" whose primary objective would be the moral and material regeneration of France, and thus of all Europe. As such it would be obliged to restrict itself to the confines of Republican legality; as it would owe its existence to the majority of the nation and not to one class, so it must fulfill its contract with that majority. For Blum, the Popular Front was not to be a revolutionary movement, not a simple defense against fascism, nor was it to be the "guardian of bourgeois society"; its mission was the salvation of the entire nation. He warned his party that this task would require time, patience, order, and caution; force would be unnecessary inasmuch as the old social order was already crumbling as a result of

[54] Léon Blum, *L'Exercice du pouvoir,* 52. Speech to the Socialist congress on May 31, 1936.

[55] *Ibid.,* 40. He declared that "we want to resurrect hope, we want to fight against poverty . . . we want France to regain confidence in the efficacity of her labor."

its inner contradictions, and dangerous because it would create panic and disorder, thereby weakening France in a period of peril. Socialism's vocation to transform society would remain unalterable, but the party, he declared, must realize that "it is not only the future of our Socialist party that is at stake, but that of the Republic itself."[56]

Blum recognized that the immensity and the urgency of this effort, undertaken at a time of acute crisis, required an exceptional leader, a leader of determination and strength. Could a man so intensely humanist, who abhorred war with passion, and who shrank from the use of force, have the will to act with firmness, even with ruthlessness? He asked his party, in an extraordinary address, whether a man who believed the functions of a leader to be primarily those of persuasion and conciliation could now exercise the full force of the party's power.

A battle such as this requires a leader; authority is under your permanent control, but it must be exercised without hindrance. I have never used language such as this. You know that whatever esteem I possess in your eyes, in the eyes of the party, I owe, to the contrary, to a constant effort of conciliation and persuasion.

Today it is quite different. Faced with new circumstances, a new man must arise in a man. I know that your confidence in me is complete, without any reservation. I deserve it and I shall deserve it in the future.

I do not know if I have the qualities of a leader for so difficult a battle; I cannot know, no more than any of you can know. . . . But if there is something which will never fail me, it is resolution, courage, and fidelity.[57]

But would resolution, courage, and fidelity be sufficient? Had Blum really persuaded his party to accept his vision of the Popular Front and his solutions to the awesome national and international problems? Did his Socialist comrades possess the confidence in him that he assumed they did? If the Socialist party, flushed with the enthusiasm of electoral victory, unanimously expressed confidence in its leader, did not its internal divisions, deeper than anyone suspected, and Blum's own hesitations and inconsistencies,

[56] *Ibid.,* 45–46, 54.   [57] *Ibid.,* 46.

so evident in his international policy, indicate that, in moments of extreme crisis, the superficiality of this confidence would be starkly exposed? Our purpose henceforth is to examine the fragmentation of an already fragile political party, and to ascertain to what extent Blum himself was responsible for the impotence and eventual disappearance, after the Munich conference, of the Socialist party as a viable force in the life of the nation.

HEART OF THE PARTY: PAUL FAURE

Paul Faure, General Secretary of the Socialist party from the schism at Tours in 1920 until the collapse of the Republic in 1940, was born in 1878, the son of a provincial lawyer of zealous republican beliefs. Attracted to socialist ideas in his early youth, Faure adhered to the Dordogne branch of the Guesdist *Parti Ouvrier Français* at the age of twenty-three, became secretary of the unified *fédération* of the S.F.I.O. in 1905, and created a socialist newspaper, *Le Travailleur du Périgord* in 1906. Entering the electoral arena in 1906, he offered himself as a candidate for the Chamber of Deputies from Périgueux, where, although defeated, he received substantial support. Shortly thereafter, Faure devoted his considerable talents as a journalist and propagandist to the Socialist organization in the Haute-Vienne, one of the most powerful *fédérations* in the party. He was appointed political director, and then promoted to editor, of the influential Socialist daily, *Le Populaire du Centre,* published at Limoges. In 1915 his many articles suggesting a negotiated peace encouraged the formation of a strong minority faction within the S.F.I.O. which was hostile to the war. He emerged as one of the leaders of this faction and, as a consequence, became a national figure. In 1920, allied with Jean Longuet, Faure was amenable to a formal adhesion of the Socialist party to the Third International, but with reservations sufficient to draw a stinging condemnation from Moscow. Designated General Secretary of the rump S.F.I.O. at the urging of Guesde after the rupture with the adherents of the Third International, Faure played perhaps the most vital role in the reconstruction of the party, and was socialism's second most prominent personality during the interwar decades. In addition to his duties as director of the party's administration, he was intermittently a member of the Chamber: elected from the

Saône-et-Loire in 1924, he retained his seat until defeated in 1932, and was not returned until 1938. Essentially, Faure's stature among Socialists was the product of his extraordinary abilities as administrator, propagandist, and organizer, and his influence with the S.F.I.O. was at least commensurate with that of Léon Blum.

If Blum was the acknowledged leader, widely respected within the party, it was Faure who personified socialism for many of the rank and file. While Blum was often overly subtle and all too frequently confusing in his articles and speeches, Faure was blunt and direct, and if Blum appeared aloof and cautious in his relations with party members, Faure was the model of amiability and fraternity.[58] Two of Blum's most trusted colleagues have attested to the fact that Faure was immeasurably more popular in the party than his chief, and have attributed this to Faure's close contact with party regulars.[59] Faure traveled extensively on whirlwind tours of Socialist sections; surely the party did not seem distant and impersonal when its General Secretary allotted time to address even the smallest gathering of the faithful.[60]

Obviously personal contact was not the only, or the most efficient, means of establishing communication with all echelons of the party. As director of the secretariat, Faure possessed a

[58] See Alexander Werth, *The Destiny of France* (London, 1937), 280: "The Socialist rank and file had a great regard for Blum; but it would be untrue to say that he was popular. He was not a *grand tribun* like Jaurès; they felt that his speeches were on a higher intellectual plane than all other Socialist speeches; and his aristocratic manner made them a little uneasy. He was not 'one of ours,' and they called him M. Blum; for 'comrade' didn't suit him, somehow."

[59] Interviews with Oreste Rosenfeld, June 29, 1962, and with Jules Moch, November 24, 1961.

[60] In an interview with Jean Castagnez, former Socialist deputy from the Cher, and a close personal friend of Faure, on June 8, 1962, he gave me this description of Faure's technique: "When Faure arrived at a meeting he was always greeted with prolonged cheering and shouts of *Vive Paul Faure! Vive le socialisme!* Immediately he would remove his coat and tie and mingle with the rank and file, eating bits of cheese and bread as he went. After a while he would stand up on a table or any convenient platform and deliver a speech which would go directly to the heart of the listener; there could be no doubt as to what he was saying or what he meant. The meeting would conclude in a wave of enthusiasm."

formidable weapon in the dissemination of information and propaganda: in collaboration with Jean-Baptiste Séverac, Deputy General Secretary, Faure composed a weekly information sheet, *Le Bulletin Socialiste,* which found its way to every Socialist outpost, and its contents customarily appeared in the organ of each departmental *fédération.* Faure also took care to establish close relationships with the secretaries of these *fédérations*—so close that many were baptized "the prefects of Paul Faure" by unkind opponents —and with the leaders of the youth movement, the *Jeunesses Socialistes.* Faure's influence within the S.F.I.O. was indeed formidable: in addition to his undeniable popularity among ordinary members, he maintained a tight grip on the party secretariat, buttressing his position by a multitude of personal ties with party officials at the local level. Here was a man who could and did wield immense power, and when he apparently agreed and cooperated with Léon Blum, the dominance of the party's Center appeared unassailable. However, investigation of Faure's beliefs and policies, particularly on international affairs, reveals that the accord between Blum and Faure was a shallow and unreliable instrument on which to build a political party; in fact, there existed between the two men differences so fundamental that they could develop easily into irreconcilable antagonists.

If Faure's importance derived essentially from his tasks as a strategist and administrator, and if, unlike Blum, he devoted scant attention to considerations of socialist theory, he did possess unshakeable convictions concerning the nature of socialism and the proper role of its partisans. Faure's socialist beliefs were starkly rudimentary: he defined socialism simply as the replacement of capitalism by a collective society, without elaborating upon the structure of the latter. By definition, then, socialism was a revolutionary doctrine, though it need not endorse violent methods. If Faure conceived of socialism as an absolute and tangible commitment to collectivism, it was also a faith: "The essential thing is to believe in socialism and to want its victory." Faure's allegiance to internationalism was purely ritualistic and perfunctory; he argued frequently that socialism was the only doctrine applicable to the French nation, citing Guesde's teachings that the social revolution in one country was quite independent of events in other lands.[61] Finally, he asserted that both bourgeois democracy and fascism had failed to solve the many problems engendered by capitalism: bourgeois democracy had failed because all middle-class parties, regardless of their place on the political spectrum, inevitably coalesced to prevent any change in the economic structure; fascism offered no remedy because, as an outgrowth of capitalism, it existed to preserve the life of its parent by force.

The victory of socialism need not be accomplished by violence: "We want to utilize all means, including legal means," he declared frequently, but asserted that if socialism should make use of the tools of "bourgeois" democracy, under no circumstances could it abandon its objective of conquering political power in order to fashion the social revolution. Faure considered that an armed assault against the existing state would be an act of lunacy, since the state possessed an arsenal of repressive measures. Circumstances required that public opinion be conquered by means of a vast campaign of enlightenment and by construction of a powerful organization of proletarian forces which would act at the propitious moment, presumably after persuasion had done its task, and only against lingering pockets of determined resistance. Meanwhile, since no estimate of the nearness of the great moment was possible, the Socialist party would not sit out the prerevolutionary period in splendid isolation, but would support those governments which adhered to democratic principles and favored social progress. Yet such support implied neither the possibility of the party's participation in power with its class enemies nor a particular fondness for the Radical party, and when the latter permitted some of its members to join the government of the elderly conservative Doumergue in 1934, Faure's scorn was without limit.[62]

Faure's most virulent attacks, however, were reserved for his enemies on the Left. Shortly after the Congress of Tours he castigated the Communist party in a brochure entitled *Le Bolchevisme en France: Farce et imposture*, a characterization from

[61] Paul Faure, *Au seuil d'une révolution* (Limoges, 1934), 121, 136, 243. Faure, to my knowledge, never mentioned Marx as a source of his socialist beliefs, but frequently cited Guesde and Jaurès.

[62] *Le Populaire*, April 1, October 6, 28, 1934.

which he took scrupulous care never to deviate. While Blum was content to consider communism a socialist heresy, Faure was adamant in his belief that it was not only an alien and undesirable import from a barbarous land, but, most important, that it was dedicated to the extirpation of all socialist values. Although Faure had conditionally supported adhesion to the Third International in 1920 and Blum had been rigorously opposed, it was Faure who emerged in the 1920's as the declared and tireless enemy of the Communist party. He denied repeatedly that there was anything French about this party; its leaders, he said, were simply "the agents of Moscow in France."[63] Naturally, Faure opposed any union between the S.F.I.O. and the Parti Communiste; union was impossible unless the wayward returned to the fold—that is, unless Communists ceased being Communists.

Faure's detractors have insisted that his attitude toward the events of February 6 was—at best—equivocal.[64] Nonetheless, his immediate response would seem to indicate the contrary; on February 7 he appealed for common action by all working-class organizations to break the "reactionary offensive." Apparently convinced that the riots were part of a plot to overthrow Republican institutions and to install a fascist regime, he maintained his appeal during the hectic days that followed the initial outburst, but he permitted himself to remark ruefully that "we have received from the Communist party a brutal refusal [to cooperate] and a new burst of insults and violence." As long as the Communists continued to reject cooperation Faure had no reason to oppose the tide of Parisian working-class sentiment for action against the apparent fascist menace, and caught in the flow of his own rhetoric, he urged the immediate formation of "a great movement of fraternization and unity."[65]

After appealing for unity with such vigor, whether from fear of a fascist *coup* or from a desire to improve the standing of his party among the working class, it would have been impossible for the General Secretary to reject Communist proposals for "unity of action," although certain of his former comrades insist that he was

[63] Paul Faure, *La Scission socialiste en France et dans l'Internationale* (Paris, 1921), 4, 6.   [64] Interviews with Oreste Rosenfeld and Jules Moch.
[65] *Le Populaire*, February 7, 9, 28 and March 3, 4, 1934.

rigorously opposed to acceptance of the Communist suggestion.[66] Presumably appealing for unity of action and denouncing the Communists for their hesitation was quite different from accepting unity in fact. At a meeting of the Socialist National Council in July, Faure restricted himself to a cautious expression of his anxieties, and he did not reveal his hostility openly until early in 1935, and only after he had questioned the assumption that there was a threat of fascism in France.

In a series of articles which appeared in *Le Populaire* late in 1934, Faure declared that the "fascists"—otherwise unidentified —had cynically exploited the popular discontent generated by economic distress, but he asserted forcefully that "the fascist peril is perhaps not so real. . . . Fascism in France is in retreat."[67] Assuming that a healthier body politic would emerge from an improvement in the economic situation, Faure reminded his readers that only Socialist economic proposals could provide the remedy. While ostensibly an attempt to secure the inclusion of support for structural reforms of the economy in the program then under consideration by the Committee of Coordination of the Socialist and Communist parties, these articles served another purpose: by downgrading the danger of fascism in France, Faure was issuing a warning against any extension of the Socialist-Communist "unity of action."

The General Secretary refrained from publicly questioning the value of the unity of action pact until a meeting of the National Council on March 4, 1935. Faure used the occasion to remind the party that, eight months previously, he had issued a warning as to the possible consequences of the pact, and he added sternly:

Now there can be no doubt: the offers of unity of action made to us were the direct result of an order given to the French Communist Party by Russia. . . .

Our painfully reconstructed house can be demolished again. . . .

[66] Interviews with Rosenfeld and Moch; interview with Jean Castagnez; interview with Lucien Laurat, July 26, 1962; interview with Alexandre Rauzy, former Socialist deputy from the Ariège, June 8, 1962; interview with Fernand Roucayrol, former Socialist deputy from the Hérault and a close colleague of Paul Faure, July 28, 1962.

[67] *Le Populaire,* November 2, 13, 1934.

And I ask myself simply, if, from the outside, they are trying to sow seeds of discord among us. When I discover within the party ideas that we fought in 1920, I am disturbed.[68]

Yet this hostility to the Communists, which intensified markedly during the early months of 1935, was not solely, or even primarily, due to Faure's fears of Communist infiltration into the S.F.I.O. or to considerations of domestic politics, but was due to his mounting suspicion of the motives of Soviet foreign policy.

Paul Faure believed, as did Léon Blum, that the cause of peace was inseparable from that of socialism; peace was necessary for the realization of socialist society, and the attainment of socialism was the only guarantee of permanent peace. But if the party's two most prominent figures shared this basic faith, and if they were in substantial agreement on many of the measures necessary to achieve peace, their respective international policies were, by 1936, quite dissimilar and were becoming increasingly more so— although this fact passed largely unperceived by the rank and file and by the two leaders themselves. If Blum's international policy was inherently ambiguous, owing to its dualism, Faure's was most coherent, unfettered by oblique *nuances,* untouched by any conflict of beliefs, and remarkably consistent with views that he had expressed since the World War.[69]

Faure wholeheartedly supported Blum's contention that disarmament was the best insurance against the danger of war, and he assailed the victorious powers of the World War with unflagging consistency for failure to honor the disarmament clauses of the Treaty of Versailles. He expressed the conviction that capitalism, by its very nature, produced imperialism and militarism, and thus, by definition, engendered war. Faure ascribed Europe's failure to disarm to the malevolent desires of a decadent capitalism; while reactionaries masquerading as nationalists invoked the spec-

[68] *Ibid.,* March 5, 1935.

[69] Faure was fiercely emotional in his hatred of war. See L. O. Frossard, *Sous le signe de Jaurès: De Jaurès à Léon Blum* (Paris, 1943), 55, in regard to Faure's attitude toward the World War. In addition to his antiwar articles already mentioned, Faure was the author of the famous manifesto of the Haute-Vienne *fédération* which demanded that the Socialist party support a plea for negotiations to end the carnage. See also Marcel Prélot, *L'Evolution politique du socialisme français,* 212–213.

ter of the "hereditary enemy," their friends the munitions makers sold their deadly products to the dictators. In a memorable speech to the Chamber, Faure sarcastically inquired of the Right: "Are you certain that your financial groups and your *marchands de canons* have no link with the Hitlerian movement?"[70] Nationalization of the armaments industry became, on Faure's initiative, a major aspect of Socialist policy.

Faure was also instrumental in securing his party's refusal to approve military budgets, a decision taken, it will be recalled, at the congress of 1931. Although he freely acknowledged the duty of national defense in case of naked aggression against France and contemptuously rejected the theories of revolutionary defeatism,[71] his position was openly pacifistic. His speech to the congress of 1931 best represents its essence:

If socialism is unable to prevent the outbreak of war, it should refuse any solidarity with those responsible, the bourgeoisie. It should denounce the crime before public opinion; simultaneously, it should seek to win a speedy end to the conflict. No, no credits for war! No, no laws for war! We must launch propaganda . . . and put constant pressure on governments to force them to organize peace.

There can be no national defense by war, only by peace!

And he repeated a sinister warning that he had issued in 1928: "In a few years, France will be, from the point of view of population as from the point of view of material capabilities, in a state of inferiority vis-à-vis many countries, in particular to Germany."[72] Thus Faure's acceptance of the principle of national defense did not mean that he would counsel the Socialist party to acquiesce automatically to a war, nor did he imply that war presented an opportunity for revolution, and his position offered only a vague prescription for ending a conflict once it had erupted. In

[70] Paul Faure, *Les Marchands de canons contre la paix* (Paris, 1932), 34; see also Paul Faure, *Le Socialisme en action* (Paris, 1928), 26.

[71] *Le Populaire,* May 29, 1931.

[72] *Ibid.* In 1928 Faure had been more explicit: "The 'nationalists' should realize that an attempt to array France against Germany [would mean] forty million Frenchmen defying sixty million Germans! That is to say, for those who know how to count on their fingers, inevitable war, crowned by invasion and defeat [of France]" (*Le Socialisme en action,* 23).

fact, Faure concerned himself essentially with the need to prevent
war, and he admonished Socialists not to relent in their demands
for general and complete disarmament accompanied by generous
rectifications of the "errors" of the Versailles settlement. In substance, he warned, should France continue in her stubborn refusal
to disarm, she would be confronted by a Germany whose demographic and industrial strength would ensure either a peaceful
rectification on Germany's terms, or, in the event of war, the
certain defeat of France.

Hitler's accession to power in no way altered Faure's fundamental convictions, but reinforced them perceptibly. The General
Secretary spared no opportunity to remind his party of awesome
German strength and of the certainty of catastrophe if France
were to maintain her intractable attitude toward disarmament.

What would be the fate reserved for a France with forty million
human beings armed to the teeth in case of conflict with a populous
Germany furnished with a war potential corresponding to her industry, which is ten times more powerful than our own?[73]

In 1934 he declared repeatedly that the arms race was leading
directly to war "in which France and Frenchmen would find total
ruin and death," and in 1935 he was the leading figure in the
Socialist campaign against an increase in arms and a prolongation
of the duration of military service. But if, like Blum, Faure sought
to alleviate international tension by supporting proposals for simultaneous and controlled disarmament, he failed to envisage the
necessity of coercive action to force recalcitrant powers to disarm;
he preferred to concentrate his polemic on the reluctance of the
French government to contemplate a reduction in armaments.

This outright condemnation of a policy of security by force of
arms was matched in intensity by a blanket condemnation of
military alliances; such alliances, he argued, could serve only to
divide the continent into opposing camps or "ideological blocs."
"Military alliances . . . lead directly and inevitably to war." Accordingly, in 1934, Faure expressed intense suspicion of Soviet
overtures to the French government, and early in 1935 he followed up a series of articles denouncing military alliances with a

[73] *Le Populaire,* March 29, 1933.

brutal critique of the motives which he presumed to be at the basis of Soviet foreign policy. Asserting that Hitler's threatening posture, particularly the rantings about living space, was directed primarily against the U.S.S.R., Faure considered Stalin's desire for a *rapprochement* with France to be a desperate bid to find an ally. He launched an ill-disguised attack—bluntness was his trademark—on the prospective Franco-Soviet Pact:

A national security which rests upon a demographic and industrial potential when in fact this potential works in favor of the "enemy" is a false security.

A national security which is obliged to count upon uncertain alliances and cooperation with a foreign power whose cooperation is precarious and doubtful is a false security.

A national security which has rout, invasion, and annihiliation as its outcome is a false security.[74]

At the very moment that Blum was appealing for an international "unity of action," Faure declared frankly that the Soviets could not be trusted:

If Russian Bolshevism returns to certain mad dreams and desires a new general war in the expectation that world-wide social revolution will result from it, we will oppose it with the socialist conceptions of Guesde and Jaurès, who struggled until the very last to preserve peace.[75]

His meaning was only too clear: the possibility that the Soviet Union was seeking to provoke a European conflagration could not be discounted.

Faure viewed Stalin's declaration of approval of the French government's national defense policy as a total vindication of his admonitions to the party, and implied that it should reappraise the value of the unity of action agreement in light of this scandal-

[74] *Ibid.*, June 19, 1934, January 13, 29, March 27, 1935.

[75] *Ibid.*, April 18, 1935. Georges Dumoulin, General Secretary of the Union des Syndicats du Nord and also prominent in Socialist circles, echoed Faure's sentiments in *Le Populaire*, May 27, 1935: "It [the Franco-Soviet Pact] is a matter of war, let us not forget it. It is a question of making war on Hitlerian Germany in order to assure the defense of the Soviet Republic."

ous pronouncement from the Kremlin. He warned the S.F.I.O. that it would be repudiating its heritage if it sanctioned any alliance, even one that was "theoretically defensive."[76] Socialism, he declared, could not realign its traditional foreign policy to meet the desires of a foreign power; security was exclusively a collective endeavor, and the vehicle of security was the League of Nations.[77] His sudden rediscovery of the League and the virtues of collective security was clearly meant to discredit the Franco-Soviet Pact. Whether he was seeking its outright rejection by the Socialist parliamentary group or merely attempting to limit its importance in the eyes of the party, there is ample evidence that he was utterly opposed to reliance upon it, and indeed feared that it was, in itself, a genuine threat to peace.[78]

Surely this abrupt invocation of the concept of collective security through the League was but a transparent effort to torpedo an arrangement with an "unscrupulous and unreliable foreign power." Moreover, Faure's concept of collective security, as evidenced by his behavior during the Ethiopian crisis, was quite different from that held by Léon Blum. Yielding to Séverac's frightened warning that the application of strenuous measures could lead to a general war,[79] Faure prescribed economic sanctions against the offender by all fifty-two members of the world organization. Thus collective action was translated to mean gentle action by fifty-two nations.

Perhaps more illustrative of the staggering differences between Blum and Faure was the latter's reaction to Hitler's military reoccupation of the Rhineland: Blum, it will be recalled, vigorously condemned Germany's move as inadmissible and appealed for joint action by France, Great Britain, and the Soviet Union; Faure declared plaintively that the event was indeed inevitable,

[76] *Ibid.,* November 9, 1935.   [77] *Ibid.,* November 7, 9, 18, 1935.

[78] Louis Lévy, *The Truth About France* (New York, 1941), 120. Lévy asserts that Faure and his supporters "were, above all, anti-Bolshevik to such an extent that they detested Stalin more than Hitler. They were opposed to the Franco-Soviet Pact, which in their view contained all the germs of war."

See also J.-B. Séverac in *Le Populaire,* February 28, 1936: "It is necessary to dare to say that the defense of the U.S.S.R. creates in no manner, for us, the duty to go to war." In my interviews with them, Roucayrol and Castagnez confirmed that Faure was resolutely hostile to any reliance upon the pact.

[79] *Le Populaire,* September 27, 1935.

and issued a fervent plea for negotiations with the Führer. Conceding that the reoccupation was a grave and brutal act, Faure asserted boldly that it was the logical consequence of the thrust of French foreign policy since 1919, and he vigorously rebuked those who were calling for a military response.[80] With an emotional flourish, he repeated that only in peace and by peaceful means could the security and independence of France be assured; France, he announced, *must* negotiate with a determination to save peace, for without peace, France, socialism, indeed civilization, could be "smashed." Faure's reaction to this crisis revealed his international policy to be simple, nationalist pacifism, heavily impregnated with defeatism and anticommunism.

It was absurd to suppose that Germany would remain disarmed for a long time to come, when, contrary to the Treaty of Versailles, the other powers failed to disarm, and when the theory of security by arms prevails everywhere . . .

It is always necessary to negotiate, no matter with whom, on no matter what question, and in no matter what circumstances, *with the fierce will to defend and save peace. . . .*

All imperialisms are hateful . . . *even those which make use of revolutionary idealism.*[81]

Paradoxically, if an assessment of Paul Faure's international policy prior to the Socialist party's "exercise of power" in 1936 appears to be a relatively uncomplicated task, it must be emphasized that his position as party tactician actually complicates the effort to extrapolate central themes from daily propaganda and polemic, inasmuch as apparent contradictions and fluctuations become all too readily detectable. Yet these may be attributed to momentary tactical necessity, and should not obscure the fact that his international policy was, in its essence—unlike Blum's—neither complex nor inconsistent. It embodied certain immutable themes: a belief that France's security and the future of socialism could be guaranteed only by the maintenance of peace was closely intertwined with a conviction that Germany's industrial

[80] *Ibid.*, March 10, 1936. Faure attacked Premier Sarraut's remark that "Strasbourg cannot remain under threat of German canons" as "maladroit and dangerous."   [81] *Ibid.*, March 8, 11, 20, 1936. (Faure's italics.)

and demographic supremacy would ensure the ruin of France in the unhappy event of armed conflict; a condemnation of armaments and alliances in the certainty that they were in themselves direct causes of war was accompanied by a feeble concept of collective security; finally—and most important—a permanent suspicion and fear of the motives of the Soviet Union colored his entire approach to international affairs. If Faure's policy appears to have consisted of a series of shallow and negative diatribes against virtually all prevailing notions of national security, it is beyond question that he possessed certain fundamental, unchanging convictions, which, taken together, amounted to a nationalist pacifism, isolationist in outlook and defeatist in spirit.

Yet his sentiments were widely promulgated as official party policy. How could it be otherwise when the party's General Secretary concluded countless speeches and articles with the cry, "There is no merit in defending peace when it is not threatened," and the party's leader continued to proclaim similar sentiments and hailed Faure's frenzied demand for negotiations with Hitler over the Rhineland as a "firm position"? As Blum meandered toward the conviction that a narrower, more sharply defined concept of collective security was necessary, one that recognized the need for the creation of a united group of powers willing to take decisive action and resolved to concede nothing under duress, Faure was increasingly the advocate of a policy whose crux was hostility toward the Soviet Union and which encouraged negotiations with the leader of the new Germany. Undoubtedly it was a rather naïve assumption to expect that agreement could be reached with Hitler simply by proposing it to him, and by swearing to one's lofty and friendly intentions. But the very simplicity of this argument was, and increasingly would be, its major asset. Negotiations were not, however, Faure's primary concern, at least not until the Rhineland episode; he was driven by a desire that France's safety be assured by avoiding chauvinism, armaments, and alliances, but should the demands of the Führer increase, his position left no alternative other than negotiations.

Faure's conception of the role and structure of the Popular Front was extremely restrained, especially in comparison to Blum's exalted vision of its historic significance. It is clear that Faure believed not for a moment that the *Rassemblement* should entail any ideological *rapprochement* with any other party. His concern was that the S.F.I.O. "remain itself," immune to Communist seduction, hostile to any permanent collaboration with the Radicals, and wary of any attempt to form a *union sacrée*.[82] In substance, Faure shared none of Blum's enthusiasm for the Popular Front as an entirely new phenomenon in French political life, and comforted himself with the belief that it was simply an enlarged *Cartel des Gauches,* necessary as a barrier against the probable coordination of the conservative parties. In his view such an arrangement would provide an excellent opportunity for the S.F.I.O. to reap profits at the ballot box, enabling the party to become a leading force in a government resolved to win important social and economic reforms and to maintain peace.

Even before the Socialist "exercise of power" in 1936 and 1937 and the ensuing international crisis, Paul Faure's international policy and, in lesser measure, domestic policies, were in sharp contrast to those of his leader; here were the seeds of harsh conflict. The differing attitudes of Blum and Faure toward the Soviet Union and the French Communist party were at the source of their discord: Blum, in response to what he believed to be the external and internal threat of "fascism," made a strenuous effort to suppress his apprehensions about Communist intentions; Faure, to the contrary, was unable and unwilling to allay his fears and suspicions, and intensified his antagonism toward the Soviet Union and its lieutenants in France. Yet it still appeared to most Socialists that their leaders were in fundamental agreement on certain broadly defined objectives; in 1936 their disagreements were neither apparent nor acknowledged, even to each other.[83] In such a situation, when Blum and Faure appeared to be basically

[82] *Ibid.,* January 2, 1936. See also J.-B. Séverac, *Lettres à Brigitte: Le Parti Socialiste, ses principes, ses tâches* (Paris, 1936) , xii.

[83] Perhaps one reason for their failure to realize or recognize the implications of each other's policies was that they were by no means intimate collaborators. Blum, the intellectual, had little patience for organization and administrative problems, and regarded these as Faure's province; in no sense did he regard Faure as one of the party's theorists. Both Rosenfeld and Moch were firm in stressing this aspect of the relationship between the two men. In addition, the dualistic character of Blum's international outlook may well have lulled Faure into believing that Blum shared fully his own pacifistic convictions.

at one, how could the rank and file, as well as most party officials, have failed to believe that Faure's policies represented a faithful implementation of the immutable tenets of socialism?

THE CAUSTIC LEFT: JEAN ZYROMSKI

Jean Zyromski, a functionary at the prefecture of the Seine Department and a major figure in the noisy Socialist *fédération* in the same department, was the forceful spokesman for the *tendance* known as the *Bataille Socialiste*,[84] after the title of its plain-speaking organ of propaganda and information. Surly and combative, and an inveterate opponent of caution, Zyromski has been characterized as hopelessly doctrinaire and utterly incapable of compromise;[85] yet even a cursory examination reveals him to be a man of supple intellect and tactical flexibility. A native of the Midi, Zyromski was drawn to socialism as a young lawyer, acknowledging that he became fully committed to its doctrines after witnessing the brutal suppression of the railway workers' strike in 1910.[86] Although schooled in the niceties of socialist theory by Guesde and Bracke, Zyromski never abandoned, perhaps as a consequence of this singular personal revelation, a belief in the efficacity, even the desirability, of direct mass action. He was doctrinaire only in his conviction that class struggle was truly the inevitable and inexorable process of history; hence he rejected

[84] The *Bataille Socialiste* was fortunate to have a large number of articulate spokesmen in the provinces as well as in the Paris region. Because of the split between Marceau Pivert and Jean Zyromski in 1935, it is difficult to gauge the relative strength of the Pivert and Zyromski factions of the *Bataille Socialiste* in that year. At the Congress of Mulhouse in 1935 the still united *tendance* won 777 *mandats* to 2,035 for the majority on the question of tactics. At the Congress of Paris in 1936, a preliminary count of the *mandats* gave 477 to the *Bataille Socialiste* (Zyromski), 457 to the *Gauche Révolutionnaire* (Pivert), and 2,396 to the Faure-Séverac majority. The congress adopted a resolution unanimously; hence no formal vote was taken. See *Le Populaire*, June 2, 1936.

The spiritual leader of the *tendance* was Alexandre Bracke (A.-M. Dessrousseaux), Hellenic scholar and professor at the Collège de France, although he was hardly as militant as most of his comrades.

[85] François Gaucher, "Contribution à l'histoire du socialisme français" (Thesis, University of Paris, 1934), 152; Charles Pivert, *Le Parti Socialiste et ses hommes* (Paris, n.d.), 29; Franz Borkenau, *European Communism* (New York, 1953), 130.

[86] Louis Lévy, *Comment Ils sont devenus socialistes* (Paris, 1932), 112–114.

any cooperation or compromise with the bourgeoisie or with the existing state. In the unlikely event that the Socialist party should capture a majority of the electorate, Zyromski argued that it should then pursue a policy of "immediate socialization"; should it fail, so much the better, for the experience would serve to unmask the hypocrisy of "bourgeois" democracy.

Quite naturally, Zyromski had no doubt that "fascism" was the legitimate offspring of a decadent capitalism, and for him its appearance heralded the opening of the final chapter of the class struggle. Socialism, he demanded, must retort to force with force:

This phase of violent war between capitalism and socialism cannot be avoided; we must be resolved and prepared for it with a full heart.

Away with the illusions of social pacifism, away with the murderous utopias . . . of gradual, legalitarian, economic democracy, of social democracy within the republican state; between capitalist power and the working class marching toward power, force will be the weapon of victory.[87]

Although Zyromski daily prescribed doses of mass action and leaned heavily toward the use of violence, he excluded the possibility of an immediate seizure of power by the French proletariat; such action presupposed a lengthy period of "revolutionary preparation," and this preparation could not be begun until all working-class organizations had been welded into a single, powerful unit. Unity of the Socialist and Communist parties was uppermost in Zyromski's frequent exhortations to his party, and his immediate reaction to the Nazi acquisition of power was to demand the union of all workers' forces. Undismayed by Communist truculence, he persisted in his impassioned plea for unity, and begged the Soviet leader to hear the fervent appeal which issued from "the heart of the masses."[88]

Zyromski greeted the "unity of action" agreement with exuberance and lavish praise, presumably in the belief that Stalin had heeded this appeal and had issued the appropriate instructions to his French vassals, and in a barrage of articles in *Le Populaire* he insisted that it be the prelude to an "organic" unity of the two

[87] *Le Populaire,* January 4, February 16, 1934.
[88] *Ibid.,* February 13, 1933, February 16, 1934.

proletarian parties. In a particularly tactless message entitled "Unity with Stalin," he observed—without a trace of humor—that "this is a vigorous personality who dominates the Communist movement," and added that "the words of Stalin deserve to be known and appreciated by all of our comrades,"[89] a suggestion which doubtless created no little disquiet among certain "comrades." With overbearing consistency Zyromski declared that no obstacles could be permitted to remain in the path of complete doctrinal and tactical unity, and he regularly chided Faure and Séverac for their lethargy and obvious lack of enthusiasm for such a project.

Yet the all-too-easy assumption that Zyromski was merely a tool of the Communists should be avoided; on several critical questions, primarily in the area of domestic policy, he was, and would continue to be, at odds with his friends on the Left, notably in regard to Communist flirtations with the Radicals. And he maintained that any fusion of the Socialist and Communist parties must be exactly that: a fusion and a synthesis of ideas, not an absorption, and party democracy, as practiced by the S.F.I.O., must be the cornerstone of unity. Despite Communist proposals for a united front which would include the Radicals, Zyromski continued to advocate struggle with the bourgeoisie; Socialism should not renounce democratic methods, nor should it refuse to envisage "the unleashing of the direct forces of the masses of workers and peasants."[90] Thus the fiery Leftist leader was quite unwilling to renounce class warfare or recourse to direct action, but the constant evolution of his international outlook which, by 1935, was clearly becoming uppermost in his considerations, tended to make this position appear anomalous and even absurd.

Zyromski's dexterity—or malleability—is apparent in the brusque evolution of his international policy, for, by 1936, his outlook was indistinguishable from that of the Communists, who had also executed a hasty and virtually indecent *volte-face*.[91] Evi-

---

[89] *Ibid.*, July 11, 29, August 5, September 4, 12, 28, October 24, November 10, 1934; January 18, 1935.

[90] Jean Zyromski, *Sur le chemin de l'unité* (Paris, 1936), 11–12, and *Le Populaire*, June 13, 1935.

[91] The details, and varying interpretations, of the change in Communist policy from revolutionary defeatism to patriotic partisanship in national

dently inconsistency presented Zyromski with no troublesome moral or intellectual dilemma, especially since his views on international affairs had always been but one or two judicious steps away from those of the other "proletarian" party. In 1931 he cosponsored the resolution of the Congress of Tours which forbade any Socialist support for the "military apparatus of the bourgeoisie," and although this policy was hardly equivalent to the Communist dictum that imperialist war must be turned into an internal class war, his support, in 1933, of a resolution which would have obligated the S.F.I.O. to decline to assist the "bourgeois regime" in any war and which demanded the constitution of an antiwar front with the Communists,[92] surely illuminates the trend of his policy.

The year 1934 marked the beginning of a decisive shift by Zyromski away from revolutionary defeatism, apparently in response to the threat posed by Hitler; but, since it was so abrupt a shift, his new international policy was badly out of joint with his internal policy. Until this time Zyromski had displayed no particular regard for the League of Nations, but the entrance of the U.S.S.R. into that organization led him to extol the concept of pacts of nonaggression within the framework of the League and to hail "the will of Soviet Russia to collaborate in the building of peace"—that is, to collaborate with the European democracies. Nonetheless, he bitterly assailed the insidious "bourgeois" practice of forming alliances:

Essentially, Soviet diplomacy at Geneva has as its basis [the signing of] pacts of nonaggression, a policy which is opposed—happily—to the old traditional techniques . . . which are characterized by negotiations of political and military alliances which divide nations into antagonistic groups.[93]

Yet early in 1935 he warned sternly against pacifism and the idea that any agreement with Germany was possible.[94] What then were

---

defense are readily available in several studies, such as Franz Borkenau, *op. cit.*; Max Beloff, *The Foreign Policy of Soviet Russia*, Vol. I (London, 1947); Jacques Fauvet, *Histoire du Parti Communiste français*, Vol. I (Paris, 1964); and Gérard Walter, *Histoire du Parti Communiste français* (Paris, 1948).

[92] *La Bataille Socialiste*, June 15, 1933.

[93] *Le Populaire*, September 24, 1934.   [94] *Ibid.*, January 30, 1935.

the obligations of the proletariat? For Zyromski there existed but one task: to protect the patrimony of the working class, Soviet Russia, whose revolutionary force was, of necessity, the fulcrum of any future proletarian revolution; the duty incumbent upon French workers was to prevent the encirclement of the U.S.S.R. by hostile powers. How? By supporting Franco-Soviet *rapprochement!* Zyromski saw nothing incompatible in his cry for proletarian approval of Soviet friendship with a government that he continued to excoriate and that the working class should be preparing to overthrow!

Moreover, Zyromski encountered formidable semantic difficulties in his attempt to define the nature of Franco-Soviet friendship: since Soviet Russia was, in his view, "the champion of disarmament," presumably any alliance between the two countries would not be in the "old style," but would be dedicated to disarmament and to the search for multilateral pacts of non-aggression. Yet he argued that *rapprochement* was necessary to prevent Hitlerian aggression in eastern Europe, and logically, to have any dissuasive value, an agreement must entail some form of mutual guarantee of a military nature. Nonetheless, he declared that "Armaments cannot guarantee peace. . . . No, the traditional systems of special alliances cannot create peace by 'equilibrium.' More than ever we must combat these perilous conceptions."[95]

Zyromski's combat, however, was short-lived: the signing of the Franco-Soviet Pact effectively muted his call for struggle against "old style" armaments and alliances. It was very obvious in any event that the differentiation between "old" and "new" types of alliances was a bit of terminology employed to assuage the delicate consciences of some Socialists. Quite simply, Zyromski jettisoned the doctrine of revolutionary defeatism—it became an "anti-Marxist attitude"—and accepted the need to support the rearmament of the democracies and the erection of an alliance system directed against Nazi Germany. Although Zyromski had long preached that capitalism was the sole cause of war, his new position was predicated upon the assumption that only one power —Germany—could be the aggressor. German victory in war, he

[95] *Ibid.*, March 28, 1935.

argued, would deliver Europe to brutal domination by Nazism; defeat of Germany, he assumed, would unleash proletarian revolution in that country, thus igniting revolution everywhere.

If war were to erupt, the supreme interest of socialism would be to insure the defeat of Fascist Germany. . . .

The welfare of the international proletariat demands the defeat of Germany.

The welfare of the international proletariat demands the defense of the Soviet Union.

To safeguard peace, the conservative capitalist governments have but one method at their disposal: to oppose against any power guilty of aggression such a superiority of force as to make any attempted attack bound to fail. Only the fear of such a coalition could intimidate Hitlerian Germany and cause it to renounce war. As long as socialism has not conquered power in the most important countries in the world, it cannot refuse its support to the peace efforts of some capitalist governments.[96]

Accordingly, Zyromski prescribed a "union and close solidarity" of Great Britain, France, and the Soviet Union to prevent Italian aggression against Ethiopia,[97] but his concern for the fate of Abyssinia was greatly overshadowed by his fears of imminent Nazi attack against the U.S.S.R. Although he condemned the German reoccupation of the Rhineland with characteristic invective, he asserted that the action was not directed against France, but was essentially a diplomatic stroke by the Führer, part of his effort to secure a superior bargaining position in order to cajole the western powers into accepting his sinister design, a coalition of capitalist states directed against Soviet Russia. Zyromski admonished his party to remain implacable in face of Hitler's blandishments, and goaded his comrades "to act for indivisible peace"— that is, to ensure the security of the U.S.S.R. In the likely event of aggression against the Soviets, he proclaimed that the duty of the French working class must be to pressure the government to apply the provisions of the Franco-Soviet Pact;[98] in this situation, revolu-

[96] Otto Bauer, Théodor Dan, Amedée Dunois, et Jean Zyromski, *L'Internationale et la guerre: Pour la discussion internationale* (Paris, 1935), 1, 5, 10–13.   [97] *Le Populaire,* September 3, 1935.

[98] *Ibid.,* February 22, March 19, 1936.

tionary defeatism or an attempt to seize power would be counter-revolutionary, since either would constitute sabotage against the Soviets.

But if Zyromski sanctioned working-class support for existing governments in their effort to prevent Nazi aggression, or, in case of war, to defeat Hitler, and if he excluded the possibility of a seizure of state power at the beginning of a conflict, he denounced the concept of *union sacrée,* and asserted blandly that revolution could be accomplished during a war, owing to its prolongation, or at its successful conclusion.[99] In other words, Zyromski attempted to conciliate his concept of class conflict with his recognition of the necessity of national defense; he was incapable of diluting or abandoning his vision of revolutionary struggle, and was compelled to employ a kind of intellectual alchemy to preserve the purity of his socialist doctrine.[100] In his effort to secure the implementation of his new international policy during the years 1936–1939, he was to be forced to dampen his revolutionary ardor even further.

Zyromski's position was essentially ambiguous: mesmerized by the mystique of proletarian unity and by the revolutionary attraction of the Soviet Union, he propagated theories of class warfare and revolution, but, persuaded that the U.S.S.R. was the inevitable object of the Nazi appetite, he advocated support for an increase in the strength of "the military apparatus of the bourgeoisie"—which, by his own admission, would serve to tighten the hold of the "bourgeoisie" on state power—and called for a military alliance of France, Great Britain, and the Soviet Union. Obviously this represented a thorough reversal in his international outlook, and it appeared to be a realistic and hardheaded response to the apparent threat of Hitler's Germany to peace. But his position was undermined by the fantasy that the existing state,

[99] *Ibid.,* October 3, 1935; Bauer *et al., op. cit.,* 12.

[100] Zyromski maintained that the Popular Front involved no prospect of permanent collaboration with the bourgeoisie, against whom, he said, "we affirm once again our irreducible opposition" (*Le Populaire,* May 9, 1936). He insisted that a Popular Front government must be a government "of combat," relying on the powerful arm of mass action, resolved to break any resistance, and equally resolved to pursue a policy of "collective security," i.e., to seek an effective alliance of Great Britain, France, and the Soviet Union.

victorious in conflict, would fall beneath the wave of proletarian revolution engendered by the defeat of Germany; if there was no war—and his policy was theoretically dedicated to the prevention of war—then the prospects of revolution in France would be inevitably sidetracked by the reinforcement of the French military. Thus, paradoxically, Zyromski's hopes for revolution seemed to be contingent upon the fact that war would occur. His willingness to support a Popular Front which included the Radicals stemmed from both fear and hope: fear of Nazi Germany and for the security of the Soviet Union, and hope that revolution somehow would be born from the coming struggle. Was Zyromski haunted by a historical example, the success of the Bolshevik revolution? Evidently Faure's apprehensions about the existence of certain alien ideas within the party were not without some foundation.

But equally paradoxical was the fact that Zyromski's international policy, viewed superficially and without serious reference to his intransigent revolutionary utterances, appeared to be perfectly compatible with much that Blum was beginning to say with increasing frequency—both men spoke, for example, of the need for "international unity of action." There was, however, a criticial difference. Blum's policy, in 1936, was concerned with the imposition of disarmament; Zyromski was already contemplating the violent destruction of the Nazi regime and the possibility, even the probability, of war.

THE IMPATIENT LEFT: MARCEAU PIVERT

To discuss Marceau Pivert after Jean Zyromski is to move from the volatile to the effervescent, for if Zyromski was combative and assertive, Pivert was the personification of dynamism: organizer, pamphleteer, orator, tactician, theoretician; this was a man insatiable in his desire for the rapid redemption of the proletariat. Born in the Seine-et-Marne in 1895,[101] Pivert was intellectually attracted to socialism in his youth, probably while a student at the

---

[101] Basic biographical information was gleaned from an obituary article by Etienne Weill-Raynal, entitled "Marceau Pivert" (Arras, 1958), a biographical sketch in L. Bodin and J. Touchard, *Front Populaire 1936* (Paris, 1961), 266; and information offered by Serge Hurtig of the Fondation Nationale des Sciences Politiques.

Ecole Normale of St. Cloud. He became a professor of physics and mathematics at the secondary level, and adhered to the Socialist party in the Department of the Yonne in 1920. He transferred to the Seine *fédération* in 1924 and was chosen secretary of the fifteenth section, located in one of the most proletarian areas of the capital. He was initially elected to the C.A.P. in 1933 as a representative of the *Bataille Socialiste,* but his period of intense activity and greatest prominence dates from 1934, when he emerged as a major figure in the national party. In 1935, owing to his profound opposition to Zyromski's stand on international policy, he became the acknowledged chief of a new faction known as the *Gauche Révolutionnaire,* a heterogeneous collection of intellectuals of varying and often sectarian shades of Marxian socialism, which, however, possessed a considerable mass following, particularly in the Department of the Seine. The Revolutionary Left did not remain an ephemeral intellectual coterie, but, under the impetus of its dynamic leader, increased its strength and appeal in Paris and in several provincial *fédérations.*[102]

Pivert has been described as "pro-Communist" and representative of an extremist "bolshevizing tendency" within the Socialist party,[103] but, less than half-truths, these assumptions constitute an arbitrary and quite misleading assessment of his character and of his brand of socialism. Very simply, Marceau Pivert was, as he readily confessed, an extremist revolutionary; he consistently proclaimed his implacable hostility to capitalism and to the existing political system, and refused to compromise with the "class enemy" or to consider the Republic as anything more than an instrument of class domination. In place of reformism and timid theories about the "exercise of power," Pivert demanded that the party pursue an exclusively class-oriented policy and prepare for the *total* conquest of political power by insurrectionary means; once established, a revolutionary dictatorship of the proletariat

---

[102] Particularly active in the ranks of the Revolutionary Left were the talented Marxist theoretician Michel Collinet, the writer Colette Audry, the journalist Daniel Guérin, André Weil-Curiel, René and Hélène Modiano, Jean Prader, Lucien Hérard, the colorful Berthe Fouchère, Lucien Weitz, René Cazanave, and Henri Goldschilde. See Daniel Guérin, *Front Populaire: Révolution manquée* (Paris, 1963), 100–102.

[103] John T. Marcus, *op. cit.,* 34–35, 73.

and peasantry would ruthlessly carry out the overdue social revolution.[104] Absolutely convinced that "fascism" was the inevitable and brutal product of a decaying capitalism, he asserted that socialism had but one retort at its disposal: revolution.

Pivert was neither so romantic as to believe that revolution would be the product of spontaneous generation, nor so unrealistic as to envisage insurrection in the heroic tradition of the barricades. Insurrection presupposed careful preparation, and preparation entailed the organization of workers' militias, the creation of popular revolutionary committees in the factories and villages, and, most important, the unity of working-class organizations. A united party of the proletariat would form—clandestinely—specially trained squadrons whose function would be to seize the vital levers of power:[105] their task accomplished, he believed that armed battalions of workers would be in a splendid position to crush pockets of resistance, or, if necessary, to fight a civil war. Pivert pleaded unsuccessfully with his party to constitute—at the very least and as the first big step toward revolution—armed groups which, if merged with similar organizations of other representatives of the proletariat, could serve as an effective combat force against the "fascist" street-gangs. Just prior to the riots of February 6, 1934, he summarized his position:

The regime is crumbling beneath the corruption which is being exposed everywhere, poverty is on the increase, the social revolution is becoming the order of the day. We want to prepare ourselves for it day and night, in mind and in practice, and . . . to utilize all occasions to muster all workers together in their struggle against the pressure of the class adversary, that is to say to prepare total unity for total revolution.[106]

Accordingly, Pivert, along with Zyromski, responded to the events of February 6 by seeking real unity with the Communists in the Paris region,[107] a unity which he considered to be the

---

[104] *Le Populaire*, January 27, June 1, August 13, 1934; see also Pivert's brochure, *Révolution d'abord!* (Paris, 1936) .

[105] John T. Marcus, *op. cit.*, 66, *Le Populaire*, January 7, 1936.

[106] *Le Populaire*, January 13, 1934.

[107] *Ibid.*, March 27, 1934; Daniel Guérin, *op. cit.*, 83–93. Guérin has revealed that Pivert and his comrades were in contact with Leon Trotsky and the leaders of the Trotskyite Fourth International; in fact, Pivert visited

prelude to a vast offensive by direct mass action against the enemies of the proletariat. Such an attitude hardly indicates that
Pivert was simply "pro-Communist"; rather it illustrates that he
was "pro-revolution" and thus, by necessity, in favor of Socialist-
Communist unity. Throughout the period which was climaxed by
the unity of action agreement, Pivert doggedly maintained that
unity could be realized only on a basis of "class"; he maintained,
that is, that any attempt by the Communists to absorb or demolish
the S.F.I.O. or the C.G.T. would be repulsed by vigorous resistance. A unified party, he argued, must retain the democratic
structure of the S.F.I.O.[108]

Pivert's total alienation from the Republic and the concept of
the *patrie* was vividly demonstrated by his outlook on international affairs. In a passionate defense of the resolution of the party
congress of 1931, Pivert argued that international rivalries were
caused solely by capitalism; hence the workers had no reason to
identify their interests with those of existing national governments. "What France? What Italy? In reality it is international
capitalism which foments rivalries."[109] The military was but a
willing instrument of bourgeois domination, and its force could
be diminished and eventually abolished only in response to pressure applied by the masses; thus, in no case should the party
approve of expenditure for armaments.

Shortly after Hitler's accession to power, Pivert urged the
S.F.I.O. to reaffirm its rejection of military credits and demanded
that it declare its intention not to support any war. The outbreak
of a war should be the signal for the beginning of the final struggle
for the victory of socialism.

We will never allow ourselves, whatever the pretext, to be dragged into
war under the direction of the capitalist class. Economic boycott,

---

Trotsky somewhere in the Department of the Isère sometime in 1935. Although there existed many areas of agreement between the *Gauche Révolutionnaire* and the followers of the exiled Soviet leader, notably with respect to
questions of war and relations with bourgeois political parties, Pivert informed Trotsky that he and his supporters could not accept the rigid organi-
zational structure of the Fourth International. Guérin also observes that
Pivert believed that the Trotskyites were leaning toward "insurrectional
adventure," which, in his opinion, would simply open the way for a brutal
suppression of the proletariat   [108] *Le Populaire,* June 1, 1934.
   [109] *Ibid.,* May 27, 1931.

general strike, insurrectional conquest of power are our replies to any attempt to force us to enter into the world imperialist war that is being prepared.[110]

Revolutionary defeatism, then, should be the proletariat's *response* to war: the immediate task was to prevent rearmament and the building of an alliance system. Pivert recommended large doses of direct, mass action to intimidate the regime, as in 1935 when he appealed for mass demonstrations against the proposed increase in military service. He derisively attacked the notion that alliances could intimidate any potential aggressor from launching war, and demonstrated his refusal to sanction any accords contracted by the existing state by issuing a vitrolic reproof to the Socialist parliamentary group for its approval of the Rome agreements.[111] The real task, he implied, was that of revolutionary preparation; until the capitalist foe was disarmed by the working class, Europe would live under the permanent threat of holocaust.

The successful conclusion of the Franco-Soviet Pact and Stalin's startling approval of French rearmament provoked Pivert to break with Zyromski, who defended the pact, and to write an incendiary brochure—appropriately entitled *Révolution d'abord!*—which, intended as a rebuttal to the allegedly heretical proposals offered by the authors of *L'Internationale et la guerre*, actually represented a succinct exposition of his socialist philosophy.

At the very beginning he challenged and categorically rejected the central assumption of his adversaries by restating his conviction that "there is *never* any case, under a capitalist regime, when the duty of national defense has an international meaning or any virtue." Pivert was saying, quite bluntly, that Zyromski and his comrades had betrayed socialism by accepting the "war policy" of the bourgeoisie; instead, the French proletariat must recognize that it possessed a single means of combat against Nazi Germany, attack upon and disarmament of its own imperialist masters and appeal to the German workers to emulate its example. He as-

[110] *Ibid.*, September 13, 1933, January 13, 1934. See also an interview by Jean Bourgogne with Pivert which appeared in *La République*, January 23, 1936. Pivert declared: "When a mobilization decree is issued, we will carry out a revolutionary movement based upon the unalterable opposition of the working class to war. Who cares about the consequences? When the working class is fighting for itself on a revolutionary and international basis, it is certain of eventual victory."   [111] *Le Populaire*, March 29, 1935.

serted that his former colleagues were fundamentally and danger-
ously in error in their desire to array a supposedly "democratic"
France against Germany, and warned that they were very wrong
in their assumption that only Germany would be the aggressor.
Support of alliances directed against Germany, he said, would
have exactly the opposite effect from that intended by Zyromski
and his friends—assuming, of course, that their intention was to
preserve peace and to undermine the Führer's position within
Germany. Pivert alleged that his opponents failed to comprehend
that Hitler owed his success to careful cultivation of German fears
of encirclement, economic suffocation, and a war of extermina-
tion; by encouraging the formation of an anti-Nazi alliance, they
were actually strengthening Hitler's grip on his people, since these
"legitimate" fears would appear to be all too real.

More important, Pivert considered that the immediate effect of
their policy, if accepted by socialism, would be to detour revolutionary preparation into a state of paralysis. To reinforce the
military was to cement capitalism in power indefinitely, an especially annoying prospect when he was convinced that it was totter-
ing on the brink of extinction. Pivert rebuked Zyromski savagely
for his idyllic assumption that the army could be democratized:
the army could be only the brutal instrument of bourgeois domination.

Thus, after having delivered the proletariat to the capitalist general
staffs, to the lies of the putrid press, to the sickening drunkenness of
nationalism . . . will they [Zyromski and his colleagues] ask the proletariat to conquer power after military victory?

Pivert reserved his heaviest scorn for the postulate that the
workers could use war to gain power:

It is not true that one can simultaneously support the war policy of the
bourgeoisie and still remain faithful to the demands of the class
struggle.
It is a mortal illusion to believe that a revolutionary war can be led
with the bourgeois army.

A belief in such a revolutionary war, he declared, revealed a fatal
misconception of the nature of elementary human psychology: in
time of war the uneducated, unprepared, and uprooted masses

would be driven by the instinct of self-preservation, thereby abdicating their inherent revolutionary fervor to the requirements of defense, thus reinforcing the domination of the class in power. Defense of the Soviet Union? Certainly, but not by war: "To defend the Soviet Union by war, by aiding our own imperialism, runs the terrible risk of a general collapse of the workers' movement."

Although Pivert admitted that the decomposition of capitalism fatally devolved from economic crisis to fascism and ultimately to war, his doctrine forbade proletarian participation in the coming "imperialist struggle." How then could the U.S.S.R. be defended and peace maintained in a Europe apparently headed inexorably toward war? Pivert had a solution: revolution—*before* the war could occur. "Against the imperialist war on the horizon, revolution everywhere!" Pointing to Zyromski's assertion that Europe was already divided into two hostile camps, he asked what further proof was needed of the necessity to unite the international proletariat in order to crush all possibility of imperialist war. Should the working class succeed in seizing power in some states before the international revolution could take place, it would offer disarmament to the remaining capitalist governments, but should the latter unleash war upon the infant socialist states, the proletariat would reply in kind. Finally, Pivert confessed that if his pleas were to go unheeded and war erupted before revolution could occur, then the proletariat had no alternative but to employ revolutionary defeatism.[112]

Pivert's response to the Rhineland crisis confirmed his estrangement from his old ally Zyromski, and revealed that the sentiments expressed in *Révolution d'abord!* were not merely theoretical—his slogan "We will not march!" left no room for doubt. Describing the reoccupation as another stage on the road to imperialist war, he declared that the workers had no stake in the controversy. But, significantly, Pivert rejected in advance any position which might be taken by the leaders of the S.F.I.O. if it failed to correspond to his own, ostensibly because the party had not discussed the issue.[113] Such a declaration of independence was surely unnec-

---

[112] Marceau Pivert, *Révolution d'abord!* (Paris, 1936), *passim*.
[113] *Le Populaire*, March 9, 1936.

essary; Paul Faure was hardly apt to suggest that punitive action be taken against Germany. Pivert's outburst demonstrated not only the reality of his faith in revolutionary defeatism, but also his readiness to defy the party's leaders; rather than a declaration of independence, his attitude amounted to an assertion of anarchy. And this was not simply a threat: his open insubordination was to embarrass two governments under Socialist direction and was partially responsible for his exit from the S.F.I.O. in 1938.

Pivert's conception of the Popular Front bore little resemblance to that held by Léon Blum; for the leader of the Revolutionary Left the "exercise of power" had no justification unless it was intended to serve as a preliminary to total conquest of power. Moreover, its achievements would be won less by a parliamentary government than by the working class prepared to wrench concessions from a frightened bourgeoisie.[114] And he placed little or no faith in the value of the party's bourgeois partners; as late as January, 1936, he attacked the Radicals as "an untrustworthy conglomeration of men, not a party."[115] Undoubtedly Pivert's acceptance of the Popular Front was attributable in part to the success of the Spanish *Frente Popular,* whose electoral victory he hailed as the advent of a socialist republic, and whose example of direct mass action, he believed, should be imitated in France. The revolt of the Asturian miners in 1934, he argued, repulsed the "fascist" threat; the electoral triumph of 1936 dislocated the bourgeoisie; now, should far-reaching reforms be delayed, the masses were prepared and willing to take drastic action. The analogy with France was all too obvious to Pivert: the defeat of "fascism" on February 12, 1934, would be followed by electoral victory in 1936, and should the Popular Front government procrastinate, the masses would do their duty. "Comrades of Spain," he wrote, "thank you for the shining confirmation that you have conferred on the methods proposed in France by the Revolutionary Left."[116]

Like Zyromski, Marceau Pivert professed and exhibited a profound contempt for existing society, and was certain that the appearance of fascism signaled the imminence of international proletarian revolution, but, unlike Zyromski, he was unwilling to

[114] Parti Socialiste S.F.I.O., *XXXIIIe Congrès National,* 163.
[115] *Le Populaire,* January 24, 1936.   [116] *Ibid.,* February 24, 1936.

mortgage his revolutionary zeal, even temporarily, for the sake of the Soviet Union. Instead of the apparently timid conception of revolution officially espoused by the Socialist party, Pivert offered a dynamic concept of total revolution, and in place of the cautious and often confusing international policy of the party's leadership —which seemed to require collusion with the class enemy—Pivert's demand for revolution now appeared to be an attractive alternative to the ominous possibility of an "imperialist war." Thus the promised land of peace and social equality could be won by the simple act of revolting against a decadent capitalism already on the verge of collapse; for Pivert, the act of revolution required only dedication, will, preparation, and a refusal to compromise with the bourgeoisie.

Of all of the leading figures of the S.F.I.O., Pivert was undoubtedly the most successful in preserving the purity of his socialist faith in his response to the challenge of fascism. But if he expressed disdain for the nineteenth-century mode of revolution and conceived of modern revolution as a meticulously planned and scientifically executed insurrection under the leadership of the party, his position was shot through with romantic illusions. With astonishing naïveté he underestimated the state's capacity for resistance, and surely his optimistic estimate of the revolutionary fervor of the workers was unsupported by available evidence. And simply because his socialism was a faith, built upon certain apparently incontestable assumptions, he made no serious effort to describe the postrevolutionary state; evidently he believed it would appear as the spontaneous product of the natural intuitive power of the proletariat. Similarly, he was incapable of perceiving that the Nazi message could also have an appeal to the working class; if he recognized that Hitler's success was attributable to a skillful exploitation of the insecurity shared by all Germans, he failed to comprehend the depth of national sentiment. It was perilous to construct an international policy upon the untested axiom that the overthrow of the existing state would lead inevitably to similar upheaval in the fascist homeland; it was equally perilous to believe that a newly created socialist state could defend itself against the onslaught of powerful foes. But, paradoxically, if Pivert's policies appear in retrospect to have been shockingly devoid of realism, his appeal and power within the party were to increase markedly during the turbulent years 1936–1938, for internal and external events were to provide a striking apparent vindication of his revolutionary doctrine.

THE SOCIALIST CLIENTELE: ELECTIONS OF 1936

The results of the first round of the balloting confirmed pre-election forecasts of a Popular Front victory, but aside from the astonishing success of the Communist party, which increased its popular vote by some 700,000 over its 1932 total, and the spectacular decline of the Radical party, which sustained a loss of 400,000 votes and saw its share of the electorate slip from 20.07 per cent in 1932 to 16.57 per cent, the most remarkable features of the election was the relative stability of public opinion.[117] The major parties of the *Front Populaire* increased their total of the vote by only 1.5 per cent, while the percentage of the parties of the Right dipped slightly. The Socialist vote, by comparison to 1932, was a model of stability: the party gained a mere 32,000 votes, and its percentage of the total of inscribed electors dropped almost imperceptibly from 17.1 per cent to 16.9 per cent.[118]

The apparent stability of the Socialist vote was, however, somewhat deceptive in that it masked extreme fluctuations in certain departments—again in comparison with the election of 1932— and measurable increases and decreases in others. Sharp fluctua-

---

[117] Georges Dupeux, *Le Front Populaire et les élections de 1936*, 126; François Goguel, *Geographie des élections françaises de 1870 à 1951* (Paris, 1951), 83. Both calculate the percentages on the basis of the total number of inscribed voters, so as to demonstrate the number of abstentions. The Socialist party, however, calculated the percentages and the electoral rank of its *fédérations* on the basis of the votes actually cast. See Parti Socialiste S.F.I.O., *XXXIVe Congrès National, 1937, Rapports* (Paris, 1937), 55. Henceforth, unless otherwise noted, all references to departmental, regional, and national percentages will follow the method used by the S.F.I.O.; e.g., rather than Goguel's figure of 35 to 40 per cent for the Socialist vote in the Haute-Garonne, we will accept the Socialist party's figure of 48.8 per cent.

[118] Georges Dupeux, *op. cit.*, 126, calculates the S.F.I.O. total in 1932 as 2,034,124; on this basis its vote fell from 17.63 per cent to 16.9 per cent. But the official results of the 1932 elections, as found in Georges Lachapelle, *Elections Legislatives, 1er et 8 Mai 1932, Résultats Officiels* (Paris, 1932), 348–351, give the S.F.I.O. 1,964,000. Thus its 1936 total of 1,996,000 represents a gain of 32,000 as opposed to Dupeux' calculation of a loss of 38,000. The S.F.I.O. won 20.68 per cent of the total vote cast in 1936.

tions to the detriment of the party were evident in the departments of the Loiret (a loss of 90% of its 1932 total), Aveyron (−75%), Indre (−64%), Moselle (−71%), Savoie (−52%), Meurthe-et-Moselle (−50%), Gironde (−48%), Lot-et-Garonne (−45%), Hérault (−41%), Var (−39%), Puy-de-Dôme (−37%), and the Loir-et-Cher (−38%). In all of these departments, except the Lot-et-Garonne, the decrease can be attributed to the presence of Neo-Socialist candidates who, in most cases, had been elected as Socialists in 1932. On the other hand, the S.F.I.O. total increased radically in the essentially rural departments of the Landes (an increase of 591% over 1932), Cantal (290%), Ain (175%), Deux-Sèvres (170%), Charente-Inférieure (158%), Haute-Marne (116%), Vendée (112%), Corrèze (78%), Sarthe (74%), Gers (50%), Manche (50%), and the Vienne (62%). Slight decreases were registered in the industrial departments of the Bouches-du-Rhône (−16%), Bas-Rhin (−20%), Seine (−12%), Pas-de-Calais (−6%), and in the largely rural department of the Drôme (−29%); in all of these departments it was the Communist party that profited by defections from the S.F.I.O. Slight and moderate progress was evident in numerous departments, as demonstrated in Table 1 (pp. 283–287), columns three and four.

Despite local variations, an examination of the electoral geography of the Socialist party will be immeasurably more profitable if it is undertaken on a regional rather than on a departmental basis. But instead of the somewhat confusing and cumbersome method employed by B. Léger in his work, *Les Opinions politiques des provinces françaises,* which groups the departments into twenty-six regions, I have grouped them here into eighteen regions according to the model established by the official census of 1936.[119] Admittedly these eighteen regions are geographically and demographically disproportionate, but they represent rough approximations of the historical provinces, and each region is composed of departments with similar economic characteristics, insofar as this is possible. These regions are listed below in descending

[119] République Française, Ministère de l'Économie Nationale, *Résultats statistiques du recensement général de la population effectué le 8 mars 1936,* I (Paris, 1938), 18–21.

order according to the percentage of the total vote received by the Socialist party on the first ballot:

1. Languedoc (30.0)
2. Rhone Valley-Provence (27.6)
3. North (26.3)
4. Garonne Basin (25.8)
5. Massif Central (25.7)
6. The Lyonnais (24.9)
7. Central France (24.6)
8. Northeast (24.2)
9. Brittany (17.1)
10. West Central France (16.6)
11. Algeria (15.5)
12. Southwest (15.3)
13. Alps Region (14.8)
14. Paris Region (14.4)
15. Eastern France (10.8)
16. The Orleanais (9.5)
17. Western France (7.9)
18. Normandy (7.0)

A cursory glance at these percentages and at Table 1 (pp. 283–287) and Table 2 (pp. 288–291) reveals the existence of three clearly defined regional categories, which may be arranged according to the degree of Socialist success in each. There were four hostile regions, comprising twenty-one departments, in which the S.F.I.O. received less than 11 per cent of the total vote cast: Normandy, Western France, The Orleanais, and Eastern France. A second category, composed of six regions (twenty-seven departments), was characterized by occasional Socialist success in widely scattered electoral *circonscriptions,* but the Socialist share of the vote amounted to less than 20 per cent of those cast: the Paris Region, the Alps Region, the Southwest, Algeria, West Central France, and Brittany. The third category, composed of eight regions (forty-four departments) was marked by considerable success of the S.F.I.O. In these regions Socialist candidates polled more than 20 per cent of the total: the Northeast, Central France, Lyonnais, Massif Central, Garonne Basin, North, Rhone Valley and Provence, and Languedoc.

Among the hostile regions should be included the departments of the Aveyron and Lozère, nominally classified in the very favorable region of the Massif Central. The presence of a popular Neo-Socialist candidate, Paul Ramadier, undoubtedly accounted for the dearth of Socialist electors in the Aveyron, and Neo-Socialist strength was responsible for the poor performance of the S.F.I.O. in the Orleanais; the Lozère, on the contrary, had been singularly unreceptive to Socialism in 1932. As Table 2 (pp. 288–291) indicates, one of the hostile areas, Eastern France, possessed a very high percentage of industrial workers, yet the region was distinctly unfavorable not only to socialism but to all of the Popular Front parties. Another region, Western France, was heavily agricultural; the third (Normandy), while essentially rural, included a concentration of industrial workers in the department of the Seine-Inférieure. Dupeux concludes that the strength of traditionalism, particularly religious faith, was the primary factor in the Socialist failure to make any inroads into these areas.[120] In any event, these meager results were not unexpected; in 1932 the three regions had produced but 6.0, 1.2, and 1.3 per cent of the entire Socialist vote respectively, as compared with 5.0, 1.4, and 1.3 per cent in 1936.

The second regional grouping was marked by extraordinary diversity, not only in regard to the degree of Socialist success or failure, but also with respect to economic characteristics. A substantial diminution of the Socialist clientele in the Department of the Seine—obviously to the benefit of the Communists—was counterbalanced by slight gains in the Seine-et-Marne and Seine-et-Oise, and although the Paris region accounted for 10.1 per cent of the Socialist total of almost two million votes, Socialist candidates won a paltry 14.4 per cent of the electorate in an area heavily populated by industrial workers. In the Alps region, overwhelmingly agricultural and sparsely populated, and despite the slender 14.8 per cent of the vote—which represented an anemic 1.3 per cent of the Socialist tabulation—five S.F.I.O. deputies were elected, exactly as many as in the Paris region. In the Southwest, spectacular Socialist inroads in the agricultural departments of the Gers, Landes, Basses-Pyrénées, were offset by catastrophic losses in the Gironde and the Charente, owing to the strength of the Neo-Socialists. It is particularly noteworthy, however, that a goodly portion of the agricultural electorate, especially independent peasant proprietors, formerly favorable to the Radicals, went over to Socialism.[121] This phenomenon was also apparent in the West-Central region, which accounted for 4.8 per cent of the Socialist total, as opposed to 2.4 per cent in 1932; nevertheless only one department in the region, the Indre-et-Loire, elected

[120] Georges Dupeux, *op. cit.*, 150.

[121] Georges Dupeux, *op. cit.*, 175. Dupeux attributes the swing to socialism to severe economic crisis in this area.

more than one S.F.I.O. deputy. Similarly, socialism was clearly on the rise in Brittany, but its advance was generally limited to urban centers such as Nantes, Saint-Nazaire, Lorient, and Saint-Malo. Algeria was also becoming a fertile ground for the S.F.I.O., notably Algiers and Oran: this region surpassed seven regions of the *métropole* in its enthusiasm for socialism. Thus, the second category of regions exhibited a complex pattern: diminution of Socialist strength in areas of heavy working-class population (Paris, Bordeaux), advance in agricultural areas, especially in those with a considerable proportion of small and medium scale independent proprietors, and sporadic success in smaller urban areas, including those with a sizable industrial proletariat (Nantes, St. Nazaire). But if socialism was definitely on the up-swing in many of these areas, the tangible results were relatively meager: only thirty S.F.I.O. deputies, or 20 per cent of the party's total, were elected in these twenty-seven departments.

The eight regions extremely favorable to the Socialist party accounted for 59.1 per cent of its total on the first ballot, and elected 112 of its deputies, or 76 per cent of the party's complement at the Palais-Bourbon. Despite the complex diversification of the agricultural population, two basic types of Socialist electors can be readily discerned: industrial workers and inhabitants of rural agricultural areas. The former—and the less important—were located primarily in the North and Northeast regions and scattered in other regions, notably in the departments of the Rhône, Loire, Isère, Bouches-du-Rhône, Gard, Haute-Garonne, and, to a lesser extent, the Allier. Although Socialist influence was relatively stable in these areas—in comparison with 1932—a slight loss was registered in the North and in the major centers of Lyons and Marseilles. Again it was the Communist party that profited from the defections from the S.F.I.O.

But the regions most favorable to socialism were essentially rural in their overall composition: Languedoc, the Garonne Basin, Massif Central, Central France, and two regions of a mixed agricultural-industrial complexion, Lyonnais and Rhone Valley and Provence. All of these regions were geographically contin-guous. The Socialist vote in these six regions was extraordinarily stable: in 1936 they accounted for 41.3 per cent of the S.F.I.O. total, as opposed to 43.1 per cent in 1932. More important, they elected eighty-one deputies, a majority of the party's parliamentary group; thus 41.3 per cent of the Socialist party's electorate was represented by 55 per cent of its deputies. If the seven departments in these six regions in which no Socialist deputy was elected are subtracted from the total, the result reveals that 39.9 per cent of the Socialist clientele elected 55 per cent of the deputies. Still more significant is the addition of the Alps region, geographically contiguous to this six-region bloc. In this case the resulting figures are even more astonishing: thirty-five departments, casting but 41.2 per cent of the party's total, elected 59 per cent of its deputies. Therefore, seven largely agricultural regions—excluding those departments in which no Socialist was elected—casting two-fifths of the Socialist vote, elected three-fifths of the parliamentary group.[122] Without doubt these deputies wielded and would con-

---

[122] These seven regions elected seventy-five S.F.I.O. deputies in 1932, or 57 per cent of the total. Unlike the departmental calculation of the percentage of industrial workers, the census of 1936 does not differentiate between the various categories of agricultural exploitation. Georges Dupeux, *op. cit.*, 162–68, attempts to delineate the categories following the example of A. Demangeon in his *La France économique et humaine,* Vol. VI, pt. 2, of *La Geographie universelle,* by P. Vidal de la Blache and L. Gallois (Paris, 1946), who utilized the agricultural census of 1929. Initially he distinguishes between two basic types of agricultural holdings: (1) capitalist ownership, either by aristocratic or bourgeois families, and (2) independent peasant proprietorship. Dupeux argues that the independent proprietors, those cultivating the land directly, were inclined to favor the Radicals and Socialists in the southwest, southeast, and in most of the Massif Central, but in the east tended to vote for candidates of the Right. Leaseholders—leasing from the capitalist owners—predominant in the Allier, Haute-Vienne, Lot-et-Garonne, and the Var, generally favored the S.F.I.O., except for the Lot-et-Garonne, where they favored the Communists. On the other hand, the sharecroppers of Vendée and Mayenne tended to support the Right. The agricultural proletariat was of sufficient size in but one department to be a determining factor; this was the department of the Aisne, which was highly favorable to socialism. It is evident that an attempt to correlate the professional categories of the agricultural population with their political behavior is frustrated by the contradictory behavior, not only of the independent proprietors, but also of the sharecroppers. Therefore, Dupeux concludes that a simple geographic division of departments into industrial or agricultural categories is more meaningful than a division according to professional categories.

Following this pattern, analysis of the Socialist parliamentary group (excluding Algeria) yields the following result:

tinue to wield a considerable amount of power in their respective departmental *fédérations,* and would serve to maintain and increase the already powerful voices of these *fédérations* within the party as a whole.

Deputies from departments with an agricultural population exceeding 52 per cent: 31, or 21 per cent of the total.

Deputies from departments with an agricultural population ranging from 45 per cent to 52 per cent: 42, or 29 per cent of the total.

Deputies from departments less than 45 per cent agricultural, but without a majority of industrial workers, thus tending to be classified as agricultural: 38, or 26 per cent of the total.

Deputies from departments with a larger percentage of industrial workers than agricultural population: 34, or 24 per cent of the total.

If we follow the characterization of the electoral *circonscriptions* by B. Léger, who has analyzed only 133 of the 147 Socialist *circonscriptions,* and who has tended to classify a *circonscription* as agricultural-industrial if it contained a smattering of industrial workers—we obtain the following results:

Deputies from heavily agricultural *circonscriptions:* 33, or 23 per cent of the total.

Deputies from agricultural-industrial *circonscriptions* (basically agricultural) : 45, or 31 per cent.

Deputies from industrial *circonscriptions:* 55, or 38 per cent of the total.

Undetermined: 13, or 8 per cent of the total.

Thus, whether we utilize the more general and—in spite of obvious difficulties—safer method of Dupeux, or the relatively unreliable estimates of Léger, we arrive at the same conclusion: the majority of the Socialist deputies were elected from agricultural areas.

2

The Popular Front Government

THE FIRST WEEKS

Immediately after the results of the second round of the legislative elections were published, *Le Populaire* feverishly announced the Socialist party's intention to head a Popular Front government,[1] and shortly thereafter Blum and Faure invited the Communists, Radicals, and C.G.T. to share the burden of power. The Communist leaders, briefly embarrassed by the bid—they clearly had anticipated that the elections would produce a government under Radical direction—refused it, arguing lamely that their presence in the government would serve as a pretext for unnamed "enemies of the people" to foment disorder, and Thorez offered Blum only platitudes, among them an unctuous declaration of support.[2] The Radicals, anxious for office as always, accepted, but intimate discussion between Blum and the testy leader of the C.G.T., Léon Jouhaux, failed to undermine the old unionist's habitual disdain for politics and politicians, and the C.G.T. declined the invitation.[3] Thus Blum's choice of ministers was limited: his cabinet was composed of Socialists, Radicals, and members of splinter parties of the Left.

Scarcely installed, the new government was confronted with a

[1] *Le Populaire,* May 4–5, 1936.

[2] Maurice Thorez, *Oeuvres,* Vol. III, Pt. II (Paris, 1953), 227. Originally appeared in *Cahiers du bolchevisme,* June 15, 1936.

[3] André Delmas, *A Gauche de la barricade: Chronique syndicale de l'avant-guerre* (Paris, 1953), 83. Gaston Cusin, Chef de cabinet of Vincent Auriol, Minister of Finance, served as unofficial representative of the C.G.T. Interview with Cusin, December 1, 1961.

double-edged crisis which threatened to topple it and to throw the country into chaos. Class warfare seemed to be an appalling reality: occupation of factories by workers spread contagiously across the country, while a frenzied flight from the franc threatened the Treasury with a massive loss of gold. Undoubtedly the twin aspects of the crisis were due to anxieties and expectations generated by Blum's accession to power. The bulk of the working class, suddenly aware of its strength, impatiently demanded the rewards promised by the *Front Populaire*. The moneyed groups, understandably apprehensive that the government would institute control over the exchange of currencies or devalue the franc, had begun to transfer massive sums to more hospitable places. Since this government widely advertised its commitment to hasten France's convalescence, it was faced with the awkward task of reassuring both camps without antagonizing either irreparably. Presumably it did not intend to tread heavily upon the interests of any of the many sectors of French society. The dilemma was frightening and demanded dramatic action, but this action could not be so dramatic as to divide the nation yet further.

The most immediate and dangerous aspect of the crisis was the wave of sit-in strikes.[4] The conservative President, Albert Lebrun, revealing his penchant for panic in moments of tension, literally begged the incoming Premier to soothe the workers with whatever promises were necessary, and, obligingly, Blum took to the radio and declared that the Parliament would be responsive to their just demands. But he concluded with an implicit reprimand:

The action of the government, to be efficacious, must be exercised in an atmosphere of public security. It would be paralysed by any attack upon order, by any interruption in the vital services of the nation.[5]

[4] On the strikes, consult Jacques Danos and Marcel Gibelin, *Juin 36* (Paris, 1952); Henri Prouteau, *Les Occupations d'usines en Italie et en France, 1920–1936* (Paris, 1938); Jean Montreuil, *Histoire du mouvement ouvrier en France* (Paris, 1946), 435–510; Marceau Pivert, "Juin 36 et les défaillances du mouvement ouvrier," in *La Revue Socialiste*, XCVIII (June, 1956), 2–33; Antoine Prost, "Les grèves de juin 1936, essai d'interprétation," in *Léon Blum, chef du gouvernement, 1936–1937* (Paris, 1967), 69–87. These commentators agree that the strikes were not provoked by agitators, but were in fact spontaneous.   [5] Léon Blum, *L'Exercice du pouvoir* (Paris, 1937), 76.

Blum's emphasis fell bluntly upon the need to maintain order, yet he was unwilling to employ the full force of the state to evacuate the factories, explaining later that recourse to police action could have precipitated outright civil war.[6] Fortunately for the new government, the conclusion of the so-called Matignon agreements, wrenched from a frightened *patronat,* the rapid enactment of accompanying legislation guaranteeing a forty-hour work week, paid vacations, and collective bargaining, and the energetic intervention of Maurice Thorez urging a return to work, assuaged the temper of the strikers.[7] By the end of June the unrest had largely dissipated. Blum himself regarded the concessions by the *patronat* and the social legislation as a victory of common sense, not of illegal proletarian pressure. Blum had not the slightest intention of violating his implicit contract with the majority of the electorate; he would not permit the development of a revolutionary situation. The conciliator of warring party factions now saw himself as the conciliator of the nation.

Successful in launching a program of social reform and firm in its role as guardian of "Republican legality," the government was to fail in its effort to revive France's lagging economy and to liquidate the financial chaos. Blum selected Vincent Auriol, party boss in the Socialist stronghold of the Haute-Garonne and longtime Socialist spokesman on financial matters, to be his Minister of Finance: evidently Auriol's political prowess and his close friendship with the Premier were his major qualifications for this sensitive post.[8] Auriol was firm only in knowing what he was not

---

[6] Léon Blum, *L'Oeuvre, 1940–1945* (Paris, 1955), 149.

[7] Representatives of the C.G.T. and the C.G.P.F. (Confédération Générale de la Production Française) met at the Hôtel Matignon on June 7, and, under Blum's guidance, the C.G.P.F. conceded the right of collective bargaining and the right of the workers to organize into unions, and granted a general increase in wages. On Thorez's instructions to the working class, see *L'Humanité,* June 12 and 13, 1936.

[8] It seems clear that during the first weeks of the government's existence Blum chose a number of key associates who were privy to every decision: they were Jules Moch, former deputy from the Drôme, appointed General Secretary to the Presidency of the Council; Auriol; Georges Monnet, the Minister of Agriculture; André Blumel, Blum's *Directeur du Cabinet;* Jean-Baptiste Lebas, who headed the powerful Socialist *fédération* in the Nord; Marx Dormoy, Under-Secretary of State and later Minister of the Interior; Oreste

going to do, and he based his financial policies upon unwarranted assumptions, which, unhappily for the government, proved to be increasingly unwarranted as time passed. Both Blum and Auriol refused to consider a devaluation: it was politically unwise. Quite naturally, they could not, also for political reasons, maintain the deflationary policy of their predecessors. Instead they pursued a policy which was grounded on the assumption that increases in salaries, plus an expanded program of public expenditure, would combine to produce a vast increase in the purchasing power of the masses, thereby increasing the level of consumption, which in turn would stimulate production. This would provide additional revenue for the state, allowing it to re-establish the hallowed balanced budget. In this ideal situation, in which the workers would have more money and business more sales, holders of capital-in-exile would be willing to invest in the French economy.

Unfortunately, the scheme failed, and for several good reasons: (1) The reform of the Bank of France, while considered necessary even in moderate political circles, was unlikely to win a vote of confidence in the government from the already suspicious financial community; (2) the franc remained overvalued in relation to the world market; (3) the social legislation raised the costs of production; (4) the cash increments received by the masses were apparently spent on basic commodities, such as foodstuffs. Thus increased spending failed to stimulate an increase in industrial production, and public expenditure increased budgetary disequilibrium. And although the flight of liquid capital slackened in the first weeks of July, the gold reserve was vulnerable to a resumption of the exodus without warning. Moreover, the government believed that it could not institute control over exchange of currencies, owing to the well-known hostility of its Popular Front partners to any measure smacking of "structural" reform of the economy.

In July the government was forced to the expedient of issuing bonds—the so-called Auriol bonds—in the vain hope that hoarders of notes would release their tight grip on what was believed to

Rosenfeld, editor of *Le Populaire;* and Georges Boris, editor of the leftist weekly, *La Lumière*. This information is based upon Jules Moch's answers to my questions, November 22, 1961; interview with Gaston Cusin; interview with Alexandre Rauzy, June 8, 1962.

be a vast sum. The venture knew only a very limited success, and the renewed outflow of gold in August persuaded Blum and Auriol that devaluation was critically necessary. The devaluation was effectuated in September, thinly disguised as an international agreement. But the financial problem was to be alleviated only briefly, and was to return to constitute a permanent harassment to the government, eventually to prove to be a source of its collapse.[9]

Despite the pressures of internal affairs, Blum was able to take several steps toward the implementation of his international policy. Necessarily his action was limited to publicizing the aspirations of his policy and to cautious diplomatic moves in the hope of restoring confidence to Anglo-French relations. Two major speeches, one delivered at the American Club prior to his assumption of power, the other given at the Assembly of the League of Nations on the thirtieth of June, represented the substance of his efforts. Both were moving summations of Blum's beliefs on international relations in a troubled Europe, both combined a magnificent idealism with a reticent admission that potentially dangerous measures might be necessary. Blum felt compelled to preface his recommendations with frank assurances that the French people were united in their will for peace; in doing so he intended to dispel lurking suspicions that the France of the Popular Front would resort to "ideological warfare" against the "fascist" powers. In short,

We want to live in peace with all nations of the world, whatever the internal policy of their regimes. We want to eliminate the causes of conflict with all nations of the world. . . . We want to work with all nations . . . provided that they want peace.[10]

The leaders of the "new" France, Blum declared, condemned the notion that there was any revolutionary virtue to war; reprisals

[9] Paul Einzig, *World Finance, 1935–1937* (New York, 1937), 188; Etienne Weill-Raynal, "Les Obstacles économiques à l'expérience Léon Blum," in *La Revue Socialiste*, XCVIII (June, 1956), 49–56; Georges Lefranc, *Histoire du Front Populaire* (Paris, 1965), 308–341, 365–387; Marguerite Perrot, *La Monnaie et l'opinion publique en France et en Angleterre 1924–1936* (Paris, 1955); Martin Wolfe, *The French Franc between the Wars, 1919–1939* (New York, 1951), 138–171.

[10] Léon Blum, *L'Exercice du pouvoir*, 126. Speech to the American Club of Paris, May 15, 1936.

against states which had persecuted their comrades were equally excluded. In substance, Europe must rid itself of its frightful obsession with the possibility of war, and devote its energies to the construction of common political and economic solidarity.

But lest France's magnanimity be construed as weakness or abandon, Blum asserted forcefully that peace must rest upon the common observance of international legality and "morality." Since assurances that this prerequisite to peace were hardly in evidence, France must rely upon the fidelity of proven friendships: none could dismiss the sincerity of her appeal, but none should doubt her willingness to preserve the security of her friends. The "pacific powers," motivated by the simple instinct of self-preservation, were in the process of reinforcing their friendship. Yet Blum ruled out a "coalition of superior forces" as a stable instrument for peace: collective security, he argued, currently involved a risk of war, which was, by definition, a dangerously abnormal situation. Thus the establishment of a real collective security, devoid of this danger, was the charge given to the "new" France. Blum's formula was simple: collective security was the condition of disarmament, disarmament was the condition of collective security. Without the certainty of assistance from others no state would disarm willingly, but without disarmament there could be no guarantee of peace. France perceived but one means to liquidate the past: the creation of a disarmed Europe with the assistance of the dictators. To the dubious, Blum replied:

Some among you think, perhaps, that by describing this image of a possible world in relation to the real world, we are pushing idealism to the point of a vision. Do not forget that all life is suspended on this vision, that it alone can reanimate enthusiasm in the hearts and minds of millions of living beings. Do not forget that, without this vision, peace will always remain uncertain and constantly threatened.[11]

Blum also began a determined effort to cooperate with Great Britain, pointedly informing Anthony Eden, the British Foreign Secretary, that his friendship with the leaders of the Labor party in no way compromised his ardent desire to establish a close

[11] *Ibid.*, 138, 142. Speech to the Assembly of the League of Nations, June 30, 1936.

relationship with the Baldwin government.[12] Apparently Eden was convinced of Blum's sincerity, for he reported to his superior that the new French leader was a marked improvement over those who had occupied the premiership during recent years. By mid-July it seemed evident to Blum that Anglo-French cooperation and friendship had been re-established.

Blum's international policy remained essentially unaltered: an appeal to international conscience and morality, a real faith in mankind's aspiration for peace, and a conviction that disarmament was the necessary prerequisite to Europe's political and economic regeneration were all tempered by the nagging reminder that the so-called pacific powers must be resolved to prevent a recurrence of armed aggression. To assure a temporary security from intimidation these powers must reinvigorate the ties which naturally bound them together, and to this end Blum honestly sought to restore France's good credit with Great Britain. Yet his emphasis lay not on force, nor even on the desirability of coercing *any* nation, but upon the future cooperation of all nations, regardless of their political regimes, for the construction of a new Europe. Granted that this was largely an ideal to be achieved, but the prominence given to it reveals that its attainment would constitute the permanent goal of his foreign policy: "Without this vision, peace will always remain uncertain and constantly threatened."

The events of the first weeks seemed to justify a certain optimism as to the ultimate success of the Popular Front experiment. A spectacular advance in social legislation and the apparent stability of the governmental coalition appeared to indicate a promising internal situation, disturbed only by the troublesome financial dilemma, which, hopefully, would be alleviated by Auriol's policy of delicate inaction. Blum's activity in the international

[12] Anthony Eden, Earl of Avon, *Memoirs: Facing the Dictators, 1923–1938* (Cambridge, Mass., 1962), 429–431. Neville Chamberlain, as Prime Minister in 1938, had no faith in Blum: "A French government in which one cannot have the slightest confidence and which I suspect to be in closish touch with our Opposition" was his description of the second Blum government. See Keith Feiling, *Neville Chamberlain* (London, 1946), 347–348. The Popular Front victory in 1936 met with scant approval from Baldwin and his entourage. See Margaret George, *The Warped Vision: British Foreign Policy, 1933–1939* (Pittsburgh, 1965), 85–87.

arena was limited to resounding declarations of France's splendid intentions and to the repair of relations with an old friend. There were few hints of the imminency of the international crisis to be born in the backwater of Europe, the Iberian peninsula. The Spanish Civil War was to create an almost insoluble dilemma for Blum, seriously compromise his government's domestic position and initiative in foreign affairs, and expose the fragility of the Popular Front.

THE SPANISH THORN

On the afternoon of July 18, Blum was meeting with André Delmas, leader of the *Syndicat des Instituteurs,* when he was abruptly interrupted by a message from the Quai d'Orsay. Delmas recalled that the Premier paled and then exclaimed with astonishment: "This is news of a military insurrection that has just erupted in Spain." Delmas was equally astonished, especially since he had already read of it in the afternoon edition of *Paris-Midi* and had credited Blum with remarkable *savoir-faire* for making no mention of it during their conversation.[13] Evidently the lines of communication between the Quai d'Orsay and the Hotel Matignon were inferior to those which linked Spain and certain newspapers in the French capital.

On July 20 Blum was the recipient of an urgent telegram from the worried Prime Minister of the Spanish Republic, José Giral, which asked for the sale of French arms and airplanes needed to crush the sedition of the Spanish military. Acting with unaccustomed decisiveness, Blum, in accord with Yvon Delbos, Minister of Foreign Affairs, and Edouard Daladier, Minister of Defense —both Radicals—was disposed to honor Giral's request. Inasmuch as Giral's Government was the legal regime of a friendly nation, and since a Franco-Spanish commercial treaty, dating from 1935, contained a proviso for the purchase of arms by Spain from France, neither legal nor ideological impediments stood in the way. But less than two weeks later the French government called for a European agreement on a convention of nonintervention in the Spanish struggle, and on August 8 it formally announced the suspension of arms shipments to its beleagured

[13] André Delmas, *op. cit.,* 110.

neighbor.[14] What events and problems arose in the interval from July 20 to August 8 which compelled Blum and his associates to reverse their position?

Apparently an urgent telephone call on July 22 from Charles Corbin, French Ambassador in London, to the Premier marked the beginning of a rapidly unfolding series of events which culminated with the adoption of the nonintervention policy. Corbin may have warned Blum that the British leaders viewed the possibility of French assistance to the Spanish Republic with no little apprehension. Blum was scheduled to meet on July 23 with British leaders on routine matters, but the war in Spain meant that his visit to London would be a significant test of Anglo-French cooperation. Upon arrival, he was driven immediately to the residence of the Prime Minister. No record of the ensuing conversation has been divulged, but it is significant that in an interview shortly afterward Blum dismissed briskly a French journalist's suggestion that Britain feared that a general European conflagration might develop from the Spanish imbroglio: "Never mind that . . . the Spanish government is a legitimate government and . . . it is a friendly government."[15] On the following day Eden explicitly counseled his French friend to be "prudent" in his actions concerning Spain, and evidently certain high-ranking members of Baldwin's entourage were even more explicit in warning Blum to remain aloof from the war in the Iberian peninsula.[16]

[14] *The Foreign Relations of the United States,* Vol. II: *1936* (Washington, 1952), 448. Ambassador Straus to the Secretary of State. See also Blum's testimony in *Les Evénements survenus en France,* I (Paris, n.d.), 216; Daniel Mayer, "Léon Blum face à Franco," in *L'Express,* December 18, 1958, 6. Delbos and Daladier's initial support for aid to Madrid is documented in Pierre Cot, *Le Procès de la République,* Vol. II (New York, 1944), 307, and confirmed to me by Rosenfeld and Moch. See also the memoir by Blum's *Directeur du Cabinet,* André Blumel, "La Non-intervention en Espagne," in Georges Lefranc, *Histoire du Front Populaire,* 460–466.

[15] Louis Lévy, *The Truth About France* (London, 1941), 113; Blum testimony in *Les Evénements survenus en France,* I, 216.

[16] Blum in *Les Evénements survenus en France,* I, 216. Moch, in our interview, recalled that Chamberlain allegedly declared: "Wherever Bolsheviks and Fascists are killing one another, it's all the better for us," meaning that the Madrid government was Communist-dominated. See also Joel Colton, *Léon Blum, Humanist in Politics* (New York, 1966), 234–269. Colton does not consider Eden's warning to be "blackmail."

Disheartened by Britain's apparent unwillingness to encourage his effort to aid the Spanish Republicans, but determined to persist in that effort, Blum returned to Paris on the evening of July 24. Landing at Le Bourget he was surprised to discover a large group of nervous politicians impatiently awaiting his arrival. Their spokesman, Camille Chautemps, Vice-President of the Council of Ministers and a Radical party leader, spoke severely, detailing the alarming consequences of the decision to honor Giral's request for aid by pointing to the upsurge of agitation in the Chamber and in right-wing newspapers. This warning was echoed emotionally by Jeanneney, the President of the Senate, who exclaimed, "How can you do this? No one understands it."[17] Later in the evening Delbos also expressed his growing uneasiness and reluctance to become involved in Spain, and President Lebrun obligingly contributed an intemperate outburst, allegedly informing his associates that "this delivery of armaments to Spain means war or revolution in France."[18]

In this increasingly dismal atmosphere the Council of Ministers convened on July 25. It was evident at the outset that substantial differences existed on the question of assistance to Madrid, but contrary to general belief the division was not along Radical-S.F.I.O. lines, but was infinitely less coherent. Chautemps, seconded by Delbos—who apparently had been influenced by the pessimistic arguments of Léger, Secretary General of the Quai d'Orsay—endorsed a policy of strict noninterference, basing his position on the British attitude, on the political effervescence created by the disclosure of the government's intentions, and on the proposition that French involvement in Spain would encourage the split of Europe into two hostile "ideological blocs."[19]

[17] Blum testimony in *Les Evénements survenus en France,* I, 216; Camille Chautemps, *Cahiers secrets de l'armistice (1939–1940)* (Paris, 1963), 33–35.

[18] Pierre Cot, *op. cit.,* 308; William Foss and Cecil Gerahty, *The Spanish Arena* (n.d.), 372–375, contains the text of a letter from the Spanish emissary de los Rios to Madrid. It reveals Delbos' nervousness over supply of the Spanish Republic. See also Louis Lévy, *op. cit.,* 114. Blumel and Moch, in our discussions, declared that the President's sentiments were conveyed to Blum on the morning after the Premier's return from London.

[19] Pierre Cot, *op. cit.,* 310; Alexander Werth, *The Destiny of France* (London, 1937), 379; *The Foreign Relations of the United States, Vol. II: 1936,* 448. Ambassador Straus placed Daladier in the noninterventionist camp,

According to Jules Moch, only Blum, Auriol, and Pierre Cot, Minister of Air, spoke in favor of the original decision to assist the Spanish Republicans. The majority of the ministers, Radicals *and* Socialists,[20] were prone to caution and were thus amenable to a compromise solution suggested by Blum. Since an initial shipment of aircraft would not be ready for some days, it was decided to announce that "France would not intervene in any manner whatever in the internal conflict in Spain," but, when ready, the aircraft would be consigned to Mexico, which in turn would effectuate their transfer to the Spanish authorities.[21] Formulation of a definitive attitude was then postponed, pending developments. The official announcement was simply a temporary expedient designed to allay the furor of the Right and to preserve the image of the unity of the cabinet.

Accordingly the French government pursued its policy of temporization. On July 31 Delbos, nettled by the dogged questioning of the Rightist Henri de Kérillis, assured the Foreign Affairs Commission of the Chamber that the Government was resolved to practice a strict noninterference in Spain.[22] But these repeated assurances failed to subdue the rumblings on the Right—and on the moderate Left. De Kérillis's newspaper, *L'Echo de Paris,* rather than tempering its indignant polemic, denounced "secret"

---

while Cot argues to the contrary. Rosenfeld informed me that Daladier favored nonintervention at the meeting of July 25 and thereafter; his interpretation was supported by Cusin, and Blum, writing in *Le Populaire,* March 9, 1939, categorically denied that Daladier was in favor of assisting the Republican forces. What seems likely is that Daladier initially took a strong stand in support of Madrid, but his determination melted quickly in face of opposition; this was a regular pattern for the "Bull of the Vaucluse"; in February 1934 he vowed to remain in office, but resigned; in 1938 he vowed to support Czechoslovakia, but went to Munich. On Delbos and Léger, see Elizabeth R. Cameron, "Alexis Saint-Léger" in Gordon Craig and Felix Gilbert, eds., *The Diplomats* (Princeton, 1953), 378–405 and Joel Colton, *op. cit.,* 247.

[20] Interviews with Moch, Blumel, and Cusin. According to Moch the only Socialists to signify their support for Blum's desire to aid Madrid were Salengro, Monnet, and Dormoy. See Joel Colton, *op. cit.,* 245–247, for details of the "caution and compromise" prevalent in the cabinet.

[21] Blum testimony in *Les Evénements survenus en France,* I, 217.

[22] *Le Journal des Débats,* August 1, 1936; interview with Alexandre Rauzy, member of the Foreign Affairs Commission of the Chamber.

French aid to the Spanish "Communists."[23] The moderate François Mauriac hysterically warned the Premier that the nation would never pardon his "crime" if he lent assistance to "butchery" in Spain,[24] and the Radical organ *La Dépêche de Toulouse* observed that assistance to Spain could turn her soil into an international battlefield.[25] Coupled with strident proclamations of support for the Spanish rebellion from several deputies on the Right, these declarations closely circumscribed the government's freedom of action.

The cabinet session of August 1 was discordant from the beginning. Blum, persuaded that evidence of Mussolini's aid to the Spanish insurgents would convince his undecided colleagues of the necessity to assist Madrid, was disagreeably surprised to discover that the involvement of the Italian dictator strengthened the hand of those who feared the Spanish war would erupt into European war. Once again, after a vigorous exchange of views between Delbos, now fully supported by Daladier,[26] and Cot, it was decided to temporize. The Government launched an appeal for the conclusion of a nonintervention agreement by the European powers, but it reserved its freedom of action pending the satisfactory conclusion of such an accord.

Blum then decided, acting on the suggestion made by the British Labor party leader Philip Noel-Baker, to make yet another effort to persuade the British government to modify its sentiments. Recognizing the futility of arguing the need to save Spanish democracy, Blum fashioned an argument designed to appeal

[23] *L'Echo de Paris*, August 2, 1936. See also the vitriolic speeches in the Chamber by members of the extreme Right, René Dommange, Pierre Taittinger, and René Delzangles, in the *Journal Officiel, Débats, Chambre des Députés*, August 1, 1936.

[24] *Le Figaro*, July 25, 1936.

[25] *La Dépêche de Toulouse*, July 31, 1936. *La République*, organ of the Radical party's right wing, remarked on August 4, 1936, that shipment of arms to Republican Spain would be considered a "hostile act" by other countries. Note also that Edouard Herriot, the Radical leader, clearly expressed his sentiments to Blum: *Ah, je t'en prie, mon petit, ne vas te fourrer là-dedans"*; see the Blum testimony in *Les Evénements survenus en France*, I, 217.

[26] See note 19 above, and *The Foreign Relations of the United States, 1936*, 454–455, Ambassador Straus to the Secretary of State.

to Britain's selfish interests, hoping to convince London that the installation of a Spanish regime servile to Hitler and Mussolini would constitute a grave threat to the entire Mediterranean region. Admiral Darlan, the Chief of the Naval Staff, in whose integrity Blum placed great confidence, was selected to carry out the task of persuasion. His mission was to convince his British opposite number, Admiral Chatfield, of the reality of the military danger in the expectation that the latter's influence would be brought to bear upon Baldwin. Unhappily for Blum, Darlan's effort was a fiasco. Admiral Chatfield confided to Darlan that his fears were illusory, since he himself knew that General Franco was "a good Spanish patriot."[27]

The total failure of Darlan's mission and the alacrity with which the British government embraced the French proposal of August 1 convinced Blum that his government was now committed to a policy which would prevent effective assistance to the *Frente Popular*.[28] Delbos' vigorous public espousal of nonintervention in a speech on August 3, and the chorus of praise for his stand in the Radical press, made it very evident that the majority of the Radical party would not tolerate a reversal of the position adopted on August 1. Moreover the temper of French public opinion, frayed by the events of June, was uncertain, and the organs of the Right were becoming alarmingly aggressive on the Spanish issue. In short, Blum believed that he was virtually isolated, within his own cabinet as well as on the diplomatic front, and faced with a divided nation. Depressed and exhausted, he

---

[27] Blum testimony in *Les Evénements survenus en France,* I, 218.

[28] Although adequate documentation is unavailable, it appears possible that the British Ambassador in Paris, Sir George Clerk, delivered a virtual ultimatum to Delbos, warning the Foreign Minister that Great Britain did not consider herself obliged to aid France if French assistance to Madrid served to provoke a general war. See Alverez del Vayo, *Freedom's Battle* (London, 1940), 70. Hugh Thomas, in *The Spanish Civil War* (New York, 1961), 258, states that Azcárate, former Spanish Ambassador to London, confirmed that Clerk had in fact delivered such a message to Delbos. Colette Audry, *Léon Blum ou la politique du juste* (Paris, 1955), 124, quotes from a letter from Blum to Suzanne Blum, written during Blum's wartime incarceration: "It is a fact that, whatever may have been my influence in London at that time, any European complications arising from French interference in Spain would have found England neutral and more than neutral."

decided to resign forthwith, although his Socialist colleagues Auriol, Rosenfeld, and Blumel urged him to force a showdown in the Chamber. His despair was temporary, as he was easily dissuaded from resigning by the Spanish emissaries de los Rios and Jiminez de Asúa, who declared that such a step would represent an incalculable loss to the cause of Spanish democracy.[29]

The Council of Ministers convened on August 8 to assess the response to its appeal of the previous week. On this occasion the tendency to temporize, characteristic of the previous sessions, was less in evidence. Rather than a situation in which the Radicals stood fast for nonintervention, while the Socialists urged aid for Madrid, the division of the cabinet did not follow party lines. Delbos, Chautemps, and Daladier insisted that France promise scrupulous fidelity to nonintervention, arguing that a rivalry among the powers in assisting the combatants in Spain could escalate the struggle into general war. Cot and Auriol, supported by the Socialists Roger Salengro, Georges Monnet, and Jean Lebas, remained adamantly in favor of assisting the Spanish Republicans, arguing that a victory of the insurgents would be a defeat for democracy and a military threat to France. The discussion was banal, as well as useless: those formerly uncommitted were now committed to nonintervention. Apparently most of the cabinet, including the Socialists Faure,[30] Charles Spinasse, and Albert Rivière rallied to the position of Delbos, Chautemps, and Daladier. After almost three weeks of deliberation and temporization, France had definitely adopted a policy of nonintervention in the Spanish strife.

Thus Blum acquiesced in the adoption of a policy which he knew would prevent effective assistance to the Spanish Republic, but recognition of the many factors which compelled this decision should vitiate the effect of the epithets which characterize much of

[29] Blum testimony in *Les Evénements survenus en France,* I, 219.

[30] On the session of the Council of Ministers, see Vincent Auriol, *Hier . . . Demain* (Tunis, 1944) , I, 50; Pierre Cot, *op. cit.,* 319; Louis Lévy, *op. cit.,* 112, which discloses that Lebrun threatened to resign unless nonintervention was adopted; *The Foreign Relations of the United States, Vol. II, 1936,* 476–477, Chargé Wilson to the Secretary of State; Jacques Debu-Bridel, *L'Agonie de la Troisième République, 1929–1939* (Paris, 1948) , 380; and interviews with Rosenfeld, Blumel, and Cusin.

the literature devoted to the problem. Blum was neither "frightened by hobgoblins" manufactured in his own imagination,[31] nor was he free to act independently as Premier, nor was he paralyzed by "ideas, sentiments, and illusions" properly belonging to another era.[32] Very simply, Blum adopted nonintervention because he had no alternative but the sterile path of resignation. He believed—quite correctly—that his desire to assist Madrid was shared by few of his colleagues, and only the naïve could expect support for the Spanish "Loyalists" from the Tory regime in London. To assume that fear of antagonizing Great Britain was "a misinterpretation of France's diplomatic and strategic assets," since Britain would be obliged to ally with France in the event of general war,[33] misses the point. One of Blum's primary aspirations was the speedy reconstruction of the Anglo-French *entente* as the prelude to pacification of the continent, and he recognized that any possibility of attaining this objective would be grievously compromised should he persist in his intention to supply the *Frente Popular,* even assuming that he had the freedom to do so. To insist that Blum could have taken forceful, independent action betrays an ignorance of elementary political realities: no government could have survived a parliamentary test against the combined opposition of the Radicals and the conservative parties. The only "independent action" open to Blum was resignation, and this would have been a negative act, insuring the installation of a government less sympathetic to the program of the *Front Populaire*—and to the Spanish Republic. Rather than this bleak certainty of failure, support of nonintervention was a potentially viable course of action. This policy, Blum hoped, would preserve the vital friendship of the British government, maintain the unity of the Popular Front, aid the Spanish Republic by depriving its enemies of their source of supply, and alleviate international tension.

But if Blum adopted nonintervention as the sole rational alter-

---

[31] Dante A. Puzzo, *Spain and the Great Powers, 1936–1941* (New York, 1962), 99.

[32] Pietro Nenni, *La Guerre d'Espagne* (Paris, 1960), 84.

[33] J. Bowyer Bell, "French Reaction to the Spanish Civil War, July–September 1936," in William C. Askew and Lillian P. Wallace, eds., *Power, Public Opinion, and Diplomacy* (Durham, N.C., 1959), 267–296.

native to the collapse of his government and of his aspirations for a new Europe, a more perplexing question remains unanswered: why, in face of cynical and systematic assistance to the Spanish insurgents by Italy and Germany, did he defend this policy and make it his own? The problem is less baffling if considered within the context of Blum's further assessment of the implications of the Spanish struggle and in light of his stubborn belief in the validity of his international policy and conception of the Popular Front. Surely Blum did not consciously desire to scuttle the Spanish Republic, but as the "interested" powers labored through their negotiations, finally producing the nonintervention agreement, he became very aware that competition among these powers in aiding their respective friends in Spain could create a spiraling arms race, itself a real source of war—as he had warned for fifteen years. The increasing tempo of Italian and German supply of the Spanish rebels in late summer 1936 apparently convinced the Premier that peace was in jeopardy, that it was even "at the mercy of an incident."[34] Moreover, Blum was fearful for France's internal stability: believing sincerely that the Spanish issue was dividing the nation perhaps irrevocably, ever mindful of what he believed to be a permanent threat to the Republic from the Right —whose renewed aggressiveness he found thoroughly alarming[35] —he was resolved to do nothing that could shatter the remnant of national unity of purpose.

Confronted with increasingly vitriolic denunciations of nonin-

[34] Speech by Blum to the Chamber of Deputies, December 5, 1936, in Léon Blum, *L'Exercice du pouvoir*, 194; Blum repeated this belief in *Le Populaire*, October 14–15, 1945, and to the parliamentary commission, *Les Evénements survenus en France*, I, 219.

[35] George C. Windell, "Léon Blum and the Crisis over Spain," in *The Historian*, XXIV (August, 1962), 423; Colette Audry, *op. cit.*, 127–128, cites Blum's letter to Suzanne Blum in which he reveals his belief that assistance to the Spanish "Loyalists" might well have provoked a civil war in France, possibly involving a revolt of the French military. Blum also mentioned the possibility of civil war in France as a result of aid to Madrid to the Socialist National Congress of 1937. See Parti Socialiste S.F.I.O., *XXXIV° Congrès National, compte rendu sténographique* (Paris, 1938), 462. In our discussions, both Moch and Rosenfeld declared that Blum genuinely believed that a right-wing uprising was possible.

tervention by the Communists, ably seconded by Zyromski and his sympathizers, and with the ill-concealed discontent of some leaders of the C.G.T.,[36] Blum felt compelled to defend his position publicly. In an impromptu speech on the evening of September 6 to the unruly militants of the Socialist *fédération* of the Seine—he was greeted with angry shouts of "guns and planes for Spain"— the Premier bared his motives with emotional fervor. With injured tone he denied being "corrupted" by power, and effectively quashed the hostility of his listeners by identifying with their sentiments: "Do you believe that my heart is less torn than yours?" Alternating between teacher and supplicant, Blum won approval by playing the card of fear—fear of another world war. Although he acknowledged that the victory of the Spanish Republic was in the interests of European democracy and French security, he warned of the inevitable consequences of competition among European powers in assisting the protagonists in the struggle, adding that, in any event, the French arsenal was unable to match the contributions made by other states. The threat of war, he asserted repeatedly, was real, and he pleaded with the doubters "to place your trust in the word of a man who has never deceived you." The following passage, which constituted a vindication of the totality of Blum's pacifist ideals, left the most profound impression upon his listeners—and upon the Socialist party:

We have some friends who consider the conduct of the government to be feeble and perilous. . . . They speak of our weakness, of our capitulation. They say that it is by this practice, this flabby practice of concessions to the bellicose powers that we have created real dangers of war in Europe. They tell us that it is necessary to resist, to stiffen and exalt the national will, that it is by the exaltation of patriotic sentiment and pride that we can maintain peace.

My friends, my friends! I know this language, I have heard it before.

I am a Frenchman—for I am French—proud of his country, proud of its history, nourished as much as anyone, in spite of my race, in its tradition. I will consent to nothing that alters the dignity of Republican France, of the France of the Popular Front. I will neglect nothing to assure its safety and defense. But when we speak of national dignity,

[36] *L'Humanité,* July 25, August 3, 22, 1936; *Le Peuple,* August 4, 6, 12, 20, 22, 24, 1936.

of national honor, of national pride, will we forget that by an unstinting effort of fifteen years we have taught our people that one of the elements of national honor is a pacific will?

Will we allow it to be forgotten that the most solid guarantee of physical security will be found in international agreements, in the international organization of assistance and disarmament? Have you forgotten that? I believe that you have not. . . .

I commend everything which strengthens the feeling of solidarity among Frenchmen against a possible danger. But the excitation of popular sentiment . . . in preparation for a conflict that one believes in his heart to be fatal and inevitable, no! For that will never have—I say it openly, at my own risk—either my cooperation or my consent. I do not believe, I will never admit that war is inevitable or fated. Until the utmost limit of my power, and until the final breath of my life, if necessary, I will do everything to keep war from this country.

You understand me very well: *everything to avert the present and future risk of war.* I refuse to consider war as possible today because it might be necessary or inevitable tomorrow. *War is possible only when one admits it to be possible; inevitable when one proclaims it to be inevitable.* As for myself, until the last, I refuse to despair of peace, and of the action of the French nation for the preservation of peace.[37]

Blum received a long and wildly enthusiastic ovation. Scattered cries of "guns and planes for Spain" were smothered with shouts of *Vive Blum! Vive la Paix!*[38] Calling upon almost magical powers of persuasion, Blum reached the innermost emotions of his audience, and his speech had a narcotic effect on working-class agitation against nonintervention. By identifying nonintervention with the preservation of peace, by professing renewed fidelity to his pacifist ideals, and by once again proclaiming the relevance of these ideals a perilous international situation, Blum set the tone of appeasement that was to be dominant in the Socialist party, at least until late in 1938.

The September speech was echoed in all of Blum's subsequent declarations on the Spanish problem during his ministry. Although the government participated in international efforts to halt assistance to the forces of General Franco and attempted to

[37] Léon Blum, *L'Exercice du pouvoir*, 176–188, *passim*. Italics mine. Speech delivered at Luna Park.

[38] Interview with Jules Moch; Alexander Werth, *op. cit.*, 388.

help the "Loyalists" by permitting a trickle of supplies to cross the frontier clandestinely,[39] Blum remained adamant in his contention that the existence of the nonintervention agreement alone confined the war to Spain. In June, 1937, shortly before the fall of the government, he declared: "For almost a year, in the midst of one of the most dangerous crises that Europe has ever known, we have preserved peace."[40]

Blum publicly equated nonintervention in Spain with the cause of peace, and the great mass of Frenchmen—including the militants of the S.F.I.O.—were unaware of the many critical factors which had necessitated the adoption of the policy. Initially Blum accepted it for want of an alternative: stymied by domestic political pressures and balked in his efforts to win British support for Madrid, he capitulated to reality. Shortly thereafter, he convinced himself that the danger of war did in fact exist, and sought to dispel the threat by appealing for international cooperation and to the "conscience" of the dictators in the hope that nonintervention could be fashioned into an effective instrument. Even when this hope was unmasked and shown to be illusory, Blum insisted publicly that nonintervention, fiction or not, preserved peace. His sense of isolation, his fear of war, his inflexible faith in the rightness of his international policy, and his conception of the Popular Front, taken together, were indeed an insurmountable barrier to reconsideration of nonintervention during his year in power. Certainly it is misleading to assert that "Blum felt in his heart that it [nonintervention] was against France's best interests."[41] Blum believed passionately that France's "best interests" required internal stability, social reform, a renaissance of democratic values, and the achievement of a pacified Europe. The Spanish conflict threatened to wreck this vision: at home, its ramifications could provoke the disintegration of the Popular Front and unleash civil strife; internationally, it threatened to precipitate a frightful arms race,

[39] See Hugh Thomas, *op. cit.*, 331–343. Gaston Cusin told me that, as a spokesman for the Customs Agents Union, he was able to instruct agents to permit passage of some contraband disguised as foodstuffs, clothing, etc.

[40] *Le Populaire*, June 7, 1937.

[41] J. Bowyer Bell, *op. cit.*, 295. Joel Colton, *op. cit.*, 265–267, argues that nonintervention in the Spanish war revealed Blum's basic weakness—the trust he placed in all men.

dashing all hopes for disarmament; and, if unchecked, it could degenerate into a general war. Given these beliefs, Blum's commitment to nonintervention was inevitable: if it was the most satisfactory solution to an awkward dilemma, it was also fully consistent with his pacifist faith and his aspirations for the France of the Popular Front. In short, Blum gambled that nonintervention would save Spain, the Popular Front, and peace, and by so doing permit him to pursue his national and international policies. Whether his fears were unreal and his policies unrealistic is another matter. Blum gambled and failed, yet the gamble appeared to be much preferable to the certainty of immediate failure.

INTERNATIONAL AFFAIRS: A LINGERING OPTIMISM

Inquiry into the foreign policy pursued by the Blum government offers dramatic confirmation of the contention that its maintenance of nonintervention in the Spanish conflict was linked closely with the sincere desire of its chief to pacify Europe; such inquiry also reveals Blum's international policy to have been inherently dualistic, perhaps even contradictory, and painfully naïve. Wise statesmen generally seek to maintain a generous supply of alternatives, but Blum was well stocked with illusions, giving him the unlimited right of expectation. In effect he believed that France could afford the luxury of noncommitment to any policy that risked her irrevocable estrangement from Germany, and, partly as a result, he worked at cross-purposes. He devoted much energy and hope to an effort to alleviate tensions between the two countries, and he combined repeated affirmations of France's pacific mission with emotional pleas for general disarmament: yet he shunned contact with Mussolini and publicized increased expenditure for French armaments. Willing to sacrifice pride and independence in an effort to cement France's ties with Great Britain, Blum refused to reinforce the Franco-Soviet Pact with a military convention, which may have undermined the credibility of France's commitments to her eastern allies. Blum later was to claim that, by 1936, he had concluded that binding military alliances were the only means of security for France; actually his policy in 1936 and 1937 was still in flux. Blum clung to a lingering optimism that good will and reason were the stuff of diplomacy, and, in consequence, he continued to employ the woolly rhetoric of pacifist idealism, which gave immense comfort to many Socialists.

Late in August, 1936, Blum greeted the arrival in Paris of Dr. Hjalmar Schacht, Hitler's Minister of Finance and Economics, as a splendid opportunity to explore the possibility of serious discussions with Germany. Despite a sharp Communist protest—which Blum dismissed with an equally sharp rejoinder[42]—the German dignitary was welcomed to the Hôtel Matignon. Blum's sincerity and zeal—and naïveté—permeated his talk with Schacht: he reminded his guest that he was a Socialist and a Jew, but avowed his determination for peace with all nations, whatever their political regimes. Apparently Dr. Schacht responded to this information by professing his own good intentions and those of the Führer, and as proof of these credentials declared that Hitler had authorized him to make concrete proposals. If France and Great Britain were to restore Germany's former colonies to her, thus insuring the Reich of an abundant source of raw materials, Schacht was prepared to guarantee Germany's participation in an international disarmament conference. Blum reacted with sheer enthusiasm, replying that he was ready to begin negotiations with Germany immediately.[43] His buoyancy was diminished only by his recollection that the colonies in question were held by Great Britain and her dominions, an inconvenience which Schacht had already considered, noting that "in the ruling circles of England the solution to this question is much better prepared than you would imagine." Warning Blum that the success of this proposal depended upon him, Schacht urged the Premier to deal directly with Baldwin, bypassing the Foreign Office. Blum protested that he could not consent to such an irregular procedure, but voiced the conviction

[42] Blum declared that "the organization of peace is one of the conditions of French security." See *Le Populaire*, August 27, 1936. Thorez's angry remarks may be found in Parti Communiste Français, *Notre Lutte pour la paix* (Paris, 1938), 71.

[43] Léon Blum in *Les Evénements survenus en France*, I, 221. See Pierre Renouvin, "La Politique extérieure du premier ministère Léon Blum," in Edouard Bonnefous, *Histoire politique de la Troisième République*, VI; *Vers la Guerre (1936–1938)* (Paris, 1965), 402. Renouvin has examined the French diplomatic documents of 1936 and 1937.

that Germany's suggestions provided a basis for fruitful discussion among the interested powers.[44]

Blum was clearly excited by his conversation with the German emissary. On September 17, just before Hitler's annual harangue to his followers at Nuremberg, Blum told the French nation by radio that "France will seek to consolidate and organize peace with all nations," adding pointedly that "there is not a single meeting, *not a single subject of discussion that France will refuse.*"[45] And when Eden paid a visit to Paris in early October, Blum was eager to relate to him the details of the Schacht proposal. Blum was taken aback and obviously embarrassed by his guest's reaction: Eden vehemently denounced the plan and the underlying assumption of British receptiveness to it, cautioning Blum, in a very patronizing manner, to be wary of cunning diplomacy. For Eden, no more should be said of the matter, and he observed that if Germany honestly desired a general European settlement she would not be deterred by an Anglo-French refusal to consider the colonial issue. Blum meekly concurred, not daring to antagonize his ally; Great Britain, after all, was sensitive about colonies. Both agreed that the German proposal was unworthy of serious consideration, and Eden extracted a promise from Blum not to pursue his exchanges with Schacht.[46]

Blum and Delbos entertained second thoughts, however. While Blum did not have another conversation with Schacht until May, 1937, both he and Delbos made a determined effort to keep open the possibility of negotiations with Nazi Germany. On December 11, Dr. Forster, the German Chargé d'affaires, reported to the Wilhelmstrasse that Delbos sought to enlist Germany's participation in mediating between the conflicting parties in Spain, and did so with the expressed aim of improving Franco-German relations. Delbos was convinced—in Forster's view—that joint mediation in Spain could serve as "a point of departure for further German-French collaboration": "After the settlement of the Spanish question, as he [Delbos] repeated several times, we could discuss all questions affecting Germany." On December 23 Delbos

---

[44] Blum, *Les Evénements survenus en France*, I, 221.

[45] Léon Blum, *L'Exercice du pouvoir*, 146.

[46] Léon Blum, *Les Evénements survenus en France*, I, 222; Anthony Eden, *op. cit.*, 568.

told Count von Welczeck, the German Ambassador, that "the entire French people [have] . . . the honest desire to reach, now or never, an understanding with Germany," and stated blandly that Great Britain would not stand in the way of Germany's colonial aspirations! Welczeck cabled Delbos's view to his superiors: "The Foreign Minister formulated his proposal as follows: We should have raw materials, colonies and loans, in return for which the only compensation required of us was peace." In short, Delbos allegedly promised "satisfaction of Germany's wishes"[47] in several areas in exchange for peace in Spain.

Surely Delbos could not have acted entirely on his own initiative in such a critical matter.[48] Very significant is the fact that these conversations were followed quickly by Blum's well-publicized speech at Lyons on January 24, 1937, in which the Premier once again appealed for a general settlement of all European problems and specifically for Franco-German understanding. Disclaiming any intention to seek a separate settlement with Germany, Blum declared that "the solution to the Franco-German problem lies within the framework of a general settlement" which would provide for economic cooperation among all European nations, thus alleviating many of Germany's economic difficulties. But, he warned, economic cooperation could not be envisaged without a "political settlement" which would require the progressive reduction of arms by all powers. Speaking directly to Germany, Blum freely admitted that disarmament might well disrupt her economy; thus France, and presumably all of Europe, should be prepared to offer her economic assistance in the forms of access to raw materials, extension of credit, and financial cooperation.

[47] *Documents on German Foreign Policy, 1918–1945*, Series D: Germany *and the Spanish Civil War, 1936–1939* (Washington, 1950), 163–165, 180–181. Delbos added that "Germany's anxiety regarding a Communist victory in Spain was comprehensible and justified." Welczeck was impressed: he told the Wilhelmstrasse that "Blum and Delbos have now . . . undertaken the attempt to reach an understanding with Germany. It is worthy of note that it is the Popular Front Government which, in spite of its anti-National Socialist attitude, . . . makes an offer and undertakes what is allegedly a final attempt to reach an understanding with Germany."

[48] Blum testified that there existed "mutual confidence" between Delbos and himself, and that he read all diplomatic correspondence. *Les Evénements survenus en France,* I, 126.

Blum refrained from insisting upon prerequisites or timetables: if Germany were to demonstrate a genuine desire for peace, France was willing to make concessions, as long as these were integrated into a "general settlement."[49] Both Delbos and Blum were committed to an accommodation with Hitler: Delbos on the condition that Germany assist in bringing hostilities in Spain to a speedy conclusion, Blum on the condition that Germany signify her will to disarm.

The Führer displayed no interest in the French proposals. On May 28, Dr. Schacht once again visited Paris and was confronted with a much chagrined Léon Blum, who opened their conversation with a rueful allusion to the "complete silence" with which Berlin had received France's suggestions. Irked by what he described as the "pugnacious behavior" of the German press, Blum lamented Hitler's failure to initiate general discussions, noting that while it was impossible for France to begin any negotiations with the colonial question, all issues could be discussed under the rubric of general disarmament. Clearly Blum's attitude had stiffened—and his hopes had diminished—since January, owing to the lack of encouragement from Berlin and his mounting suspicions of Hitler's motives. Speaking bluntly, he told Schacht that the leaders of Germany must rid themselves of two illusions: "The first is that they will succeed in separating Great Britain and France; the second is that, through a latent revolutionary crisis, France is being destroyed as a factor in European affairs."[50] In substance, Blum informed his visitor that he was willing to make one final effort to establish the groundwork for an eventual Franco-German *rapprochement,* although he was much less sanguine about the prospects of success than heretofore. Germany had not demonstrated the necessary "desire for peace," and he feared that she believed she could split France from Great Britain, or, failing this, was content to stand by and witness France's internal disintegration.

Undoubtedly these nagging suspicions were at the core of

[49] Léon Blum, *L'Exercice du pouvoir,* 168–169, and Joel Colton, *op. cit.,* 221–222.

[50] Both Blum's and Schacht's account of the meeting are published in *Documents on German Foreign Policy, Germany and the Spanish Civil War,* Blum's on pp. 136–141, Schacht's on pp. 120–121.

Blum's insistence that Paris and London maintain a common diplomatic posture and were instrumental in his decision to accelerate the pace of French rearmament. With the exception of his effort to persuade Germany to be reasonable, Blum was content to follow the British lead in international affairs, especially in regard to Spain, and he took care to establish a close personal relationship with Anthony Eden.[51] Augmentation of military expenditure was doctrinally unpalatable to Blum, and his record of stern opposition to arms increases prior to 1936 provided a basis for the Vichy regime's allegations that the Popular Front was responsible for the deplorable state of France's defenses in 1940. At the famous Riom trial he handily acquitted himself of accusations to this effect, and since the details of his government's arms policy are now well known, there is little useful purpose in repeating them here.[52] It is sufficient to note that, skeptical of de Gaulle's proposals for the creation of highly mobile armored units and acting upon the advice of Daladier, Minister of Defense,[53] Blum secured passage by the Chamber in October, 1936, of an increment of fourteen billion francs in the military budget. He also was willing to divert funds from the appropriation for public works to military purposes, and in March, 1937, the government launched a drive for public subscriptions to a "Loan for National Defense." Thus Blum acted to build an image of a pacific and strong France, practicing almost complete fidelity to her surest ally.

Yet Blum's peace offensive failed to make contact with the Italian dictator, and his search for binding alliances did not extend to the Soviet Union. Blum protested that Italy was unreliable: ideologically predisposed against "the assassin of Matteotti," Blum testified that Mussolini's Ethiopian adventure signaled Italy's irreversible orientation toward Germany, effectively prohib-

[51] Pierre Renouvin, *op. cit.*, 403; Anthony Eden, *op. cit.*, 429–431.

[52] See Léon Blum, *L'Oeuvre, 1940–1945*, 253; Pierre Renouvin, *op. cit.*, 408; Georges Lefranc, *Histoire du Front Populaire*, 392–399; Pierre Cot, *L'Armée de l'air 1936–1938* (Paris, 1938) ; General Maurice Gustave Gamelin, *Servir: Le Prologue du drame (1930–aout 1939)* (Paris, 1946), 240–246; Paul Reynaud, *Mémories*, II: *Envers et contre tous* (Paris, 1963), 130–152.

[53] Léon Blum, in *Les Evénements survenus en France*, I, 223; Edouard Daladier, *Ibid.*, 17; Paul Reynaud, *op. cit.*, 133–140; General Charles de Gaulle, *The Call to Honour* (New York, 1955), 24–26.

iting any Franco-Italian *rapprochement*.[54] Unmoved by Mussolini's trenchant warning that unless France changed her "harsh
attitude" Italy would seek satisfaction in alliance with Hitler, and
curtly rejecting the Italian Ambassador's suggestion that France
abandon the Spanish Republic in return for an alliance with Italy
and the promise of Franco's friendship,[55] Blum showed himself
totally unresponsive to the Duce's overtures. Blum boasted that he
had "no illusions about Mussolini";[56] yet he had them about
Hitler, surely the more sinister opponent. It is difficult to recon-
cile Blum's deliberate aloofness toward Italy with his willingness
to be flexible toward Germany and with his oft-repeated intention
to negotiate with any nation "regardless of its regime." Pierre
Renouvin has argued that Blum's rigidity was the product of his
personal antipathy to Mussolini;[57] it might be added that this
hostility was of long standing—fourteen years—and that Blum
had denounced Laval's dealings with the Duce with unaccustomed severity, precluding, for political reasons, any effort by his
government to court Italy's friendship. Finally, Italy's activities in
Spain demonstrated how little she respected international agreements.

Initially favorable to bolstering the Franco-Soviet Pact with a
military convention, Blum was confronted with a combination of
obstacles, suspicions, and hopes which prevented realization of
this aim. Blum was hamstrung from the outset by the attitudes of
some of his colleagues and the military: Delbos made little secret
of his suspicion that Stalin might be planning to push France into
a war with Germany;[58] Daladier shared the lack of esteem held by
the High Command for the Red Army; and Ambassador Coulondre repeatedly instructed the Soviets that France would not contemplate reinforcement of the alliance until the Comintern de-

[54] Léon Blum, *Les Evénements survenus en France*, I, 125.

[55] Lucien Lamoureux, "Mussolini et la France en 1936: Une Mission
officieuse de M. J.-L. Malvy, (député, ancien ministre)," in Edouard Bonnefous, *Histoire politique de la Troisième République*, VI, 410–411, Pierre
Renouvin, *op. cit.*, 403, and Joel Colton, *op. cit.*, 223.

[56] Léon Blum, in *Les Evénements survenus en France*, I, 220; *Le Populaire*,
June 30, 1935.   [57] Pierre Renouvin, *op. cit.*, 409.

[58] Robert Coulondre, *De Staline à Hitler: Souvenirs de deux Ambassades
1936–1939* (Paris, 1950), 13.

sisted from its alleged interference in France's internal affairs.[59] Such sentiments and actions were hardly indicative of a French desire to create a climate of confidence between the two powers, and the Soviets more than once voiced their irritation with the inaction of the French government.[60] Moreover Blum was visibly alarmed by the apparent bellicosity of the French Communist party—note his speech at Luna Park and rejection of Thorez's protest over the visit of Dr. Schacht—and he was easily persuaded, late in 1936, that a private warning from President Beneš of Czechoslovakia to the effect that the upper echelons of the Soviet Army were infiltrated with Nazi sympathizers justified a cautious pace in relations with Moscow.[61] In fact Blum never openly challenged the assumptions of Delbos or the military and was not averse to allowing the question of a military convention to become moribund; the most likely single explanation for his behavior is that he was anxious to avoid rigid commitment to the Soviets as long as any hope remained for a peaceful settlement with Germany.

Thus Blum's international policy during his first ministry followed a well-prepared pattern: he combined passionate appeals to international "conscience" and a constant emphasis upon the theme that war was possible only if men should believe it to be possible with the reluctant concession that Germany's intransigence and threatening posture necessitated a display of strength. But the display was only that, meant not to intimidate but to persuade: Blum refused to choose between firmness and conciliation and gave priority to the latter; his insurance against failure was alliance with Great Britain. If, as he argued at Riom in 1942,[62] he had embarked upon a determined policy of a collective

[59] *Ibid.*, 22, 31–32, 47; Léon Blum, in *Les Evénements survenus en France,* I, 128; Paul Reynaud, *op. cit.*, 160–162.

[60] Léon Blum, in *Les Evénements survenus en France,* I, 129; Pierre Renouvin, *op. cit.*, 406.

[61] Léon Blum in *Les Evénements survenus en France,* I, 129.

[62] Léon Blum, *L'Oeuvre, 1940–1945,* 300–307: "But the peace that we wanted and hoped to organize was an indivisible peace, extending to all of Europe, requiring a general and equitable settlement of all differences; this was a peace based upon the freedom of all peoples. . . . And on the day when we saw the independence of nations menaced, obligations violated, the world handed over to designs of conquest and hegemony, then these men who had

security rooted in military alliances, such action was barely implicit in his public pronouncements; explicit was the need to drive the very idea of war from men's minds and to secure disarmament and international cooperation. "Socialism," he declared, "incarnates the struggle against war, incarnates the will to extirpate the roots of war from the human mind."[63] Blum was to abandon his vision of a Europe pacified by reason and mutual accommodation only in 1938, and not before—although his attempt to negotiate with Germany had been a sobering experience. In 1936 and 1937 he continued to proclaim his ideals to be the proper prescription for a troubled continent. In other words, Blum persisted in his effort to instruct the French nation in the fundamentals of Socialist pacifism and genuinely sought international understanding. The deeper significance of rearmament and fidelity to Great Britain was effectively hidden from the nation—and from himself—by his exaltation of pacifist idealism.

FROM IMMOBILITY TO ABDICATION

Early in the fall of 1936 it became evident that the Popular Front Program was no longer attuned to reality: created out of fear of "fascism" and need for social reform, it provided no blueprint to revive a sagging economy and no formula for dealing with the sudden intrusion of foreign affairs as an ideological issue in politics. While the government was able to survive the impact of the Spanish crisis, both it and the spirit of the Popular Front were to suffer a painfully slow death, caused primarily by domestic difficulties but also by suspicions and tensions generated, at least in part, by the war in Spain. Buffeted by a complex of problems—the plight of the franc, the absence, despite shifts in

---

been characterized as bleating pacifists recognized that if peace rested upon collective security, then collective security could rest only upon force of arms."

[63] Léon Blum, speech to the nation during the electoral campaign, *L'Exercice du pouvoir,* 15. Here are examples of such rhetoric, selected at random: "To want peace is to want it despite all obstacles, despite all dangers, despite all risks" (*Le Populaire,* August 10, 1936) ; "For almost a year, in the midst of one of the most dangerous crises that Europe has ever known, we have kept the peace" (*Le Populaire,* June 7, 1937) ; "War is never necessary" (*Le Populaire,* December 15, 1936) ; "Socialism is necessary for peace, peace is necessary for socialism" (*Le Populaire,* November 16, 1936) .

government policy, of economic revival, and a renewal of social discontent—hampered by the remarkable convalescence of the conservative forces, revealed by the confident intransigence of the *patronat* and the unyielding hostility of financial circles, and undermined by the increasing fragility of its political base, the Blum government stumbled for nine months along a downward path into immobility and ultimately to abdication.

Compelled to devalue the franc by a sudden acceleration of the outflow of gold in September and a steady rise in wholesale and retail prices, which intensified the disparity between French and world prices, the government also signaled a change of its economic policy. Devaluation promised a great deal: by making French prices competitive on the world market, it aided the export and tourist industries; abandonment of the gold bullion standard relieved the Bank of France of its obligation to redeem its notes in gold and revalorization added seventeen billion francs to the value of the Bank's dwindling gold reserves, ten billion of which were assigned to the newly created Exchange Stabilization Fund, designed to prevent fluctuations in the currency. But speculators, in the absence of exchange control,[64] were free to obtain other currencies redeemable in gold, and since the franc still was defined as a gold currency the Treasury was vulnerable to a renewed hemorrhage without warning. The devaluation marked as well an end to faith in the purchasing power theory: the government now staked its hopes for economic improvement on the good will of the holders of liquid capital. Blum's new policy sought massive investment in French business by possessors of capital-in-exile in the belief that their confidence would be won by opportunities afforded by the devaluation and by government refusal to impose restraints upon exchange control. New investment, it was assumed, would stimulate the economy as a whole.

These expectations proved illusory: the benefits of the devaluation were few and temporary, and the government's wager on the benevolence of the financial community was shown to be ill-founded. A continuing rise in prices undercut a moderate im-

[64] M. Wolfe, *op. cit.*, 152; P. Einzig, *op. cit.*, 192; F. Goguel, *La Politique des partis sous la Troisième République,* 3rd ed. (Paris, 1958) , 348. According to Wolfe and Goguel, Blum rejected exchange control because it might be resented by Great Britain and the United States—and by the Senate.

provement in business conditions, and in January, 1937, speculative pressure against the franc's exchange value exhausted the coffers of the Exchange Stabilization Fund.[65] New investments were not forthcoming. Thus in February the government opted for further concessions to liberal capitalism, this time in the hope of securing at least the neutrality of the financial groups. The "pause," announced by Blum on February 14, promised that the government would do nothing to alarm its detractors: abandoned, albeit provisionally, were new social welfare schemes and public works projects for which funds already had been allocated, and three experts highly esteemed in financial circles—Rist, Rueff, and Baudouin—were appointed to oversee the workings of the Exchange Stabilization Fund. The "pause," in substance, was a promise to do nothing at all: it was a desperate bid to halt speculation against the franc.[66] Henceforth the government survived only on the sufferance of its most inveterate opponents.

Blum was also ill-treated by his political allies: the victim of sniping from both flanks of the Popular Front in 1936, he received better treatment in the spring of 1937 only because neither Communists nor Radicals could propose a viable alternative to his remaining in power. The Communists, angered by their inability to force a change in Spanish policy and by the devaluation, which struck hardest at their working-class clientele, mounted a sharp assault upon the Premier in the fall of 1936, with Thorez delivering a slashing speech in which he accused Blum of "capitulation" to Hitler.[67] But the Communists could do little else but launch verbal tirades and embarrassing strikes: they were the prisoners of their own limited aspirations. Their failure to vote against the government in the Chamber debate of December 5 on

[65] F. Goguel, *op. cit.*, 356ff.; P. Einzig, *op. cit.*, 269ff.; M. Wolfe, *op. cit.*, 152.

[66] Bodin and Touchard, *op. cit.*, 242; Jacques Chastenet, *Histoire de la Troisième République*, VI: *Déclin de la Troisième* (Paris, 1962), 167; Alexander Werth, *France and Munich* (London, 1939), 102; M. Wolfe, *op. cit.*, 152–155. Technically Rist, Rueff, and Baudouin headed the Exchange Stabilization Fund, but their appointment was intended to give the impression that no action in matters of finance would be undertaken without their approval.

[67] Edouard Bonnefous, *op. cit.*, 57–58: see *L'Humanité*, October 12, October 23, November 2, November 16, November 28, 1936.

nonintervention in Spain demonstrated that, whatever their talent for invective and nuisance, they would not risk a rupture of the Popular Front.[68] The Radicals, visibly worried by Communist bellicosity over Spain, alarmed by Communist-inspired labor difficulties, and increasingly susceptible to the strident anti-Popular Front warnings of their right wing,[69] appeared to pose a threat to the government's continued existence in October. Blum countered with a potent threat of his own—new elections. It was effective: at the Radical Congress, held at the end of the month, irritation with the Popular Front was confined to a harmless orgy of anticommunism.[70] When the government settled into immobility early in 1937 the Radicals had neither reason nor occasion to topple it; yet they clearly had begun their journey away from the Popular Front which was to culminate, in 1938, with their outright alliance with the conservative camp.[71]

There is little useful purpose in subjecting all of Blum's problems to careful scrutiny, but several deserve mention: the leaders of the C.G.T., mesmerized by the redemptive myth of the forty-hour week, pushed for immediate and full implementation of the forty-hour law and for other measures dear to their hearts; the *patronat*, reorganized by tough-minded businessmen and rejuvenated by the cracks in the Popular Front, brusquely rejected renewal of the bargaining contracts which had followed the Matig-

[68] Georges Dupeux, "Léon Blum et la majorité parlementaire," *Colloque des 26 et 27 mars 1965: Léon Blum, chef de gouvernement 1936–37*, 9. See also Jacques Fauvet, *Histoire du Parti Communiste Français*, I: *De la guerre à la guerre, 1917–1939* (Paris, 1964), 205–208.

[69] Dupeux, *op. cit.*, 6–7; Peter J. Larmour, *The French Radical Party in the 1930's* (Stanford, 1964), 208–212. The assault on the Popular Front was led by Pierre Dominque and Emile Roche in the columns of *La République;* see the numbers for September 9, 16, 1936, as examples.

[70] Speech by Léon Blum to the Radical *fédération* of the Loiret at Orléans, October 18, 1936, in *L'Exercice du pouvoir*, 318–329; on the congress see Dupeux, *op. cit.*, 7; P. Larmour, *op. cit.*, 215; *La Dépêche de Toulouse*, October 24, 1936.

[71] P. Larmour, *op. cit.*, 220, argues that the anti-Communist and anti-Popular Front tone of the Radical Congress of 1936 influenced Daladier to become the chief of the anti-Popular Front forces within the Radical party. G. Dupeux, "Léon Blum et la majorite parlementaire," 15, notes that once the "pause" was obtained, the Radicals had no reason to leave the government.

non Agreements;[72] work on the International Exposition of 1937 in Paris, intended to symbolize France's revival, fell far behind schedule owing to workers' slowdowns; and the bloody riots at Clichy on March 16, whether due to exasperation of the working class with the lassitude of the government, Communist or Rightist provocation, or simple blunder, dealt a sharp blow to Blum's withering self-confidence.[73] Blum's vision of the Popular Front, which presupposed for its success a minimum of national cohesiveness, ran aground on the refusal of each sector of French society to look beyond its own narrow interests.

These problems, however, were subsidiary to the interlocking problems of economic stagnation and financial instability. The government's patient efforts at conciliating its antagonists failed to ameliorate the illness of the franc, and lack of economic revival increased budgetary disequilibrium. In May a new speculative assault upon the franc began, and the more the government vowed that another devaluation was out of the question the more certain did devaluation appear to the speculators. The crisis became a panic early in June, and the money-market refused to absorb short-term government bonds to replace those falling due.[74] Rist, Rueff, and Baudouin attempted to extort from Blum a pledge to make rigid economies in expenditure and to refuse to consider control over monetary exchanges. Blum had to reject their demands: acceptance implied a full-fledged return to conservative economics, involving not merely renunciation of further

---

[72] *Ibid.*, 216; René Rémond and Janine Bourdin, "Les Forces adverses," *Colloque des 26 et 27 mars 1965, Léon Blum, chef du gouvernement 1936–37,* 12.

[73] For details and varying interpretations of the Clichy riots see G. Lefranc, *op. cit.,* 237, who argues that Blum was prepared to resign in favor of Georges Monnet; E. Bonnefous, *op. cit.,* 126, who argues that Blum's performance in the Chamber in the subsequent debate over the incident revealed him to be a disillusioned man. Louise E. Dalby, *Léon Blum: Evolution of a Socialist* (New York, 1963), 312, offers a similar description of Blum's mood; Daniel Guérin, *Front Populaire: Revolution manquée* (Paris, 1963), a follower of Marceau Pivert, describes Clichy as "the poisoned fruits of the 'exercise of power.'"

[74] M. Wolfe, *op. cit.,* 153–154; A. Werth, *op. cit.,* 105. The 1937 Budget was unbalanced on paper in the sum of 25.1 billion francs. By March the Treasury had just enough funds to meet its payments only as long as short-term bonds were subscribed to by the money-market.

social measures but repeal of some of those already enacted. Their subsequent resignation appeared to be the first act in a showdown between Blum and his assailants.

But the showdown was not forthcoming: Blum chose to abdicate with honor, and honor required that the parliamentary game be played out. The Premier asked the Parliament for decree powers to deal with the financial panic, but made no effort to reassure the financial community as he had done in October and February. While Auriol was muddled in his explanations of what would be done with these powers should they be granted, it was no secret that the government would institute a rigid control over exchanges, anathema to the Radicals as well as to the Conservatives. The Chamber voted its approval of the proposal, as most of the Radicals maintained the fiction of support for the government serenely confident that their elderly colleagues in the Senate would administer the defeat.[75] The Senate obliged with a massive rejection of the legislation, and rather than appealing to the Chamber for a vote of confidence—which would have provoked a constitutional crisis—Blum submitted his resignation to the President of the Republic. The great "experiment" was over.

Why did Blum succumb to the will of the Senate—and the financial community—without making any use of the legal and extralegal weapons at his disposal? Several of Blum's Socialist colleagues may have counseled their leader to demand a vote of confidence from the Chamber,[76] thereby pitting the Chamber against the Senate, and to ask for a dissolution of the Chamber. Elections would be fought on an emotional issue, the right of the Senate to overthrow a government resting upon a majority elected by universal suffrage; a Popular Front electoral victory would enable the government to smash the obstructionist Senate and to carry out structural reforms of the economy. Others, especially on the left of the S.F.I.O.,[77] demanded that Blum employ the threat of popular force against the Senate. Blum calmly refused to follow

[75] G. Dupeux, "Léon Blum et la majorité parlementaire," 16.

[76] Interviews with Moch, Rosenfeld, and Blumel.

[77] Zyromski and Pivert. See Zyromski's article in *Le Populaire*, July 1, 1937, in which he decried the failure to utilize mass pressure. See Pivert's speech to the Socialist National Congress in *XXXIV⁰ Congrès National*, 411–443, and his article in *Les Cahiers Rouges*, August–September, 1937.

either course, and withdrew. Many observers have seen in Blum's refusal to do battle a confession of fatigue and have assumed that the action of the Senate handed him the opportunity he had been seeking to abandon power.[78] This may well be true, but several other considerations figured in his decision.

Blum was mindful of harsh political realities: neither Communists nor Radicals were prepared to enter the lists to keep the government in office. *L'Humanité* demonstrated little enthusiasm for Blum's request for special powers, and hardly lamented the government's departure.[79] The Communists had no desire to see France plunge into internal strife; a weak France was of no use to the Soviet Union. Moreover the Communists rightly feared a new election: recent by-elections had revealed the disenchantment of the Radicals with the Popular Front and the resilience of the conservative parties.[80] The Radical ministers urged Blum not to call for a vote of confidence,[81] clearly implying that a majority of their party might not support the government. Finally, even had Blum survived a new test in the Chamber, dissolution of the Chamber required the assent of the President of the Republic and of the Senate.

More important than purely political factors were Blum's fidelity to his socialist beliefs and his conception of the Popular Front, and his assessment of the international situation. At the Socialist National Congress, held in July, Blum asserted forcefully that "if we had engaged in battle [by putting popular pressure on the Senate] it would have been necessary to push it to its conclusion —to victory."[82] But the very nature of Blum's socialism compelled him to oppose such a venture: he believed that the proletariat could not take political power until it was totally prepared to implement the social revolution. Surely he had given no indica-

[78] A. Werth, *op. cit.*, 107; C. Audry, *op. cit.*, 147; Daniel Guérin, *op. cit.*, 168; L. E. Dalby, *op. cit.*, 312.

[79] *L'Humanité*, June 23, 1937; see Rosenfeld in *Le Populaire*, June 16, 1937, for a Socialist comment on the Communist attitude.

[80] G. Lefranc, *op. cit.*, 253.

[81] Vincent Auriol in *L'Express*, September 21, 1961; Georges Dupeux, "Léon Blum et la majorté parlementaire," 17; Georges Dupeux, "L'Echec du premier gouvernement Léon Blum," *Revue d'Histoire Moderne et Contemporaine*, X (January–March, 1963), 37.

[82] *XXXIVe Congrès National*, 468–469.

tion, either before his accession to power or during his tenure of office, that the propitious moment had in fact arrived, and on numerous occasions he had carefully instructed his followers and the working class to confine their activities within the boundaries of "legality." Thus Blum's commitment to socialist formula precluded illegal action against the Senate. But Blum's conception of the Popular Front represented an even more formidable barrier to the use of mass pressure; likewise it militated against the deliberate provocation of a constitutional crisis. Blum had stated repeatedly that the Popular Front would adhere strictly to "Republican legality"; unlike the general strike of February 12, 1934, demonstrations in June, 1937, would not be in defense of this legality but in opposition to it. For Blum the Popular Front was responsible not to the proletariat, but to the entire nation: its aim was national *rapprochement*. Illegal proletarian action, or a constitutional crisis, could, in Blum's eyes, provoke a social crisis, dividing the nation yet further. Finally, Blum's assessment of the international situation and his conviction that France must be a major force in international affairs bulked large in his decision to resign. Only a month previously he had pointedly reminded Dr. Schacht that Germany must rid herself of the illusion that France was disintegrating from within. To his Socialist comrades Blum declared bluntly that, had he chosen any other course of action,

into what state would we have thrown the country? A *social crisis* would remove France, for long months and perhaps indefinitely, as a factor in international affairs.

Considering the internal condition of the nation, considering its political state, considering its psychological state, *considering the external danger*, we said: *no, we do not have the right to do that*, [to provoke a crisis]; we do not have the right, vis-à-vis our party or vis-à-vis our country.[83]

By themselves, Blum's reasons for his resignation—fear of civil disorder, the external danger, and lack of cohesion of the Popular Front—are not, as Dupeux concedes, wholly persuasive.[84] Blum

[83] *XXXIVe Congrès National*, 470. (Italics mine.)
[84] G. Dupeux, "L'Echec du premier gouvernement Léon Blum," 39. G. Lefranc, *op. cit.*, 251–252, essentially accepts Blum's reasons and adds that the government would have encountered insurmountable obstacles had it attempted to remain in power.

knew that he was defeated and that his vision of the Popular
Front was doomed to partial fulfillment. He was not obsessed with
a scrupulous care for "legality," but he was determined that the
nation should not be divided irreparably in an era of international turmoil. Long before he had assured his countrymen that
he would not play the role of Kerensky; neither was he prepared
to play Robespierre. The task of the Popular Front was finished:
it had won great social gains for the masses, and the Radicals
could be the custodians of the achievement; if it had failed to
pacify Europe, it had, if only for a brief moment, symbolized the
aspiration for good will and understanding among all nations.
Blum simply had no reason to hang on to power: unless the
liberal capitalistic institutions were to be altered drastically—and
the time was not one for revolutionary alterations—enactment of
further reforms was impossible. Blum already was concerned that
a new political alignment, broader than the Popular Front, could
give the nation the unity and strength that the Popular Front
could no longer hope to provide.

3

The Socialist Party and the Popular Front Government

Certain of his powers of persuasion, Léon Blum confidently anticipated general approval of his stewardship of the "exercise of power" by the Socialist party, and at its official gatherings the party obligingly confirmed his expectations with expressions of support and confidence. And *Le Populaire*, displaying the mature serenity habitually associated with government organs, gladly hailed the many accomplishments of his regime, although the generous optimism of the first weeks gave way to defensiveness and acrimonious thrusts at its adversaries as the pace of reform slackened and expired, and as the focus of attention shifted dramatically from internal affairs to international policy after the outbreak of the Spanish Civil War. Despite elaborate camouflage, however, the Socialist party was deteriorating from within: its shaky façade of unity was eroded steadily by accumulating disappointments, suspicions, and divisions. The *Gauche Révolutionnaire*, drawing ideological sustenance from the sit-down strikes and from revolutionary Spain, hastened to prepare, at least verbally, its own revolutionary offensive, while Jean Zyromski, exasperated by the nonintervention policy, regularly fulminated against the government's alleged capitulation to "fascism." But the rumblings on the Left were not at all surprising and hardly constituted an immediate threat to the stability of the party. With the developing primacy of international affairs, differing reactions to the war in Spain among the leadership marked in fact the beginnings of the inner collapse of the S.F.I.O. On the one hand the Spanish struggle sharply reinforced the pacifist and anti-Soviet tendencies of Paul Faure and a majority of the Socialist parliamentarians, who became wholly persuaded that any French involvement in Spain would trigger the general European war which they suspected to be the aim of Soviet policy, while on the other hand many of Blum's close associates, whose initial acceptance of nonintervention was at best reluctant, became increasingly irritated by the obvious shortcomings of this policy and worried by the implications of the apparent failure to resist the "fascist" enterprise below the Pyrenees. This cleavage of opinion was not restricted to the upper echelons of party leadership but was reproduced at all levels of membership, and the pattern of division among the *fédérations* was indicative of a ready potential for the splintering of the S.F.I.O. on a regional basis. In fact, dissimilar responses to the war in Spain within the Center majority signaled the onset of its decomposition, although a sensible hardening of positions taken at this time, which transformed the two camps into bitterly opposed *tendances,* did not occur until well after the fall of the Blum government. Thus the impact of the "exercise of power" and the Spanish Civil War stirred latent differences within the Socialist party so profoundly that, at the very moment of its greatest victory, it had entered upon the road to its own collapse.

TRIUMPH OF FEAR: THE "FAURISTES"

Ostensibly Léon Blum had no more loyal collaborator than Paul Faure. Throughout the duration of Blum's ministry Faure consistently, and often fervently, defended his chief's actions. Yet in many instances the General Secretary of the S.F.I.O. was prone to embellish Blum's policies with the imprint of his own beliefs and fears, and in these Faure was truly representative of much of his party. His position unified those who were dominated by fear: fear of war, of Stalin, and of Hitler; fear of disturbing the comfortable inertia of neutrality in a Europe threatened by ideological conflict; and fear of the demise of the sheltered parochialism that had for so long characterized their Socialist party.

Faure did not play a critical role in the formulation of government policy, although he was Minister of State; rather he conceived his task to be that of guardian of party interests in deliberations of the Council of Ministers as well as that of transmitter of the government's wishes to the S.F.I.O.[1] In short, he was to watch, to defend, and to prod when necessary. In domestic affairs he was quick to come to Blum's defense and equally quick to criticize the Communist party. Although suspicious of Communist instigation of the sit-down strikes, Faure was highly pleased with the flood of social legislation which they precipitated, and his Guesdist instinct persuaded him that simple reforms would neither satiate the working class nor provide a permanent solution to the economic crisis. He delighted in holding out the promise that "structural reforms" of the economy would soon be the order of the day: "After the realization of the Popular Front program," he warned, "history will not stop in its course,"[2] and he was hard put to restrain his zeal for the nationalization of banks, insurance companies, and the armaments industries—he was a principal mover in the nationalization of the latter in the summer of 1936.[3] But he made it clear to Socialists that revolution was not imminent and they should respect "Republican legality"[4] during the indeterminate interlude of the Popular Front which, he argued, must be maintained, even though he advertised regularly his conviction that the Radicals were more reliable partners than the Communists. Finally, Faure placed the weight of his prestige behind the most unpopular of Blum's policies, the "pause";[5] mounted an attack upon leftist malcontents within the party whose lacerating criticisms of the government became embarrassing to Blum;[6] and, after the fall of the government, seconded Blum's request for Socialist participation in the Chautemps ministry. Thus, at least in domestic affairs, Faure's loyalty to Blum's "experiment" seems to have been complete. Loyalty, however, did not obligate Faure to be a partisan of dramatic innovation: his own proposals were

[1] Interview with Jean Castagnez, June 29, 1962, and with Fernand Roucayrol, July 28, 1962.   [2] *Le Populaire,* July 11, 1936.

[3] Interviws with Castagnez and Roucayrol; interview with Oreste Rosenfeld, June 29, 1962.   [4] *Le Populaire,* May 3, June 14, 1937.

[5] *Ibid.,* February 14, 1937.

[6] See Faure's speech at the National Council of April, 1937, in which he accused the *Gauche Révolutionnaire* of "treason and crime" against Blum, in *Le Populaire,* April 19, 1937.

old Socialist shibboleths, and he stoutly opposed both a broadening of the Popular Front alliance and closer ties between Socialists and Communists.[7] In substance, Faure was concerned that, despite the lure of power, the S.F.I.O. "remain itself," autonomous and aloof, traditionally organized, and free from the corrosive effects of change. Defense of Blum and preservation of the old party were the essence of his efforts on the domestic front.

Faure's attitude toward international affairs and particularly toward the Spanish Civil War had a much more critical impact upon the Socialist party. Although it is apparent that Faure was not privy to the details of the discussions between Blum and Dr. Schacht, he gave vigorous public support to Blum's effort to secure the pacification of Europe by negotiation and probable concessions to Germany. Faure's praise for Blum's speech at Lyons in January, 1937, was lavish: he credited the President of the Council of Ministers with opening a new era in world history. Blum, he asserted,

wants to place France at the head of all the peaceful states of the world and to make her the principal artisan of peace. . . .

Is there any other government in the world that has done more to reinvigorate the forces of peace?

But the General Secretary carried his interpretation of the speech to the point where it could no longer be recognized as Blum's handiwork: "If economic accords are being studied, if disarmament is again in sight, it is all due to French policy. Even if we were certain of victory, we would *never* agree to go to war."[8] In the first place, economic accords were *not* being studied; Blum had merely agreed to consider them in conjunction with discussions on disarmament. Second, Blum had never demonstrated such optimism about the nearness of a disarmament accord, and certainly he had never rejected the proposition that war might some day be necessary. By a process of simplification and by the

---

[7] *Le Populaire,* June 14, 1937; interviews with Castagnez, Roucayrol, and Rosenfeld; interview with Jules Moch, November 24, 1961.

[8] *Le Populaire,* February 1, May 25, 1937; Paul Faure, "Les Intrus du Capitole" (unpublished ms.), 43–47, and speech at Lyons, reported by *Le Temps,* June 15, 1937.

1. Paul Faure. (Photo from Aral-Pix.)

2. General view of the Socialist National Council. (Photo from Aral-Pix.)

3. Popular Front demonstration, Paris, July 14, 1935. (Photo from Keystone.)

4. The Blum ministry on the steps of the Elysée Palace, Paris, June 12, 1936. (Photo from United Press International.)

5. Jean Zyromski with leftist and Communist leaders, 1936 (*left to right*: Paul Langevin, Eugène Hénaff, Jacques Duclos, and Zyromski). (Photo from United Press International.)

6. Blum conferring with party leaders at a Socialist National Council (*left to right*: Vincent Auriol, Blum, Paul Faure, and Jean-Baptiste Séverac). (Photo from European.)

7. Blum giving a speech, Paris, July 14, 1936. At his left is Marceau Pivert. (Photo from Keystone.)

8. Popular Front demonstration, Paris, July 14, 1936. (Photo from Keystone.)

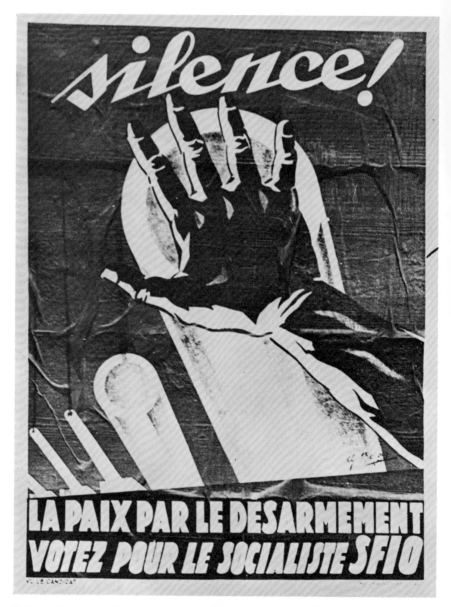

9. Socialist poster denouncing war. (Photo from United Press International.)

use of adept slogans, Faure was able to adapt Blum's words to his own conceptions—and no one challenged him.[9]

Earlier Faure had exhibited a marked hesitancy about support-ing Blum's rearmament program, and only after he was taunted publicly by the conservative editorialists of *Le Temps* did he attempt to explain why he had suddenly dropped his long-stand-ing opposition to French rearmament. Even then his explanation was not wholly persuasive. He asserted lamely that he had never questioned the duty of Frenchmen to defend the *pays*—which was true—and declared that his many votes against military budgets had been simply manifestations of distrust of the men then in power. Since the Popular Front government was, as he put it, "ardently pacifist," he had no fear that France's arsenal would be misused.[10] But in the spring of 1937 Faure freely predicted that disarmament was around the corner, and disclosed that the gov-ernment was making plans for those workers who would be dis-placed by the imminent slowdown in arms production.[11] Such declarations represented something less than an endorsement of the government's decision to accelerate rearmament.

The reaction of Paul Faure to the Spanish Civil War was a fundamental factor in the fracturing of the S.F.I.O.'s Center ma-jority in that it confirmed and encouraged the pacifist and anti-So-viet sentiments of a substantial segment of that majority. The war in Spain and its international ramifications convinced the Gen-eral Secretary of the absolute correctness of his pacifist convic-tions, and Soviet activities in Spain, coupled with the virulent assault upon the nonintervention policy by the French Commu-nists, persuaded him that his deepest fears about the motives of Soviet foreign policy were thoroughly justified. Nonintervention, then, was admirably suited to Faure's international outlook: con-vinced that it attenuated a serious danger of general war, he was

[9] Faure's interpretation of Blum's speech was repeated by his associates, e.g., Charles Spinasse in *Le Populaire*, March 29, 1937; Louis L'Hévéder in *Le Rappel du Morbihan*, January 23, February 13, May 8, 1937; and *Syndicats*, organ of the anti-Communist groups within the C.G.T. used Blum's speech to launch a campaign for a "new peace treaty with Germany," January 21, 1937.

[10] *Le Populaire*, February 5, 1937.

[11] Speech delivered at Montaubon, published in *Le Populaire*, May 25, 1937.

also certain that its maintenance served to thwart a Soviet design to provoke a conflict between France and Germany. And in these beliefs Faure was the spokesman for much of the Socialist party.

Of Faure's fervent advocacy of nonintervention there can be no doubt whatever: his public pronouncements alone constitute ample demonstration that he considered this policy to be both necessary and advantageous. Although he did not play a major role in the cabinet's decision to adopt nonintervention, he is alleged to have concurred with the opinion of the Minister of Foreign Affairs—that assistance to the Spanish Republic could unleash a general war—and to have spoken out, as did several other Socialist ministers, in support of nonintervention.[12] And once neutrality in the Spanish strife had become the official policy of the French government, it had no more ardent champion than Paul Faure.

Shortly after the Second World War, in a little-noticed volume of memoirs, Faure summarized his reasons for championing the nonintervention policy, and in so doing revealed the critical effect made by the Spanish Civil War upon the development of his international outlook during the years 1936–1940.

A government under Socialist direction practiced a policy of nonintervention toward Spain, despite the active presence of foreign elements in both camps. Why? Because, above any other consideration, . . . the consequences [of intervening] were the determining factors. . . .

[Had we intervened] it would have been necessary for us to face military attacks upon all of our frontiers at once—for it [intervention] meant war. . . .

We could not have saved Republican Spain and we would have gone to our own annihilation.

All of these observations, deduced from indisputable realities, remained valid in our eyes for the totality of European problems until September, 1939. . . .

If we were incapable of aiding Republican Spain, by what miracle could we have given salutary aid to Czechoslovakia and Poland? . . . In all of these instances, the consequences were invasion and defeat [of France].[13]

[12] Interviews with Castagnez, Roucayrol, and Jules Moch.
[13] Paul Faure, *De Munich à la Cinquième République* (Paris, 1948), 57.

Thus the Spanish conflict satisfied Faure that France could take no initiative which involved a risk of war; "annihilation," "invasion," and "defeat" loomed as the ineluctable consequences of the fulfillment of France's commitments to her friends. This conviction of France's permanent inferiority to Germany lay at the core of much that Faure said and believed about the necessity for abstention from the Spanish struggle. While the weekly propaganda sheet issued by the party secretariat, *Le Bulletin Socialiste*, regularly churned out such articles as "Yes! The Léon Blum Government Has Saved Peace," and "We Have Repeated Several Times: The Neutrality Policy Has Saved European Peace,"[14] Faure himself wrote extensively and spoke before innumerable Socialist audiences in support of nonintervention. At Lille on December 11, 1936, he declared that

Blum has said that he believes that he prevented war last August. Our leader has never lied. We believe him. We will fight with all our strength against war—war, which would mean the end of all socialist and human aspirations.

Four days later, at Saint-Armand (Cher), he asserted that

we do not want war. We do not believe it to be inevitable. We will tolerate no imprudence which could provoke war. Like Léon Blum, I am convinced that if we had not adopted nonintervention last August . . . war would have broken out.[15]

Faure's capacity to repeat the same argument was evidently limitless, and no effort need be made to emulate him in that respect here. It suffices to note that his vigorous support for nonintervention never diminished: in May he told a crowd of enthusiastic Socialists in his personal stronghold of the Saône-et-Loire that "more than ever, nonintervention is a necessity," and at a rally in Lyons in June he reaffirmed his belief that "nonintervention has saved the peace of the world."[16]

[14] *Le Bulletin Socialiste* (*Hebdomadaire à l'usage de la presse du Parti*), December 7, 21, 1936.

[15] *Le Populaire*, December 12, 16, 1936.

[16] *La Dépêche Socialiste* (Saône-et-Loire), May 29, 1937. Paul Faure devoted a great number of speeches to the Spanish question, and his effort

That Faure should uphold the nonintervention policy with fervor and undeniable conviction is not in the least surprising: his stand was but the inevitable outgrowth of his views since the First World War on the question of war. As in the crisis over the Rhineland, Faure rejected absolutely *any* action which contained the slightest risk of war. Convinced that the maintenance of peace took precedence over every other consideration—he displayed, for example, not the slightest concern for the fate of the fledgling social revolution in Spain—he insisted that France must remain aloof from this struggle. His pacifism was reinforced by his gloomy insistence that France would suffer certain defeat at the hands of a more powerful adversary in the event of a general war. This pacifist faith, combined with defeatism, could produce only a champion of nonintervention.

Yet there was another vital aspect to Faure's response to the Spanish Civil War, and it too was tightly bound up with his beliefs and fears. Obsessed by a perpetual suspicion of Moscow's intentions, Faure had little hesitation in ascribing Soviet intervention in Spain and the French Communist party's attack upon nonintervention to a Soviet desire to provoke a Franco-German war. It must be recalled that Faure had steadfastly refused to discount the possibility that the Soviet Union's ultimate objective was war, either to create an opportunity for world revolution or simply to divert Nazi Germany from the Soviet homeland. In the

---

amounted to the most sustained effort by any Socialist leader, including Blum himself, to defend nonintervention. These speeches were the most noteworthy: at St.-Etienne (Loire), reported in *Le Temps,* February 8, 1937; in the Pas-de-Calais, reported in *L'Eglantine,* March, 1937; to the National Congress of the *Jeunesses Socialistes,* reported in *Le Temps,* March 30, 1937; and to the Socialist *fédération* of the Somme, reported in *Le Cri du Peuple* (Somme), June 12, 1937. Also indicative of Faure's attitude was his introduction to a reprint of Blum's speech to the Chamber on December 5, 1936, entitled *Léon Blum en 'action' pour la paix* (Paris, 1936), pages 3–5, in which he declared, "It is necessary to defend peace at any price . . . to prevent from being dragged into a conflict, and to place her at the head of those nations and peoples who are fighting against war." And he went on to declare that the Communists "cannot be permitted to attack and denature the tenacious and laudable work for peace led by Léon Blum in the darkest and most difficult hours of our history." See also *L'Avenir Socialiste* (Rhône), June 19, 1937, and the *Bulletin Socialiste* for December 28, 1936.

fall of 1939 Faure stated publicly that the Communist party "did everything possible—on the command of its masters in Moscow— to push France into war over Spain, then over Czechoslovakia, and now over Poland."[17]

But earlier, aside from expressing broad hints,[18] Faure was obliged to stifle these suspicions in public. He was less reticent in

[17] *Le Pays Socialiste*, October 13, 1939.

[18] The timing of Faure's impassioned pacifist declarations offers some indication of his sentiments about Soviet motives regarding Spain and Nazi Germany. His first extensive speaking tour devoted almost exclusively to the defense of nonintervention took place when the Communists attacked this policy in the Chamber in December, 1936, and the second after the Barcelona affair of May, 1937, which resulted in Prime Minister Largo Caballero's replacement by Juan Negrín. Roucayrol has told me that the Barcelona events "proved" to Faure that the Soviets were attempting to seize total control of the Spanish Republic. In the second half of 1937, Faure dropped some public hints as to his suspicions. In a speech at Masseret in the Corrèze, reported in *Le Populaire*, the journal of the Socialist *fédération* of the Loir-et-Cher on September 4, 1937, he asserted that "if the Léon Blum government had followed the suggestions of the Communist party at the moment that the Spanish Civil War broke out, France would have found herself alone, facing the fascist peoples. . . . Socialists, we are by definition free and independent men. That is why we must look at Russia without a bandana over our eyes and a gag over our mouths."

And in a speech to the Montmartre section of the *fédération* of the Seine, reported by *Le Temps* on November 12, 1937, Faure remarked that "a year ago we were two fingers away from war, and it is thanks to the inflexibility of Léon Blum that it was avoided. In August, 1936, France was alone. . . . And Russia? She has shot, by the thousands, her generals and her colonels. And for what motive? For being foreign agents? If this accusation is true, the affair is truly terrible, and if by chance it is false and thousands of innocents have been shot, what could we hope for from such a country?"

Le Bulletin Socialiste, under Faure's editorial eye, also did its best to discredit the Communists: in its issue of May 31, 1937, it openly suggested that fascism and Communism were opposite sides of the same coin. And in the November 15, 1937 number, an article bearing the unmistakable imprint of Paul Faure pounced upon some intemperate remarks of the Communist leader Marcel Cachin: "No, comrade Marcel Cachin, Jaurès never said or wrote that war would inevitably create a revolutionary situation. . . . No, a hundred times no, it is not true that a new war would break the chains of the proletariat. . . . Let us suppress this appalling and depressing idea that the supreme cry of deliverance will be launched by a few survivors in the silence of a vast cemetery, let us suppress this senseless paradox [which holds] that humanity can find its salvation in its own annihilation."

private: Fernand Roucayrol has recalled that Faure warned several Socialist deputies and federal secretaries that Communist propaganda over the Spanish issue was directed toward precipitating a general war. Jean Castagnez stated flatly that Faure took him aside just prior to the debate in the Chamber on December 5, 1936, and said: "Jean, you know as well as I that the Communists are using Spain to exacerbate [international] tension, and probably want to drag France into a war."[19]

Nonintervention found a ready defender in Paul Faure. His advocacy of this policy was fully consistent with his international outlook: his pacifism, heavily impregnated with defeatism, plus a virulent anticommunism, caused him to be hostile to any other view of the Spanish problem. Whatever specific fear was dominant in his mind—fear of war, or of defeat, or of Communist revolution—fear was the basis of his policy. His response to the Spanish Civil War could have been none other than what it was. And paradoxically, although Blum's approach to the Spanish issue had been quite different, the public declarations of the S.F.I.O.'s General Secretary appeared to complement much that Blum said about the necessity for nonintervention in the conflict. Once again, Blum and Faure seemed to be at one.

Faure was not alone among Socialists in his views. His cautious and defensive posture toward the work of the Popular Front was not uncommon and, taken as an isolated factor, has little significance; most Socialists were uneasy about the prospect of closer collaboration with the Communists and unsure about the future of the Blum "experiment." Very significant is the fact that a great many of the Socialist deputies and local party officials shared fully their General Secretary's attitude toward international affairs, especially with respect to the Spanish Civil War. Faure's stand, by confirming and encouraging that of others, marked the emergence of a new *tendance,* later to be labeled the "Fauristes." In 1936 and 1937 the Fauristes were yet a very loose grouping of like-minded individuals bound together by their fears and inclinations, bearing only slight resemblance to an organized *tendance* in the style of the *Gauche Révolutionnaire* or the *Bataille Socialiste.* Although the extent of the Fauriste sentiment cannot be properly

[19] Interviews with Roucayrol and Castagnez. See also Faure's statements in *Le Pays Socialiste,* October 3 and 10, 1939.

measured until the *fédérations* have been investigated, it should be illuminating to introduce several of the key figures who constituted the core of the Fauriste *tendance* in 1938 and thereafter, and to examine their responses to the Spanish Civil War. These men were: Justin Arnol, deputy from the Isère; Fernand Roucayrol, deputy from the Hérault; Charles Spinasse, deputy from the Corrèze and Minister of the National Economy; Louis L'Hévéder, deputy from the Morbihan; Bernard Chochoy, head of the Socialist Youth; and André Delmas, General Secretary of the *Syndicat des Instituteurs*.[20] The parliamentarians among them also served as secretaries of their respective *fédérations*.

Justin Arnol apparently believed himself eminently qualified to interpret provincial opinion, and cast himself in the role of its spokesman: he entitled his articles in *Le Populaire* "Report from the Provinces." Firmly in command of his own *fédération*,[21] Arnol confidently reported that the population of his region calmly supported the government's Spanish policy despite the "alarmist campaign" being waged by the Communists, and noted that it was openly hostile to "any recklessness in foreign policy." His arguments and motives were those of Paul Faure: he told his own *fédération* that

the Socialist party remains faithful to its doctrine. . . . It know that nothing fruitful or human can result from murderous civil wars or international conflicts. . . . The French people want peace. Léon Blum and Yvon Delbos are searching for it with every means. They avoid taking part in the polemics between Berlin and Rome on the one hand, and Moscow on the other. They want France to be disengaged from all this, and want to create a truly French policy—a policy of peace. Are the Communists so unaware that a war psychosis can be created quite easily?[22]

This was naked xenophobia: France had no stake in the quarrel between Communism and "fascism"; hence she should undertake

[20] For a complete list of "Fauriste" personalities, consult the list of signatories of the Paul Faure motion for the Congresses of Montrouge and Nantes, *Le Populaire*, November 29, 1938, and May 5, 1939, respectively.

[21] See the numbers of *Le Droit du Peuple* (Isère) for the period.

[22] *Le Populaire*, August 29 and September 29, 1936, and *Le Droit du Peuple*, September 5, 1936.

no commitments to the Soviet Union, whose agents in France were attempting to prepare the public mind for war!

Equally averse to alignment with Soviet Russia and to any French interference in the Spanish war was Fernand Roucayrol, leader of the Hérault *fédération* and evidently a very influential personality among the Socialist deputies.[23] Roucayrol bluntly warned that any departure from nonintervention would be "insanity," and summarily lumped the "fascist" powers and the U.S.S.R. into the same category as disturbers of peace. Protesting vigorously that France *must* remain at peace, he argued regularly that France should not become involved in the Spanish struggle, which he characterized as a contest between two totalitarian ideologies.[24] In 1939 he explained why he had taken this position: "When the Spanish war broke out, no effort was spared [by the Communists] to throw France into an adventure on a terrain admirably chosen to oppose her squarely against Germany and Italy."[25]

Holder of an important ministerial portfolio and a major political figure in his home bastion of the Massif Central, Charles Spinasse appeared to be on the ascendancy within the Socialist party. Austere and aloof, Spinasse kept himself apart from party squabbles and sought to cultivate an image of leadership.[26] Most

[23] Interviews with Rosenfeld, Moch, and Castagnez; interview with Alexandre Rauzy, June 8, 1962; interview with Daniel Mayer, June 17, 1962.

[24] *L'Aube Sociale* (Hérault), December 19, 1936. See also the issues of October 17, 1936, and April 24, 1937, and Roucayrol's speech to the National Council, as reported by *Le Populaire* on November 9, 1936.

[25] *Le Pays Socialiste*, October 6, 1939.

[26] Louis Gros, a Socialist senator, wrote in his memoirs, *République toujours* (Avignon, 1945), 158–159, that "Spinasse presented a monastic appearance, silent and reserved. . . . He sought to create a choice place for himself in the Socialist party. He made a few brilliant speeches . . . that he had practiced, polished, and repolished beforehand . . . and repeated several times without doubt before a mirror. . . . He was considered to be a distinguished economist, but . . . he did not convince many persons of this, particularly the Socialist deputies."

Much of the controversy that has surrounded Spinasse's record since 1945 has centered around his activities at Vichy in July, 1940, and during the Vichy regime. He is reported to have convinced many Socialists to vote for full powers to Marshal Pétain. In this regard, see Léon Blum, *L'Oeuvre, 1940–1945* (Paris, 1955), 72, 76, 79; the testimony of Louis Noguères, Socialist

of his communications to the party took the form of learned analyses of economic conditions, and, as late as March, 1937, he was still confidently predicting that the government's economic policy would stimulate an upturn in the economy. Spinasse was very cautious in his public statements dealing with foreign affairs, but he was quick to endorse nonintervention: "By intervening in Spain, we would take responsibility for a world conflict which would not fail to erupt."[27] Whether he shared, in 1936 and 1937, the virulent anti-Communist sentiments of Faure and the others is still open to question, but he raised no opposition to an outpouring of pacifist and anti-Communist feelings directed by his lieutenant within his own *fédération* of the Corrèze.[28]

Indefatigable propagandist, prolific contributor to the "Free Tribune" of *Le Populaire,* and perennial speaker at Socialist congresses, Louis L'Hévéder was very well known to the militants of the S.F.I.O. An avid pacifist, L'Hévéder was even more outspoken than Faure and Arnol in his advocacy of nonintervention and was extraordinarily proficient in directing suspicion toward the Communists for their opposition to this policy. He also took care to make his position unmistakably clear.

deputy from the Pyrénées-Orientales, in *Les Evénements survenus en France,* VII, 2234–2238, in which Noguerès accused Spinasse and Rauzy of desiring to install a Nazi regime in France; and Vincent Auriol, *Hier . . . Demain* (Tunis, 1944), 97. During the early months of the Vichy regime, Spinasse published a journal called *L'Effort,* for which he received, according to Auriol, a stipend of 150,000 francs per month. From November 1, 1941, to August 22, 1942, Spinasse directed a journal called *Le Rouge et le Bleu: Revue de la Pensée Socialiste française;* occasional contributors to this journal, published in occupied Paris, were Arnol, Peschadour, Marcel Roy, and Roucayrol.

[27] *La Voix Corrèzienne,* October 21, 1936. See also *Le Mémorial de la Creuse,* October 10, 1936, and Spinasse's speeches at Limoges, reported in *Le Populaire,* January 25, 1937, and at Tulle, reported in the *Populaire* on March 29, 1937.

[28] Alexandre Rauzy has told me that Spinasse was "Blum's man" in 1936 and 1937 and that "he did not join us until 1938." In an interview on July 26, 1962, Lucien Laurat told me that Spinasse let it be known that he shared Faure's views on nonintervention. Spinasse later declared that he wanted a complete break with the Communists as early as June, 1936; see *Le Rouge et le Bleu,* February 7, 1942. Consult *La Voix Corrèzienne,* especially the articles by Julien Peschadour.

The attitude of the Communists in foreign policy is determined by the needs of Russia. The Russian government considers war to be inevitable and believes that the U.S.S.R. will be directly involved, and hence is looking for allies. . . . Our government rejects any action which could crystallize Europe into opposing blocs. . . . More than ever, I think that the French government, by its prudent attitude [toward the Spanish problem] has avoided the worst and is continuing to safeguard the last chance for peace by preventing an atrocious civil war from degenerating into an international war.[29]

But as the Spanish Civil War dragged on through the spring of 1937, L'Hévéder became convinced that nonintervention could not by itself prevent a general war, and he recommended that the League of Nations mediate between the opposing parties in Spain. In other words, concessions must be made to the Spanish rebels. He added that

we must not count on war to extirpate the roots of fascism. Fascism is the fruit of poverty, of disorder. . . . It will disappear *only* if all peoples, triumphing over their prejudices, join in accord to construct a harmonious human society.[30]

L'Hévéder's proposal was not merely a prescription for terminating hostilities in Spain, but was a call for the *rapprochement* of all nations. And the route to *rapprochement* must begin with concessions to the "fascist" powers in the confident expectation that an amelioration of the conditions that produced fascism would be conducive to its eventual disappearance. L'Hévéder excluded war as an instrument of policy, or even as a last resort; the Spanish conflict persuaded him that the danger of general war, so frightfully real, could be eliminated only by a policy of appeasement.

Nonintervention in Spain was proudly supported by the leadership of the S.F.I.O.'s powerful appendage, the *Jeunesses Socialistes,* and, once again, the ingredients of that support were pacifism, defeatism, and unremitting suspicion of the Communists. The national leader of the Socialist Youth, Bernard Cho-

[29] *Le Rappel du Morbihan,* December 5, 1936. L'Hévéder called for a full-fledged Socialist attack upon the Communists; see the *Populaire,* December 7, 1936.

[30] *Le Populaire,* June 10, 1937; *Le Rappel du Morbihan,* May 8, 1937.

choy, was a close friend of the party's General Secretary and a member of his ministerial cabinet. In collaboration with Danielle Liegeois, Chochoy directed the uncompromisingly pacifist organ *Le Cri des Jeunes,*[31] which served as the primary weapon in an apparently successful effort to fashion the youth organization into the exclusive patrimony of Paul Faure. In its pages the cult of the personality took shape: Paul Faure was described as the soul of French socialism.[32] Although disgruntled by the government's failure to reduce the term of military service, the editorialists of *Le Cri des Jeunes* delighted in coupling their approval of nonintervention with slashing attacks upon the Communists:

The only reproach that . . . the Communists can direct against the leader of our party is that he attaches no virtue to war and wants peace with all nations. . . .
Long live Léon Blum, apostle of peace!

Chochoy confidently predicted total disaster—as did Paul Faure —in the absence of nonintervention:

Two months ago, at the moment when the Spanish Civil War erupted, Léon Blum saved the French proletariat from an adventure . . . in which it would have been decimated and utterly destroyed.[33]

[31] Louis Lévy, *The Truth About France* (London, 1941), 121: "As Secretary of the Party, Paul Faure had considerable influence over the young people of the Socialist Youth Movement. . . . Through the activities of himself and his friends, the Socialist Youth Movement became a nursery of defeatism." *Le Cri des Jeunes* was the "Organe National des Jeunesses Socialistes (S.F.I.O.)."

[32] Consult, for example, the first of two numbers for March, 1937. Faure's portrait enveloped two-thirds of the front page. Many issues contained select quotations from Faure's articles and speeches, and only rarely did a quotation from Léon Blum gain prominence. Faure was also the main speaker at congresses of the *Jeunesses Socialistes,* and his speech to the 1937 gathering at Creil (Oise) was devoted largely to a defense of nonintervention.

[33] *Le Cri des Jeunes,* November 11 and the first of two numbers for December, 1936. See also the September issue which described the Communist proposal for a "front des français" as follows: "We will not march for a union sacrée. . . . We will not participate in an antifascist crusade. We will not subscribe to the idea that war is inevitable. . . . Let us refuse to descend to the depths of chauvinism and neo-patriotism."

The Fauristes were ably seconded in their views by the avowedly anti-Communist elements in the C.G.T. responsible for the publication of the influential weekly *Syndicats*. Although the animators of this journal were in theory politically unaffiliated— its official *raison d'être* was to alert the C.G.T. to the threatened loss of its traditional independence from all political parties— many of them were active members of the Socialist party: René Belin, Assistant Secretary of the C.G.T.; Georges Dumoulin, General Secretary of the C.G.T. in the Department of the Nord; Marcel Roy, one of the secretaries of the Metal Workers Union; Lucien Laurat, a professor of political economy; and André Delmas, General Secretary of the *Syndicat des Instituteurs*, the teachers' union.[34] All of these men became, in varying degrees, upholders of the Fauriste position on international affairs, as evidenced by their vigorous defense of the nonintervention policy. Initially skeptical, Belin was easily persuaded of the merits of noninvolvement in Spain: this policy, he declared, preserved peace and offered the hope of a "new Peace Treaty with Germany."[35] Dumoulin, fearing that Republican Spain was, by 1937, "totally Bolshevized," warned against assisting the Communists in their destruction of Spanish liberty.[36] Roy and Laurat were certain that any French assistance to Madrid would unleash an international conflict, and they too were highly suspicious of Soviet motives for

[34] André Delmas was a member of the S.F.I.O., and directed his union throughout the years in question. Many Socialists were also prominent in the C.G.T.; e.g., until the elections of 1936, Peschadour was the secretary of the C.G.T. in the Corrèze, and Robert Vielle occupied the same position in the Gironde.

[35] *Syndicats*, January 21, 1937. Lucien Laurat, in an interview on July 26, 1962, told me that "in the beginning we in the *Syndicats* group favored assistance to the Spanish Republic, but we were compelled to take account of the fact that Bolshevism was making serious inroads into Spain, and this led us to believe that the U.S.S.R. desired to use the Spanish war to provoke a general war, a war in which France would do the fighting. Hence we became ardent supporters of nonintervention in order to thwart this Soviet plan."

[36] *Le Pays Socialiste*, July 14, 1939, and *Syndicats*, December 31, 1936. Dumoulin also told the National Committee of the C.G.T. that any war which might erupt over Spain would be an "imperialist war," and he would urge the French proletariat not to participate in it. See *Le Peuple*, December 8, 1936.

assisting the Spanish Republicans.[37] But it was André Delmas who was the most spirited advocate of nonintervention among the staff of *Syndicats*. From the very beginning of the Spanish war Delmas was obsessed by the specter of a general war, and he insisted repeatedly that the peace of Europe hinged upon the maintenance of nonintervention. At a meeting of the National Committee of the C.G.T. Delmas angered part of his audience by challenging the pacifist credentials of the opponents of nonintervention:

Some of our comrades think that we cannot avoid a European war. But one cannot build a policy based upon the inevitability of war.

Those who think, to the contrary, that the unfortunate conflict [in Spain] can be localized judge it useless and dangerous to question the principle of nonintervention. . . . Only the application of the plan of nonintervention can save peace.[38]

Admittedly Delmas paid tribute to the niceties of argumentation by urging the "application" of the original "plan" of nonintervention, but the burden of his message lay elsewhere: those who called for aid to Republican Spain and, by implication, for a fighting stance against "international fascism," were guilty of believing in the inevitability of war and of constructing their policy accordingly. And the attitude of the effective leader of this union must have either bulked large in shaping the views of its members or been profoundly representative of their own views, or else these were mutually shaped and shared. Significantly, the *instituteurs* are reckoned to have constituted a large segment of the rank and file of the S.F.I.O.[39]

Although our sample has been limited to several leading figures of the developing Fauriste *tendance*, there can be no doubt that their position received applause and emulation from those who

[37] On Marcel Roy, consult *Syndicats* for November 20, 1936; *Le Peuple*, September 9, 1936; and *Le Populaire*, September 9, 1936.

[38] *Le Peuple*, September 13 and December 8, 1936; *Syndicats*, October 17, November 27, 1936.

[39] Interviews with Roucayrol, Laurat, Moch, and Rosenfeld. On the post-1945 S.F.I.O. see Pierre Rimbert, "Le Parti Socialiste S.F.I.O.," in Maurice Duverger, ed., *Partis politiques et classes sociales en France* (Paris, 1955), 195–208.

later were to be counted among the ranks of the "appeasers."[40] Swiftly and brutally, these men were diverted in the summer of 1936 away from confident speculation about domestic affairs; suddenly their paramount concern became the preservation of European peace, or, at least, the abstention by France from dangerous entanglements that could involve her in war. Their reaction to the Spanish Civil War was an unsubtle blend of idealism and fear: all were hopeful that France's display of pacific will would illuminate the way toward permanent peace; yet all were frightened by the prospect of any French participation—even indirect —in the conflict, were stubbornly convinced that the danger of a general war was perilously real, and were distrustful of the motives of the Soviet Union. Thus at the time of the Spanish Civil War the Fauristes stood fast on a course charted long before and under different circumstances. By categorically refusing to accept any risk of war, by reaffirming their pacifist ideal as an inviolable socialist orthodoxy, and by rejecting the Soviets as partners for peace, they were to have no other policy, when confronted with new and harsher threats to peace, than "appeasement" of the dictators.

CAUTIOUS DISSENTERS

Despite the duty of discretion, imposed by their membership in the cabinet or by their position as prominent party spokesmen, certain key members of Blum's entourage were noticeably appre-

[40] It would serve no useful purpose to run the gamut of all the signers of the Faure "pacifist" resolutions in 1938 and 1939 in order to correlate support of appeasement with support of nonintervention in the Spanish Civil War. A few outstanding figures may serve as examples; all were appeasers in 1938; their Fauriste view on nonintervention may be found as follows: René Brunet, *La Volonté Socialiste* (Drôme) January 23, May 8, 1937; Felix Gouin, *La Provence Socialiste* (Bouches-du-Rhône), April 8, 1938; Jean Castagnez, *Le Réveil Socialiste du Cher,* February 6, June 12, 1937; Max Lejeune, *Le Cri du Peuple* (Somme), February 6, 1937; Camille Planche, who was one of the major proponents for "mediation" in Spain and a leader of the *Comité d'Action pour la Paix en Espagne,* see *Les Cahiers des Droits de l'Homme,* July 15, 1937, and *Le Combat Social* (Allier) August 8, December 12, 1937; Jean Le Bail, *Le Populaire du Centre* (Haute-Vienne), September 2, 1939; Julien Peschadour, *La Voix Corrèzienne,* November 1, December 6 and 13, 1936; Léon Silvestre *Le Combat Social* (Gard) September 5, November 7, December 5, 1936.

hensive about, and even antagonistic toward, the government's Spanish policy. These men shared in the rewards and frustrations of power with their chief, and frequently gave him diverse counsel; but they were united in their disquiet over the implications of French abstention from the Spanish strife. They expressed their dissent in different ways. Some, like Vincent Auriol, kept a stony silence while their mouthpieces critized or weakly rationalized the government's action; others, like Georges Monnet, openly blamed the British government and the Radicals for compelling the government to accept the nonintervention policy. Yet all were convinced that France's failure to combat "fascist aggression" in Spain compromised her effort to quarantine the dictators, and all were prepared to resolve to resist any further challenge from them. For these men—Auriol, Monnet, Rosenfeld, Blumel, Moch, Lebas, Salomon Grumbach, deputy from the Tarn, and Marx Dormoy (chosen Minister of the Interior after Salengro's suicide) —the lesson of Spain was precisely the opposite of that preached by Paul Faure and his sympathizers: Spain demonstrated the need to accept the risk of war to halt the spread of "fascism."

We have observed that Auriol, Blumel, and Rosenfeld were privy to Blum's decision to adopt nonintervention, although all were vigorously opposed to it; Moch aligned himself with them. Significantly, during the months following, of this group only Rosenfeld, editor of *Le Populaire,* spoke out publicly in defense of the government's stand on Spain, and his efforts were obviously uninspired.[41] Personal and party loyalty should have commanded a spirited espousal of Blum's policy from such a ranking personage as Auriol, but not only did he refrain from any public commentary on the issue, he made no effort to silence the clamorous campaign against nonintervention waged by the organ of his own *fédération* of the Haute-Garonne, *Le Midi Socialiste*—of which he was a director. The masthead of this powerful provincial daily frequently was dotted with curt warnings—for example, "If Franco wins, whose fault? Ours!" and "Can this game of dupes last any longer?" Its editor, Léon Hudelle, was permitted to release his "tears of rage" against "a neutrality which is disastrous for European democracy" without challenge from the titular

[41] *Le Populaire,* September 3, December 19, 1936.

leader of the *fédération,* Auriol himself.[42] Whether instigator of or approving witness to this blunt reproof to the government, Auriol's position was clear.

Similarly, Georges Monnet studiously abstained from making public declarations on the Spanish question throughout the fall of 1936, and the weekly publication of his left-leaning *fédération* of the Aisne, *Le Réveil Populaire*—which Monnet directed—seemed to pretend that the Spanish Civil War was not taking place. In January, 1937, however, in response to mounting and extremely vocal discontent among Socialists in the Aisne, Monnet was moved to confess at their congress that the government's position with respect to Spain was "difficult," noting that *"direct* intervention in Spain could have provoked European war. And in July and August England would not have followed us on the path of intervention."[43] Of course Monnet was evading the issue and shifting the blame: everyone knew that the phrase "direct intervention" was comfortably ambiguous, signifying anything from the involvement of French troops to the sale of weapons to Madrid; furthermore, Monnet was simply loading the onus of responsibility for an unpopular policy onto another government. In fact, Monnet's explanation was merely an embarrassed way of confirming the obvious: France could do nothing without assurances of support from London. In any event, this lame rationalization counted for little with Monnet's local comrades, for in July, 1937, the Aisne *fédération* categorically demanded the immediate abandonment of the nonintervention policy. More significant was the fact that Monnet's sole public defense of nonintervention was delivered in the seclusion of a local congress, and only after he was prodded on the question by his supporters. Surely Monnet's action was something less than a tribute to Blum's prowess as a statesman, and his words contrasted sharply with the benevolent accolades bestowed upon nonintervention by Faure and his friends; equally, they contrasted with Blum's own assessment of his policy.

[42] *Le Midi Socialiste* (Toulouse), August 16, 21, October 11, December 8, 1936. Editor Hudelle's overall posture in foreign policy matters during the years 1936–1939 was most singular in comparison with other Socialists. Perhaps one of the most vitriolic opponents of nonintervention, in 1938 he fully approved of the Munich pact and the position of Paul Faure.

[43] *Le Réveil Populaire,* February 6, 1937.

Although hardly a confident of Blum like Rosenfeld or Blumel, the Minister of Labor, Jean-Baptiste Lebas, must be counted among his important backers. Uncontested leader of the party's largest *fédération*—the Nord—Lebas was among the powerful personalities of the S.F.I.O. Sharp of tongue if not of mind, Lebas was a veteran of many years of vicious political struggle in the Nord, where his principal competitors were Communists. Consequently, he nursed a steady suspicion of the Communist party. Whether from choice or owing to force of circumstance, Lebas seems to have regarded foreign affairs as outside his competence, and his muteness over Spain was entirely in character. But the editorial columns of the official Socialist organs of the Nord *fédération, La Bataille* of Lille and *La Bataille Ouvrière* of Roubaix, provide clues to his attitude. Both journals exhibited unswerving loyalty to their leader often citing Blum's own defense of nonintervention, but both stressed that this policy was a hardheaded response to a critical situation. Conscious of the impact among workers of continuing Communist invective against the government's Spanish policy, *La Bataille Ouvrière* carried an editorial entitled "Heart and Reason"—unsigned and written in the first person—which maintained that

any policy other than the one chosen on August 8 would break the Popular Front. As a result of an instinctive fear, three Popular Front parties did not want to assist the Spanish government. . . . Any official aid to Red Spain would separate us from England, thereby dangerously increasing the threat of war. . . . We approve [the policy] of Léon Blum. After weighing all of these facts, and some others that I am unable to mention, our *fédération* congress has given its approval to Léon Blum's policy, the only possible policy. Blum can reconsider his policy only if he convinces England and the Radicals.[44]

[44] *La Bataille Ouvrière,* November 29, 1936; a similar article will be found in *La Bataille,* December 27, 1936. These weekly publications were under the editorial administration of the "administrative secretary" of the *fédération,* Lebas's lieutenant Victor Provo. Two other Socialist journals in the Nord were under individual direction: *L'Avenir du Nord* (Lille) frequently spoke for Augustin Laurent, deputy, and Léo Lagrange, deputy; *Le Peuple Libre* (Lille) was the mouthpiece of Roger Salengro and Charles Saint-Venant, deputies, and after Roger Salengro's suicide, of his brother, the deputy Henri Salengro.

Whether written by Lebas or one of his assistants, this statement expressed the candid opinion of the leadership of the Socialist forces in the Nord. Actually it contained a startling confession: it concurred with the Communist contention that nonintervention was the product of fear and was injurious to the Spanish Republican cause, but it argued that the interests of the Popular Front and French security were paramount. From putting responsibility for nonintervention squarely upon the Radicals and the British government, several deductions followed easily. (1) Blum himself was really opposed to nonintervention and was attempting to persuade its proponents to "reconsider"; (2) a bad decision in foreign policy was preferable to no Popular Front in France; and (3) France was unable to stand alone. Like Monnet, Lebas and his aides acknowledged publicly that nonintervention was not a matter of choice—and especially not of their choice—and that its maintenance was due to negative reasons.

Ranking Socialist member of the Foreign Affairs Commission of the Chamber and customarily the party's chief spokesman in parliamentary debates on foreign affairs, Salomon Grumbach enjoyed the respect and confidence of his colleagues. Like Auriol, Lebas, and the others, Grumbach was worried by Italian and German involvement in Spain, but he was careful to temper his hostility to the policy of nonintervention with the reminder that it was "inspired by circumstances"—presumably beyond the control of the French government, which, he said, "can take no initiative which would isolate France from Great Britain." Thus London bore the brunt of his invective: in the spring of 1937 he mocked what he described as "the inexplicable passivity of England" and demanded to know why nonintervention had been permitted to become a "mockery."[45] One might suspect with justification that the British government was not the only object of his rancor: one need only read "France" for "England"!

Alone of this group Marx Dormoy, deputy from the Allier and Minister of the Interior, publicly defended nonintervention with vigor. He had been, like Grumbach, one of Renaudel's principal supporters, but, remaining within the Socialist fold, he had be-

[45] *Le Populaire du Centre* (Socialist daily published at Limoges), December 8, 1936, March 19, 1937.

come one of Blum's closest personal friends.[46] But his defense of government policy was double-edged: "The ideal of peace," he declared in a well-publicized speech at Lille, "has guided us in all of our international action. . . . *In spite of our preferences, in spite of our sympathies,* it is this ideal alone which determined our attitude in the Spanish affair." Why was peace endangered? Not, as Faure would have it, because of the threat of an international conflict erupting over Spain, but because France would be isolated, cut off from Great Britain, should she become embroiled in the Spanish war. "We have maintained peace," he confided to members of the *fédérations* of the Creuse and the Allier, "only by doing violence to our hearts."[47]

This small group of influential Socialists, all closely identified with the S.F.I.O.'s Center majority—except perhaps for Georges Monnet, who occasionally sided with the *Bataille Socialiste*—was deeply troubled by the nonintervention policy. In substance, the impact of the Spanish Civil War was to shape this group into the core of a new *tendance,* later to be called the "Blumistes," although an open split with the Fauristes was avoided until 1938. All of these men were closely associated with Léon Blum, and this association foreclosed the possibility of overt dissent from his policy. Keenly aware of political realities, none believed that exposure of his fear that nonintervention would yield only disaster—the defeat of a friendly government of a strategically placed nation and an increase in the audacity of the "fascist" powers—would be fruitful. All accepted nonintervention with great reluctance: Moch, Rosenfeld, Blumel, and Auriol opposed it at its inception, and only Dormoy could persuade himself that it was a contribution to peace. Unlike Zyromski and Pivert, none demonstrated any special concern for the class character of the war in Spain, but viewed it as a stage of "fascist" aggression, and all of them assigned paramount importance to the preservation of close Franco-British collaboration in case of another confrontation with Germany and Italy. The logic of their assessment of nonin-

[46] Marx Dormoy, member of a politically prominent family in the Allier, remained one of Blum's closest friends until his assassination by fascist terrorists in 1941. See Léon Blum, *L'Oeuvre, 1940–1945,* 182.

[47] *Le Populaire,* April 5, June 6, 1937; *Le Combat Social* (Allier), September 26, 1937.

tervention precluded any other alternative: surely they did not consider this policy to be a model of international cooperation, and its cynical violation by Germany and Italy justified skepticism about Blum's dream of a pacification of Europe by negotiation; its sole asset, in their eyes, was a negative one—it preserved the Anglo-French entente.

ON THE LEFT

The year of the Popular Front government brought both promise and frustration to the Socialist Left. While often at odds, Zyromski and Pivert traveled the same path from peaks of exhilaration to despondency and outright anger. In different ways both were sharply influenced by events in which they were only the most peripheral actors: the sit-in strikes, the Spanish Civil War, the "pause," and the fall of the government. Zyromski's behavior made all the more evident the disparity between the violence of his language and his carefully limited aims, although he was hard pressed to contain his natural passion for movement. Zyromski wanted both government action and mass action, each serving as a catalyst to the other, while intent that the actions of both should be circumscribed by the precise goal of turning back the wave of "international fascism." Pivert and his swelling band of followers, their revolutionary zeal sparked by the strikes and apparent social revolution in Spain, sought to mobilize a forced march to the Socialist utopia. Failing of their objective, they hastened to assign blame to the government, working classes, and even to themselves, and by the spring of 1937 had taken refuge in a campaign of ideological annoyance, which gained them many fresh recruits to their extremist creed. Paradoxically, while the Popular Front experience seemed to yield a harvest of despair for Zyromski and Pivert and drove new wedges between the rival camps on the Socialist Left, its shortcomings gave both significantly wider audiences within the S.F.I.O.

Buoyed by the election returns, which he took pleasure in describing as a "profound antifascist surge from the depths of the masses," Zyromski issued a call for combat, for a Socialist-led government which would "attack the root of capitalist property" and would seek to head an international anti-Hitler coalition. But, as usual, his message was ambiguous: did he mean that

France was on the threshold of social revolution? "The Popular Front," he boasted, "is for us a point of departure toward bolder and greater steps." But when would the steps be taken, and could they be taken if they were to interfere with the need to build a France sufficiently strong to face the adversary across the Rhine? The sit-down strikes pointed up the dilemma: while he rejoiced over the activism of the workers, Zyromski was relieved by the conclusion of the Matignon Agreements, which, he conceded, represented a "good start" on the road to socialism.[48] Like the Communists, Zyromski was apprehensive that social upheaval could prejudice the achievement of foreign policy aims; he desired mass ferment only insofar as it could be channeled in accordance with his will. This was especially evident in his response to the government's handling of the Spanish Civil War.

Judging from the ferocity of his utterances, Zyromski was, from the outset, the most formidable and dogged opponent of the nonintervention policy within the Socialist party. As early as August 4, he unhesitatingly labeled the Spanish rebellion "fascist," freely predicting that its victory would complete the "encirclement" of France by "international fascism." Evidently deficient in both geography and geometry, Zyromski nonetheless played upon a single theme: France's military security was at stake, and he regularly exhorted the Blum government to deliver arms to "our Spanish brothers."[49] Decrying what he characterized as the "complacent weakness" and "blindness" of the democratic powers in regard to Nazi Germany—whose ruler, he asserted, had instigated the military sedition in Spain—the leader of the *Bataille Socialiste* urged the working class to employ its "specific techniques"—that is, mass demonstrations—in order to coerce the government to lift its "embargo" upon shipments to Republican

---

[48] *Le Populaire,* May 9, 11, 22, June 15, 1936.

[49] *Ibid.,* August 4, 17, September 15, 24, 1936. It is noteworthy that Zyromski was quick to emulate the Communist example. *L'Humanité* of August 3, 1936, argued that France must assist the Spanish Republic in order to defend her own security. In order to embarrass the Socialist leaders, *L'Humanité* of September 17, 1936, headlined the "accord of Duclos [Jacques Duclos, veteran Communist leader] and Zyromski on the Spanish question," and on September 23 the same journal prominently announced Zyromski's resignation from the central bureau of the Socialist *fédération* of the Seine in protest against nonintervention in Spain.

Spain.[50] But demonstrations were meant to pressure, not to over-whelm the government; at numerous mass meetings Zyromski was careful to emphasize that the duty of the working class was to persuade Blum to do what was right.

Zyromski's initial assessment of the significance of the Spanish struggle was evidently unalterable: thoughout the year of the Blum government the heart of his position remained the simple assertion that the insurrection in Spain was merely the prelude to a total assault upon European democracy; thus France must assist democratic Spain since her very existence as a nation depended upon the defeat of "fascism" on Spanish battlefields. The risk of war? Zyromski denounced fears of war with characteristic arro-gance:

To protest against the idea of war has become a meaningless affirma-tion. To oppose all kinds of war . . . is to fall into an abstract pacifism which is ignorant of the multiple and varied means of fascist strategy and tactics. Such a pacifism leaves the field free to fascism and permits it to establish its hegemony.

This unremitting antagonism toward nonintervention, deriving from the facile assumption that the Spanish rebellion was but one stage of a vast plot, was wholly consistent with Zyromski's earlier views. The Spanish Civil War stiffened his conviction that Nazi Germany must be opposed by a firm military alliance of France, Great Britain, and the U.S.S.R., and he pointed with pride to Soviet intervention in Spain, explaining that it was motivated by the desire both to save Spanish democracy and to spur London and Paris into action against "fascism."[51]

[50] *Le Populaire,* September 15, 1936. Zyromski referred to nonintervention repeatedly as "the embargo, a unilateral measure which the French govern-ment has thought its duty to impose—for reasons which I do not understand."

[51] *Ibid.,* September 24, October 2, 15, December 9, 23, 1936, January 25, 1937; and *L'Espagne Socialiste: Organe franco-espagnol illustré du Comité d'Action Socialiste pour l'Espagne* (C.A.S.P.E.), April 16, 1937. The major figures who organized this committee and published this organ were: Zyrom-ski, Director; Jean Prader (G.R.), General Secretary; Simone Kahn, Adminis-trative Secretary; Colette Audry (G.R.); Michel Collinet (G.R.); Berthe Fouchère (G.R.); Jean Longuet (Center); Edouard Serre (G.R.); André Weil-Curiel (G.R.); Lucien Weitz (G.R.); Amedée Guy (B.S.), deputy from the Haute-Savoie; Audeguil (B.S.), deputy from the Gironde; Andraud

Although Zyromski's position on Spain was unwavering and apparently coherent, it was studded with ambiguities. Publicly impervious to political and diplomatic realities, Zyromski ignored the many factors which had dictated the adoption of the nonintervention policy, and his brutal dismissal of a pacifism cherished by many Socialists was ill calculated to rally the party to his views. While he described the Spanish Republic as the front line of European democracy, he made, presumably out of deference to his leftist followers and his own conscience, occasional mention of the socialist and revolutionary character of the Spanish conflict; yet he declined to specify whether Republican Spain was basically "bourgeois-democratic" or "revolutionary-socialist."[52] The ambiguity of his revolutionary posture was further underlined by his continued insistence that adherence to proletarian internationalism was not compromised by advocacy of an old-fashioned alliance system, and as well by his acknowledgment that limitations upon mass action were imposed by the need to keep Blum in power. Zyromski actually minimized proletarian participation in the international and national struggle against "fascism" by restricting such participation to demonstrations geared to achieve a specific purpose. Zyromski was being checkmated by the conflict between his better judgment and his revolutionary aspirations. While his attitude toward nonintervention was to win him a wider audience within the S.F.I.O. by default—since those around Blum who were antagonistic to this policy were obliged to remain

(Center), deputy from the Puy-de-Dôme; Amédée Dunois (B.S.); Louis Lévy, and Marceau Pivert. Six issues of *L'Espagne Socialiste* are available, dating from April 16, 1937, to November 1, 1937. An unsigned editorial in the first number declared that the C.A.S.P.E. had been formed to "let the truth be known," because "certain people" had used the pacifist sentiments of Socialists to win support for nonintervention.

[52] Zyromski's most elaborate analysis of the Spanish Republic was published in the *Populaire* on September 15, 1936. He acknowledged that this Republic must have "a substantial social aspect" and that "it must not be a simple bourgeois democratic Republic." But Zyromski made little mention of the socialist aspects of Republican Spain. Even the title of the journal which he directed—*L'Espagne Socialiste*—was obviously a concession to Pivert. It is noteworthy that in a letter to the author, dated June 22, 1962, Zyromski said that his major effort in behalf of Spain was confined to the columns of *Le Populaire*.

silent—the very ambiguity of his position was to rob him of a larger clientele on the Left, impatient of deliverance. On several critical questions—the sit-in strikes and the subsequent role of the working class, the nature of the war in Spain, and the means necessary to liquidate the "fascist" threat—Zyromski differed substantially from Marceau Pivert.

While Zyromski was outwardly committed to an effort to coordinate the momentum of the Popular Front's twin elements—government action and mass action—Pivert presupposed a fundamental cleavage between them, believing that they were susceptible only of fleeting alliance. The theme "two Popular Fronts," the official political alignment and the union of the masses, was very popular on the Revolutionary Left; the latter was to come to the rescue of the former in moments of need, but its primary mission was to speed the pace toward socialist revolution—irrespective of the actions of the government. "Absolute confidence in the masses," declared Pivert, "and rapid progress toward the Socialist Republic of workers and peasants of France."[53] But the amplitude of the sit-in strikes caught even Pivert by surprise, and he lamented his lack of preparation: "The proletarian revolution slipped through our hands," he wrote two years later; "we did not know how to seize upon our chance."[54] Comfortable as theorizers of revolution, the men of the *Gauche Révolutionnaire* seemed divorced from the current in which they placed their hopes; none were prepared to capture or even to influence the flow of proletarian discontent. Yet Pivert was thrilled with the depth of the apparent consciousness of the working class of its unity and its tasks; clearly he sensed that the sudden eruption of mass action signaled that revolution could not be far behind.

Pivert was absolutely convinced that events in Spain constituted a thorough vindication of his socialist beliefs. Like Zyromski, Pivert perceived the sinister hand of "international fascism" behind the revolt of the Spanish generals, and he too demanded that the anti-Franco camp receive help from abroad. But the

[53] Speech at the National Council of May 10, 1936, reported in *Le Populaire*, May 11, 1936.

[54] *Juin 36,* June 11, 1938; see also Marceau Pivert, "Juin 36 et les défaillances du mouvement ouvrier," *La Revue Socialiste, Nouvelle Série* (98), 1956, 2–33.

similarities between the two leftist leaders on the Spanish question were shallow indeed. Zyromski refused to dismiss the possibility of a general war; Pivert denounced such a war as the worst conceivable response to the new "fascist" danger. Zyromski attacked nonintervention as a shameful surrender; Pivert argued that it mitigated against the outbreak of "imperialist war." Zyromski was decidedly equivocal about the social import of the struggle in Spain; Pivert hailed the Spanish "revolution" as the vanguard of world revolution. Zyromski renewed his support for a powerful military alliance against Hitler; Pivert assailed the "Hitlerian notion" of pitting nations against one another, offering revolution as the sole alternative to war.[55] And Zyromski increasingly minimized the role of the masses, while Pivert increasingly appealed for direct proletarian action. Thus, despite their cosponsorship of an organ devoted to the Spanish "Loyalist" cause—*L'Espagne Socialiste*—the war in Spain widened the breach between the leaders of the *Bataille Socialiste* and the *Gauche Révolutionnaire*.

In a report from Barcelona, Pivert joyously announced that the final struggle for the international liberation of the proletariat had begun:

The capitalist world is oscillating, before dying, between socialist revolution and fascist counterrevolution. . . . The supreme hope of the counterrevolution is imperialist war. . . . By provoking the fascist *putsch* of Franco against the Spanish workers . . . capitalism has itself chosen the road to its defeat. . . . Now the revolutionary forces are on the march; a new humanity is being born—a new invincible proletarian consciousness is being formed. . . . At the center of this new wave of world socialist revolution, Red Barcelona, we can perceive this new world. . . . *Révolution d'abord!* The Spanish proletarian revolution is going to be an impregnable bastion of the world revolution.[56]

[55] *Le Populaire*, August 14, 1936: "*There is no worse crime than to consent to war to rid ourselves of fascism.*" (Italics in original). Also *Le Populaire*, September 21, October 28, 1936.

[56] *Le Populaire*, August 24, 1936: "And now all of Catalonia and Valencia are in the process of socializing their economies. . . . Whether we want it or not, power belongs to workers, peasants, and militias in Catalonia: the real power is in the hands of a people in arms, who are directing their own destiny. *Révolution d'abord!*"

Pivert sharply rejected Zyromski's gloomy assessment of nonintervention; it prevented, he believed, the "exasperated imperialists" from unleashing an "international catastrophe."

It is not the fleet of the British Admiralty nor the French Air Force which will save the Revolution [in Spain]. It is the revolutionary solidarity of the international proletariat.[57]

Obviously delighted by the events in Spain during the summer and fall of 1936, Pivert was apprehensive only that the oft-predicted "imperialist war" would develop before the international proletarian revolution, ignited in Spain, could sweep over the continent. Certainly he had substantial justification for his delight: had not his persistent demands for direct proletarian action —organization of militias and armed battalions of workers— found an apparent vindication in the revolutionary upheaval in Catalonia? And, he reasoned, if these people in arms were capable, simultaneously, of crushing their oppressors, fighting Franco, and launching a social revolution, why should the French proletariat not be eager to emulate their heroic example? By forming their own militias and aiding the Spanish revolutionaries directly, while the government stood aloof from the war, thereby preventing "imperialist war," the French working masses, he believed, would be preparing admirably for their own revolutionary task.

Unhappily for Pivert, subsequent events failed to confirm his apocalyptic vision of impending world revolution. Early in 1937, the euphoria of mid-1936 having ebbed, Pivert lamented that his counsel had gone unheeded by the great majority of the working class, whose reaction to the Spanish "revolution" had, he confessed, been lethargic. "The gravest obstacles [to the pursuit of revolutionary struggle]," he declared, "seem to come from ourselves as much as from our class enemies. . . . The proletariat lacks an offensive spirit."[58] Why? Pivert began to suspect that the workers had been lulled by the promise of the "exercise of power," and he slowly turned his wrath against the Government. As early as October, 1936, Pivert, aided by his comrades Hélène

[57] *Ibid.*, March 13, 1937; *La Vague: Organe de rassemblement révolutionnaire,* April 1, 1937.
[58] *Le Populaire,* March 13, 1937.

and René Modiano, castigated Blum's rearmament proposals, and the excitable organ of the Jeunesses Socialistes of the Seine *fédération, Jeune Garde,* openly Pivertiste, launched a noisy propaganda assault against any rearmament.[59] While Pivert was willing to issue cryptic warnings,[60] he was reluctant to force a break with Blum; until the climactic events of March 16, 1937, the Pivertistes seemed to maintain a grudging confidence in Blum's pacifism— "Blum put us to sleep with his pacifist rhetoric," as one of them noted in retrospect[61]—and a dwindling hope in the "official" Popular Front. But the issuance of the so-called Bonds for National Defense and the announcement of the "pause" threatened to sever the overtaxed links between the government and the Revolutionary Left. Pivert wrote:

The Popular Front was not created to make the proletariat swallow the pill of military credits and national union. No! I will not be a silent and timid accomplice. No! I will not accept capitulation to militarism and the banks. No! I will agree neither to social peace nor to *union sacrée.*[62]

Sensing an unsavory connection between concessions to the financial community and stepped-up rearmament, Pivert feared that social reform was being sacrificed for national defense. Yet even this could be excused if the "pause" was but a transitory phase preparatory to the introduction of legislation to nationalize key industries; how splendid it would be if the government should fall on such an issue! "The way to combat would then be open, and the masses could be mobilized for action." But any lingering

[59] *Jeune Garde: Organe des Jeunesses Socialistes* (S.F.I.O.) *de la Seine,* September 12, 26, November 7, 1936, February 19, 1937.

[60] Pivert and the Modianos also warned Zyromski: "If an international war which certain people [Zyromski and the Communists?] secretly desire to erupt over Spain is actually unleashed, it will not be a war for a 'democratic crusade,' nor still less will it be a war of 'revolutionary defense' against fascism, but it will clearly be a war provoked by a conflict between rival imperialisms. We are at the side of our Spanish brothers; we want a class victory in a civil war. . . . *It is not by preparing for war that we will keep peace. We remain Socialists—we continue to reject all war, and prepare the revolution*" (*Le Populaire,* October 2, 1936; Pivert's italics).

[61] Daniel Guérin, *Front Populaire, Révolution manquée* (Paris, 1963), 151.

[62] *La Vague,* March 1, 1937.

optimism was snuffed out by the bloody clash in Clichy between the police and leftist demonstrators on the night of March 16, in which one member of the *Gauche Révolutionnaire* was killed. It was "the hour of truth." Placards plastered by the *Gauche Révolutionnaire* on walls of the working-class sectors of Paris read:

At Clichy, five dead, 200 wounded! Police fire on antifascist workers— under a Popular Front government. Is this the ransom demanded by the banks for their confidence? No, this cannot last![63]

Pivert issued the anticipated declaration in behalf of his *tendance:* the Popular Front experiment, he said, "is terminated at the parliamentary level."[64] In short, the "official" Popular Front was dead.

This action was to give Pivert a free rein for intransigence in rhetoric and suppleness in tactics, and was to permit him to reknit the Revolutionary Left around his leadership—which had not been without challenge. Pivert's stance on Spain had illuminated the awkward illogic of his reluctance to cut loose his moorings from the "official" Popular Front while simultaneously calling for direct mass action; the government's apparent lurch toward the right simply brought matters to a head. The Spanish War, in several ways, cut deeply into the framework of faith upon which the Revolutionary Left was constructed: it brought renewed questioning of the problems of revolution and internationalism, war and pacifism, and the role of the avowed revolutionary in a prerevolutionary situation.

There can be no doubt that the *Gauche Révolutionnaire* was convinced that a far-reaching social revolution was triggered by the uprising of the Spanish military, and all concurred that the Spanish "revolution" could be the catalyst of revolution in France. But two of the more prominent members of the *tendance* were utterly opposed to Pivert's apologia for nonintervention by the government and dismissed his fears of "imperialist war" as

[63] *Le Populaire,* April 6, 1937.

[64] *Le Populaire,* April 19, 1937. Pivert did not demand, however, the immediate end to Socialist direction of the government, and vowed that he did not want an end to the Popular Front experience.

unwarranted. They were Michel Collinet, a young Marxist theoretician, and Jean Prader, a member of the influential *Comité des Intellectuels Antifascistes* and General Secretary of the C.A.S.P.E. (Comité d'Action Socialiste pour l'Espagne), publisher of *L'Espagne Socialiste.*

Although more sophisticated and carefully reasoned, Collinet's interpretation of the meaning of the Spanish struggle closely paralleled Pivert's: the contest was, from the outset, between socialism and "fascism." Collinet incorporated Zyromski's plea for pressure on the government to supply Madrid with Pivert's appeal for direct assistance by the working class to their Spanish comrades. Unlike Pivert, he saw weakness and fear, rather than pacifist idealism, as the motive for Blum's action. "The Blum government," he asserted, "truckled under to the pressure of capitalist England and the French bourgeoisie."[65]

This allegation was taken up by Jean Prader in a provocative brochure suitably entitled *Au secours de l'Espagne Socialiste!* Prader indicted the government and the Socialist party for their alleged surrender, not merely to Hitler, but to the sordid "reactionary" French bourgeoisie, and he assailed Pivert's position as both illogical and inherently pacifist rather than socialist. Pivert's proposal for direct proletarian assistance to the Spanish Republic was, Prader asserted, paradoxical: it amounted to a declaration of war against the government, yet Pivert continued to believe that a rupture between the masses and government could be avoided. Pivert's position, he reasoned, contained an even more fundamental contradiction: if, as Pivert acknowledged, the Spanish Republic was a socialist Republic, it was inconceivable that an "imperialist war" could erupt over Spain. Hence the bourgeoisie would practice—in Prader's jargon—"reactionary defeatism" and launch a civil war; in fact, he argued, aid to Spain by the Blum government would produce the same reaction. By this act the final revolutionary struggle would begin, and thus any war would be a "revolutionary war" and no Socialist, least of all Marceau Pivert, should fear this eventuality. If socialism refused to accept the prospect of revolutionary war, Prader offered this grim prediction:

[65] *La Vague,* November 15, 1936; *Idée et Action, Revue Mensuelle du Mouvement socialiste et syndicaliste,* December, 1936, 56–61.

If we prefer peace today to defending Spain against fascism, who does not see that tomorrow we will be compelled to sacrifice ourselves? What will we do, if tomorrow, Hitler threatens to unleash war on account of a political situation in France which is not to his liking? . . . Would we sacrifice socialism in France in order to avoid war? Then what reason would we have to exist?[66]

The examples of Pivert, Collinet, and Prader readily attest to prodigious intellectual activity and revolutionary faith among the ranks of the Revolutionary Left, but they also demonstrate that the *tendance* remained essentially a heterogeneous collection of intellectuals whose commitment to sectarian brands of socialism and helpless confidence in imminent deliverance from the bourgeois yoke thwarted their effort to grasp political realities. All of them lived in a world of slightly differing, but congenial, illusions: Prader was eminently justified in some of his accusations against Pivert; it was illogical to support nonintervention and yet to appeal for direct mass action to circumvent this policy—and to ask the government to bless the venture with benign noninterference! But Pivert's assumption that a war over Spain would be "imperialist" and not "revolutionary" was fully consistent with his criticism of Zyromski in 1935: in the event of war, he asserted then, the unprepared proletariat would abdicate its revolutionary zeal in favor of the demands of national defense, and thus revolution must occur *before* war could erupt. Pivert and the Modianos were much less disturbed by nonintervention than by Blum's rearmament program, which seemed to point the way to *union sacrée* and "imperialist" war. Prader did deliver a telling blow when he implied that Pivert's desire to prevent "imperialist" war revealed him to be more of a pacifist than a revolutionary, and Pivert could retort only that the French working class, as demonstrated by its apathy over Spain—in the sense that it did not hasten to emulate the Spanish example—was unprepared for revolution. Neither, however, recognized that he had permitted assumptions to become facts; "revolution" and "imperialist war" were serious realities to both Pivert and Prader. Victims of their own beliefs, they were apparently convinced that only the slightest push was needed to send the world tumbling in one direction or

[66] Jean Prader, *Au Secours de l'Espagne Socialiste!* (Paris, 1936), 62.

another; how or whether to administer the push were subjects of dispute. Thus while the Spanish "revolution" initially appeared to the men of the Revolutionary Left to herald the advent of world-wide socialist revolution, or at the very least of revolution in France, they were unable to agree upon a single course of action or to refrain from bitter polemics among themselves. In one respect, Prader was quite right: the *Gauche Révolutionnaire* was reduced to "verbal gymnastics" over the Spanish Civil War.

With Pivert purged of his embarrassing obligations to the government, some of the ambiguities of his position seemed resolved: he was free to enlist a clientele with renewed reliance upon theories of direct action, could repair his ideological bonds with his friends in the *Gauche Révolutionnaire,* and was able to take the government severely to task for its immobility. Yet Pivert had no desire to see the government toppled: "It is foolish to condemn a government, which, by its very existence, permits the development of the revolutionary capacity of the masses." Similarly, he had no wish to secede from the S.F.I.O., in which, he believed, the Revolutionary Left represented "an increasingly strong current of opinion, irrepressible opinion";[67] party meetings and publications were also splendid vehicles of propaganda. But Paul Faure was in no mood to permit the Revolutionary Left to continue its actions, which he regarded as mutinous, unchecked. Early in 1937 Faure responded to Pivert's indiscreet criticism by issuing a severe reproof, admonishing the Revolutionary Left to refrain from any further acts of "indiscipline." Pivert retorted that he was being muzzled under threat of expulsion from the party.[68] The rebellious posture of the Revolutionary Left after Clichy compelled the Secretariat to take more stringent measures against the offenders —much to their delight, since the General Secretary's action was so much free publicity for their cause—and Faure drew up a stern indictment in which he insisted upon the immediate dissolution of the *tendance*. In a highly emotional speech to the National Council gathered at Puteaux on April 18, Faure accused the Revolutionary Left of "treason and crime" against both party and government.[69] Pivert replied with irony that he was "surprised" at the severity of the allegations, and he assured the National Coun-

[67] *Le Populaire,* April 19, 23, 1937.   [68] *Ibid.,* January 22, 1937.
[69] *Ibid.,* April 19, 1937.

cil that while he had no intention of violating party discipline, great care must be exercised not to confuse the S.F.I.O with the government. The Council, however, obliged Faure by voting, 4,620 to 25, with 583 abstentions, to dissolve the *Gauche Révolutionnaire* and to censure its "inadmissible attacks upon our comrades in the government." Faure had won the battle, but at the cost of publicizing the Revolutionary Left, which simply maintained its organization by changing its name, rather facetiously, to the "Minority of the C.A.P.," and pledged to "maintain the fires of socialist revolution."[70] In subsequent months, judging from its apparent inability to forge firm ties to the masses, the Revolutionary Left was more successful in stoking the fires of discontent within the S.F.I.O. than in unleashing a revolutionary conflagration.

Zyromski, meanwhile, pursued his course of selected criticism and prodding of party and government; notable was his abstention from the general acclaim which greeted Blum's speech at Lyons in January, and shortly thereafter he ridiculed the thought that any doubts remained about Hitler's intentions to establish his hegemony over the continent.[71] Although the robust leader of the *Bataille Socialiste* devoted most of his attention to the Spanish question and to awakening the working class to the plans of "international fascism," he persisted in his effort to encourage the union of the Socialist and Communist parties. Zyromski's optimistic prediction that unity was imminent was not welcomed by all Socialists, particularly when it was very clear that his project for union was merely a corollary to his international policy. A united party, Zyromski predicted, would (1) liquidate "integral pacifism" from its ranks, (2) defend the Soviet Union against all aggressors, and (3) give its full support to "collective security," that is, a system of armed alliances directed against Germany.[72] On the domestic front Zyromski figured as a wary supporter of the government, although he was angered by the indefinite prolongation of the "pause." Yet he sought to preserve his revolutionary purity by perfunctory reference to the need to perfect the "fighting techniques" of the proletariat, and by continuing to hold out

[70] *Ibid.*, and April 23, 1937.   [71] *Ibid.*, January 25, February 9, 19, 1937.
[72] *Ibid.*, March 17, April 3, 16, May 5, 13, June 2, 3, 1937.

the promise of an early conquest of power.[73] But Zyromski was very willing to keep the masses in reserve, at least most of the time; along with Pivert he urged the employment of mass demonstrations in June, 1937, to intimidate the Senate, but since Blum rejected popular coercion of the Senators, Zyromski's words were not put to the test of action. This was but another instance of his continuing dilemma: how to conciliate his faith in mass action and predilection for movement with the need to employ the "bourgeois" Republic in defense of the U.S.S.R.

THE CONGRESS OF MARSEILLES

The thirty-fourth National Congress of the Socialist party began its deliberations on July 10, 1937, during an oppressive heat wave that served to exacerbate tempers already much frayed by the fall of the Blum government. The three resolutions originally drawn up for presentation to the Congress underwent hasty revision as a consequence of Blum's exit from office, and were resubmitted as follows: A "Blum-Faure" motion on "General Policy" noted the disappointment throughout the country over the end of the Blum ministry, but pledged full and loyal collaboration by the S.F.I.O. in the Chautemps government, concluding with the confident declaration that the Popular Front would continue with its tasks. The resolution of the *Bataille Socialiste*— signed by Bracke as well as by Zyromski—expressed deep regret that a decisive confrontation with the Senate had been avoided, and called upon the Socialist members of the new government to seek the propitious moment to overthrow Chautemps so that a new government "in the image of the Popular Front" might be installed in power. In international policy, the resolution carefully avoided inflammatory statements, and confined itself to vague phrases about the necessity for "organized peace and collective security."[74] The Minority of the C.A.P.—that is, the *Gauche*

---

[73] *Ibid.*, April 6, May 5, 1937.

[74] *Ibid.*, June 26, 27, 1937. In the same journal on July 1, Zyromski clarified his demand for mass action, intimating that the struggle of the Popular Front would no longer be confined to the parliamentary arena. He composed this curious formula: "The conjunction of parliamentary and governmental action with the movement of the masses must be realized." Apparently this meant that the masses should provide a push when appropriate. Zyromski was silent about Communist refusal to join in demonstrations against the Senate.

Révolutionnaire—offered a scathing resolution which demanded the immediate withdrawal of the Socialist ministers from the government, urged that plans for revolutionary mass action be prepared for imminent use, and appealed for the constitution of a "government of combat" which would ruthlessly carry out the nationalization of key industries. In international policy it repeated the familiar shibboleths of the Revolutionary Left—for example, the elimination of a collective security based upon a belief in rival power blocs, and an immediate halt to French rearmament.[75] Clearly, however, the key issues before the Congress were to be the problem of participation, the future of the Popular Front, and the thorny issue of nonintervention in the Spanish Civil War.

The Spanish question was deliberately kept apart from the problems of "General Policy" by the *Bataille Socialiste* and the *Gauche Révolutionnaire,* so as to win as many *mandats* as possible on the strength of their domestic policies, and the leaders of the Blum-Faure bloc were compelled to follow suit. The C.A.S.P.E. offered a surprisingly mild resolution, signed both by Pivert and Zyromski, which was studded with deferential references to the sanctity of proletarian internationalism. It noted wryly that nonintervention "has not fulfilled the objectives envisioned by its initiators," and requested the Congress to demonstrate its fidelity to the resolution of the Socialist International by declaring itself in favor of the right of Republican Spain to purchase war materials without restriction.[76] Faure and Séverac responded with a resolution, signed by several of Blum's associates —S. Grumbach, Moch, Dormoy, Monnet, and Lebas—which devoted much energetic rhetoric to condemning the violations of nonintervention, but concluded with a simple expression of confidence in the will of the government to do everything to ensure "the strict application of nonintervention in the future."[77] A third resolution was placed before the Congress, closer to the sentiments

[75] *Ibid.,* June 29, 1937.

[76] *Ibid.,* May 13, 1937; for arguments among members of the C.A.S.P.E., see *L'Espagne Socialiste,* numbers for May 1, June 16–30, 1937.

[77] *Le Populaire,* June 3, 1937. The resolution was prepared while the Blum government was still in power, and Blum's associates were naturally obliged to maintain their public support of Blum.

of Faure and Séverac, by Camille Planche, deputy from the Allier and president of the Ligue des Anciens Combattants Pacifistes: it proudly proclaimed that the Socialist party "is unreservedly in favor of the policy of nonintervention," and concluded with the slogan popularized by Faure—*"Tout pour l'Espagne républicaine, rien contre la paix!"*[78]

With these motions before the Congress it appeared that a direct confrontation between the supporters and adversaries of nonintervention was in the offing, and the passionate debates of the first afternoon seemed to indicate that such would be the case. Louis Lévy, charged with delivering a perfunctory report on the party's relations with the International, laid down the challenge by declaring flatly that nonintervention could not continue for another day. Lévy was eagerly seconded by Zyromski, who, after divesting himself of his cumbersome jacket and shirt, delivered a brutal attack on nonintervention. With characteristic bombast— and with no little pride—he pointed out that he had been correct all along about the Spanish problem, and he reminded his wilting listeners that "the Spanish Civil War is not simply an internal civil war, but it is—above all—a stage in the great aggressive war waged by international fascism against the democratic forces." Warming yet more to his subject, the ebullient chief of the *Bataille Socialiste* charged Blum with leading the workers to their graves or to "fascist" concentration camps via his "ill-conceived" Spanish policy. Finally, he demanded that the Spanish Republic receive the rights to which it was entitled by international law, requesting that France urge the League of Nations to consider immediate retaliatory action against the "fascist" powers for their intervention in Spain.[79]

The delegates were then treated to a violent diatribe against the armaments policy of the Blum government by a young enthusiast of the Revolutionary Left, René Cazanave, who asserted—to the accompaniment of a chorus of howls—that "preparation for war is fascism." Encouraged by the cheers of his comrades, the speaker attacked armaments and alliances, and called for a force-

[78] Parti Socialiste S.F.I.O., *XXXIV° Congrès National, Marseille, Compte rendu sténographique* (Paris, 1938), 445. This resolution was signed also by Castagnez, L'Hévéder, and Mauger, deputy from the Loir-et-Cher.

[79] *XXXIV° Congrès National*, 46–55, *passim*.

ful leader who would propose a "just peace" to Germany.[80] After Cazanave had left the platform—amid general relief—the presiding officer introduced the distinguished aviator Edouard Serre of the Seine *fédération,* who wished to speak in the name of the *Gauche Révolutionnaire.* The Congress erupted: cries of "No! No! Not the Seine again! Enough!" filled the hall. When the din finally subsided, Serre declared that his *tendance,* despite its opposition to armaments and national defense, was supporting the C.A.S.P.E. resolution because, as he put it, the Socialist party could not continue to be a partner to the assassination of Republican Spain. But, he added, taking care to preserve the ideological purity of the Revolutionary Left, direct assistance by the working class to its Spanish brothers was unquestionably the better solution.[81]

A more moderate tone was introduced into the proceedings by the speeches of the Socialist veterans Jean Longuet and Salomon Grumbach. The aging Longuet, in an emotional address, stated regretfully that Blum was mistaken in his Spanish policy. While admitting that the attitudes of the Radicals and "conservative England" had undoubtedly been major factors in the adoption of nonintervention, Longuet charged that pressures exercised by certain members of the government had constituted a formidable obstacle to assisting the Spanish Republic. Since Longuet had already mentioned the role of the Radicals, and since he apparently considered this to be an additional factor, it would seem obvious that he was referring to the position taken by some Socialist members of the government. Longuet's allegation, however, passed unchallenged or unnoticed, and he concluded his speech with a vigorous appeal for a prompt end to nonintervention, warning against the idea that *any* agreements could be reached with either Hitler or Mussolini.

Grumbach's brief speech concentrated on the scandalous propositions made by Cazanave, and he reaffirmed, as if it were necessary, the party's adherence to national defense and collective security. Then the deputy from the Tarn voiced his doubt that assistance to the Madrid government would have led to a European catastrophe, but, turning to Zyromski, he declared that it was impossible to prove it. In conclusion he reiterated his familiar theme: whatever the case, France was compelled to preserve the friendship of Great Britain.[82]

The torrid session was brought to a close by a brief declaration of the obscure Vergnolles, a member of the delegation from the *fédération* of the Dordogne. He simply reminded the Congress that Planche had submitted a motion which fully supported the policy of nonintervention! After such a vigorous presentation of the arguments against nonintervention, and after a reluctant and colorless defense of this policy, it was logical to assume that the Fauristes would retort on the following day. But the Spanish question was not brought to the floor for purposes of debate again: the problem was assigned to a committee which worked out a so-called synthesis resolution behind closed doors. On July 12, Jamet, of the Vienne *fédération,* and Planche hailed the "peace policy" of the Blum government, and singled out the nonintervention policy for special commendation.[83] But that was all.

The Fauristes, however, had no need to take the rostrum to defend nonintervention: they could count on Blum to do their work for them. Very late in the afternoon of July 12, the leader of the S.F.I.O., amid enthusiastic acclaim, began a spirited and often emotional defense of his actions as head of the government. At the very beginning of his address, he directed his attention to the Spanish problem:

I admit that many of our expectations have been invalidated [by events]. I confess that many of our hopes have been mistaken and deceived. *But in spite of everything,* the *one fact* which should prevail in your minds, *over all others,* is that for a year Europe has not known war, that is to say general war. . . . Armed conflict has been avoided for the majority of Europe's peoples. Some say to us, "Yes, you said that last August, but in fact war would not have broken out." Believe me! It takes a great deal of assurance to say that. I still do not know today. . . .

To resign one's self to actions containing an immediate danger of war because if one does not do so the danger could be more redoubtable tomorrow—*never will I do that!* Do you understand what this

---

[82] *Ibid.,* 81, 85–86.   [83] *Ibid.,* 398–410, 445–446.

argument means? This argument is a justification of preventive wars! *No, No, it is not by war that liberty is going to be defended.*[84]

The majority of the delegates rose and applauded wildly, and "the thunder of bravos" rang through the hall.[85] Clearly there was no need for the Fauristes to speak in behalf of nonintervention.

At the final session of an exhausted Congress, Louis Lévy presented a "compromise" resolution on the Spanish problem. It was duly adopted without debate and by acclamation—by raised hands—and, superficially, it appeared to favor the opponents of nonintervention:

The Congress of the Socialist party, considering that the policy of nonintervention has not yielded all the results anticipated by its initiators;

Associates itself fully with the decisions of the I.O.S. and F.S.I. which request full freedom of commerce in armaments . . . for Republican Spain, engaged in its struggle against fascism.[86]

Although apparently much stronger than the resolution on Spain adopted previously by the National Council,[87] the Marseilles resolution was just as deceptive and unenforceable. Very simply, it was another toothless resolution: the party merely "associated" itself with the resolutions of the Internationals; it conceded that nonintervention had achieved something—"nonintervention has not yielded *all* the results." Rather than directing the Socialist members of the government to work for the end of this policy, it went on to request them "to work against any recognition of belligerency rights for the rebel armies." In essence, it declared that the Spanish Republic should have the right to purchase means of defense, but it was totally silent as to how and when the restitution of this right should be attained.

Once again a meaningless "synthesis" resolution had been adopted; a potentially divisive issue was simply glossed over. Zyromski, recognizing that the C.A.S.P.E. motion stood little chance

[84] *Ibid.,* 461–463, *passim.* (Italics mine.)   [85] *L'Oeuvre,* July 13, 1937.
[86] *Le Populaire,* July 14, 1937. The I.O.S. was the Socialist International, and the F.S.I. the International Federation of Trade Unions.
[87] Especially the resolution of the National Council in February, 1937.

of winning acceptance by the Congress, was willing to settle for a declaration of the party's desire to aid Republican Spain.[88] Rather than continue the explosive debate of the first day of the Congress, the Socialist chieftains were ready to purchase Zyromski's silence by supporting this ambiguous resolution, and, in any event, Blum's speech not only represented a vindication of nonintervention, but also implied strongly that this policy would continue. Thus the adoption of this resolution did not signify that the Socialist party had suddenly condemned nonintervention, nor did it mean that the profound differences over the Spanish problem within the party had been genuinely compromised.

The proceedings of the Congress took place in an atmosphere of continuous uproar: fist fights among the delegates were commonplace, chairs were hurled down onto the main floor from the balcony—an act attributed to Italian newsmen—and at one point Blum, on the verge of tears, mounted a table to beseech his comrades to preserve the decorum worthy of a "party of government." Blum's eviction from power and the question of participation in the Chautemps government were the coresponsibles of the acrimonious debates on the three motions before the Congress. The National Council of June 22 had sanctioned participation by a large margin, 3,972 to 1,369, but this action was only narrowly approved by the Congress, 2,946 to 2,459.[89] Obviously participation in a government headed by a Radical, with little hope for further social reform, was highly unpopular with many "centrist" stalwarts, and their sentiments found expression in the voting on the resolutions. The "Blum-Faure" motion received 2,946 *mandats* (54.7% of the total), the *Bataille Socialiste* motion 1,545 (28.7%), and the *Gauche Révolutionnaire* motion 894 (16.6%).[90] Superficially it would appear that the Left constituted a formidable 45.3 per cent of the party, but it would seem more likely that the strength of the *Bataille Socialiste* was inflated by the votes of many "centrists" antagonistic to participation under a Radical leader. In fact the *Bataille Socialiste* resolution was well calculated to attract the dissidents: deliberately vague on international

[88] Zyromski remarked shortly afterward that it had not been easy for him to accept this resolution, and that he had gone to the limit in making concessions. See *L'Espagne Socialiste*, August 1–15, 1937.

[89] *XXXIVᵉ Congrès National*, 606–607.   [90] *Ibid.*

policy, its demand for a new Popular Front government under Socialist leadership was admirably tailored to reap the rewards of frustration. This hypothesis is substantiated by the following: (1) the vote reaffirming the decision of the National Council of June 22 was virtually identical with the vote on "General Policy"— 2,946 affirmative *mandats* in the first instance as compared with 2,946 in favor of the "Blum-Faure" resolution, and 2,459 negative *mandats* as compared with a joint leftist total of 2,439; (2) many "centrists" publicly expressed their disdain for participation; (3) participation had long been anathema in all segments of the S.F.I.O.; (4) examination of the Socialist *fédérations,* undertaken below, reveals no widespread surge of sentiment in support of Zyromski's international policy, thus indicating that much of his strength was due to his domestic policies; and (5) comparison of the tally at Marseilles with that of a National Council held the following November demonstrates that the vote cast for the *Bataille Socialiste* resolution at the Congress of Marseilles was very definitely a distorted indication of the actual strength of the *tendance* itself (see Table 9, pp. 314–318). In July the *Bataille Socialiste* won 28.7 per cent of the *mandats,*[91] while at the National Council in November its share fell to 18.4 per cent, a decline of over 10 per cent. At the latter meeting the "centrists" bettered their showing by increasing their percentage to 64.6, a gain of nearly 10 per cent over their performance at Marseilles.[92] But in January, 1938, on a vote concerned exclusively with participation—necessitated by the fall of Chautemps and his request for Socialist participation in a new ministry—the "centrists" garnered only 49.2 per cent of the total, while the percentage won by the *Bataille Socialiste* jumped to 32.4.[93] Therefore the hypothesis

[91] These percentages are calculated on the basis of the total number of *mandats* cast for the three resolutions; abstentions and absentees are not counted in the calculations.

[92] *La Vie du Parti,* supplement to *Le Populaire,* November 25, 1937. Account of the vote of the National Council of November 6 and 7, 1937. The numerical result was: "Séverac Motion" (Center), 3, 448; *Bataille Socialiste,* 978; "Pivert" (*Gauche Révolutionnaire*), 909.

[93] *Ibid.,* February 15, 1938. Account of the vote at the National Council of January 17, 1938. The numerical result was as follows: "Sérol Motion" (Center), 4,035; "Zyromski," 2,659; "Pivert," 1,496. The increased number of outstanding *mandats* was due to the increase in party membership during 1937.

that the considerable success of the *Bataille Socialiste* at the Congress of Marseilles was primarily attributable to the participation issue would appear to be vindicated by the weight of considerable evidence.

Thus the "Blum-Faure" majority possessed a firmer grip on the party than the vote at the Marseilles Congress would indicate. Yet this majority was itself progressively deteriorating from within, as was demonstrated by its response to the Spanish Civil War, and it was certainly ill prepared to withstand any further shocks. Although the National Congress adjourned on a note of timid optimism, the S.F.I.O. had been profoundly shaken by the "exercise of power": The euphoria of May, 1936, had vanished beneath a wave of accumulated disappointments: the party's leader had continued to pursue a dualistic and frequently contradictory international policy, reassuring some with his pacifist fervor, disturbing his intimate colleagues by his reluctance to take a stronger stand against "fascism," and outraging much of the Socialist Left by failing to permit assistance to Republican Spain and by refusing to enlist the aid of the masses; the "great ministry" had been the easy victim of the old men of the Senate. The prospects for further spectacular reform appeared nil, and much of the party chafed at the burden of participation in a government which embodied the Popular Front only in name. The period from the Congress of Marseilles to the Sudeten crisis of September, 1938, was to be one of final preparation within the S.F.I.O for the split of the party, a break which, although inevitable and irrevocable after the Munich conference, was the product of a long period of gestation.

SOCIALIST DEPUTIES

An occasional visitor to the Chamber of Deputies would have been hard put to distinguish the Socialists from most of their colleagues: their very indistinguishability in terms of social backgrounds was one mark of their easy blending into the petty bourgeois world of Third Republican politics. Socialists were almost uniformly "respectable" in this political arena: the champions of social democracy, self-proclaimed representatives of the working class, counted but eleven "workers" among their ranks, and of these most long since had had no profession but politics. Remarkable, then, was the social homogeneity of the Socialist delegation:

virtually all were drawn from provincial elites, and 60 per cent figured among the professions—40 per cent were lawyers, professors, or teachers. Even among those who advertised themselves as farmers few were of modest means, as most were directors of cooperatives or wine-growers. The following list indicates the number of Socialist deputies in each professional category;[94] "regions 1–7" are those in which Socialist candidates were the most successful in 1936, according to criteria employed earlier.

Profession	Regions 1-7	Remainder	Total
Farmers	10	7	17
Commerce, Industry	13	7	20
Employees (state and private)	10	5	15
Professional			
Lawyers	20	1	21
Professors	15	7	22
Teachers	9	6	15
Doctors	5	4	9
Journalists	6	1	7
Accountants	3	1	4
Publicists	2	1	3
Engineers	0	1	1
(Total professional)	60	22	82
Workers	9	2	11
Miscellaneous	2	0	2
Totals	104	43	147

Of itself, the social homogeneity of the Socialist parliamentarians serves to point up the regularity with which Socialist *fédérations* and electors selected their deputies from among the professional layers of French society, the backbone of the Republican political class. Taken with other factors, however, this would seem to substantiate the view that the S.F.I.O., at least on the regional level, was more a part of the political system than apart from it. Unlike the Communists who were, until 1936, confined to sullen and intransigent isolation, the Socialists participated fully in poli-

[94] Drawn from a list of the Socialist deputies in Georges Lefranc, *Le Mouvement socialiste sous la Troisième République* (*1875–1940*) (Paris, 1963), 409–411.

tics and observed the rules of the game with some care. Most
Socialist deputies were immensely political beings, supple, oppor-
tunistic, and doctrinaire only when it was necessary to preserve
their Socialist credentials. Since 1921 the S.F.I.O. had acquired a
regional power base, habits, and beliefs which identified it as a
party of the established political order. By 1936 many Socialist
deputies were veteran politicians with a vested interest in the
continued functioning of that order; habits and reflexes of a
decade and a half determined that in areas where the Socialist
party was an established political force it was cautious, even
narrowly defensive, and inclined to resemble its most powerful
regional or departmental adversary on the left of the political
spectrum. Hardly a formula for a party that espoused dramatic
innovation, but splendid for courting electoral success. Hence it
should be no surprise to discover that most Socialist deputies, in
matters of prime concern such as the Spanish Civil War, inclined
toward the Radicals rather than their ideological kindred, the
Communists. Equally unsurprising was the nature of Socialist
propaganda at the local level—in areas of Socialist success at the
ballot box—which stressed protection and defense of the interests
of its varied clientele; threats of socialization were made only
against easily identifiable and unpopular groups, such as insurance companies and the armaments industries.[95] Evidently "advanced radicalism" corresponded to the desires of Socialist deputies and voters alike.

We have already demonstrated the consistency of the pattern of
Socialist electoral geography with reference to the elections of
1932 and 1936. Table 3 (pp. 291–295) and Table 4 (pp.
296–300), the former concerned with the number of Socialist
deputies elected from each department and region, the latter with
a comparison of Socialist, Communist, Radical, and splinter Left
votes, extend examination to the elections of 1924 and 1928, and
in both regions are arranged in order of Socialist success in 1936.
Both tables reinforce the contentions that the S.F.I.O. was a powerful, established political force only in certain regions—the first
seven, from Languedoc through Central France—and that the
overwhelming majority of the party's deputies were elected from

[95] A conclusion reached after examination of seventy-one local Socialist
journals, representing seventy-one *fédérations*.

those regions. Yet Table 4 reveals that the S.F.I.O. apparently had reached the peak of its electoral appeal in all seven regions in 1932, if not in 1928.

These tables permit further observations on the political posture of the Socialist parliamentarians. In the four legislative elections from 1924 through 1936, the S.F.I.O. returned 479 deputies, and 340 of them, or 71 per cent, were returned from the first seven regions; little wonder that 71 per cent of the Socialist deputies in 1936 were selected from these same seven regions! The veteran character of the Socialist delegation is further underlined by the fact that of the 104 men elected from these regions in 1936, fourteen had been elected from the same department three times previously, fifteen twice previously, and twenty-eight once previously, for a total of fifty-seven re-elected, while forty-seven were freshman legislators. Contrast these figures with those drawn from the remaining eleven regions: in these only two men had been elected three times previously, five twice previously, and six once previously, for a total of thirteen experienced parliamentarians, while thirty were to serve their freshman terms. Although Socialist newcomers narrowly outnumbered the veterans, seventy-seven to seventy, freshmen were a minority among the *élus* from the first seven regions.

The stability—or the stagnation—of the Socialist vote in the first seven regions, with the exception of the Massif Central, suggests that henceforth the Socialists may well have believed themselves to be on the defensive, especially in view of the astonishing Communist increase everywhere—in the departments of the Dordogne, Lot, Alpes-Maritimes, Var, Lot-et-Garonne, Aveyron, Lozère, Loire, Rhône, and the Cher, for example, the Communists outdistanced the S.F.I.O. on the first ballot. The Socialists seemed to have attained a plateau of electoral strength as early as 1928, and were unable to climb substantially above it in subsequent elections. This does not imply the inflexible stability of the Socialist clientele: if the Communists were the chief gainers in the elections of 1936 it was no secret that the Radicals met with disaster, indicating that, in large measure, Socialist losses to the Communists were compensated for by recruits from the Radicals. What had occurred was a reshuffling of the leftist electorate, a sharp swing in its center of gravity toward the Left: Communist gain, Socialist stagnation, Radical loss—this was the electoral balance sheet of the Popular Front formula. In some instances, however, both Radicals and Socialists were bypassed by angry voters in favor of the Communists, as in the Lot. Such instances do not deny the rule: in the seven regions of Socialist strength the S.F.I.O. evidently lost as many votes to the apparently dynamic competitor on its left as it won from its traditional electoral partners on its right. The point was not lost on many Socialists: the Communists, by their spectacular advance, emerged from the elections of 1936 as serious rivals to the S.F.I.O. in areas that constituted the very heartland of its electoral strength. If only for this reason, Socialists in these seven regions—with the possible exception of the North—were to find it congenial and prudent to revert to their traditional anti-Communist posture. And events during the first months of the Popular Front government were to make the reversion to form all the easier.

The pattern of stability was not too dissimilar in the scattered pockets of Socialist strength in the next six regions, from the Northeast through the Alps. Certain departments exhibited characteristics similar to those in the first seven regions—for example, the Indre-et-Loire, a modest Socialist stronghold, where a slight Socialist increase was matched by the Communists to the overall detriment of the Radicals, or the Savoie, where, as in the Lot, Socialist desertions to the Communists were not matched by compensation from Radical voters. In the Northeast, however, especially in the Aisne, the S.F.I.O. worked in tandem with the Communist party to secure an unprecedented leftist victory, while in Brittany, with the exception of the Finistère, Socialists welcomed substantial gains without fear of being overtaken by the Communists in the near future—in the Morbihan, for example, the S.F.I.O. had simply supplanted the Radicals as the party of the traditional Left. Thus the major characteristic of these six regions, insofar as Socialists were concerned, was diversity: in older Socialist strongholds, especially where veteran party *élus* were in control, the Communists were to be seen once again as the Socialists' main antagonists; in areas of new Socialist strength, like the Aisne, where the Communists and the Popular Front spirit had helped to fashion the Socialist victory, Socialists were inclined to look upon the Communists as partners in the defense against fascism.

Tables 5 (pp. 300–303) and 6 (pp. 303–307) offer added confirmation of several of our assertions: the first compares the election of Socialist deputies in 1936 and 1932; the second shows how Socialists were elected in 1936.

Table 5 demonstrates that while sixty-four Socialists held their seats, fifteen were elevated to seats won by Socialists in 1932, and sixty-eight new seats were captured, the S.F.I.O. lost fifty-one of the seats it had won in 1932; thus the overall gain was seventeen seats. The summary at the end of the table indicates that major Socialist gains came at the expense of the Radicals (twenty-three seats) and of the Right (twenty seats), and that major Socialist losses were to the Communists (eighteen seats) and the Neo-Socialists (thirteen seats); in fact the S.F.I.O. won no seats from either Communists or Neo-Socialists. Forty-three, or two out of three of the new seats were won in the seven regions of regular Socialist strength, while twenty-seven of the fifty-one seats lost were in the same regions. Gains and losses in these regions were as follows:

Gained From		Lost to	Balance
0	Independents	1	−1
19	Radicals	6	+13
0	Communists	9	−9
16	Right	5	+11
8	U.S.R. (Socialist and Republican Union)	0	+8
0	Neo-Socialists	6	−6
43		27	+16

Socialist advances in Brittany, West Central France, and Algeria were countered by heavy losses in Paris—where eight Socialist seats fell to the Communists—and in Eastern France.

Table 6 shows that twenty-four Socialists were returned on the first ballot; that forty-four would have been returned on the second ballot without either Radical or Communist withdrawal, so sufficient was their plurality; that twenty-seven might have been defeated had a Radical candidate remained in the race on the second ballot, an unlikely confrontation given the Popular Front alliance and the cozy habit of electoral arrangements between Socialists and Radicals. Thus ninety-five of the 147 Socialist deputies probably would have been returned even without the formal Popular Front electoral agreement, and to this total should be added the five Socialists elected owing to unique local desistances. But forty-seven Socialist deputies might have met with defeat had Communists remained in competition, siphoning off enough votes to doom the Socialist candidacy. The importance of Communist fidelity to the Popular Front pact is underscored by reference to the seven regions of Socialist strength: although seventy-three Socialists would have been returned without Communist assistance, thirty-one owed their election to the discipline of the Communists. Communist votes were decisive in electing Socialist candidates in the North (thirteen), Central France (six), and the Loire (two), all areas of substantial working-class population; in some instances Communist support was decisive only because of the splintering of the normal Socialist vote due to the presence of popular Neo-Socialist candidates—for example, in the Hérault, Var, and the Gironde.

The election of 1936, then, gave many Socialist deputies more cause for apprehension than for celebration: their party emerged as the largest in the Chamber, yet its electoral foundation was decidedly weaker than in 1932, and nearly one-third of its deputies owed their places to Communist votes. The S.F.I.O. had lost 40 per cent of the seats it had won in 1932, and not a single one of its new seats had been garnered from the Communists. Most striking, despite the apparent fidelity to the S.F.I.O. of the areas comprising its electoral stronghold, was the degree of Communist penetration into them, and the likelihood that such penetration signaled the onset of sharp Socialist decline. Socialists had been outdistanced and then smothered by Communists in Paris in the elections of 1932 and 1936 respectively; were the Nord, Bouches-du-Rhône, even the Corrèze, about to follow the same path? Evidently many Socialist deputies were deeply troubled by that nightmare, although ambivalence toward their "comrades" on the Left persisted well into the summer of 1936. Theirs was a double fear: fear that the Popular Front spirit might represent the first stage of a quick decomposition of the old shell of politics, local and national, for the Communists seemed to be immensely skillful in making the tired system of left-wing politics vital, active, popular, and even a bit Jacobin; and a fear that antagonizing the Communists could cast the S.F.I.O. in the unenviable role of saboteur of the Popular Front. Hence the cautious attitude of Socialist deputies toward their ostensible allies on the Left during the first two months of the Blum government.[96] But foreign affairs, specifically the Spanish Civil War, stirred them from caution into action. The Spanish Civil War was, for the Socialist party as for the Popular Front itself, the watershed: for most Socialist deputies its international impact necessitated an end to the nebulous antifascist slogans which had prevailed at election time, and most took congenial shelter in traditional Socialist pacifism and vague talk about an "international settlement." The Spanish Civil War also provided an opportunity to deal with the Communists: most Socialist deputies had no hesitation in privately describing the Communists as warmongers and castigating them publicly as disruptive superpatriots of dubious credentials who refused to recognize the dangers inherent in their stand against nonintervention. It would be no exaggeration to add that such interpretations of Communist agitation over Spain provided a happy solution to the political dilemma posed by Communist success in the elections of 1936.

SOCIALIST MILITANTS

It is worth recalling that the S.F.I.O. was a fully democratic party in its organization. The National Congress, sovereign representative of the rank and file, was composed of delegates from the ninety-two departmental *fédérations,* with each *fédération* entitled to *mandats,* or votes, in proportion to its membership. For example, the *fédération* of the Nord, the largest, had 567 votes at the Congress of Marseilles, while the *fédération* of the Mayenne, the smallest, had but eight. The party allotted one *mandat* for every twenty-five members. Membership was determined not by the number of annual membership cards but by the total annual

[96] This is clear from examination of the Socialist journals in the departments.

number of membership stamps purchased in a *fédération*. To determine the number of votes assigned to any given *fédération* the party divided the number of stamps sold by twelve and divided the result by twenty-five. These calculations were based on the previous year's sale of stamps, and a *fédération* which experienced a sharp increase in membership during a year would not be rewarded with additional *mandats* until the following January 1. Conversely a *fédération* retained its *mandats* even if it suffered an abrupt decline during a year; the reckoning was always postponed until the new year.

The use of the term *mandat* was deliberate: a delegate was given a mandate by his *fédération* to follow its instructions. The *fédération* theoretically was the most important unit of the Socialist party, since *fédérations,* meeting in congress, decided what party policies would be. The structure of the *fédération* was also democratic: sections, usually town, village, or neighborhood organizations, were entitled to votes at the "federal congress" equal to their membership. The federal congress, sovereign representative of the *fédération,* was held annually and in emergencies in the *mairie* or café of a friendly town, and it instructed its delegates to the National Congress how to vote on the several resolutions scheduled to be presented there. Occasionally a federal congress would give a blank check to its emissaries to vote as they saw fit, but in most instances delegates were committed to apportion the *mandats* of their *fédération* according to the decision taken beforehand by their local comrades. The federal congress also elected a federal secretary for the coming year, selected the editor of the local Socialist journal—who frequently was the "federal secretary"—chose the "federal bureau," a body designed to oversee the executive authority of the secretary, and selected the party's candidates. On paper, then, the *fédération,* democratically composed of grass-roots sections, was free to choose its own officers, direct its own affairs, and employ its *mandats* at the National Congress as it desired.

Of course the members of the democratic *fédération* were subject to many and diverse forms of democratic pressure upon their decision making. The site of the federal congress, for example, may have been chosen by the secretary so as to favor supporters of a certain position or candidate by permitting an outpouring of local zeal in favor of that position or candidate.[97] The congress was also the place where the Socialist deputies from the department could be assured of a captive audience and a lengthy hearing, and they were often persuasive. The secretary frequently invited national figures to address the congress. They too were persuasive; Paul Faure took care to appear at as many federal congresses as possible. The secretary also directed the flow of information reaching the militant by editing the Socialist journal, and it should be remembered that much of the information was supplied to the secretary by the national secretariat. Most secretaries permitted a limited amount of lively discussion on party policy in these journals, but the tone was determined by the secretary, who was supported by the majority at the most recent congress. It is instructive to note that many deputies doubled as federal secretaries in those departments where socialism was powerful electorally, and many secretaries were ex-deputies. The secretary also traveled the circuit of the sections, and most deputies paid regular visits to sections throughout their *fédération,* not just those within their electoral district. Deputies also wrote frequent, sometimes weekly articles for the *fédération* journal, and some controlled their journals outright. Thus the average militant's freedom of choice was circumscribed by numerous pressures—from the secretary, the Socialist journal, the deputies, the national secretariat, and from the atmosphere of the federal congress—and in most *fédérations* these forms of persuasion worked to the decided advantage of the dominant force in the Socialist party, the "Blum-

[97] Candidates for parliamentary elections were ordinarily selected prior to the meeting of the "federal congress" by the secretary and the "federal bureau," and occasionally by the sections within a constituency. In many instances the names of the candidates were revealed in the Socialist journal without any indication as to how they had been chosen; presumably the task of the federal congress was to greet the chosen with acclamation. In any case, the *fédération* theoretically chose its candidates. For some representative cases, see *Le Travailleur des Alpes* (Basses-Alpes), January 25, 1936; *La Volonté Socialiste* (Drôme), January 26, 1936; *L'Aube Sociale* (Hérault), February 1, 1936; *Le Cri Populaire de l'Oise,* March 1, 1936; *L'Auvergne Socialiste* (Puy-de-Dôme), February 1, 1936; *Le Travail* (Basses-Pyrénées), March 8, 1936; *Germinal* (Belfort), April 11, 1936; and *La Dépêche Socialiste* (Saône-et-Loire), March 28, 1936.

Faure" majority. The Nord *fédération,* for example, which counted 23,000 adherents in 1937, cast 560 of its 567 *mandats* at Marseilles for the Blum-Faure resolution. However, in *fédérations* without powerful Socialist *élus,* such as the Meurthe-et-Moselle, and indeed in some with deputies of a leftist persuasion, such as the Aisne, some of these forms of pressure were utilized to the advantage of the *Bataille Socialiste* and the *Gauche Révolutionnaire.* A habit of authority had been established in most *fédérations* well before the electoral triumph of 1936, and it ensured .that the Socialist deputies would have the major share in determining the political posture of their respective *fédérations;* the secession of the Neo-Socialists and Renaudelians in 1933 was engineered by deputies who carried their *fédérations* out of the party with them. But crisis and success opened cracks in the habit of authority and the pattern of stability in several *fédérations:* the threat of fascism, the international crisis, the Popular Front and its victory, brought many enthusiastic recruits to socialism, many of whom were vulnerable to the rhetoric of dynamism characteristic of the Left. Many *fédérations,* however, were to resist the invasion only too well by retreating into the rhetoric of the past.

The Membership

We shall not follow the official party method of determining membership, for its rigor results in an underestimate of the size of the rank and file. It is unrealistic to assume, as did the party, that a loyal Socialist had to prove his fidelity monthly. The discrepancy between the total number of membership cards issued and the annual membership as determined by the party formula in any *fédération* is substantial. In 1936, for example, the Ain *fédération* delivered 1,291 cards, but on the basis of twelve stamps for each member it counted only 797 members. Following the lead of Antoine Prost in his study of the C.G.T.,[98] we shall employ the arbitrary figure of ten stamps per member per year, allowing for the zealous who filled their quota and the laggards who undersubscribed theirs. On this basis, for example, the Ain *fédération* had 956 members in 1936. Table 7 (pp. 307–310), indicating the

[98] Antoine Prost, *La C.G.T. à l'époque du Front Populaire* (Paris, 1964), 10.

membership of the S.F.I.O. by *fédérations* for the years 1935–1938, is calculated according to ten stamps per member.

This table demonstrates the striking increase in Socialist party membership during 1936 and 1937, of 56,757 and 84,172 respectively. The total membership advanced from 100,700 in 1935 to 241,629 in 1937, and even after a decline of 22,055 in 1938 the Socialists closed their books with a registration more than double that of 1935. In general the increase has to be attributed to the revived vigor of the French Left as well as the S.F.I.O. itself, to their newly found sense of purpose, a quality that seemed to be missing for some time. Furthermore, as Prost believes, to join a working-class organization was to signal one's commitment to antifascism, and, in some instances, to revolution.[99] The Popular Front, after all, held out the promise of participation in meaningful accomplishment. Many people, then, must have been stimulated to join the S.F.I.O. by the ideological climate of these years. Many, of course, were prompt to abandon the Popular Front and its constituent elements when the Popular Front experiment went on the rocks in 1938, and Socialist losses in membership in that year probably exceeded the above figure, owing to departures unaccounted for by the stamp method of reckoning membership.

Table 8 (pp. 311–314) indicates the increases and decreases for the years 1936–1938 in percentage terms. The percentage calculated is that of the increase above, or decrease below, the previous year's total membership. For example, if a *fédération* shows an increase of 30 per cent, then 30 per cent of its militants were new. In 1936 the all-party increase was 36.3 per cent, in 1937 it was 34.9 per cent, and the loss in 1938 was 9.1 per cent.

A majority of the S.F.I.O. membership in 1936, 1937, and 1938 adhered to *fédérations* within the seven regions of Socialist strength in the 1936 and previous elections. In 1936 these seven regions counted 85,937 Socialists, as against 71,520 elsewhere; in 1937, 126,829 as against 114,800; and in 1938, 121,177 as against 98,397. In percentages, regions one through seven held a majority of 54.5 per cent in 1936, 52.5 per cent in 1937, and 55.2 per cent in 1938.[100] But while these seven regions retained a majority of the

[99] *Ibid.*, 156.

[100] Of course these percentages are influenced by the weight of the large *fédération du Nord*.

party's members, the other regions showed a larger percentage increase in 1936 and 1937 and a larger percentage decrease in 1938 when the Popular Front had run its course. Membership in the first seven regions increased 29.9 per cent in 1936, 32.3 per cent in 1937, and decreased only 4.3 per cent in 1938; membership in the remaining regions increased 43.5 per cent in 1936, 37.7 per cent in 1937, and decreased 16.7 per cent in 1938. Clearly the Popular Front atmosphere stimulated Socialist recruitment everywhere, but most markedly in those areas where socialism had not been strong at the ballot box.

As the following figures indicate, the overwhelming majority of Socialist *fédérations,* even in 1937, counted fewer than 3,000 members. (Figures in parentheses denote *fédérations* in regions one through seven; the first figure given is the total for the entire party.)

Members	*1936*	*1937*	*1938*
20,000+		1 (1)	1 (1)
15,000–20,000	1 (1)	1	
10,000–15,000	1	2 (1)	2 (1)
5,000–10,000	2 (1)	2 (1)	2 (1)
4,000–5,000	2 (2)	6 (4)	2 (2)
3,000–4,000	3 (1)	9 (6)	10 (6)
2,000–3,000	15 (11)	15 (8)	16 (8)
1,000–2,000	23 (10)	38 (14)	37 (16)
Under 1,000	45 (14)	18 (5)	21 (5)

We also see that in 1936 almost half the *fédérations* had fewer than 1,000 members, but of these only fourteen were among the seven regions of Socialist political strength. Rapid growth elevated the great majority of *fédérations* above the one thousand level in 1937 and 1938, but very few were composed of more than 3,000 members, even in the banner year of 1937, and there were only six very large ones—the Nord, Pas-de-Calais, and Bouches-du-Rhône, in the heartland of Socialist electoral vigor; the Seine, Gironde, and Seine-et-Oise, in areas of meager political reward for the S.F.I.O.—in the same year. As early as 1936 *fédérations* in the seven key regions were in the 1,000–3,000 category, and most remained there; despite the larger percentage increases in other areas, their *fédérations* were attempting to catch up to levels already attained elsewhere.

We may conclude that *fédérations* in departments of Socialist electoral strength were, in most instances, stronger units than those in other areas. A majority of S.F.I.O. members belonged to *fédérations* in seven important regions, although this majority rested upon the colossal *fédération du Nord;* while membership increased in these *fédérations,* they were not vulnerable to the disrupting impact of a massive influx of new members and their membership lists did not dip sharply in 1938; and most of these *fédérations* were quite responsive to management by their leaders, owing to several factors, including the established structure of power and the relative stability of their size—in 1937 only seven ranged above 4,000 members and only five had fewer than 1,000.

While we may be permitted to draw these conclusions from membership figures, and may attribute the party's growth to its success and the Popular Front atmosphere, we can offer only suppositions concerning the social character of the rank and file. It has been assumed by many observers that the Socialist party was the home of functionaries, teachers, professors, some lawyers and doctors, white-collar workers in private enterprise, and even of a goodly number of workers, both skilled and unskilled. Certainly many national leaders were drawn from the first-mentioned categories—Zyromski was a functionary, Pivert a teacher, Bracke a professor—and many of the local Socialist elites were from the same categories—L'Hévéder was a professor, as were Arnol and Zoretti, leader of the Calvados *fédération.* But we have no evidence that the rank and file, or a majority of the rank and file in any given *fédération,* were drawn from one or several of certain occupations. The S.F.I.O. did not maintain extensive files on its members, and whatever files may exist have not reached this author. We are able, then, only to point to the great number of teachers, professors, functionaires, and lawyers among the Socialist leadership, both national and local.

Party Power

Not surprisingly, the heartland of the S.F.I.O.'s electoral strength was also the heartland of its Center majority. At the Congress of Marseilles, as demonstrated by Table 9 (pp.

314–318), 71 per cent of the *mandats* cast for the Blum-Faure resolution on general policy came from the seven regions of Socialist political power, while only 38 per cent of the Left vote—combining, for the sake of argument, the tallies of the *Bataille Socialiste* and *Gauche Révolutionnaire*—came from these areas. At the National Council of November 7, 1937, when participation in a Radical government was not a primary issue, the Center increased its vote at the expense of the Left, and fully 64.5 per cent of its total was delivered by the same seven regions while the Left declined to 33.9 per cent. It should be noted that *fédérations* in these regions commanded 53.9 per cent of the outstanding *mandats* in 1937.

As Table 9 indicates, there were many exceptions to the general pattern: the *fédération* of the Alpes-Maritimes, in a department where socialism was nonexistent politically although in a region generally very favorable to the S.F.I.O., voted heavily to the Left at Marseilles, while the *fédération* of the Indre-et-Loire, a bastion of Socialist power in a region generally unfavorable to the S.F.I.O., swung to the Center majority. These examples tend to reinforce the equation of electoral success with moderation in party politics, and conversely, the coincidence of electoral insignificance with a tendency toward radicalism. The Left won a majority in forty-five of the ninety-two *fédérations,* but of these forty-five only thirteen were among the seven politically important regions. Of these thirteen *fédérations* only seven maintained their orientation to the Left at the National Council. Comparison of Tables 8 and 9 reveals another factor: of the thirty-two *fédérations* won by the Left at Marseilles which were located outside the zones of Socialist political strength, twenty-six increased their membership over the all-party average in 1936 or 1937, and seventeen did so in both years; hence the coincidence of a dramatically increasing membership with an inclination toward the Left.

The Left, of course, was not unified, and its twin components attracted rather different clienteles. The *Bataille Socialiste* won at least a third of the *mandats* of thirty-six *fédérations* at Marseilles, but dipped below that level in nineteen of them at the National Council. The *Gauche Révolutionnaire* on the other hand won at least a third of the *mandats* in twenty-one *fédérations* at Marseilles, but dropped below this level in only one of these *fédéra-*

tions in November. Support for Zyromski at Marseilles was attributable in part to his opposition to Socialist participation in the Chautemps government, since many Socialists, anxious to register their opposition to participation, had no alternative but to vote for the *Bataille Socialiste* resolution; many of them returned to the "centrist" ranks in the fall.[101] Moreover the *Bataille Socialiste* won its *mandats* in differing types of *fédérations,* although its principal base was the Paris region. A vote for Zyromski did not necessarily signify ideological identification with him; to side with his opposition to Blum's Spanish policy, for example, was a respectable and hardly revolutionary affirmation. Protest rather than commitment was the rule, explaining in some measure the fluctuating nature of the *Bataille Socialiste* following. Zyromski's *tendance* was also an extremely important vehicle for those who favored closer Socialist-Communist relations and those who demanded that Socialism pursue an intransigently antifascist international policy. Nevertheless, the *Bataille Socialiste* was winning support primarily among *fédérations* in areas where socialism was a waning or spent political force.

The *Gauche Révolutionnaire* was recruiting dedicated followers in departments where socialism was a dead issue politically, with, inevitably, several exceptions, such as the *fédérations* of the Aisne, Oise, Seine, Seine-et-Oise, and Côte d'Or. Most Pivertiste strongholds were politically moribund *fédérations* in agricultural departments such as the Lot, Marne, Maine-et-Loire, Vosges, Orne, Vendée, Calvados, Manche; a few were in areas of great working-class concentration such as the Meurthe-et-Moselle, where Socialists were rebuilding their organization anew. Key personalities played a vital role in securing converts to Pivert's message of anger and redemption—Lucien Hérard in the Côte d'Or, for example. Most Pivertiste *fédérations* were very small; in the Orne or Loiret, for example, where, in a clublike atmosphere, to be revolutionary was to indulge in flamboyant talk and heady theorizing. The local *Gauche Révolutionnaire* leaders were young, volatile, and impatient, like Pivert himself, and many were teachers. These were young men drawn by Pivert's promise of revolution and pacifism. Revolution, reasoned Pivertistes, elim-

[101] In the first seven regions, Zyromski's resolution polled 574 *mandats* at Marseilles, but only 358 in November.

inated the possibility of war; the official Socialist ideology was old-fashioned as well as dangerous; and the *Bataille Socialiste* position was dangerous because it promised war without revolution. The failure of the Popular Front and the lesson of Spain reinforced their revolutionary strivings, strivings which only rarely were translated into action.

A CASE IN POINT: THE RESPONSE OF THE *FEDERATIONS* TO THE
SPANISH CIVIL WAR

Debates at the National Councils of November, 1936, and February, 1937, and the resolutions adopted at these gatherings on the Spanish issue, hardly reflect the turbulence created by that issue within the Socialist party. The November meeting of the National Council supported an innocuous resolution prepared by a special committee (Salomon Grumbach, L'Hévéder, Bracke, and Roucayrol) that pleased almost everyone by its splendid ambiguity. It sustained Blum's action over Spain with enthusiasm while it meekly requested the government to align its Spanish policy, in accord with England's, along lines prescribed by the I.O.S. and F.S.I.; that is, it requested an end to nonintervention. Obviously the resolution meant absolutely nothing in practical terms except that nonintervention would remain the French government's policy: everyone knew that His Majesty's government was highly unlikely to abandon a policy that it supported with unaccustomed zeal. Yet the motion temporarily satisfied the followers of Zyromski in that it put the S.F.I.O. on record as favoring the free supply of the Spanish Republic; equally it assuaged Socialist consciences by demonstrating that the French Socialist party was not unfaithful to the instructions of the International. Such a resolution was not at all out of character for the S.F.I.O.; this was simply its habitual practice of the "black-white" motion, one which combined the essences of all positions, however incompatible, into one unintelligible resolution which was utterly useless as a practical guide for future action. In other words, party unity habitually took precedence over coherence, and resolutions adopted by the National Councils and National Congresses are, as we have seen, of very little value in determining the position of the party as a whole.

In February, 1937, the National Council repeated its evasive

behavior of November: after a desultory debate it approved a
resolution very similar to the worthless one adopted previously.
But this time Zyromski tactlessly persisted in offering his own
motion, which, since it was designed to win as many *mandats* as
possible, suggested very gently that the government should dis-
pense with nonintervention—regardless of London's opinion—
should control of the Spanish frontiers prove to be ineffectual, as
everyone fully expected it would be. Zyromski's proposal was
soundly rejected by a vote of 4,221 to 907, and further discussion
of the Spanish question at party gatherings did not take place
until the Congress of Marseilles.

Real discussion of the Spanish problem was confined to the
columns of *Le Populaire* and to various nationwide publications,
and particularly to the journals of the ninety-two Socialist *fédérations*. Unhappily, it is nearly impossible to assess the response of
these *fédérations* to the Spanish Civil War. The chief difficulty
derives from the appalling complexity of the situation within
many of them—for example, the lack of a clearly defined majority
opinion, disparity between the opinions expressed by the leaders
and those of the militants, and the paradoxical, often contradictory opinions of the leaders themselves. Generalizations, quite
obviously, are extremely hazardous. Documentation too is occasionally a perplexing matter: although seventy-seven journals,
representing seventy-one *fédérations*, are available, some are of
inferior quality and others demonstrate that their editors possessed an admirable dexterity in camouflaging acute differences
within their respective *fédérations*. The third problem—and perhaps the most crucial—is simply a lack of knowledge in most cases
about the social composition of a *fédération*. It may be assumed,
for example, that most of the militants of the *fédérations* of the
Nord and Pas-de-Calais were recruited from among the industrial
working class, but does it follow that a majority of the members of
the *fédérations* of the Creuse and the Corrèze belonged to the
agricultural population? Thus we are confronted with several
problems for which we have no answer. In an agricultural *fédération* such as that of the Corrèze, for example, how many of the
rank and file were actively engaged in agricultural pursuits, and
further, what was their status: peasant proprietors, agricultural
laborers, or leaseholders? And, for that matter, how many adher-

ents were to be found among the ranks of the shopkeepers, civil servants (especially teachers), and workers from small industrial establishments? Even when we know the profession of the leaders of a *fédération*—the Calvados, for example, where the party was firmly in the hands of teachers and other civil servants—it is still impossible to ascertain the profession of the militants. Incomplete information about the composition of each *fédération* excludes the possibility of a comparison of purely "industrial" *fédérations* with purely "agricultural" ones.

All of these deficiencies, however, do not eliminate the *fédérations* as extremely valuable—and perhaps the most valuable—units of study. In scrutinizing the journals of the *fédérations,* a great deal of otherwise unobtainable information about the nature of the Socialist party, as well as about its reaction to the Spanish Civil War, is revealed. It is possible to discover the structure of power within each *fédération* and to ascertain the ideological posture of its leaders: this affords a legitimate opportunity for comparison and generalization. Once the structure of leadership in any *fédération* is known—unfortunately this cannot be determined in every *fédération*—comparison is no longer so dangerous. If it is known, for example, that the Socialist deputies from a predominantly agricultural department were in control of the local party organization, and if it is conceded that these deputies also considered themselves to be responsible to their electorate, it is justifiable to label their *fédération* as "agricultural" and to compare it with similar *fédérations,* or with an "industrial" *fédération,* assuming, of course, that the structure of power was similar in these other *fédérations.* Moreover, even in most of the *fédérations* which cannot be labeled according to the above criteria— since either the department elected no Socialist deputies or the deputies were not the major figures in the *fédération*—much can be learned about the leaders and their interpretation of the Spanish struggle. Hence the emphasis must be necessarily on personalities rather than on social and economic groupings: lack of certain information compels the adoption of this type of analysis. The critical tasks, then, are (1) to ascertain the identity of the leaders of each *fédération* and the strength of their positions; (2) to investigate their response to the Spanish problem, especially in regard to the thorny issue of nonintervention, and to attempt to classify this response according to the four currents of thought on the Spanish question which have been discussed; (3) to compare the reactions of the *fédérations* to the Spanish Civil War and to draw certain conclusions from these comparisons.

Doubtless the most striking single factor which would emerge from any inquiry into the workings of the Socialist *fédération* during the years in question would be the critical role exercised by key personalities, usually the deputies, in the activities and decisions of each *fédération*. In this instance, equally striking is the fact that an overwhelming majority of the Socialist parliamentarians were prone to caution on the Spanish issue, and indeed many—sixty-two at the very least—openly espoused the views of the leading Fauristes,[102] while few deputies were critical of nonintervention—only Rives, Andraud, and Guy supported the C.A.S.P.E. And in most of the *fédérations* with deputies the response of the deputies to the Spanish Civil War was decisive in determining the attitude of the rank and file. In many *fédérations* this response triggered a reaction against both Communism and a policy of resistance to "international fascism"; in a lesser number it had exactly the opposite impact. Brief examination of the response of the *fédérations* to the Spanish Civil War may permit the drawing of several conclusions which, hopefully, may point the way to an understanding of the S.F.I.O.'s rapid decline as a political unit.

Table 10 (pp. 318–321) is a summary interpretation of the response of the *fédérations* to the war in Spain and its interna-

---

[102] On the basis of my research in *fédération* newspapers, the following deputies were consistent in following a "Fauriste" interpretation of the events in Spain and their significance for France: Rauzy, Soula, Silvestre, Hubert-Rouger, Larguier, Roucayrol, Salette, Majurel, Vidal, Lucchini, Brunet, Vaillandet, Biondi, Vantielcke, Esparbès, Berlia, David, Spinasse, Peschadour, Roumajon, Rivière, Riffaterre, Blanchet, Vardelle, Valière, Roche, Debrégeas, Quinson, Arnol, Ravanat, Hussel, Pétrus Faure (from the Loire, joined Socialist parliamentary group after the elections), Février, Nouelle, Burtin, J.-M. Thomas, Boulay, Planche, Jardiller, Chasseigne (deputy from the Indre, joined the Socialist parliamentary group after the elections), Rolland, L'Hévéder, Lazurick, Castagnez, Maffray, Morin, Meunier, Baron, Muret, Sibué, Pringolliet (deputy from the Savoie, joined the Socialist parliamentary group after the elections), Allemane, Beaugrand, Dupont, Lejeune, Henri Salengro, Chouffet, Mabrut, Saint-Venant, Boudet, Thivrier, and Gardiol. Joel Colton argues that nonintervention ran counter to the wishes of the party (*Léon Blum: Humanist in Politics* [New York, 1966], 256, 481).

tional implications. The table can be only partially accurate, and thus only marginally helpful, since opinion within a *fédération* was rarely unanimous, and only in a few instances did a "federal congress" register its sympathies toward the war. I have employed my judgment in selecting the dominant opinion within a given *fédération,* but this judgment is based upon debates at federal congresses, the vote on the Zyromski resolution at the February, 1937, session of the National Council, and, most important, upon my investigation of the local Socialist press.

The heaviest support for nonintervention in the Spanish struggle came unmistakably from *fédérations* in the seven regions where socialism was an established political force, which, with two sharply defined exceptions, assumed a moderate position toward Spain. The exceptions were (1) *fédérations* which were either without Socialist parliamentarians or in which the *élus* were unable to assure their own predominance, and (2) *fédérations* in departments located close to the Spanish frontier.

In Languedoc, Fauriste sympathizers on the Spanish issue were dominant in the *fédérations* of the Ariège,[103] Gard,[104] and the Hérault,[105] while the cautious dissenters from Blum's nonintervention policy—men who were close to Blum personally and who were to be his chief supporters when he declared for a "firm" policy toward Nazi Germany in 1938 and who then were to be called Blumistes—were firmly supported by the *fédérations* of the Aude[106] and the Tarn.[107] Only the *fédération* of the Pyrénées-Or-

---

[103] Articles in *La Montagne Socialiste,* November 15, 1936, and February 7, 1937, by Rauzy, deputy, argued that nonintervention had saved peace and asked for negotiations with all nations; official editorial on September 13, 1936, attacked Thorez's posture on nonintervention as being motivated by the interests of the U.S.S.R.

[104] In articles for *Le Combat Social,* September 5, 1936, December 5, 1936, Silvestre, deputy, freely predicted France's defeat in the war that would erupt if nonintervention were abandoned; official editorials of the *fédération* denounced the "militaristic policy" of the French Communist party, September 12, 1936.

[105] *L'Aube Sociale;* articles by Fernard Roucayrol, whose leadership of the Fauriste point of view has already been discussed.

[106] *La République Sociale,* edited by Montel, "federal secretary" and a close associate of Léon Blum, attempted to present all points of view on the Spanish question.

[107] The *fédération* was led by Salomon Grumbach and Malroux, deputies; Grumbach's views have already been discussed.

ientales,[108] strategically situated on the Catalan frontier, exhibited any profound discontent with the policy of nonintervention.

In the Rhone Valley and Provence, only the politically anemic *fédération* of the Alpes-Maritimes[109] opted for the radical theories of the *Gauche Révolutionnaire* and, to a lesser extent, of the *Bataille Socialiste*. The leaders of the strong *fédérations* of the Bouches-du-Rhône[110] and the Vaucluse[111] clearly leaned toward the Fauriste viewpoint, but in the two *fédérations* which had witnessed a substantial diminution of their popular appeal in 1936—the Drôme[112] and the Var[113]—all four principal positions found adherents, although the Blumiste point of view was predominant.

In the North, a twofold pattern is apparent. In the industrial

[108] *Le Socialiste* carried perfunctory defenses of Blum's position; e.g., January 14, 1937. Noguères, "federal secretary," showed his displeasure with nonintervention by ignoring the issue.

[109] *L'Alerte,* carried exuberant editorials announcing that the Spanish struggle represented the beginning of the "final battle," presumably for socialism; see, e.g., the issue for September 5, 1936. The *fédération* denounced nonintervention openly on May 22 and 29, 1937, and swung rapidly to the Left.

[110] *La Provence Socialiste,* in editorials by Paul Quilici, spokesman for the leadership of Cavelli, Tasso, and Gouin, denounced the dangers inherent in the Communist opposition to nonintervention in Spain, see, e.g., the issues for September 5 and 12, 1936. Articles by deputies indicated solidarity with Fauriste position and heavy grip of the deputies on the *fédération;* see, e.g., issues for January 1 and June 11, 1937.

[111] *Le Réveil Socialiste,* under the close scrutiny of the deputy Vaillandet and the secretary Cluchier, launched a pacifist campaign in response to the possibility of French assistance to the Spanish Republicans; see, e.g., the issues for August 20 and October 29, 1936. The Communist motives in attacking nonintervention were attacked on December 10, 1936. Deputy Lussy joined the campaign on October 17 and November 5, 1936.

[112] *La Volonté Socialiste* revealed the fragmentation of the *fédération* in three categories: (1) the deputies were split, Brunet for the Fauriste position, Moutet for the Blumiste; (2) the secretariat leaned to Zyromski; and (3) there was a large group of young Pivertistes. See the number for May 8, 1937, as an example.

[113] *Le Populaire du Var* was the organ of a *fédération* under reconstruction after the schism of the Neos, and the deputies Zunino and Collomp failed to have an established political base. Henri Michel, the regular editorialist, leaned toward criticism of nonintervention, much in the manner of the Blumistes (November 7, December 19, 1936). Zunino's view was close to that of the Fauristes; see his article on March 27, 1937.

departments of the Nord[114] and the Pas-de-Calais,[115] where the Socialist *fédérations* constituted the dominant political force despite an increasingly serious Communist challenge, the Blumiste interpretation won wide acceptance among Socialist leaders. In the less industrialized departments of the Oise[116] and the Somme,[117] where socialism had been less successful in 1936, the Socialist deputies who spoke out in support of nonintervention were under heavy attack from the *Bataille Socialiste* and the *Gauche Révolutionnaire.* It is tempting to conclude that in highly industrialized departments where the S.F.I.O. had a strong electoral appeal and a well-organized *fédération,* and was confronted with a powerful Communist organization, the Socialist leaders turned to the Blumiste position in order to mitigate the effect of Communist attacks upon a policy which was highly unpopular with the working class, while at the same time it enabled them to maintain their loyalty to the leader of the party. Unfortunately this hypothesis will not stand the test of comparison: under similar conditions, the leaders of the Bouches-du-Rhône *fédération* favored the Fauriste position, and in the *fédération* of the Nord itself, Fauriste sentiment was on the upswing in the sections of Lille![118] One generalization, however, can be made with some assurance: in highly industrialized departments where socialism still commanded the electoral allegiance of much of the working class—and where several Socialists were elected—neither the *Bataille Socialiste* nor the *Gauche Révolutionnaire* had any influence

[114] The attitude of Lebas, the leader of this *fédération,* has already been discussed; Fauriste opinion in Lille centered around Henri Salengro and Charles Saint-Venant, both deputies. See *La Bataille, La Bataille Ouvrière, L'Avenir du Nord,* and *Le Peuple Libre.*

[115] *L'Eclaireur* followed the government's line on Spain closely, but without ouvert enthusiasm.

[116] *Le Cri Populaire de l'Oise* revealed a three-way split of this *fédération,* similar to that in the Drôme. Biondi, a deputy, was in the Fauriste camp; note, e.g., his article of November 8, 1936. There were also strong leftist currents, under the leadership of strong personalities such as Berthe Fouchère.

[117] Although Max Lejeune was the single most powerful figure in this *fédération,* he took little part in its activities until 1938. A "federal congress' endorsed nonintervention in Spain by a healthy majority—see the number of *Le Cri du Peuple* for October 25, 1936—but a sharp period of internal strife erupted over the Spanish issue in mid-1937.

[118] See *Le Peuple Libre,* September 4, 11, April 23, 1937.

in the *fédérations,* either among the leaders or among the rank and file. As a corollary to this general rule, it is equally clear that in highly industrialized departments where socialism was being rapidly outdistanced by the Communists, and where few Socialists were elected—for example, the Seine and the Seine-et-Oise—the two Socialist Lefts, taken together, possessed a decisive majority in the *fédérations.*

In the Garonne Basin, the leaders of the Dordogne[119] *fédération* were definitely Fauriste in their view of the Spanish problem, and the critically important *fédération* of the Haute-Garonne[120] was split three ways: the Fauristes were in the ascendancy in the vital sections of Toulouse; the Blumiste position found an aggressive exponent in the person of Hudelle; finally, there existed a group of sentimentalists whose affection for Spain took precedence over every other consideration—including the need for caution. But in this region only the Lot-et-Garonne[121] *fédération,* submerged under a Communist avalanche in the elections of 1936, was overtly partisan to the *Bataille Socialiste,* and in part to the *Gauche Révolutionnaire.* As in the Nord, Socialist electoral success barred the way to these groups, although the region was much less industrial in character.

[119] *La Voix Socialiste* apparently expressed the voice of the leaders only, as secretary Bayol's articles on September 5 and November 28, 1936, attacking the Communists for their posture in international affairs, and those of one of his associates, Guérin—who on September 12, 1936, asked if the Communists wanted France to declare war on Germany—were countered by the growth of leftist sentiments. The *fédération* cast thirteen of its thirty-nine *mandats* for the Zyromski motion at the February, 1937, National Council.

[120] Auriol and his editor of the Socialist daily, *Le Midi Socialiste,* obviously opposed nonintervention, but the deputies Bedouce and Esparbès warned against adventure abroad and the Communist international policy; see, e.g., the numbers for August 18 and December 13, 1936. The Toulouse section unanimously hailed nonintervention in the manner of the Fauristes (reported in the number of December 19, 1936). Only in the southernmost regions of the department was there appreciable hostility among Socialists to nonintervention; see the organ of the Socialist section of Saint-Gaudens, *L'Emancipation,* September 6, October 11, 1936, and February 28, 1937.

[121] A tiny *fédération,* lacking any deputies. Socialists in this department were relatively unimportant in its political life, and consequently their organization was largely a debating society. For an outpouring of commentary on Spain, most of it very hostile to nonintervention, consult *Le Réveil Socialiste* for August 22, 1936, and May 8, July 10, 1937.

This leads us to the regions of the Massif Central and the Lyonnais, which, with two exceptions— (1) *fédérations* without Socialist deputies (the Aveyron, Cantal, Lot, and the Lozére) ; (2) *fédérations* in departments which contained a large working-class population, which had either lost ground electorally or had witnessed an alarming upsurge of Communist votes in 1936 (the Puy-de-Dôme and the Rhône, respectively) —were unquestionably the bastions of Fauriste sentiment.[122] All of these *fédérations*

[122] For the Ardèche *fédération,* consult *Le Réveil Populaire,* especially the numbers of January 2 and 30, 1937, for commentary on the Spanish question. In general, nonintervention was accepted and faithfully defended, especially by the leaders Froment, a deputy, and Souchier, the secretary.

The Aveyron *fédération* had been seriously depleted by the schism of 1933, and *Le Socialiste Aveyronnais* demonstrated that Socialists in this department engaged in political activity largely by discussion among themselves. There was considerable difference of opinion over Spain; see the numbers of January 16 and July 24, 1937.

The *fédération* of the Cantal is another which is difficult to classify; its leader, Maurice Deixonne, did not give his open allegiance to the Revolutionary Left until some time in 1937. Both Deixonne and the ex-deputy Fontanier attacked the Communist position with ferocity; see, e.g., *Le Socialiste du Cantal* for November 8 and December 13, 1936, and March 7, 1937.

The Corrèze was a bastion of Fauriste sentiment, as illustrated by the attitudes of Spinasse and Peschadour. See *La Voix Corrèzienne,* especially the article by Peschadour on November 1, 1936, which asserted that a victory of Franco would not harm France.

The Creuse was another Fauriste stronghold; as in the Corrèze the S.F.I.O. was the dominant party in the department. All the Socialist deputies—Rivière, Riffaterre, and Blanchet—adopted the Fauriste view on Spain. See *Le Mémorial de la Creuse,* June 5, 1937, and *Le Populaire* (Paris), May 17, 1937.

No information is available on the Haute-Loire *fédération,* but Socialists in the Lot, where the S.F.I.O. had suffered heavy losses to the Neos in 1933 and to the Communists in the elections of 1936, veered to the Left. See *Le Travail du Lot,* August 22 and September 5, 1936, and February 13 and June 5, 1937, for fervent discussion on Spain. The G.R. captured the *fédération* in February, 1937.

There was no Socialist journal in the Lozère.

There was considerable division among the leaders of the *fédération* of the Puy-de-Dôme over Spain, as demonstrated by the pages of *L'Auvergne Socialiste,* but key personalities, such as the deputy Mabrut, openly feared war over Spain; see, e.g., the number for October 30, 1937.

The leaders of the Haute-Vienne, one of the oldest and most powerful Socialist *fédérations,* were solidly Fauriste in their views on Spain. The Socialist daily *Le Populaire du Centre,* through the pen of the deputy Maurice Vardelle, accused the Communists of believing war to be inevitable;

were under the control of their deputies, and all—with the exception of the Loire and the Isère—were situated in basically agricultural departments. Hence, aside from demonstrating once again the power of the deputies, a series of conclusions can be drawn: (1) socialist electoral success excluded the possibility of serious penetration into these *fédérations* by the *Bataille Socialiste* and *Gauche Révolutionnaire;* (2) in *fédérations* which constituted an entrenched and powerful political force in basically agricultural departments, the Spanish Civil War and the debate over nonintervention reinforced a deep-seated pacifism and reactivated a virulent anti-Communism among the leaders—usually deputies —precluding the acceptance of any interpretation of the Spanish question other than that of the Fauristes; (3) while the leaders of strong *fédérations* in industrial departments frequently turned to

see, e.g., the number for September 22, 1936. Note also the enthusiastic approval of nonintervention by the "federal congress" on April 26, 1937. Consult also *Le Petit Limousin,* directed to the agricultural population, which attacked the Communists as the war party—e.g., on December 5, 1936, and June 28, 1937—and the *Bulletin d'Informations Socialistes,* which in June, 1937, warned that the Communists wanted to send French troops to Spain.

In the Ain, both the deputy, Quinson, and the secretary, Chatagner, were Fauriste in their sympathies. Note *Le Travailleur de l'Ain* for December 12, 1936; this journal also carried a regular column entitled "Pacifist Tribune."

Justin Arnol seems to have controlled the *fédération* of the Isère very well; if any opposition to such control was present, it did not appear in the pages of the *Droit du Peuple.*

Upon joining the S.F.I.O. in January, 1937, the deputy Pétrus Faure rapidly emerged as the leader of the Loire *fédération.* And he shared the attitude of his namesake, Paul Faure, on the Spanish question and the Communists: see *Le Courrier de l'Ondaine,* August 29 and September 5 and 12, 1936, and July 17, 1937.

Eugène Gendre, secretary of the Rhône *fédération,* was most adept in preserving a façade of Socialist unity in the pages of *L'Avenir Socialiste.* Gendre himself was a Fauriste in his views on Spain—see, e.g., his article on March 13, 1937—as was the deputy Février, but André Philip, a cautious dissenter from nonintervention, seems to have had the upper hand, at least on the Spanish issue.

The Saône-et-Loire *fédération,* in a department which must count as a Socialist stronghold, was virtually Paul Faure's personal fief. Consult lavish approval of nonintervention and harsh criticism of the Communists in *La Dépêche Socialiste,* September 12 and 26, 1936, and June 19 and July 3, 1937.

the Blumiste position partly as a consequence of increasing Communist influence with the working class (although, as we have noted, this was not always the case), the absence of a large working-class population, and, in most cases, the appearance of a serious Communist challenge in the elections of 1936, actually served to facilitate a return by the leaders of strong *fédérations* in agricultural departments to the traditional Socialist values of the pre-Popular Front era—an inflexible pacifism and a conviction that socialism and communism were fundamentally and irrevocably incompatible.

In the region which we have designated as Central France, the *fédération* of the overwhelmingly agricultural department of the Indre[123] was firmly in the Fauriste camp, while Socialists in the Cher[124] were, in large part, under the direction of two avowedly Fauriste deputies. The influence of personalities was definitely evident in the *fédérations* of the Allier[125] and Côte d'Or,[126] where all four points of view on the Spanish problem found articulate champions; it should be noted that Socialism appeared to have reached its saturation point at the ballot box, in both of these departments, while communism was becoming an increasingly formidable electoral force.

Finally, the Northeast was the only one of the regions favorable to the S.F.I.O. in the elections of 1936 that demonstrated an overt hostility to the government's Spanish policy as well as a vulnera-

[123] It was not until the deputy François Chasseigne, who was to be a minister in the Vichy regime, rejoined the S.F.I.O. in early 1937, that this *fédération* had any coherence as a political grouping. Both Chasseigne and the secretary, Parpais, were overtly hostile to the Communist international policy and attitude toward Spain: see *Le Berry Républicain*, August 30 and September 13, 1936.

[124] The deputy Castagnez said, with regard to Spain, "We want peace at any price," in *Le Réveil Socialiste du Cher*, February 6, 1937, and the deputy Lazurick echoed Castagnez's suspicions of the motives of the Communists; see, e.g., the number for December 12, 1936. See also *Le Sancerrois*. Both men were spokesmen for the *fédération*, although they were not masters of it.

[125] See *Le Combat Social* for the views of the Fauriste Camille Planche, a deputy, the C.A.S.P.E. supporter Paul Rives, and Marx Dormoy.

[126] The ideological confusion endemic in this *fédération* is clear from the pages of *Le Socialiste Côte d'Orien;* all four camps had able supporters on the Spanish problem. Lucien Hérard, a very popular figure, won many converts to the *Gauche Révolutionnaire*.

bility to the appeals of the two Socialist Lefts. In the Aisne,[127] where six Socialist deputies had been elected in 1936, even the Blumiste position of cautious dissent was scorned—primarily because of the character of its leaders, many of whom were known partisans of the *Bataille Socialiste*. Paradoxically, the Ardennes *fédération*,[128] in a department which elected but one deputy in 1936, was avowedly pacifist—perhaps owing to memories of 1914–1918.

The second major category of regions—those areas in which socialism had met with intermittent success in the elections of 1936 (28 per cent of the total Socialist vote on the first ballot, and from which 20 per cent of the party's deputies had been elected) —was characterized by a great deal more skepticism about nonintervention than were most of the *fédérations* in the first category of regions. In these regions, opinion varied from a smattering of Fauriste opinion in the Morbihan,[129] Indre-et-Loire,[130] Basses-Alpes,[131] and the Savoie[132]—all of which were heavily influenced

[127] This *fédération* was split almost evenly between supporters of Zyromski and Pivert. See *Le Réveil Populaire* for the views of Georges Monnet and the deputies who leaned toward the *Bataille Socialiste*, Pierre—Bloch and Bloncourt.

[128] There was difference of opinion on the Spanish question in this *fédération*, but *Le Socialiste Ardennais* was peppered with articles hailing nonintervention as a "magnificent effort" and warning the Communists of "pacifist convictions" held by Socialists. Consult the numbers of September 10 and 24, 1936, and January 7, 1937.

[129] L'Hévéder's attitude needs no further elaboration. It is significant that the "federal congress" supported his view by a vote of 850–72 in February, but by a margin of only 519–459 in July. Consult *Le Rappel du Morbihan*, February 13 and July 10, 1937.

[130] The S.F.I.O. was an entrenched and powerful political force in this department, and the *fédération* was under the control of three Socialist deputies and the secretary. All were ardent pacifists and vigorous anti-Communists; e.g., the *Réveil* of August 22, 1936, boasted that "this government will not wage ideological war"—a direct slap at the Communists. See also vehement denunciations of the Communists on October 31, 1936, and March 20, 1937.

[131] See warnings against the "bellicose" Communists and attacks against the "fratricidal war" launched against the Spanish Republicans by the Communists in *Le Travailleur des Alpes*, October 17 and 31, 1936, and May 29, 1937. Stalin was also assailed as a "bloody dictator" on December 13, 1936.

[132] Louis Sibué, deputy, echoed the Fauriste viewpoint in *Le Socialiste Savoyard*, January 9 and 23, and July 3, 1937.

by veteran Socialist deputies, and, moreover, all of which were located in agricultural departments—to outright condemnation of the policies of the government in, for example, the Paris region. The majority of the *fédérations* with deputies—the Finistère,[133] Côtes du Nord,[134] Loire-Inférieure,[135] Charente-Inférieure,[136] Deux-Sèvres,[137] and the Gers[138]—generally were inclined toward the Blumiste position. But these last-mentioned *fédérations* demonstrate the futility of any comparison based exclusively upon the economic character of the departments; all of these departments, with the exception of the Loire-Inférieure, were largely agricultural. The perceptible difference between the *fédérations* in these departments and those which constituted the Fauriste bastions was simply that socialism was a relatively new force in the former; none was a habitual Socialist stronghold like the Creuse or the Indre-et-Loire, and most Socialist deputies elected from these departments were not veteran members of the Socialist contingent at the Palais-Bourbon. For example, in Finistère the newly elected Tanguy-Prigent was the moving force of the *fédération*, but he

[133] The deputy Tanguy-Prigent believed that the Spanish example demonstrated that a policy of alliances and force could halt "fascism." See *Le Breton Socialiste*, January 16, March 6, 1937. On Rolland, see the same journal for November 13, 1937.

[134] A "federal congress" invited the government to "raise the blockade." See *Le Combat Social*, October 11, 1936.

[135] One of the most successful Socialist *fédérations* in Brittany, and one of the fastest growing in the party. A variety of opinion on the Spanish war was expressed in *Le Travailleur de l'Ouest*, but it was predominantly Fauriste or Blumiste. One editorialist went so far as to inquire if the Communists were plotting war; see the numbers of August 29, September 26, and December 5, 1936.

[136] *La Voix Socialiste* featured articles by the secretary Grasset, whose aim was to defend the Blum government against Communist sniping, but neither he nor any of his associates employed the arguments popularized by the Fauristes in, e.g., the numbers of October 24 and November 7, 1936.

[137] In a *fédération* which was sympathetic in part to the *Bataille Socialiste* and *Gauche Révolutionnaire*, only the deputy, Bèche, was lavish in his praise of nonintervention. The "federal congress" voted, not by a wide margin, its approval of the government. See *Le Travail*, November 7, 1936, February 13, 1937.

[138] The deputies Saint-Martin and Dubosc played a minor role in the activities of the *fédération* in 1936 and early 1937, and *Le Gers Socialiste* was most reluctant to endorse nonintervention; see, e.g., the numbers for October 17, 1936, and June 19, 1937.

was completely estranged from another, and older, Socialist deputy from the Finistère, Rolland—who supported the Fauriste position. Essentially these new men were not willing to consider traditional Socialist values as immutable, and were motivated by an enthusiasm for the idea of the Popular Front, especially by its implied willingness to halt "fascist" encroachment, both nationally and internationally. These new men, distressed by the failure of nonintervention yet unable to reproach Blum directly, tended to adopt the position of the Blumistes. Hence our criteria must also include the questions of the relative newness of Socialist strength in a particular department and the very real differences in temperament between the newly elected and the veteran Socialist deputies.

Fortunately it is a much simpler task to account for the opposition to nonintervention in these regions. There is little doubt, for example, that Socialists in Algeria[139] were influenced by emotional ties to Spain as well as by a fear of the implications which were inherent in any increase of Italian power in the Mediterranean. Similarly, the *fédérations* of departments close to the Spanish frontiers—the Landes,[140] Basses-Pyrénées,[141] and the Hautes-Pyrénées[142]—were visibly distressed by the possibility of a "fascist" neighbor to the south. Furthermore, and significantly, none of these *fédérations* possessed the restraining influence of one or more Socialist deputies, as was the case in the Hérault, Pyrénées-

---

[139] The Algiers *fédération* voted unanimously for the Zyromski resolution at the February, 1937, National Council. *Alger Socialiste* called for "reconsideration" of nonintervention, and after the fall of the Blum government openly attacked "the comedy of nonintervention." See the numbers for October 24 and November 21, 1936, and March 27, April 24, and December 4, 1937.

[140] The "federal congress" called for an end to nonintervention in 1937, and the *Bataille Socialiste* made considerable headway in this *fédération* in 1938. See *Le Travailleur Landais*, November 6, 1937.

[141] *Le Travail* featured articles by Gaston Chaze, the secretary and long-time socialist organizer in the department. The "federal congress," after having been exposed to Chaze's opposition to the government's Spanish policy, asked for "reconsideration" of that policy. See the numbers for September 6 and November 22, 1936.

[142] *La Bigorre Socialiste* featured articles by the secretary, Cazaubon, and virtually no one else. The "federal congress" demanded an end to nonintervention, while Cazaubon increasingly leaned toward Pivert's position. See the number for March 20, 1937.

Orientales, and the Haute-Garonne—departments which were equally imperiled by the prospect of a victory of the Spanish rebels and their foreign accomplices. The *fédération* of the Gironde,[143] however, was an exceptional case: its deputies were openly critical of nonintervention and freely utilized the arguments popularized by Zyromski. But the Gironde *fédération* was not stable in the same sense as those of the Haute-Garonne or the Corrèze: it was engaged in a bitter conflict with a powerful "neo" organization—led by the renegade Marquet—which supported nonintervention with considerable warmth.[144] In addition, it was compelled to compete with a virile Communist *fédération* for the allegiance of the working class. Caught between these two forces, it is not at all surprising that the *fédération* adopted a more aggressive posture against the "threat" of an audacious "international fascism."

There remains the Paris region, the heart of *Bataille Socialiste* and *Gauche Révolutionnaire* sentiment. The *fédération* of the Seine was particularly vulnerable to the appeal of the two Socialist Lefts. Badly outclassed by the Communists in the elections of 1932, and smothered by them in 1936, the S.F.I.O. had clearly lost its grip on its working-class clientele. The effort to recapture the proletariat had been led in the years 1933–1935 by the united *Bataille Socialiste,* and its tactic had been to emulate the Communists, and, if possible, to appear more radical. But when the Communists had shifted and accepted the Popular Front—with Zyromski following in their wake—Pivert and the *Gauche Révolutionnaire* retained their radical stance, and in 1938 were rewarded for their perseverance by gaining an absolute majority in the *fédération.* In 1936 only the acceptance of nonintervention by Marceau Pivert prevented the *fédération* from adopting Zyromski's demand for an immediate end to nonintervention, and in 1937 when the leader of the *Gauche Révolutionnaire* reluctantly signed the C.A.S.P.E. resolution, the noninterventionists, led by

[143] Most editorialists of *L'Unité Socialiste* demanded an end to nonintervention, much in the manner of Zyromski, and the journal admitted that the *fédération* was solidly opposed to the government's policy. See the numbers for August 22 and November 21, 1936, and June, 1937.

[144] Consult *Le Socialiste Girondin: Organe Officiel de la fédération du Parti Socialiste de France,* August–December, 1936.

the Fauriste deputy Gaston Allemane, were swamped by the united vote of the Left. In the Seine-et-Oise,[145] the situation was much the same: the Communist vote in 1936 was double that of the S.F.I.O., and thus the *fédération* was increasingly vulnerable to the theories of the two Socialist Lefts.

The third category of regions, those areas in which the Socialist party had fared extremely poorly in 1936—accounting for a mere 9 per cent of the total Socialist vote, represented by only 5 per cent of the party's deputies—was characterized by confusion and a sharp diversity of opinion on the Spanish problem. The moribund *fédérations* of the Bas-Rhin and the Haut-Rhin[146] supported non-intervention without noticeable enthusiasm as a matter of loyalty to Blum, while only two *fédérations* accepted the Fauriste viewpoint. These were the Jura,[147] where Socialist candidates had polled 21 per cent of the total vote in 1936 (the highest percentage of all twenty-one departments in this category) and where one Socialist deputy had been elected, and the *fédération* of the Territory of Belfort,[148] whose leaders were ardent pacifists. But the most stratling fact is the large number of *fédérations* which aligned themselves with the *Gauche Révolutionnaire:* the Meurthe-et-Moselle, Moselle, Vosges, Mayenne, Orne, Vendée, and the Calvados.[149] In all of these departments, socialism had met with

[145] Although technically one of the S.F.I.O.'s largest *fédérations,* the Socialist party in this department was basically a conglomeration of semiautonomous sections. Almost half of the rank and file voted for the C.A.S.P.E. resolution in July, 1937.

[146] Consult *La Presse Libre* (Bas-Rhin) and *Der Republikaner* (Haut-Rhin).

[147] *Le Jura Socialiste* was under the thumb of the secretary, LaCroix, and his views on Spain and the Communist demand for an end to nonintervention were very similar to those of Louis L'Hévéder. Consult the number for June 5, 1937.

[148] This tiny *fédération* was under the tight control of three men, the secretary René Naegelen, Cuénat, and Paul Rassiner. All suspected that the Communist goal in the Spanish affair was to provoke a war between France and Germany. See *Germinal,* September 19 and October 17, 1936, and May 1, 1937.

[149] For the Meurthe-et-Moselle *fédération* see *Le Populaire de l'Est;* for the Vosges *fédération, Le Travailleur Vosgien.* Both, but especially the latter offer examples of Pivertiste views. For the Calvados and Zoretti's articles, consult *Le Pays Normand.*

utter disaster at the polls in 1936—with the unlikely exception of the Vendée—and in all of them socialism was an insignificant political force. With the exception of the Meurthe-et-Moselle and the Moselle, these *fédérations* were extremely small, and all were led by articulate intellectuals, usually teachers. Thus a corollary should be added to the general rule that the degree of vulnerability of a *fédération* to the theories of the *Bataille Socialiste* or the *Gauche Révolutionnaire* was in inverse proportion to the electoral strength of the S.F.I.O. in a department: in those departments where socialism was virtually nonexistent as a political force, the *fédérations,* ordinarily led by a small coterie of intellectuals, increasingly gravitated toward the *Gauche Révolutionnaire.* The reasons for this swing to Marceau Pivert are not difficult to surmise: convinced of the futility of the parliamentary road to socialism by dismal electoral performances of the S.F.I.O. in their departments and by the apparent inability of the government to carry out any truly revolutionary measures, these individuals found Pivert's solution for the easy elimination of a whole series of frustrations—particularly the frustration created by the desire to save peace and the Spanish "revolution" at the same time—to be extremely congenial.

In summary, two definite conclusions may be drawn about the Socialist party and its reaction to the Spanish Civil War during the period of the first Blum government. First, the personal inclinations of key individuals, both at the highest levels of leadership and in the *fédérations,* constituted the paramount factor in the S.F.I.O.'s response to the Spanish struggle, and however significant other considerations may have been—for example, the economic characteristics of the departments—they were of secondary importance. Second, although a numerical majority of the Socialist party officially accepted nonintervention, it was an extremely heterogeneous majority, whose sentiments ranged from enthusiastic approval to the barest toleration of this policy; thus the crisis over Spain deepened the division in the party over matters of international policy.

Our examination of the party's *fédérations* has confirmed both of these conclusions: in those departments where the Socialist party was an entrenched political force, its deputies, many of whom were veteran party wheelhorses, were looked upon as the natural leaders of their *fédérations*. In many of these departments, particularly those in agricultural areas, the deputies, when confronted by the implications of the Spanish Civil War, were quick to revert to the old habit of equating socialism with pacifism and anticommunism, and quite naturally became avid partisans of nonintervention; in others, especially in the highly industrialized departments where Communist influence among the working class appeared to be on the upswing, the deputies generally were much more reserved in their approval of nonintervention. In the departments in which socialism was a relatively new political force, the Socialist deputies emerged rapidly as the commanding figures in their *fédérations*, but, in general, these new men were less concerned with the threat of war and the potential threat of communism than with what they believed to be the necessity to put a stop to the increasing audacity of "fascism." Yet, despite their will and their impatience, they too could envisage no solution to the Spanish problem other than nonintervention—at least not in this period.

Demands for assistance to the Spanish Republicans took two forms: overt opposition to nonintervention and pleas for direct proletarian action in order to circumvent this policy. The strength of the former demand was concentrated primarily in *fédérations* without deputies—with certain exceptions—which were faced with a vigorous Communist challenge, and in some *fédérations* of departments in close proximity to the Spanish frontier; the latter demand found its audience principally—again with certain exceptions—among Socialists in departments where the electoral future of the S.F.I.O. appeared to be extremely bleak, particularly in small *fédérations* which were led by persons with little experience—or interest—in practical politics.

In brief, the Spanish Civil War accelerated the trend toward fragmentation within the Socialist party in two ways: first, it accentuated latent differences over international policy, thereby further dividing the Center and widening the gulf between the *Bataille Socialiste* and the *Gauche Révolutionnaire;* second, and perhaps most important, it brought the question of international policy before the entire party, and the divisions that existed on the national level were increasingly paralleled by divisions among —and within—the *fédérations*.

4

Illusion, Division, and Compromise, 1937–1938

The immediate result of the Congress of Marseilles was an outpouring of discussion within Socialist ranks over international affairs, uninhibited by the restraints imposed formerly by the "exercise of power." Few Socialists suspected that the debate, which was rapidly transformed into a bitter polemical contest, was the onset of a long period of uninterrupted inner turmoil for their party. Whatever Socialists may have desired, international developments and, ultimately, the question of resistance or non-resistance to aggression were to shape their future, a future over which they were to have no control, despite their extravagant rhetoric, platitudinous resolutions, and steadfast determination to act as if their decisions had to be France's as well. The interlude from Congress to Congress, from Marseilles to Royan in 1938, saw the Socialist party progressively turn inward under the force of external events. The party's agony was dreary, lamentable, and prolonged, and its record is filled with unchecked illusions. We must examine that record in these final chapters.

FROM MARSEILLES TO A SECOND "EXERCISE OF POWER"

During the months following the National Congress the debate over international policy tended to harden positions which had crystallized during the early stages of the Spanish Civil War, with one very notable exception: only at the moment of Blum's accession to power for a second time did his international outlook shed much of its ambiguity. Prior to March, 1938, Blum took part only intermittently in the controversy. After a brief—but vigorous—flurry of activity from August through mid-October, 1937, the Socialist leader was largely absent from public as well as party affairs, owing to the terminal illness of his wife. Apart from an appearance at the National Council held in November and an unsuccessful effort to form a ministry in January, 1938, Blum remained largely aloof from political life until late February.

Our immediate concern is with Blum during this period prior to his return to power in March, 1938. In the late summer and early fall of 1937, Blum made what was to be his final effort, itself almost pathetic and desperate, to maintain his faith in the ideals of his international policy. In a lengthy series of articles in *Le Populaire* and in two major speeches, Blum sought to account for the unsettled state of European affairs, and also to demonstrate the continuing validity of his ideals.[1] Blum lamented that Europe had undergone a sharp regression in her modes of thought and behavior, and he pointed sorrowfully to the alarming decline in the "spirit of internationalism." The threat of war, he thought, was frightfully real, and the existing system of collective security was capable of providing neither peace nor security. The "pacific powers"—whose specific identity Blum neglected to mention— were everywhere on the defensive; instead of extinguishing conflicts, they were reduced to mere expediency in every emergency, as the case of Spain demonstrated all too clearly.[2] Such a system could never guarantee peace permanently, particularly when the primary responsibility for the danger of war was to be found in the inherently aggressive nature of the "fascist regimes." Therefore, Blum asserted, the "close union" of the "pacific powers" was

[1] *Le Populaire*, August 16, 17, 19, 20, 23, 24, 27, 28, 1937. Although these articles were signed simply "P," Blum's authorship is beyond doubt. The style is unmistakably his, and the articles are published, on pages 152–162, in the collection chosen by Suzanne Blum which appeared under the title *L'Histoire jugera* (Paris and Montreal, 1945). As for the speeches, the first was delivered at Velizy (Seine-et-Oise) on September 5, and the second at Roubaix (Nord) on September 19, 1937.

[2] During this period Blum staunchly defended nonintervention. He repeated that this policy had been adopted because of the danger of a general conflagration in Europe (*Le Populaire*, August 19, 1937). At Roubaix, Blum declared: "Even those among you who continue to think that we committed an error [by adopting nonintervention] can explain it only as an excess of our peaceful will, and I continue to believe, for my part, that the complete destruction of the system of 'nonintervention' would usher Europe into a more dangerous period" (*ibid.*, September 20, 1937).

critically necessary if Europe were ever again to live in tranquility; thus the concept of collective security must be reborn and made a reality.[3]

The leader of the S.F.I.O. did not imply, however, that "dictator states" should be excluded from the system of collective security. The crucial task for the "peaceful powers," Blum argued, was to reanimate their own faith in disarmament, the organization of peace, and in the idea of a general settlement of all outstanding problems. In substance, Blum said, the vital question was extremely simple: "Does there remain a means, does there remain a hope of enrolling the authoritarian dictatorships [in the system of collective security]?" Blum was unable to offer a categorical answer to his own query, but he declared emphatically that the peace of Europe was solely dependent upon the universal acceptance of "peaceful coexistence." He charged France and her peaceful partners with the responsibility for achieving this "peaceful coexistence":

Whatever may be her judgment on the past, whatever may be her hopes for the future, democratic France, desirous of peace, can spare no effort to make this *modus vivendi* possible. . . . France is disposed to seek all conditions of coexistence with the dictators. Always on the same condition. This is that the coexistence be peaceful.

They [the peaceful powers] are ready, for the sake of peace . . . to consider all forms of entente and collaboration.[4]

Basically this was a poignant restatement of what Blum had said at Geneva and Lyons, and of what he had suggested to Dr. Schacht: if the "fascist" powers should demonstrate their will for peace by accepting a disarmament convention, France and, he hoped, all the "peaceful" nations, should be prepared to make

[3] *Ibid.,* August 17, 20, 28, 1937.

[4] *Ibid.,* August 20, 23, 27, 28, 1937. In his speech at Velizy, Blum defined his position with utmost care: "Peace cannot be established on day-to-day remedies. . . . A solid international community, including the participation of the dictatorial states, is necessary. . . . I believe that we must escape this tragic dilemma which obliges us today to envisage all the consequences [of war], and there is only one way of escaping it, that is by general disarmament. . . . The more that peace is menaced and compromised, the more we must conserve in ourselves the will to make it stable and durable." Consult *Le Populaire,* September 6, 1937.

concessions to them in the interests of a general settlement of all problems. Blum's effort was a reassertion of his belief that his ideals and aspirations were shared by most of mankind, and that they were indeed realistic solutions to the awesome dilemma confronting Europe. Moreover, this appeal had a definite touch of finality: peace could not be preserved indefinitely by the present system, which to him was little more than expediency raised to the level of official policy. In sum, Blum required a system of collective security which would be all-embracing: if disarmament and a general settlement were achieved, then Europe would constitute a pacific and interdependent community of nations, regardless of the political regimes of the member states.

Yet there was something else in this appeal. Almost submerged beneath the flood of idealism was another familiar theme: the necessity for the "peaceful powers" to unite. At the very least Blum required a system of collective security which would become fully operative in case of need along lines established in advance; the weak must be insured against aggression. Blum insisted that the present situation, characterized by uncertainty, could not be perpetuated indefinitely, and, by the logic of his arguments, if the "peaceful powers" should be unsuccessful in their effort to secure a general settlement, their very unity would either deter aggression or put a stop to it. In fact this aspect of Blum's international policy was gradually becoming more noticeable in his considerations: in October he despaired openly over the disunity of the "pacific powers," for, he asserted, if they were united, "they could *impose* peace."[5] But it would require the brutal shock of the *Anschluss* to convince Blum that the union of certain powers, determined to meet force with force, was the only viable alternative to "fascist" hegemony in Europe.

Characteristically, the Blumistes, those men close to Blum who had dissented cautiously from his Spanish policy, refrained from active participation in the discussion within the party, owing initially perhaps to the renewed appeal of their chief in favor of disarmament and a general settlement. It would seem more likely, however, that, as in the case of the Spanish Civil War, their disquiet was manifested—and masked—by silence. Only the

[5] *Ibid.,* October 7, 1937. Italics mine.

crusty veteran Salomon Grumbach spoke out loudly: he told the National Council in November that he was extremely apprehensive about the course of international affairs, and declared in all frankness that the only option remaining open to France was to build a firm alliance system in partnership with Great Britain and the Soviet Union.[6] Louis Lévy, a close friend of Blum but not a member of the inner circle of Blum's associates—although he was elected to the C.A.P. in 1936 and 1937 as a representative of the Blum-Faure majority—renewed his bitter assault on nonintervention and demanded that France speak the only language intelligible to Berlin and Rome—force. Lévy urged that the S.F.I.O. speak out in favor of French participation in a mighty coalition of powers directed against "fascism"; such a coalition must include the U.S.S.R., which, he argued, "despite the opinion of some poorly informed comrades, is a peaceful power."[7] But aside from Grumbach and Lévy, the Blumistes maintained their public silence.

Paul Faure and his colleagues, however, were anything but silent. The General Secretary of the Socialist party toured hospitable *fédérations* extensively and contributed a great number of articles to *Le Populaire* in an apparently successful effort to win wide support for his international policy. Faure's activities may be summarized under three headings: the first consisted of a vigorous defense of nonintervention; the second of a total reaffirmation of pacifism, bordering on the complete rejection of participation in war; and the third of an energetic counterattack against the suggestion that an alliance system be constructed against Germany and Italy. Faure's action was hardly surprising, inasmuch as it represented the logical evolution of his international policy.

Little more need be said concerning Faure's warm espousal of nonintervention. He was absolutely determined to assure the continuance of this policy, and for the same reasons as before: his fear of war and of the intentions of the Soviet Union. Faure delivered countless speeches in which he stressed his belief that nonintervention had saved France from war. And war, he cried again and again, was the greatest of human tragedies: "Even if we were

[6] *Ibid.*, November 8, 1937.

[7] *Ibid.*, November 7, 1937, January 10, 1938. Lévy was a fiery writer: he told the party that it must finish with what he described as "this abominable policy of capitulations to fascism" (*ibid.*, February 18, 1938).

certain of military victory, we would *never* give our signature to war."[8] As if the Socialist "signature" would matter! The Socialist party, Faure asserted interminably, was *the* party of peace; it alone possessed the will to maintain peace. Taken literally, the General Secretary's ringing speeches virtually constituted a total rejection of the use of war, regardless of the circumstances. Faure was careful to direct much of his appeal to youth. He told a congress of the *Jeunesses Socialistes*—to the accompaniment of wild applause—that

youth is unanimous in its revulsion at the idea of war. . . . Its revulsion is both instinctive and rational. . . .

To live, not to accept the idea of killing or of being killed, to pick the roses of life in tranquility, to feel threatened no longer. . . . These sentiments beat in the hearts of the young and give them courage and virility for tasks other than the murder of men and destruction.[9]

In an address to the Economic Commission of the League of Nations in September, 1937, Faure resurrected the offer made by Blum in his speech at Lyons and subsequently restated by the Socialist leader: in return for her pledge of peace, Germany would be the beneficiary of economic accords with France. The range of these accords, Faure declared, could be unlimited, but they should deal with the problems of raw materials and financial credits.[10] In February, 1938, in reaction to a growing demand spearheaded by Grumbach, Lévy, and the *Bataille Socialiste* for Socialist support of military alliances directed against the "fascist" powers, Faure asserted vehemently that the Socialist party should stand firmly behind the "peace policy" enunciated by Blum at Lyons. As positive evidence of Socialism's peaceful will,

[8] Speech at Masseret (Corrèze), published in the *Populaire* of the Loir-et-Cher, September 4, 1937; speech at Aubusson (Creuse), published in *Le Populaire*, September 20, 1937; speech at Montmartre, published in *Le Populaire*, November 12, 1937; speech at Epernay (Marne), published in *Le Populaire*, November 20, 1937; speech at Saint-Denis, published in *Le Populaire*, November 21, 1937; speech at Milleu (Aveyron), published in *Le Socialiste Aveyronnais*, December 23, 1937; speech at Tours, published in *Le Réveil* (Indre-et-Loire), March 5, 1938; speech at Montmartre, *Le Populaire*, November 12, 1937.   [9] *Le Populaire*, November 6, 1937.

[10] Paul Faure, *De Munich à la V° République* (Paris, 1948), 24–25; *Le Populaire*, September 28, 1937.

Faure declared without hesitation that the S.F.I.O. would support *"direct* conversations" between France and Germany on all outstanding questions. And at the very moment that Hitler was beginning to press his demands on the hapless Austrian Chancellor Schuschnigg, Paul Faure heaped scorn and vituperation on the idea of an antifascist coalition of powers. France, he said, would never adhere to any "aggressive pact," and moreover,

She has never thought of entering into an antifascist coalition. . . .

She is ready to offer her collaboration in anything which could consolidate and organize peace; [she is] ready to seek all possible agreements on the questions of credits, economic assistance, demography, and colonial territories.[11]

In other words, France should be prepared to make every conceivable concession in order to preserve peace!

Faure's pacifist offensive attracted eager and vocal enthusiasts who tirelessly propagated the message of the General Secretary. Séverac hailed the "wise and judicious policy of nonintervention," and sarcastically inquired whether any confidence could be placed in the word of the Soviet Union.[12] Arnol praised the "sacred cause of peace," which, he declared loftily, was so admirably defended by the policy of nonintervention: "We Socialists," he wrote proudly, "refuse to accept war."[13] L'Hévéder proclaimed that none could ever suspect the Socialist party of receiving its instructions from a foreign power, and he told the militants of the Morbihan *fédération* that the primary task facing Socialism was to keep France from war.[14] Julien Peschadour, a confidant of Charles Spinasse and soon to be an influential figure in his own right, asserted that it was inconceivable that anyone could consider the abandonment of nonintervention, and he publicly characterized Stalin as a "bloody despot," adding that he much preferred "bourgeois" France to "the so-called Soviet paradise."[15]

[11] *Le Populaire,* February 23, 25, 26, 1938.

[12] *Ibid.,* December 22, 1937; March 7, 1938.

[13] *Le Droit du Peuple* (Isère) , November 13, 1937.

[14] *Le Populaire,* November 2, December 4, 1937; *Le Rappel du Morbihan,* March 26, 1938.

[15] *La Voix Socialiste* (Charente-Inférieure), November 27, 1937, and *La Voix Corrèzienne,* January 6, March 18, 1938.

Roucayrol reminded the delegates to the National Council in January, 1938, that the Communists entered the Popular Front on orders from Soviet Russia in a desperate search for allies against Germany.[16] And Camille Planche launched a violent attack on the idea of antifascist alliance: "We must," he said, "condemn any policy which aims at the encirclement of Germany."[17]

Similarly, the rapidly emerging "Fauriste" international policy received wide currency, in much the same manner as the Fauriste position on Spain, within the Socialist Youth Movement and among the anti-Communist ranks of the C.G.T. Bernard Chochoy, the national leader of the *Jeunesses Socialistes,* unleashed a stinging attack on what he alleged to be a glorification of militarism by the Communist party.[18] *Le Cri des Jeunes* asked why the Spanish Communists should not be classified among the enemies of Republican Spain.[19] Marcel Roy, writing in *Syndicats,* bitterly assailed those "who believe in armed conflict as a means to secure the liberation of the proletariat"—that is, the Communists—and he urged the C.G.T. "to do everything to put an end to those [conflicts] which already exist." Raymond Froideval found the latter suggestion to be especially valuable, and he admonished the Spanish Republicans to cease their struggle and accept a "compromise" which would end the war. Froideval also repulsed the suggestion of an antifascist coalition and he pleaded with the C.G.T. to use all its strength to ensure that France and Germany arrived at an entente.[20] Certainly both the *Jeunesses Socialistes* and the *Syndicats* wing of the C.G.T. were fertile breeding grounds for "Fauriste" ideas.

Recognizing their close affinity on international policy—as manifested by the mushrooming of support for Faure's position— the Fauristes sought to create a journal of opinion, in the style of the *Bataille Socialiste,* which would serve as a forum for their ideas. To be sure, their arsenal was already well stocked: Faure

[16] *Le Populaire,* January 19, 1938.

[17] *Le Combat Social* (Allier), February 27, 1938.

[18] *Le Populaire,* November 20, 1937.

[19] November, 1937, second number. This journal continued its glorification of Paul Faure: its first number for January, 1938, carried a lead article entitled "Vive Paul Faure," which said "the Young Socialist is proud of Paul Faure, who has always had the courage of his words."

[20] *Syndicats,* October 7, 1937; February 9, 1938.

controlled the powerful arm of the Secretariat, and its publication, *Le Bulletin Socialiste,* was indeed an efficacious instrument of propaganda;[21] the many deputies and secretaries of *fédérations* who were in sympathy with Faure's outlook ordinarily exercised a firm grip on the local Socialist periodicals; the columns of *Le Cri des Jeunes* were unswerving in their loyalty to the General Secretary; and finally, the *Syndicats* group appeared to be in close sympathy with the ideas of Paul Faure. But in the fall of 1937, the Fauristes added yet another cog to their already formidable propaganda machine. This was the periodical *Le Socialiste,*[22] which was created ostensibly for the purpose of combating the creeping menace of the *Gauche Révolutionnaire* in the huge *fédération* of the Seine, but judging from its roster of contributors—Paz, Séverac, Belin, and Peschadour among others—it was fully intended for party-wide circulation. Thus, while maintaining their posture as the stalwarts of the party's Center majority, the Fauristes were fast becoming an organized *tendance* in their own right.

The *Bataille Socialiste* group, in the person of its fiery chief Jean Zyromski, carried on its public campaign against the "scandalous" retention of nonintervention and in favor of a closer relationship between France and the Soviet Russia. Zyromski had little confidence in the Chautemps government, and had no hesitation about saying so; plainly he was anticipating its early demise, and he concentrated his efforts on international policy, hoping that the S.F.I.O. would have completed a full-fledged revision of its outlook on international affairs by the time it returned to power. Zyromski repeated the same old tired clichés incessantly: Spain was the victim of an international "fascist" plot; the Spanish Republicans were fighting a heroic struggle in defense of European democracy, and unless they were permitted to purchase arms, French socialism and France would perish with them. The leftist leader renewed his attacks on pacifism and

[21] Several articles, all of which were widely reprinted in the local Socialist press, may serve to document this statement: an article describing terrorism in the U.S.S.R. appeared on August 30, 1937; an article lavishly approving nonintervention on November 8, 1937; the already cited "No, Comrade Marcel Cachin" on November 15, 1937; a story purporting to reveal that the Soviet Union was shipping oil to Italy on February 7, 1938.

[22] The first issue appeared on November 15, 1937, and its lead article was entitled "The Stalinization of Spain."

argued that "to deny the existence of international blocs is to deny the existence of the class struggle"; in other words, a military alliance of so-called "democratic" states directed against the "fascist" states represented the class struggle pure and simple. Finally, Zyromski demanded the unification of the Socialist and Communist parties, the cessation of attempts to seek agreement with either Germany or Italy, and closer Franco-Soviet collaboration.[23] In sum, the policies of the *Bataille Socialiste* remained unaltered, and Zyromski continued to be the outstanding and aggressive spokesman for his *tendance*.

Bolstered by concrete evidence of its increasing strength within the S.F.I.O.,[24] the *Gauche Révolutionnaire* joined the intraparty debate with obvious exuberance. Once again its battle cries were direct mass action and preparation for total revolution, and its leaders exhibited for once a truly remarkable degree of unity among themselves. In domestic affairs, the *tendance* pursued two immediate aims: the unleashing of this direct mass action in order to install a "Government of Combat" or "Government of Public Safety," and the achievement of unity of the working-class parties.[25]

[23] Zyromski adopted a very literal interpretation of the motion on Spain passed at Marseilles: "The party has unanimously condemned nonintervention and mediation," and he criticized Blum for disregarding the law of the party (*L'Espagne Socialiste*, August 1–15, 1937).

Zyromski's major pronouncements on Spain were as follows: *Le Populaire*, August 24, October 5, October 31, November 4 and 18, December 22, 1937; February 16, March 2 and 18, 1938. Zyromski was also extremely sensitive to the attacks made by the *Gauche Révolutionnaire* on the repression of certain groups in Republican Spain, and he was compelled to defend this action by accusing Pivert of wanting to interfere in Spanish affairs (*Le Populaire*, October 5, December 22, 1937; *Clarté*, December, 1937, 502–504).

[24] The steady increase in strength of the *Gauche Révolutionnaire* may be demonstrated by its share of *mandats* at successive Socialist gatherings: at the National Council of April, 1937, the G.R. won 11.6 per cent of the *mandats;* at Marseilles 16.6 per cent, at the November National Council 17.0 per cent, and at the January, 1938, National Council, 18.4 per cent. In January the *tendance* won control of the *fédération* of the Seine (*Le Temps*, January 25, 1938), and shortly thereafter it published a new periodical, *Juin 36,* which became the organ of the *fédération* and of the *tendance* itself.

[25] Marceau Pivert in *Les Cahiers Rouges*, August-September, 1937, and in *Le Populaire*, January 14, 1938. Addressing the congress of the *fédération* of the Seine shortly after the fall of the Chautemps government in January 1938,

The Revolutionary Left gave its closest scrutiny to the problems of the Spanish "revolution" and the threat of European war, and in both cases Marceau Pivert was the uncontested spokesman for his *tendance*. In Pivert's eyes, the Spanish "revolution" had suffered a double betrayal: first, lack of assistance from the international proletariat and the French government's obstinacy in clinging to nonintervention had deprived the "revolutionary vanguard" in Spain of the means to fight; second, the Communists, profiting from their position as sole supplier of arms, were crushing the "revolutionaries" and restoring capitalism. Pivert asserted that Soviet diplomacy was "oriented toward the hypothesis of a world war," and implied that the extirpation of "revolution" in Spain was an integral part of Moscow's plan to woo England and "bourgeois" France as allies in the coming struggle. Thus, he argued, while it was imperative that nonintervention be scrapped and that arms be sent to Republican Spain, it was also mandatory that these arms be delivered into the hands of the "revolutionaires." To accomplish this, only one sure road was open: direct action by the proletariat.[26]

If only direct working-class assistance could rescue the dying Spanish "revolution," only an active "revolutionary policy" could prevent the catastrophe of European war, which, Pivert still believed, would be launched by capitalism in its death throes. Pivert and his eager comrades poured a steady stream of abuse on everything which they considered to be preparation for war—rearmament, military alliances, and the dreaded *union sacrée*. The leader of the "Minority of the C.A.P." reiterated much that he had said in *Révolution d'Abord!* in 1935: only direct action, culminating in revolution, could halt the race toward war; Pivert added that revolution not only would liberate the Germany people from "fascism," but also would free the Russian people from

Pivert cheered "The Popular Front is dead! Long live the Revolutionary Front" (*Le Temps*, January 25, 1938).

[26] *Les Cahiers Rouges,* August-September, 1937; Marceau Pivert and Daniel Guérin in *Le Populaire,* August 31, September 7, 1937; Pivert in *Le Populaire,* November 29, 1937. Pivert's assessment of Communist policy in Spain was fully supported by Michel Collinet (*La Vague,* November 15, 1937; *Le Populaire,* November 11, 1937), and by Colette Audry (*Le Socialiste Savoyard,* August 21, December 11, 1937).

the yoke of Stalinism.[27] Thus with an ideology essentially unchanged since 1935, and freed from the restraint imposed by the
existence of a government under Socialist direction, the *Gauche
Révolutionnaire* was making its voice heard within the Socialist
party.

During this period of effervescence and tension within the
party, two National Councils were convoked, the first on November 6 and 7, 1937, and the second on January 17 and 18, 1938.
Despite the vigorous discussion on international policy then
under way in virtually all of the party's publications and on
public platforms, the earlier meeting was a drab and perfunctory
affair. A motley succession of speakers trooped to the rostrum:
Lévy politely suggested that the party had not met with much
success in implementing the resolution of the Marseilles Congress
on Spain; Longuet shrieked that the "abominable comedy of
nonintervention must cease"; and Zyromski denounced those
who, he said, blindly refused to recognize the existence of two
irrevocably opposed ideological blocs in Europe. The Fauristes
saw no need to assign the task of rebuttal to a first-rate speaker:
instead the colorless Quinson, deputy from the Ain, remarked
placidly that the S.F.I.O. had been successful in the recent can-
tonal elections[28] because of "the peasants' belief that the Léon
Blum government kept the peace." Séverac pointed out legalisti-
cally that the discussion was quite senseless since a National
Council had no power to initiate policies and was restricted to the
task of insuring that the policies laid down by the Congress were
being executed. This sober reminder prompted the National
Council to adopt a resolution—unanimously—asking that the
Socialist ministers do their best to see that the resolution on Spain
was carried out. Clearly no one, except Pivert, was anxious to
provoke an open crisis: Pivert demanded the immediate with-

---

[27] *Le Populaire,* August 21, 1937; *La Vague,* November 15, 1937. Pivert and
René Modiano charged that Blum's attempt to form a ministry which would
include Thorez and Paul Reynaud was a naked effort to pursue a war policy
(*Le Populaire,* February 14, 1938; see also Pivert in the same journal on
March 9, 1938, and an article in *Le Temps,* March 16, 1938, dealing with a
meeting of the council of the Seine *fédération*).

[28] The S.F.I.O. polled 21.32 per cent of the total vote cast on the first ballot.
For complete election results, consult *Le Temps,* October 16, 1937.

drawl of the Socialist ministers from the government and the adoption of a policy of revolutionary preparation. His suggestion received 909 *mandats*, while Zyromski's appeal for a government including the Communists won 978 *mandats*. The majority, with 3,448 *mandats*, settled for a motion which expressed full confidence in the Socialist ministers and put the party on record as favoring a new series of reforms.[29] The latter provision was a fine gesture, but of little value since the Socialist delegates to the committee of the *Rassemblement Populaire* had been attempting, since August—without success—to persuade the Radicals and Communists to support further reform.

While the November National Council was reluctant to engage in decisive debate on problems of international policy, the hastily convoked National Council of January, 1938, was in no position to do so. The resignation of the government, precipitated by Chautemps' outburst against the Communists, caused a severe ministerial crisis. President Lebrun's favorite, Georges Bonnet, was unable to form a ministry, owing to unanimous Socialist opposition to his candidacy. Blum then was designated by Lebrun, but his effort was unsuccessful: Blum sought to install a government ranging in political complexion "from Thorez to Reynaud," hoping that the selection of the latter would appease the financial community, but the Radicals were definitely antipathetic to the inclusion of the Communists, and Reynaud insisted that Louis Marin also be included, a proposal unacceptable to Blum.[30] Chautemps was charged with forming another ministry, and he appealed for Socialist participation. At the National Council which was called to consider his request, many "centrists," like the Blumiste Lebas and the Fauriste Roucayrol, opposed participation, fearing that Chautemps' action against the Communists, as well as the Radicals' refusal to accept Commu-

[29] *Le Populaire,* November 7, 8, 1937.

[30] *Le Populaire,* January 16, 18, 1938. Blum, Sérol, and Auriol claimed that the Radicals would not accept Communist participation. The Communists retorted that "Comrade Léon Blum has been badly misinformed on the real thought of the Radical group." Quite obviously the Communists were still staking their fortunes on the Radicals. Blum's impression of the Radical attitude was substantiated by Daladier and Chautemps. See *La Vie du Parti,* supplement to *Le Populaire,* February 15, 1938.

nists as partners in the government, constituted an attempt by the Radicals to break the Popular Front majority in the Chamber. Despite a compromise solution hammered out by Blum, Lebas, Faure, and others, which stated that the S.F.I.O. would participate only if the government rested upon the Popular Front majority, Chautemps' invitation was rejected by the National Council.[31] Chautemps then formed a homogeneous Radical ministry as a temporary expedient, and the Council gave the Socialist parliamentary group a free hand to support or oppose this government as it saw fit.

Thus on the eve of Blum's second "exercise of power," the Socialist party was beset with uncertainty and increasing internal division. In Parliament, the party was desperately attempting to preserve the fiction of Popular Front solidarity, yet many "centrists" were resolutely hostile to any further participation under a Radical *Président du Conseil*. In international policy, which was unquestionably uppermost in the considerations of all segments of the party, long-developing differences, manifested and sharpened in the crisis over Spain, hardened perceptibly after the Congress of Marseilles. Léon Blum's position still gave solace, by its dual character, to much of the party, but from the moment of the *Anschluss,* Blum was to commit himself more and more to the international policy of one of the contending groups. Hence the significance of the second Blum government lies not so much in Blum's effort to rally all parties—and the nation—against the threat of "fascist" aggression, but in the undeniable fact that his action constituted the beginning of the final agony of the Socialist party, an agony which was to consign it to impotence.

THE SECOND "EXERCISE OF POWER," MARCH 12–APRIL 8, 1938

At the very moment when the Austro-German crisis was fast approaching its denouement, French political life was plunged into chaos by the resignation of Camille Chautemps. Blum was doubly shocked: France, he believed, appeared weak and woefully divided, while Germany displayed her eagerness to use brutal force to satisfy her aggressive ambitions. The Socialist leader immediately drew two critical conclusions from these events: first,

[31] *Le Populaire,* January 18, 1938.

a Popular Front ministry was now totally out of date and must be superseded by a government of "National Union"; second, only the firm and determined will of an antifascist coalition of powers could thwart further Nazi expansion. And although Blum was extremely dubious that he could be the man to accomplish the feat of constructing this vitally urgent government of National Union, he accepted President Lebrun's commission to form a ministry.[32]

On the morning of March 12, Blum declared to an abbreviated session of the National Council that the crisis over Austria had upset all of his previous calculations and that the new situation obligated the Socialist party to launch an appeal to all Frenchmen. A Government of National Union, which would include representatives of all political parties, he said, using his skill at semantic subterfuge, would be by no means the forbidden *union sacrée*, but would be a "national rallying" around the Popular Front majority. Without being more explicit, Blum appealed for an unlimited mandate from the party in order to carry out this task. Faure nervously called for an immediate vote, but Zyromski interrupted noisily to give his blessing to the project.[33] With only Pivert and his angry followers opposed, Blum's request was approved by a vote of 6,575 *mandats* to 1,684.[34]

[32] Léon Blum, *L'Oeuvre, 1940–1945* (Paris, 1955), 125: "In accord with the Radicals and undoubtedly with the leaders of the moderate and reactionary opposition, M. Albert Lebrun called me to take power quickly so as to eliminate me from the political scene entirely and thus leave the way open for Daladier." Blum told the court at Riom that "everyone knew that it [the government] would be short when it began, and I assure you that I knew it as well as anyone" (*ibid.*, 241).

[33] *Le Populaire*, March 13, 1938. The previous afternoon Blum had told the Socialist parliamentary group that a ministry in the image of the Popular Front was out of the question, and had stated that the "National Union" was absolutely mandatory in face of the new Nazi threat. See *Le Temps*, March 13, 1938. The sole indication of Faure's attitude at this time may be found in an article by Blum in *Le Populaire* on July 9, 1938, written in response to an article by the ex-Pivertiste Maurice Deixonne. Blum wrote that Faure had been reluctant to convoke the National Council, fearing that Blum's proposals would be rejected.

[34] Pivert declared that *union nationale* was equivalent to *union sacrée;* i.e., he accused Blum of preparing for war in cooperation with the bourgeoisie. See *Le Populaire*, March 13, 1938.

Armed with this handsome vote of confidence, Blum addressed a pathetic appeal for a "political Matignon accord" to the parties to the right of the Radicals.[35] In a meeting held at the Palais-Bourbon, Blum called for the speedy installation of his proposed Government of National Union, for this was, he declared forcefully, "the only guarantee of peace." Blum promised categorically not to initiate any legislation for structural reforms in the economy— "there are more vital matters," he said, and he disclosed to his attentive listeners that they would find his choice for Minister of Finance most reassuring. Finally, asserting that his appeal was directed to their reason, not to their sentiments, he volunteered to withdraw his own candidacy if they believed another man to be more acceptable. At the conclusion of his talk Blum was warmly congratulated by several of his political enemies, and he departed confident of success. But Paul Reynaud was the sole speaker among those who followed to urge complete acceptance of Blum's request, which was rejected by a large margin.[36] Late in the evening, Blum announced to President Lebrun that he had formed a ministry composed of Socialists, Radicals, and members of the Socialist and Republican Union.[37]

Blum's ministerial declaration and his speech to the Chamber vividly demonstrated the reorientation of his international policy. The declaration read, in part,

[35] Blum decided to address these parties after receiving assurances from Louis Marin and Pierre-Etienne Flandin that his proposal would receive the utmost consideration. See the testimony of Léon Blum in *Les Evénements survenus en France*, I, 253.

Flandin, testifying before the same commission, denied that he gave any assurance to Blum that he would do his best to secure approval of Blum's request (*ibid.*, IX, 2, 596).

[36] *Ibid.*, I, 253; Léon Blum, *L'Oeuvre, 1940–1945*, 242; *Le Temps*, March 14, 1938.

[37] The most significant appointment was that of Joseph Paul-Boncour to the Quai d'Orsay. Paul-Boncour had never hidden his disquiet over nonintervention and the absence of a "hard" line toward Germany and Italy. See, for example, his speech published in *Le Solognot* (Loir-et-Cher) on April 10, 1937, in which he attacked what he described as "our policy of abdication." Consult also the third volume of his memoirs, *Entre deux guerres* (Paris, 1946), 7off.

We have assumed power in the aftermath of a striking event which has shaken and staggered all of Europe, and which could engender, or could be the prelude to, awesome developments.

A unanimous France passionately wants peace. When it is a question of peace in Europe, there is no initiative that she is not resolved to take or to accept. She also wants to safeguard her complete independence and her vital interests, to preserve the security of her frontiers and her [lines of] communication, and to honor fully the obligations . . . to which she is bound by her signature. . . .

Since the circumstances force our country to do so, we intend to increase our military force. . . .

We will strive to maintain and to refashion our alliances . . . which [are] a pledge of peace for the world. Peace in honor and freedom was always France's rule. Integrity and international solidarity do not cease to be her principles. The *rapprochement* of all the peaceful powers in the world in behalf of collective security will not cease to be her aim.

In his speech Blum declared unequivocally that France would fulfill all her treaty obligations, and he stated that if Czechoslovakia were to be menaced with aggression, France would be at her side. And France would not be alone: the Soviet government, he asserted, was friendly and, in case of conflict in Europe, "would be found in the same camp as France."[38]

Blum made an energetic effort to translate these intentions into reality: acting on instructions from Blum, Paul-Boncour gave verbal assurances to the Czechoslovakian Ambassador that France would stand by all of her commitments to Czechoslovakia; furthermore, the government closed its eyes completely to the transit of war materials across the frontier into Catalonia.[39] At a meeting of the Permanent Committee of National Defense held on the evening of March 15, Blum asked the military chiefs (Marshal Pétain, General Gamelin, and General Vuillemin) if France could reply to a German attack on Czechoslovakia. Daladier interposed that France could not assist the Czechs directly, and should

[38] *Le Populaire*, March 18, 1938; Léon Blum, *L'Histoire jugera* (Paris, 1945) 165–167.

[39] J. Paul-Boncour, testimony to the parliamentary commission, *Les Evénements survenus en France*, II, 801; Léon Blum in *Le Populaire*, July 12, August 10, 1938.

prepare to engage the German forces on the French frontier. According to Daladier, Blum accepted this conclusion, but added that he was confident that the U.S.S.R. would intervene immediately on the side of France. General Vuillemin was hardly as confident, and his dissent received a nodding approval from the Marshal. Blum then turned to the Spanish problem, and although the four existing accounts of this meeting are not in agreement on this question, it would appear that the *Président du Conseil* suggested that an ultimatum be delivered to General Franco, stipulating that unless he renounced foreign assistance and expedited the removal of Italian troops from Spain, France would ship arms to the Republicans and take any other steps which might be necessary. Paul-Boncour vigorously seconded the suggestion, and asked consideration of a plan by which France would invade Spanish Morocco in the event that Franco were to reject the ultimatum. Apparently for purposes of discussion, Blum inquired about the possibility of sending a French military expedition to the rescue of Catalonia. Both suggestions were vigorously condemned by the military leaders and by Daladier, and the meeting ended on an inconclusive note. As a consequence the government was forced to settle for public declarations of France's fidelity to her engagements to Czechoslovakia, and for a policy of "relaxed" nonintervention in the case of Spain.[40]

Blum's other major effort, his attempt to accelerate arms production, ran afoul of the financial problem. Blum recognized that new bonds must be offered for public subscription, but he also saw quite clearly that the state must impose strict regulations, and establish control over monetary exchange in order to prevent a drain on the franc. Such a program, he believed, would permit the state to pour capital into the armaments industry. Blum's dilemma was cruel but simple: without special powers at his dis-

---

[40] Edouard Daladier, testimony to the parliamentary commission, *Les Evénements survenus en France*, I, 27; J. Paul-Boncour, *ibid.*, III, 802; General Maurice Gustave Gamelin, *Servir*, II: *Le Pologue du drame* (Paris, 1946) 325–327; Léon Blum, *Les Evénements survenus en France*, I, 253.

According to Paul-Boncour, *Les Evénements survenus en France*, III, 802, Blum simply inquired whether France should send several divisions to the Spanish frontiers. It would seem most likely that a military expedition was but one of several possible alternatives offered by Blum for discussion.

posal, which would allow him to institute the needed control over exchanges, his program had but a dim chance of success; however, he was certain that the Senate would never grant him such powers, and he was alarmed by the outbreak of a rash of sit-down strikes which threatened to crush any lingering hopes of realizing a semblance of national unity in a time of international crisis.[41] Blum chose to ask for special powers to deal with the economic situation, and he proposed a far-reaching series of reforms, knowing that he would be defeated.[42] His goal was not simply to depart from office on a question of principle, but to leave in the hope that his successor, undoubtedly a Radical, would be given powers which would enable him to cope with the situation effectively. As anticipated, the Senate overwhelmingly rejected Blum's request for special powers, and Blum resigned on the evening of April 8.

Again Léon Blum bowed to "republican legality," once more incarnated somewhat incongruously by the old men of the Senate; the Socialist chief absolutely rejected the suggestion that popular force be brought into the fray—although Pivert organized a militant demonstration anyway. At an emergency meeting of the National Council, a visibly tired Blum condemned an appeal to force:

An appeal to the workers and republicans would have created—deliberately—a revolutionary situation. We did not think that it was possible, in the present state of France and of Europe . . . to create events of this kind. . . .

During these four weeks . . . we exercised on foreign policy an action which has already produced results.[43]

---

[41] Little is known about the origins of these strikes. One of the best sources of information is a series of articles by Vincent Auriol in *Le Populaire* on April 18, 19, 20, 21, and 22, 1938. Auriol places the burden of responsibility on the *patronat*, and Rosenfeld was of the opinion that the strikes were deliberately fomented by the *patronat* in order to embarrass the government (interview with Rosenfeld). The Communist role is equally difficult to ascertain. The majority of the C.A.P. accused the Seine *fédération*, under the control of Pivert, of using the *Amicales Socialistes* to spread the strikes. See *Le Temps*, April 2, 1938.

[42] *Le Populaire*, April 5, 1938; Léon Blum, *Les Evénements survenus en France*, I, 255; interview with Rosenfeld. See also *Le Temps*, April 8, 1938.

[43] *Le Populaire*, April 10, 1938.

With dramatic suddenness Blum had reoriented his international policy: the brutal shock of the *Anschluss* had prompted him to seek the constitution of a Government of National Union, a vast increase in France's armaments, and the realization of an antifascist coalition of powers. In practice, however, Blum's government had achieved little: it had declared that France intended to protect Czechoslovakia against aggression and it had attempted to increase the trickle of aid to the Spanish Republic. The vital significance of this second "exercise of power" lay rather in its effect upon Blum and the Socialist party. Although in the following months prior to the Sudeten crisis Blum's international policy was devoid neither of equivocation nor of duality, and while he was still prone to occasional lapses into his familiar pacifist rhetoric, he had finally arrived at the reluctant conclusion that only a willingness to meet force with force could save Europe from "fascist" aggression and hegemony. If this decision was the almost inevitable, though belated, accession to dominance of one strand of Blum's international policy, much of his party was taken by surprise. Yet by the end of these four weeks, a profound reaction to Blum's apparent *volte-face* was well under way, and the final and often bitter struggle within the S.F.I.O. was beginning in earnest.

DIVISION OF THE RANKS

The National Council which convened on April 9 was but the prelude to the strife that was soon to consume all the energies of the Socialist party. Ostensibly the question under consideration was what attitude the party should take toward the new government of Edouard Daladier, but the real question was international policy. Although Blum's actions during his month in office had stunned most of the "Fauristes" into numbed silence—with some exceptions[44]—two of the most prominent Fauristes, L'Hévéder and Roucayrol, took advantage of the occasion to issue a stern warning to the party. L'Hévéder loudly denounced any international policy which presupposed the division of Europe into antagonistic blocs of powers, and Roucayrol declared that the

[44] J. B. Séverac wrote—at the same time that Blum's ministerial declaration appeared—that "France is ready to go to the extreme limit for peace," and that "our hatred of war is profound" (*Le Populaire*, March 17, 22, 1938).

party would betray its heritage and ideals if it were to support any government whose international policy was based upon force. Zyromski announced glumly that he would favor Socialist approval of the Daladier government only if it declared its aim to be the construction of an antifascist alliance system and if it terminated the policy of nonintervention. Grumbach replied, not without logic, that the party must support Daladier if it wanted the aspirations mentioned by Zyromski to be realized. Pivert made known his suspicion that the Daladier government represented the first stage in the constitution of a "fascist dictatorship in France," and he informed the National Council that the party must "run a revolutionary risk," cease its advocacy of rearmament and military alliances, and launch a direct appeal to the working masses. At voting time, Zyromski amended his proposal so that it tacitly approved the Daladier government at the same time that it called for a campaign to install "a government conforming to the will of the nation"—that is, a government in the image of the Popular Front majority. His tactic was quite successful, and his motion received 2,107 *mandats* (26.1%), while Séverac's—which stated that opposition to Daladier would be inadmissible in the present situation—received 4,320 *mandats* (53.4%), and Pivert's uncompromising motion garnered 1,656 *mandats* (20.5%).[45] The delegates to the National Council dispersed on a note of uncertainty and uneasiness; the meeting had revealed the acuteness of their differences over international policy. The next two months were to be a period of preparation for the National Congress, scheduled to be held at the resort town of Royan early in June.

The "Blumistes" were very much at a disadvantage during these two months, owing to several factors: Blum himself withdrew from active participation in public life until late in May, at which time he readily confessed that his long period of rest had left him badly out of touch with the rank and file; Zyromski and his associates cleverly capitalized upon the very obvious similarities between their international policy and the position assumed by Blum in March and April, thereby blurring the distinctions between them; finally, the Fauristes were in command of a mighty propaganda apparatus, whereas the Blumistes—who were, of course, still no more than the nucleus of a *tendance*—had no

[45] *Ibid.*, April 10, 11, 1938.

organization and only limited means of communication with the party as a whole. Among the Blumistes, Dormoy and Monnet— who were ably seconded by Lévy[46]—were the most outspoken in advocating a policy of "firmness" toward the "fascist" powers. Dormoy asserted that France "must not be the dupe of the dictators," and responding to the challenge of the Fauriste leader Camille Planche, he told the militants of the Allier *fédération* that the sole barrier to "fascist" ambition was the union of all the "democratic" powers.[47] Monnet publicly attacked the heart of the Fauriste position by declaring that *any* concessions to the "fascist" powers would simply increase their appetite for further aggression.[48] This "firm" international policy quickly gained support in a large number of *fédérations,* particularly among those where nonintervention had been reluctantly accepted in 1936 and 1937, and it appealed especially to many of the party's younger deputies, such as Tanguy-Prigent, André Philip, and Eugène Thomas.[49] But as yet neither a Blumiste international policy nor a Blumiste *tendance* was well developed, and until Blum made his position perfectly clear in the summer and fall of 1938, the Fauristes appeared to dominate the party's Center majority.

Paul Faure passed the months immediately prior to the Royan Congress locked in mortal combat with the *Gauche Révolutionnaire,* and in consequence the pace of his speechmaking slackened perceptibly. Although the General Secretary delivered three major speeches primarily devoted to international affairs—in which he reiterated his support of nonintervention and his determination to avoid war, as he said, "at any price"[50]—the publiciz-

[46] *Ibid.,* May 2, 1938.

[47] *Ibid.,* May 9, 1938, and *Le Combat Social* (Allier) , June 5, 1938.

[48] *Le Réveil Populaire* (Aisne) , May 21, 1938.

[49] Blumiste sentiment, as distinct from support for the *Bataille Socialiste,* was definitely in the ascendant in many of these *fédérations*—e.g., the Aude. See the account of the federal congress in *La République Sociale,* March 10, 1938; for the Finistère *fédération,* see the account of its congress in *Le Breton Socialiste,* June 4, 1938; see also *L'Avenir Socialiste* (Rhône) , May 21, 1938; *L'Avenir du Nord,* February 27, 1938.

[50] *La Dépêche Socialiste* (Saône-et-Loire) , March 12, 1938; an address to the so-called Ecole Supérieure Socialiste de Paris, reported in *Le Socialiste,* May 15, 1938; speech to the National Conference of Socialist Youth, published in *Le Cri des Jeunes,* the first number for May, 1938.

ing of his position devolved upon L'Hévéder, Peschadour, Planche, Chochoy, and the editors of the organ *Le Socialiste*. L'Hévéder attributed the tension in Europe not to the dictators but to the "errors of the Treaty of Versailles" and to a general refusal to satisfy Germany's "legitimate need for raw materials"; in the opinion of the popular deputy from the Morbihan, the Congress of Royan should disassociate socialism from those who, he declared, "believe in ideological war," and it should announce that the S.F.I.O. would support a French initiative for negotiations with Germany.[51] While L'Hévéder's statements were perhaps a more extreme manifestation of Fauriste sentiment, Peschadour's declarations were equally categorical and almost as startling: in a widely cited article entitled "Intervention in Spain? NO!" the deputy from the Corrèze asserted that the Communists could afford to sponsor a policy which ran the risk of war because "in a general war the factory workers would remain at their jobs. The peasants would bear the brunt of the fighting."[52]

Camille Planche and the editors of *Le Socialiste* composed separate resolutions on international policy for presentation to the Congress of Royan, but aside from differences in phraseology they were nearly identical. Both refused to accept the view that peace and security could be had by recourse to armaments, and both requested the opening of negotiations with the "fascist" regimes in the hope of securing disarmament and economic agreements.[53] The Planche resolution conceded that nonintervention had not met with complete success, but it went on to recommend a joint Franco-British effort "to end the war in Spain," that is, mediation of the conflict; the resolution of *Le Socialiste* ignored the Spanish question.

Chochoy and his cohorts stepped up their support of Faure's position in *Le Cri des Jeunes,* and the National Conference of Young Socialists enthusiastically adopted a resolution which condemned any alliance designed to encircle any nation and suggested an international accord which would reduce the risk of war

[51] *Le Populaire,* April 4, May 10, 1938.

[52] *La Voix Corrèzienne,* May 1, 1938. Peschadour reaffirmed this conviction in the same journal on June 5, 1938.

[53] *Le Socialiste,* May 15, June 1, 1938; *Le Combat Social* (Allier), June 5, 1938.

by providing for an equitable division of raw materials among all nations.[54]

The *Syndicats* group was not to be left behind in this outpouring of pacifist sentiment: an official editorial, published on March 23—while Blum was still in power—hinted broadly that France should make a declaration of her intent to remain neutral in the event of war. In the same number Froideval suggested that war could be avoided if the C.G.T. spoke "in French and not in Russian," and Marcel Roy accused the Communists of manufacturing what he described as a "war psychosis" in order to prepare France for war "in behalf of a cause which is not her own."[55] The *Anschluss* appears to have increased the desire of the *Syndicats* group for negotiations with Germany: Belin characterized Schuchnigg as "just another dictator," ascribed most of Europe's difficulties to the "odious" Treaty of Versailles, and repeatedly demanded the opening of negotiations with Germany in the interest of securing a general settlement of all outstanding problems. And Liochon, President of the *Fédération du Livre,* declared bluntly that he preferred "peace with Germany and Italy" to war in alliance with "the so-called front of democratic nations."[56]

The reaction by the Fauristes to Blum's sudden reorientation of his international policy, like their position on the Spanish Civil War, received enthusiastic approval from most of the leaders of *fédérations* in departments where socialism constituted an entrenched and powerful electoral force, particularly—but not exclusively—in agricultural areas. In the Languedoc, the leaders of *fédérations* of the Ariège[57] and the Hérault[58] were nearly unani-

---

[54] See the first number for May, 1938, and also an article by Chochoy in *Le Populaire,* April 21, 1938.   [55] *Syndicats,* March 23, 1938.

[56] *Ibid.,* April 6, 13, May 4, 18, 1938. Unlike some of his comrades, Belin did not condemn rearmament and the concept of national defense. He argued that "integral pacifism" would not prevent the unleashing of war, but neither would the preaching of hatred against Germany. His solution was "a negotiated peace before war can occur."

[57] Consult *La Montagne Socialiste* for this period, especially an article by Alexandre Rauzy which appeared on March 6 and in which he argued that France could never have recourse to force because her potential was inferior. See also an article by the same author on April 3, in which he urged immediate negotiations with Germany.

[58] *L'Aube Sociale,* March 12, May 21, 1938.

mous in their opposition to an international policy based upon military alliances, and in the Rhone Valley and in Provence, key figures in the *fédérations* of the Bouches-du-Rhône,[59] Var,[60] and the Vaucluse[61] persisted in speaking of disarmament and negotiation as the only realistic road to peace and took obvious pleasure in accusing the Communists of warmongering. Even in the industrialized areas of the north, Fauriste sentiment was widespread,[62] while in the Socialist stronghold of the Massif Central, Peschadour's undisguised assault on the Soviet Union and his direct appeal to the latent pacifism of the peasantry was greeted with general approval.[63] Socialists in the Lyonnais, with the exception of part of the Rhône *fédération*,[64] were solidly in the Fauriste camp,[65] and in the area designated as Central France, the Fauriste position had many articulate and devoted champions. In numer-

[59] See, for example, the article by Félix Gouin in *La Provence Socialiste*, April 8, 1938.

[60] J. Toesca, the secretary of the *fédération*, claimed in an editorial in *Le Populaire du Var*, March 26, 1938, that many Communists desired war, and this journal carried a headline on May 23, 1938, which read, "To superarm is war, to negotiate is peace."

[61] *Le Réveil Socialiste* published numerous anti-Communist and pacifist articles; see, e.g., the numbers for December 23, 1937, and April 14, 1938.

[62] In the *fédération* of the Nord, Henri Salengro championed the Fauriste position; see, e.g., his article in *Le Peuple Libre*, February 25, 1938, in which he expressed his horror of a "hard policy toward Germany." In the Oise, the deputy Jean Biondi was busy propagating the ideas of Paul Faure: see *Le Cri Populaire de l'Oise*, April 3, 1938.

[63] *Le Petit Limousin*, published in the Haute-Vienne, but designed to appeal to the peasantry in the surrounding departments, was a powerful Fauriste organ. See its lead article of April 30, 1938: "All accords for peace, none for war." Further supporting evidence may be found in *Le Mémorial de Creuse*, May 28, 1938; *Le Socialiste Aveyronnais*, June 5, 1938.

[64] Eugène Gendre, the secretary, and André Février, a deputy, were unqualified in their support of Paul Faure and his policy; see, e.g., Gendre's article in *L'Avenir Socialiste*, May 28, 1938, in which he called for negotiations with Germany. André Philip led the Blumistes in the Rhône.

[65] The Saône-et-Loire *fédération* was unanimous in its support of Faure's international policy: consult *La Dépêche Socialiste*, May 28, 1938, for details of its congress. Arnol still dominated the Isère *fédération;* in the Loire, Pétrus Faure, a deputy, was the most prominent figure in the *fédération,* and he suggested that the Czechs should be prepared to make all concessions in the interests of peace (*Le Courrier de l'Ondaine*, May 28, 1938) .

ous other *fédérations,* geographically scattered but in departments which had exhibited strong sympathies for the S.F.I.O. in the elections of 1936—for example, the Basses-Alpes,[66] Savoie,[67] Indre-et-Loire,[68] and Jura[69]—the Fauriste appeal was rewarded by generous acclaim. Thus, as this very abbreviated survey demonstrates clearly, the pattern of support among the *fédérations,* in the spring of 1938, for the essential aspects of the international policy of the Fauristes coincided with that established in 1936 and 1937 for their Spanish policy.

The *Bataille Socialiste* engaged in the polemics with the righteous conviction that recent international developments had confirmed the validity of its position, and it employed its familiar slogans with renewed vigor. Zyromski increased the tempo of his assault on nonintervention, decried what he derisively characterized as France's "successive capitulations to fascism," and savagely attacked the Fauristes for their "pseudo-pacifist illusions," which, he explained, were at the source of the discord within the S.F.I.O. The leftist leader emphasized the newest slogan in his well-stocked repertoire: the existence of two opposing "ideological blocs" in Europe, he asserted, represented the internationalization of the class struggle; thus negotiations with the "fascist" powers, which could result only in concessions by the "democracies," would constitute a treasonous betrayal of Socialist beliefs

[66] *Le Travailleur des Alpes* published several unmistakably Fauriste articles in this period; e.g., on March 26, 1938, Dr. Goudard, the assistant secretary of the *fédération,* wrote that "it is no longer permissible to send our young to war." Several articles by "André" violently assailed the Communists, attacked the concept of alliances, and equated communism with fascism (December 11, 1937, and January 29 and April 2, 1938).

[67] A. Pringolliet, a former Neo-Socialist, returned to the S.F.I.O. in 1937, and working with the other deputy from the Savoie, Louis Sibué, made the *fédération* clearly Fauriste in its international outlook. Consult *Le Socialiste Savoyard.*

[68] Consult *Le Réveil Socialiste,* November 6, 20, 1937; January 22, May 24, 1938. This *fédération* was virulently anti-Communist; its journal published articles by its secretary which denounced the "fratricidal action" of the Communists in Spain, further characterizing it as "a war to the death on socialism." Nonintervention was approved "with pride" by two congresses of the *fédération.*

[69] *Le Jura Socialiste,* March 26, 1938: "We must subordinate everything to the necessity to keep peace."

and aspirations. Zyromski's supporters demanded that the party support a firm alliance between the "bourgois democracies" and the U.S.S.R., for such an alliance would give force to an "ideological bloc" which already existed.[70]

Although the position of the *Bataille Socialiste* bore external resemblance to that held by the Blumistes, it was much more radical in character: it was more explicit in its demand for an end to nonintervention, gave a very prominent place to unity between Communists and Socialists, and called for the replacement of Daladier by a new Popular Front government, which, with the powerful assistance of the masses, would suppress the Senate and initiate far-reaching economic reforms.[71] Instead of Blum's reluctant espousal of a policy which carried with it the danger of war, the *Bataille Socialiste* welcomed and even exalted this policy as if it were a recognition by the Socialist leader that the class struggle was now transferred to the international arena. Much of this, of course, could have been little more than ideological camouflage or plain wishful thinking, indicative of the continuing need felt by Zyromski and his partisans to conciliate their revolutionary dreams with their demand for a "hard" policy toward Nazi Germany. A revolutionary crisis in France would hardly prepare the nation to withstand Axis aggression, and it is exceedingly unlikely that the *Bataille Socialiste* seriously contemplated such a situation. It seems clear that Zyromski actually wanted to utilize the threat of working-class action to pressure the government into dropping nonintervention and to prevent it from making any concessions to the "fascist" states. On the other hand, the concept of "the internationalization of the class struggle" represented a useful weapon in that it could facilitate the acceptance by the working class of a policy which contained the risk of war, as well as offset the appeal of the antiwar doctrine of the *Gauche Révolutionnaire*.

In the early months of 1938 the *Bataille Socialiste* suffered severe losses to the *Gauche Révolutionnaire* in the *fédérations* of the Seine and Seine-et-Oise, but maintained its firm grip on the

[70] *Le Populaire,* April 2, 28, May 4, 5, 19, 1938.

[71] Resolution presented by the *Bataille Socialiste* to the Congress of Royan, Parti Socialiste S.F.I.O., *XXXVᵉ Congrès National, Compte rendu sténographique* (Paris, 1939), 566–573.

important *fédérations* of the Seine-et-Marne and Gironde, and its energetic spokesmen in the Aisne[72] commanded the allegiance of at least half the Socialists in that department. Otherwise its strength was both scattered and restricted: it was unable to penetrate deeply into such large and strong *fédérations* in industrial areas as the Nord, Pas-de-Calais, Bouches-du-Rhône, or into such medium-size *fédérations* in areas of considerable Socialist electoral success as the Corrèze, Creuse, Haute-Vienne. There were, however, exceptions to this rule, particularly in those *fédérations* where socialism appeared to be declining in the face of a vigorous Communist challenge, such as the Puy-de-Dôme,[73] Drôme,[74] and Rhône,[75] although in none of these *fédérations* did the *Bataille Socialiste* possess a majority. Zyromski's Spanish policy undoubtedly accounted for his remarkable appeal in the *fédérations* of the Basses-Pyrénées,[76] Hautes-Pyrénées, Algiers,[77] and the Landes;[78] similarly, earlier rumblings against nonintervention were translated into open approval of his international policy in the *fédérations* of the Côtes-du-Nord[79] and Ille-et-Vilaine.[80] In numerous other *fédérations* where the *Bataille Socialiste* was represented by

[72] Pierre-Bloch and Bloncourt, both deputies, were the major personalities who supported Zyromski in this *fédération*.

[73] Although *L'Auvergne Socialiste* increasingly criticized nonintervention, Albert Paulin, a deputy and Vice-President of the Chamber, managed to hold the "centrists" together in this *fédération*. At its congress Paulin's compromise resolution won out over the *Bataille Socialiste* by 179 to 52 *mandats*. See *L'Auvergne Socialiste*, June 4, 1938. The deputies Andraud, Villedieu, and Mabrut were Fauristes.

[74] The Drôme *fédération* suffered from serious fragmentation. The deputy René Brunet was an avowed Fauriste, and Marius Moutet was a Blumiste sympathizer. At the congress of the *fédération,* these men supported a compromise resolution.

[75] The Rhône *fédération* was split four ways: at its congress the Blumiste position received 42 *mandats*, the Fauriste, 49, the B.S. 75, and the G.R. 17 (*L'Avenir Socialiste*, June 4, 1938).

[76] *Le Travail*, April 17, 1938.

[77] *Alger Socialiste*, March 12, May 21, 1938. The lead editorial on March 12 warned that the freedom of Algeria was bound up with the fate of the Spanish Republicans.

[78] *Le Travailleur Landais*, November 6, 1937. The congress of the *fédération* unanimously condemned nonintervention.

[79] *Le Combat Social*, April 10, 1938.

[80] *L'Aurore*, February 5, June 18, 1938.

highly articulate and popular personalities, such as in the Aube, Deux-Sèvres,[81] Sarthe,[82] and Haute-Savoie,[83] the *tendance* received powerful support from the rank and file. But, with few exceptions, Zyromski was unable to enlist a bloc of followers among the *fédérations* in departments where Socialism was an entrenched and overwhelmingly powerful political force; his strength was scattered and variable, and he was losing ground to the *Gauche Révolutionnaire*, despite the revolutionary veneer grafted onto his international policy.

Anguished by the National Council's hasty approval of Blum's proposal for a Government of National Union, and fully aware of the implications of Blum's action, Marceau Pivert and his comrades circulated among the *fédérations*, in defiance of an explicit prohibition by Paul Faure, a tract which bore the signature of the *fédération* of the Seine. Entitled "Alert! The Party is in Danger!" it assailed "national union" as a decisive step toward war and a betrayal of the party's heritage and internationalism.[84] Summoned before a session of the C.A.P. on March 30, Pivert declared bluntly that he would continue to circulate the tract, regardless of any decision by the C.A.P., whereupon Faure allegedly retorted that "the G.R. should be shoved out the door."[85] On March 31 the Council of the Seine *fédération* precipitated an open struggle with the C.A.P. by sustaining Pivert's action. On April 11, after Pivert had refused to counsel the *Amicales Socialistes* to encourage a general return to work and had led a demonstration against the Senate in defiance of a ban imposed by Dormoy, the Minister of the Interior, the party's "National Commission of Conflicts" suspended the leaders of the Seine *fédération* from the S.F.I.O. for

[81] Consult articles by Georges Girard in *Le Travail*. This journal loudly denounced what it believed to be France's submission to Great Britain in matters of international policy. See the numbers of March 5, 26, May 7, 1938.

[82] *La République Sociale de l'Ouest*, June 3, 1938. The congress of the *fédération* cast 113 *mandats* for the Zyromski motion to 73 for that of Camille Planche.

[83] Dr. A. Guy, a deputy, was an outspoken supporter of the *Bataille Socialiste* in this *fédération*.

[84] *Juin 36*, 18 March–1 April, 1938; Daniel Guérin, *Front Populaire: Révolution manquée* (Paris, 1963), 207; *Le Populaire*, April 14, 1938; *Le Socialiste*, May 15, 1938.   [85] D. Guérin, *op. cit.*, 208.

their insubordination. The Council of the Seine *fédération* voted overwhelmingly to retain Pivert as secretary; the C.A.P. responded by declaring the *fédération* dissolved.[86] Although the *Gauche Révolutionnaire* was to make a determined effort to have Pivert's suspension countermanded by the Congress of Royan, the *tendance* had been dealt a mortal blow; Marceau Pivert and many of his followers were, in effect, expelled from the Socialist party.

Certainly Pivert's truculent refusal to accept party discipline was not the sole cause of his departure from the S.F.I.O., although his long record of independent action undoubtedly figured prominently among Faure's motives for initiating the suspension. The *Gauche Révolutionnaire* had irritated and embarrassed the party's leadership before—Faure had threatened severe sanctions against the *tendance* in 1937—but perhaps its activities and propaganda during Blum's second "exercise of power," plus Pivert's readiness to circumvent the national Secretariat, simply broke the patience of the General Secretary. In addition, however, there are plausible grounds for believing that Pivert actually welcomed, and even may have sought to provoke, his exit from a party which, as he declared later, had deviated so far from the "revolutionary" path.[87] Daniel Guérin's work suggests that the S.F.I.O.'s acceptance of "national union" rendered impossible any further cohabitation between this doctrine—which Guérin qualifies as "social patriotism"—and that of "revolution," and Lucien Hérard insisted in 1938 that the issue of national union was responsible for the schism. But Guérin's own reflections, and the attempt by the *Gauche Révolutionnaire* at Royan to secure a reversal of the action taken against it, would seem to indicate that Pivert and many of his colleagues were quite reluctant to depart from the

[86] D. Guérin, *op. cit.*, 209; *Le Populaire*, April 14, 1938. Followers of Pivert seized the headquarters of the Seine *fédération*, and Costedoat and Allemane, chosen by Faure to be co-secretaries of the new *fédération*, were compelled to set up their headquarters at the national Secretariat.

[87] Madeline Hérard, Marceau Pivert, and Lucien Hérard, *Rupture nécessaire* (Paris, 1938), 12–15. Pivert argued that the Socialist party had chosen the "nationalist" path, and declared that his was "a painful but *necessary* task: the constitution of a party devoted to class struggle and revolution." (Italics mine.)

Socialist party. The best single explanation is that offered by Guérin: "We had become really dangerous."[88]

Indeed the *Gauche Révolutionnaire* had become dangerous; not only had it conquered the Seine *fédération* and several of the relatively unimportant ones[89]—particularly those in departments where socialism was moribund politically—but it was making inroads into entrenched and politically powerful *fédérations*.[90] This *tendance* was no longer simply a haven for dilettantish intellectuals, nor did it merely attract the discontented; its appeal was beginning to take firm root. What was most striking—and most alarming for the rest of the party—was its undeniable appeal to youth. Daniel Guérin draws a vivid contrast between the youthful and dynamic appearance of the *Gauche Révolutionnaire* delegates to the Royan Congress with that of the "old fossils" who dominated the S.F.I.O.[91] Although documentation is extremely difficult, owing to the absence of records, it seems clear that the large majority of the "Pivertistes" at the local level were quite young, men whose abhorrence of war and disappointment with the failure of the Popular Front to begin the construction of a new society led them directly to the seductive doctrines of the

[88] M. Hérard, M. Pivert, and L. Hérard, *op. cit.,* 19; D. Guérin, *op. cit.,* 172. Guérin declares that he was not convinced that a schism was either beneficial or desirable, and "we neither wanted nor created the schism" (211). But, he adds significantly, the Congress of Royan would have had to condemn "national union" explicitly and categorically in order for the *Gauche Révolutionnaire* to remain in the S.F.I.O.

[89] Based upon the tabulation of the vote at Royan which may be found in the *Compte rendu sténographique,* 612–614, the *Gauche Révolutionnaire* held a majority in the following *fédérations* (the percentages represent the share of the total *mandats* held by the G.R.): Calvados (95%); Cantal (67%); Haute-Loire (79%); Loiret (67%); Maine-et-Loire (65%); Morocco (60%); Meurthe-et-Moselle (67%); Orne (70%); Haute-Savoie (57%); Vendée (52%); Ain (60%).

[90] Again based upon the vote at Royan, the *fédérations* were the Aisne (50%); Côte d'Or (46%); Oise (35%); Seine-et-Oise (48%); Allier (20%); Charente (23%); Charente-Inférieure (25%); Cher (24%); Côtes-du-Nord (25%); Creuse (15%); Hérault (15%); Indre (19%); Jura (44%); Loire (29%); Morbihan (20%); Belfort (24%); Seine-Inférieure (37%); Deux-Sèvres (40%); Somme (36%); Vosges (33%).

[91] D. Guérin, *op. cit.,* 216.

Gauche Révolutionnaire. And in the spring of 1938, that *tend-ance* had a single powerful message: war would be prevented not by alliances, armaments, "national union" or negotiations, but by revolution.[92] Thus the *Gauche Révolutionnaire* was dangerous as well as mutinous: it posed a very real threat to the established leadership in many *fédérations,* and in Paris it was capable of creating incidents which were highly embarrassing to the party. No wonder that the great majority of the party viewed Pivert's departure with relief.[93] Although the last act was to take place at Royan, the *Gauche Révolutionnaire* reached its high-water mark in March and early April, 1938; many of its partisans refused to follow Pivert out of the S.F.I.O., and the faithful who established the Parti Socialiste Ouvrier et Paysan (P.S.O.P.) soon fell prey to the familiar diseases of dogmatism and sterile ideological conflict among themselves.

RETREAT INTO AMBIGUITY: THE CONGRESS OF ROYAN

The thirty-fifth National Congress of the Socialist party convened on the fourth of June, 1938, in an elegant hall located on the outskirts of the resort town of Royan. While such pacific surroundings should have been conducive to reasoned and harmonious discussion, the debates at this congress were marked by unparalleled bluntness and dissonance. For the first time, the increasingly profound division within the Center majority was exposed to public view. But once more conflict was smothered by ambiguity; the resolution adopted by the congress possessed the sole but splendid merit of leaving the unity of the old majority unimpaired—at least superficially. The product of secret, and undoubtedly weary discussion, this resolution was plainly an awkward amalgamation of two contending positions, and a clumsy confession that the Socialist party had, in fact, no international policy.

The problem of the *Gauche Révolutionnaire,* euphemistically

[92] *Juin 36,* May 1, 1938.

[93] In our discussion, Roucayrol related that Faure later regretted the amputation of the *Gauche Révolutionnaire,* because, as he said, "Pivert was close to us on international policy." Guérin denounces Zyromski in his book for the latter's lack of support (205). At Royan, the Blumistes voted to suppress the *Gauche Révolutionnaire.* See the Lebas motion, *Compte rendu sténographique,* 609–610.

referred to on the agenda as "the incidents of the Seine," monopo-
lized the proceedings for the entire first day.[94] On June 5, the
delegates began their consideration of international policy, unquestionably the central issue facing the congress. The crusty
veteran Jean Longuet, attending his last congress, took advantage
of his position as spokesman for the delegation to the Socialist
International to declare that the threat of war over Czechoslovakia and Spain was due to a single problem: the increasingly
blatant nature of "fascist" aggression. Recalling his actions for
peace during the world war, Longuet heatedly denied that anyone
could challenge his pacifist credentials. But, he added passionately, never would he accept "the domination of German militarism in the world"; thus French socialism must resolve to halt the
march of "fascism," by force if necessary.[95]

Longuet was answered, with equal passion, by Jean Le Bail, a
powerful figure of the Haute-Vienne *fédération* and hereafter one
of the major spokesmen for the Fauristes. Le Bail did not mince
his words: using Zyromski as his ostensible target, he identified
the Spanish and international policies of the leader of the *Bataille
Socialiste* with those of the Communists, and declared savagely
that both policies could lead only to war.[96] Since the positions of
Zyromski and Longuet were very similar, Le Bail's attack on
Zyromski was obviously a transparent assault on Longuet and the
Blumistes.

But the speaker who attracted the most attention was Louis
L'Hévéder, who delivered, on the morning of June 6, a complete
and often brutally frank exposition of his ideas. The deputy from
the Morbihan pointed to the tremendous disagreement within the
party over international policy, but he concurred with Longuet's
opinion that the Czechoslovakian and Spanish problems were
closely intertwined. The similarity of views, however, went no
further: both problems, L'Hévéder claimed, would find their solution only within the framework of a general settlement of all
European problems. Describing the belief that these problems

---

[94] The details of the debate on the *Gauche Révolutionnaire* need not
concern us. Sanctions against Pivert and the bureau of the Seine *fédération*
were upheld by a vote of 4,904, to 3,033, with 298 abstentions (*ibid.*,
609–610).

[95] *Ibid.*, 202–203.   [96] *Ibid.*, 283–287, *passim.*

were attributable solely to "fascism" as simplistic and nonsensical, he asserted that Europe's difficulties, which originated with the Treaty of Versailles, were due to the perpetuation of the iniquities and errors of that treaty. L'Hévéder prescribed negotiations as the only alternative to war:

Let us negotiate with the totalitarian states to put an end to the abominable Spanish Civil War. . . .
Peace is a possession so precious that it is worth very great sacrifices. Everything must be done to avoid a general war.

France, he concluded, must recognize the limitations of her resources; no longer could she be "the policeman of Europe." In other words, France must renounce the fiction that she was able to protect her central and east European allies; she must exercise the only option left to her—she must negotiate with, and make concessions to, Nazi Germany.[97]

L'Hévéder's sensational speech opened a period of unrestrained debate—so unrestrained that it threatened to degenerate into an imbroglio. Lévy denounced L'Hévéder's ideas as "dangerous and illogical," and asked how a policy such as his could preserve "our island of democratic liberty" in a Europe dominated by "fascism."[98] Zyromski angrily castigated L'Hévéder's "pseudo-pacifist illusions," which he considered as erroneous as the "revolutionary infantilism" of the *Gauche Révolutionnaire*,[99] and he restated his familiar demand for the construction of a powerful coalition of the "democratic" powers as the only conceivable means of opposing "fascist" aggression. The voluble leader of the *Bataille Socialiste* then paused to enumerate—and to assail—several more "pseudo-pacifist illusions": to deny the existence of "international blocs," he said, making use of his newly manufac-

[97] Longuet interrupted L'Hévéder with the cry "Impossible! . . . this is completely utopian." L'Hévéder responded, amid cheers and laughter, "If we are speaking of utopias, I am quite willing to compare mine with yours!" (*ibid.*, 337–339) . [98] *Ibid.*, 349.

[99] *Ibid.*, 355. "But against international fascism, against the force of the totalitarian states, against their armies and against their fleets . . . do you believe that direct action by the working class is the only adequate means of resistance? Certainly not!"

tured doctrine, was to deny the existence of the class struggle itself, and to refuse to accept the idea of war was fallacious and utopian. "Comrades," he declared to a chorus of howls, "whether you want it or not, war is here, it is a fact . . . *war is here.*" Zyromski remarked with mock astonishment that he was appalled to discover Socialists who could demand peace with all peoples, whatever their political regime; the totalitarian states, he cried, were fundamentally incompatible with any workable and peaceful international community. The speaker concluded with an earnest appeal for Socialist endorsement of a reinforcement of the Franco-Soviet Pact, aid to Republican Spain, and a firm commitment to guarantee Czechoslovakia against aggression; this international policy alone, he said, could save the peace of the world. Zyromski's summation was of unaccustomed eloquence:

Whatever you can say about it [this policy] . . . it means peace for socialism, a peace which respects spiritual, democratic, and national values . . . but if by peace you mean peace in slavery [and] a peace which respects the domination of international fascism, know that there are yet some international Socialists in this party who are opposed to this kind of peace.[100]

After a welcome respite for luncheon, the debate resumed in mid-afternoon. Albert Rivière, deputy from the Creuse and very sympathetic to the Fauriste position, praised L'Hévéder's speech, declaring that his own sentiments were very close to those of the deputy from the Morbihan.[101] Rivière was followed to the rostrum by Lucien Hérard—who was shortly to accompany Pivert out of the S.F.I.O.—the spokesman for the besieged *Gauche Révolutionnaire*. Although hardly a colorful orator like Pivert, Hérard skillfully—if drearily—defended his *tendance* against Zyromski's assault: he acknowledged that once war was unleashed, the general strike was utterly worthless, and he explained that his was the chief argument in favor of preventing war at all costs. On the question of "ideological blocs," Hérard declared that "we fully

[100] *Ibid.*, 366. In a letter to the author, Zyromski declared that he considers this speech to have been the most successful exposition of his ideas during the period 1936–1939.   [101] *Ibid.*, 391–392.

share the view of L'Hévéder," but "we deny the duty of national defense under the capitalist regime." The proletariat, he said, should fight its own battles, not those of its oppressors; once it had seized power in the nation, then, and only then, could it engage in war against the "fascist powers."[102]

But Hérard and his arguments were only of passing interest and of secondary importance; the fate of the *Gauche Révolutionnaire* had already been decided. There followed one of the shortest, but unquestionably one of the most important, speeches of the congress. Camille Planche rose to present his motion. The deputy from the Allier, crippled by wounds received in the World War, was at once an impressive and pathetic figure. Praising L'Hévéder's attitude, which, he announced, must represent that of the majority of the congress, Planche asserted that the concept of opposing blocs was laden with frightful consequences. "What is this 'bloc of democracies' supposed to do," he inquired sarcastically; "will it carry out the provisions of the Treaty of Versailles, or will it offer peace to the world?" For Planche, the way remained open for coexistence, conciliation, and understanding among all nations. The idea of opposing blocs, and the demand for intervention in Spain

implies the acceptance of war. . . . We do not accept war. [Applause.] We will never allow ourselves to be shut up in the dilemma of either fascism or war, for we will risk having both war *and* fascism.

But we say: *neither fascism nor war, but peace!* [Applause.][103]

Planche concluded by reading his resolution and pleading for its adoption.

The hall erupted into bedlam. Salomon Grumbach cried, "This is scandalous! Then it is we who want war?"[104] This was indeed a curious reaction, for Planche simply had restated much

[102] *Ibid.*, 399–402, *passim.*

[103] *Ibid.*, 419–424. (Italics mine.) In brief, Planche's resolutions stated that arms could not assure the maintenance of peace, that the S.F.I.O. could not support any action which would preserve the iniquities of the Treaty of Versailles, and recommended the opening of negotiations on international problems. On Spain, it urged an effort by the "great powers" to put an end to the bloodshed, but it conceded that nonintervention, in its present form, must cease. However, the overwhelming emphasis of this section on Spain was on the necessity to put an immediate end to the fighting.   [104] *Ibid.*, 424.

that Blum had said for years—and had continued to say until the *Anschluss.*

Calm was restored quickly, thanks to a stern warning from the chair and a dull speech by Spinasse. André Philip then took the floor in behalf of a motion cosponsored by Monnet and himself, but which actually reflected the thought of the Blumistes. The Socialist party, Philip declared, must scrupulously avoid two dangers: the first was the Fauriste postion—"an isolationist attitude, which, under the guise of pacifism, goes as far as to say . . . that the essential thing for us is to remain out of a conflict at any price"; the second was the Zyromski position—an outlook which, "under the guise of antifascism, opens the way to . . . a kind of *neopoincarisme.*" Although Philip rejected the notion of two hostile blocs inescapably opposed to each other, he asserted forcefully that the Socialist party must resolve itself to resist the demands of "fascism"—"capitulation must cease!" And while he was not opposed in principle to negotiations with the "fascist" powers, Philip declared that France must be prepared to assist Czechoslovakia against agression and must not permit the travesty of nonintervention to continue.[105]

Although the succeeding speakers sustained the emotional pace set by L'Hévéder, Zyromski, Planche, and Philip, their speeches merely filled a lull between peaks of excitement. Paz, supporting Planche, argued that even a victorious war would retard socialism's development for many years; Zoretti expressed his "profound shock" over Zyromski's speech; Naegelen, speaking in behalf of the lethargic Alsatian *fédérations,* warned that concessions to Hitler would not secure peace; and Bracke expressed his complete solidarity with Zyromski's position. But these speeches were superfluous: a confrontation between Fauristes and Blumistes had taken place. The questions now were: what would be the position of Léon Blum, and would the confrontation lead to an open split of the Center majority?

On the morning of its final day, a nervous congress heard Blum

[105] *Ibid.,* 435–439, *passim.* At the close of the congress Philip admitted that his position was close to that of Zyromski (*ibid.,* 591). The Philip-Monnet resolution also urged that immediate steps be taken to realize the unity of the Socialist and Communist Parties. Monnet claimed that his resolution had 670 *mandats* committed to it. *Ibid.,* 588.

deliver his major address, and once again the leader of the S.F.I.O. conceived his task to be one of conciliation. Blum devoted a lengthy segment of his speech to the Spanish question: he recapitulated the several factors which had figured in the decision to adopt nonintervention, and he confessed that if any possibility still existed that this policy could become a reality it would have his complete support. But, he added firmly, under no circumstances could "the cruel dupery" (a phrase plagiarized from his adversaries) be permitted to persist, and thus *"perhaps* the only pacific reply available to France consists precisely in the official resumption of her freedom [to send arms to Spain]." Then Blum began his tedious effort at conciliation. Turning to L'Hévéder, he warmly seconded the proposition that the Treaty of Versailles bore the ultimate responsibility for Europe's difficulties. Nonetheless, he warned in an uncharacteristically stern manner, one must acknowledge that the immediate responsibility for the threat of war lay exclusively with the Axis, and if freedom and peace were to be preserved, France must accept the risk of war.

L'Hévéder shouted that he would never accept "the idea of war," to which Blum replied evasively that he too did not accept the "idea of war." Blum promised solemnly that he would never forsake the ideals of disarmament and collective security, and that he would never refuse to accept negotiations with the "fascist" states; but, he lamented, the present situation demanded a policy of firmness, and France's role was "to be the bridge between London and Moscow." It was clear that Blum's sympathies were with Philip and Monnet, but he was zealous only in his prudent care not to alienate the Fauristes. Altogether it was an undistinguished performance, climaxed by an emotional appeal for fraternity and unity within the party: "We must," he said pathetically, "have confidence in ourselves."[106]

The commission assigned the onerous task of formulating resolution that would offend the least possible number of Socialists was quite successful. Neither the Fauristes nor the Blumistes were ready to risk a decisive confrontation; Faure and Philip withdrew

---

[106] *Ibid.*, 501–532, *passim*. Blum mentioned the danger of a general war and the harsh fact that any other policy would have dislocated the Popular Front.

their motions in favor of a so-called synthesis resolution. But the *Bataille Socialiste* and the *Gauche Révolutionnaire* were unwilling to surrender their motions in the interest of "fraternity." The resolution adopted by the majority—4,872 *mandats* (60.6%) to 1,735 (21.5%) for that of the *Bataille Socialiste* and 1,430 (17.8%) for that of the *Gauche Révolutionnaire* (see Table 11, pp. 321–325)—was a frank confession of an inability to agree.[107] The "law of the party" was not the product of synthesis but of division; rather than guidance, it offered confusion. Its principal sections read as follows:

The Socialist party wants peace. It will shrink from no effort, from no sacrifice, to avoid war. . . .

In order to build a solid and just peace it will hear any appeal, it is ready for any combat, for any negotiation, notably those which could establish economic cooperation among all peoples.

It proclaims once again that the surest guarantee of peace resides in collective security. That is to say in the binding together of the international community, of which the League of Nations is the necessary organ; in the generalization of pacts of assistance, and in the conclusion of disarmament conventions which are their indispensable complement.

However, the circumstances oblige it to recall that peace is indivisible, and that the will for peace must be reciprocal.

French socialism wants peace, even with the totalitarian imperialisms, but it is not disposed to acquiesce to all of their undertakings. If it should be reduced to this extremity—which it will try to prevent by all means—it will defend the independence of the national soil and the independence of all nations guaranteed by the signature of France.[108]

More specifically with respect to the Spanish drama, it recalls that the policy called nonintervention has had as its essential goal the cessation of the intervention of the totalitarian powers in behalf of the military rebellion. . . . The party declared in its Marseilles resolution

[107] Table 11 (pp. 321–325) is a tabulation of the vote at Royan, arranged by areas in descending order of electoral success in 1936—as in Table 1. It demonstrates clearly that the strength of both the *Bataille Socialiste* and the *Gauche Révolutionnaire* was located primarily in those areas where the Socialist party was weakest electorally.

[108] Faure asserted later that the "real significance" of this statement escaped him (*De Munich à la Ve République*, 55) .

and repeats with force: this state of things [intervention in support of Franco] must cease, primarily because it is revolting to any sense of justice, and because the independence of the Spanish nation is an essential element of the security of France.[109]

Thus the Socialist party would make every sacrifice for peace and would support negotiations with the potential aggressors, but it would defend the independence of France's allies; it condemned Axis intervention in Spain, but merely warned that this must cease; nowhere did it specify whether it accorded primacy to negotiations or to the construction of an antifascist alliance. Such a resolution might have been fully consonant with Blum's international policy prior to the *Anschluss,* for its reflected the dualism and ambiguity so evident in his position; surely it did not correspond to his words and actions since March 10, 1938. The Royan resolution represented neither the firm policy desired by the Blumistes nor the endorsement of pacifism wanted by the Fauristes, but amalgamated both positions into a meaningless resolution on which both groups could justifiably base their future appeal. The significance of the Congress of Royan is not to be found in its majority resolution, nor in its sanction of disciplinary action against the *Gauche Révolutionnaire:* rather it lies in the fact that the latent and increasingly irreconcilable differences between the two groups composing the Center majority over international policy were exposed publicly, and were not resolved. After the Congress of Royan the dispute moved feverishly and inexorably toward its climax; as a consequence of the Sudeten crisis there would be created, in fact if not in name, two Socialist parties.

[109] *XXXVe Congrès National, Compte rendu sténographique,* 578.

5

The Collapse of the
Socialist Party

MUNICH

During the months between the indecisive Congress of Royan and the Sudeten crisis of September, strife within the Socialist party over the critical question of international policy intensified rapidly.

Léon Blum, who had been inactive politically since the fall of his second ministry, spelled out his position with unprecedented clarity. In a flood of articles in the party's daily organ, he declared repeatedly that only the close cooperation of Britain and France with the Soviet Union could thwart the designs of the German dictator: "Today, as twenty-five years ago, it is the menacing progress of German might which threatens peace." Blum described the Franco-Soviet Pact as an essential ingredient in European stability, and warned that abandonment of Czechoslovakia to Hitler would place the fate of *all* of Europe in question. The proletariat, he said with resignation, must be prepared to fight: "We can go no further [in the way of conciliation] for we have gone too far already."[1]

For the party's General Secretary, however, conciliation had not been carried far enough: "We desire," he announced, "a pact with the Devil if necessary!" Faure coupled attacks against the Communists for their "duplicity" with pointed reminders that any policy other than nonintervention in the Spanish affair would lead directly to war. Conveniently recalling Blum's speech at Lyons, he alleged that the unequal division of the world's raw

[1] *Le Populaire,* July 20, 26, August 19, September 2, 8, 9, 1938.

225

materials was a legitimate object of Germany's discontent, and he prescribed international accords to settle this problem, thus eliminating a permanent threat to peace. Since, Faure argued, pointing an accusing finger at the Communists, the Socialist party had never sanctioned the concept of an "ideological crusade," it would support all negotiations with the Axis powers: "The parties that *directed* the Popular Front governments," he noted, "have never denied the right of any people to give itself the government of its choice." Unlike Blum, Faure believed the territorial integrity of Czechoslovakia to count less than the maintenance of peace: "We must find means other than war to settle the Sudeten problem . . . to avoid war is the *most urgent* duty."[2] Clearly, by the beginning of September, 1938, the differences separating the Socialist party's two most prominent figures were so great as to be virtually irreconcilable.

While Blum and Faure were offering contradictory advice to the party, Zyromski was busily propagating his refurbished doctrine of class warfare. In July the leader of the *Bataille Socialiste* published a fiery pamphlet entitled *Comment lutter contre le fascisme international,* which, under the guise of theoretical analysis, was simply a reaffirmation of his familiar demand for a "firm" policy toward the "fascist" powers.[3]

Also in July, Marceau Pivert and many of his partisans[4]—Gué-

[2] *Ibid.,* July 22, 23, 24, August 12, September 3, 1938; speech in the Lot-et-Garonne, reported by *Le Temps,* July 19, 1938, and by *Le Réveil Socialiste* (Lot-et-Garonne) , July 23, 1938.

[3] This pamphlet demonstrated the care taken by Zyromski to preserve his standing as a man of the Left by camouflaging his policy with revolutionary verbiage. He argued that while fascism was assuredly the "terminal period" of capitalism, the workers' movements were still able to operate within the framework of "bourgeois" democracy. Hence the Socialist party should combine all means of democratic action with the use of direct mass action against the "fascist" beast. The struggle against "fascism," Zyromski said, was international in character; thus the proletariat must fight on the same field as the "fascists." Therefore international "ideological blocs" did exist as a result of the increase in the tempo of the class struggle; i.e., the class struggle was now truly international.

[4] Many of Pivert's adherents refused to follow him out of the Socialist party, particularly those who occupied prominent positions in provincial *fédérations,* notably Maurice Deixonne (Cantal), Berthe Fouchère (Oise), and L.-O. Zoretti (Calvados) . In July, Zoretti formed a new *tendance* known as

rin, Collinet, Weil-Curiel, Hélène and René Modiano, Hérard, Cazanave, and Prader—convoked the first congress of the Workers and Peasants Socialist Party *(Parti Socialiste Ouvrier et Paysan, P.S.O.P.)*, among whose leaders, incidentally, figured neither workers nor peasants. *Juin 36,* which became the official organ of the new party, savagely attacked armaments and alliances, and bitterly criticized the Communist party for its "perilous chauvinism," an attitude which, the Pivertistes believed, was designed to rouse proletarian enthusiasm for war. *Juin 36* also accused Blum of preparing for war, and Guérin denounced the idea that war would be a justifiable means of saving Czechoslovakia. Pivert added that "we will be neither dupes nor accomplices to an imperialist war," which, by his definition, meant all wars except "revolutionary" wars. But, despite Pivert's magnetic personality, the P.S.O.P. suffered the fate of most splinter parties, attracting little attention and few adherents. Once excluded from the S.F.I.O., Pivert's influence on its rank and file was negligible.[5]

The frightful crisis of September, 1938, demolished the S.F.I.O. as a viable political entity. Blum and Faure were the principal actors in a ludicrous comedy played out in the pages of *Le Populaire;* these men, spokesmen for socialism since 1920, offered such conflicting counsel that the honest Socialist must have despaired

---

Redressement, which attracted many disciples of the ostracized *Gauche Révolutionnaire.* Its program demanded immediate "structural reforms" in the economy, attacked the futile "parliamentary game," denounced the concept of "national union," assailed the "war economy" which it believed to exist, and refused to approve of a foreign policy based upon alliances. Consult *Le Pays Normand* (Calvados), July 24, 1938.

[5] *Le Temps,* July 18, 1938; Daniel Guérin, *Front Populaire: Révolution manquée* (Paris, 1963), 224–229; *Juin 36,* June 11, July 22, September 10, 1938. The P.S.O.P. recruited most of its adherents from the *fédération* of the Seine. This was the only *fédération* to show a sharp diminution in the number of adherents during 1938. Consult the report of the Secretariat which was submitted to the Congress of Nantes in 1939, published as Parti Socialiste S.F.I.O., *XXXVIᵉ Congrès National, Rapports* (Paris, 1939), 142–143. In the provincial *fédérations* where the *Gauche Révolutionnaire* had demonstrated strength, *Redressement* was able to capture a majority of Pivert's supporters, e.g., the Calvados, Cantal, the Oise. Where *Redressement* possessed no strong personality, as in the *fédération* of the Côte d'Or, its strength was negligible. At the same time, the leaders of *Redressement* engaged in bitter polemics with Pivert.

for the future of his party. Faure at least was consistent, but once again at a critical moment Blum surrendered to his instinctive pacifist reflex and momentarily appeared to support Faure's intransigent pacifist position.

During the first weeks of September it seemed as if Blum would hold fast to his firm position on the Sudeten question: he demanded "strong language from London" and emotionally urged Roosevelt to declare that the United States would stand behind Britain and France in their determination to support Czechoslovakia. Yet Blum greeted Chamberlain's flight to Berchtesgaden as an act of "noble audacity," and upon learning that London and Paris had urged Prague to bow to Hitler's ultimatum, he confessed that he was divided between "a cowardly sense of relief and shame." Nonetheless, two days later Blum protested the failure of France to honor her commitment to the Czechs, and appealing again for a declaration of support from Roosevelt, he vigorously expressed his "indignation and revulsion" over the abandonment of Czechoslovakia. But on September 29, Blum's will faltered: declaring that it would be "a crime against humanity" to break off negotiations, he described the Munich conference as "an armful of wood thrown into the fire at the moment that the fire was dying and in danger of being snuffed out." And on October 1, Blum announced that "there is not a man or woman in France who can refuse to Mr. Chamberlain and Edouard Daladier his just tribute of gratitude."[6]

Paul Faure followed a much less circuitous path to an identical conclusion, and, unlike Blum, his favorable interpretation of the Munich conference was not temporary: he fiercely defended it until the end of his life.[7] During September the General Secretary clamored loudly for negotiations with Germany, and taking care not to conceal his sentiment, he recalled that it was the hated Poincaré who had undertaken France's obligation to Czechoslovakia. The Sudeten problem, Faure argued, could be solved peacefully by "conciliation and concessions," and although the Munich settlement was characterized almost entirely by concessions to the

[6] *Le Populaire,* September 11, 15, 18, 20, 22, 26, 27, 29, October 1, 1938.

[7] *La République Libre,* January 4, 18, 1957; July 11, 1958; Paul Faure, "Les Intrus du capitole" (unpublished ms.), 40–43; Paul Faure, *De Munich à la Ve République* (Paris, 1948), 44.

Führer, he hailed it with unrestrained joy. It was, he declared, "the victory of Peace."[8]

Blum, however, quickly recovered his composure after the shock of being so close to war had dissipated, and was shortly to resume his offensive for a firm policy toward Germany. Nonetheless the crisis itself created serious disarray within the ranks of the Socialist parliamentary group and the C.A.P. At a joint meeting of these two bodies on September 29, held in the absence of Blum, the division of the party became starkly evident. Faure and Zyromski engaged in a tumultuous argument: the former, who was warmly applauded, defended the arguments that he had expressed in *Le Populaire,* while Zyromski assailed the action of the French government and all those who were sympathetic to it, declaring that France should run the risk of war and defend Czechoslovakia, even without British assistance. Very significantly, Moch and Grumbach voiced their support of Zyromski's position, as did a number of former ministers, with the exception of Spinasse and Février.[9]

A similar confrontation between Fauristes and Blumistes took place on October 4, and the Fauristes were unquestionably the victors. The majority of the parliamentary group, acting against the advice of Blum, voted to express its approval of the Munich settlement. Blum performed what he later described as a "painful effort" by informing the Chamber that the Socialists would vote to approve the government's action at Munich, although he tempered the endorsement by demanding that in the future France honor her pledge to protect smaller European nations.[10] Only one Socialist—Jean Bouhey of the Côte d'Or—violated the tradition

---

[8] *Le Populaire,* September 10, 11, 17, 18, 24, October 2, 1938. Faure remarked that "we applauded the Pope for his efforts. We would have applauded the Devil."

[9] *Le Temps,* September 30, 1938; *Le Petit Parisien,* September 30, 1938.

[10] Testimony of Léon Blum in *Les Evénements survenus en France,* I, 258: "I spoke in the name of a group which had just had a singularly ardent debate, where division was profound and bitter. This difficult mission, to take the floor [in the Chamber] not to express a personal sentiment, but that of the majority of the group, I fulfilled . . . but never with a heavier heart."

See also Blum's article explaining his speech in *Le Populaire,* October 13, 1945. In our discussion, Rosenfeld declared that a clear majority of the parliamentary group voted to support the Munich settlement.

of a united Socialist vote and cast his ballot against the government.

A third confrontation followed quickly. This time the scene was a meeting of the C.A.P. on October 5. Zyromski seized the initiative by proposing a resolution condemning the foreign policy of Daladier and Bonnet in unequivocal terms, but withdrew it in favor of a similar motion sponsored by Lévy. Salomon Grumbach declared himself in full agreement with Zyromski and Lévy, but suggested that, in the interest of party unity, no vote be taken. Arnol, speaking in behalf of Faure, speedily concurred with Grumbach's suggestion. A vote was taken on whether a vote should take place on the Lévy motion: fifteen voted no, twelve voted yes, and three abstained. Faure, having failed to secure an absolute majority, performed the ritual of resigning his post as General Secretary, but was easily dissuaded by a unanimous vote urging him to reconsider—and by the fact that the three members who had abstained changed their votes to "no."[11] Then the C.A.P. decided to establish a special commission which would study "the peace policy of the party" and report to a special congress to be held at the end of the year.

Thus the acute problem of international policy was left temporarily in abeyance; unwilling to push the question to a quick decision, Dormoy and Grumbach—but not Blumel, Lebas, and Lévy—tipped the balance in favor of delay. Nonetheless the damage had been done: in three critical instances, the Fauristes had been pitted squarely against the Blumistes—who had received a powerful boost from Zyromski and his partisans. The split of the party's majority, which had been developing over a lengthy period, had occurred with dramatic swiftness under the stress of the

[11] *Le Temps,* October 8, 1938; *Le Populaire,* October 7, 1938. The division was as follows: Voting "no" were Allemane (Fauriste), Arnol (Fauriste), M. Caille (Fauriste), René Chateau (Fauriste), Dormoy (Blumiste), Prieur (Fauriste), Théo-Bretin (Fauriste), Faure, Favier (Fauriste), Gaillard (Fauriste), Granvallet (Fauriste), Graziani (Blumiste), S. Grumbach (Blumiste), L'Hévéder (Fauriste), Charles Pivert (now a Fauriste), Paz (Fauriste), Roucayrol (Fauriste), Chochoy (Fauriste). Voting "yes" were Blumel (Blumiste), Bloch (*Bataille Socialiste*), Dufour (*Bataille Socialiste*), Girard (*Bataille Socialiste*), Jacques Grumbach (*Bataille Socialiste*), A. Laurent (Blumiste), Lebas (Blumiste), Lévy (Blumiste), Veillard (*Bataille Socialiste*), Zyromski, Joublot (*Bataille Socialiste*), Degronde (*Bataille Socialiste*).

Sudeten crisis and Munich. The break was not to be healed by time, discussion, or the evasive tactic of "synthesis"; in fact, the Socialist party had entered into a period of agony which was to culminate in a final and lamentable drama at Vichy in July, 1940.

THE CONFRONTATION SHARPENS

Neither the Blumistes nor the Fauristes were willing to permit the party's internal crisis to simmer quietly, and both camps began to engage in frenzied polemic. Blum himself emerged immediately as the undisguised leader of a *tendance* determined to enlist socialism on the side of a vigorously antifascist international policy. As early as October 8, Blum reasserted his belief that *only* the close collaboration of Britain, France, and the Soviet Union could prevent the threat of further aggression by Germany, and he suggested that the Franco-Soviet Pact receive "its full force and efficacity"—that is, it should be strengthened by the addition of precise military conventions. Blum pleaded for a rapid acceleration of airplane production, condemned categorically the idea that France should negotiate a bilateral accord with Germany on all outstanding differences, and declared that France must retain *all* her pacts of mutual assistance. This time Blum left no doubt as to the depth of his commitment; pacifism, he maintained, must not be equated with submission:

A nation is always able to avoid war. It is even able to do so without any effort, without any risk, provided that it is willing to pay every price demanded of it to keep peace.

Do you believe that socialism can grow and prosper in an international situation which is denuded progressively of every spirit of liberty, of every spirit of human freedom and generosity?[12]

The Blumistes declared their sentiments with unusual frankness. Monnet asserted flatly that Munich was nothing more than a victory of German force which, in fact, could have been prevented had Britain and France demonstrated a will to resist.[13] Auriol characterized the Fauriste position as "flabby sentimentalism,"[14]

[12] *Le Populaire*, October 8, 20, 28, November 1, 2, 14, and December 7, 1938, for the passage cited.   [13] *Ibid.*, November 1, 1938.
[14] *Le Midi Socialiste* (Haute-Garonne), December 15, 1938.

and the crusty Lebas challenged the followers of Paul Faure to have the courage to tell the "truth" about Munich. The settlement, Lebas said, was peace by mutilation; Socialism must revise its international policy and must accept the risk of war by supporting an antifascist coalition of powers, or, he warned, France would be handed over to "fascism."[15] But it was the ex-Renaudelian Marx Dormoy—who had once accused the Soviet Union of pursuing a "tsarist" foreign policy—who stated the Blumiste case most succinctly:

Peace at any price is inevitably war at any price. . . . I know that they say to us "a bad peace is better than war." [This is] pure sophistry. A bad peace never assures peace, it only prepares for war. . . . We will find peace by justice and by force. Alas! Yes, force. For those who oppose us will yield only to that. They are ignorant of reason, they laugh and mock at law. . . . Let us look at things as they are and not as we wish to see them. Fascism is a reality, Germany's dream of hegemony is a reality. It is futile to bury our heads in the sand.[16]

The *Bataille Socialiste* greeted the post-Munich developments within the party with undisguised glee, for its leaders correctly recognized that the increasingly bitter dispute between Blumistes and Fauristes was creating a situation which conceivably could make their *tendance* the decisive force in the S.F.I.O. Without hesitation, Zyromski rallied the *Bataille Socialiste* to the Blumistes; stripped of its revolutionary veneer, Zyromski's international policy was now virtually identical with that of his allies. In addition to supporting Lévy's proposal on October 5, Zyromski swung his forces behind Blum's idea of "national union," declaring that it was an absolute necessity in the struggle against Germany.[17] Finally, Zyromski gave his full endorsement to the resolu-

---

[15] *L'Avenir du Nord,* October 9, 16, 1938; *La Bataille Ouvrière* (Nord), November 13, 1938; and *Le Populaire,* October 29, 1938.

[16] *Le Populaire,* November 3, 1938. Faure singled out this article as typical of the "bellicose mentality" of the Blumistes in *De Munich à la Ve République,* 55.

The Blumistes also launched an organ, *La Paix Socialiste.* The contributors to the December, 1938, issue—which apparently was the only one to appear—were Auriol, Monnet, Dormoy, and Sérol (deputy from the Loire).

[17] Zyromski called for the "maintenance and development" of the Franco-Soviet Pact, rejected any entente between France and Germany, and reiter-

tion submitted by Léon Blum for consideration by the special
party congress, and, in effect, adopted it as his own.[18]

After Faure's outburst of jubilation over the outcome of the
Munich conference, his name virtually disappeared from the
pages of *Le Populaire,* and although in October and early November he was campaigning for a seat in the Chamber in a by-election
in the Saône-et-Loire—which he won—his activities were conspic-
uously ignored by the party's organ. Yet this may have been partly
of the General Secretary's own choosing: while his able and vocal
lieutenants were propagandizing freely in behalf of his position
on international policy, Faure himself was increasingly reluctant
to clash with Blum personally. The aftermath of Munich made it
starkly apparent to Faure, perhaps for the first time, that his
position was in direct conflict with that of the man with whom he
had cooperated for eighteen years. His dilemma was both practical and personal: could he, for the sake of his beliefs, risk splitting
permanently a party which had been so laboriously constructed
and which had become only recently the largest party in the
Chamber? Faure had no desire to see Blum replaced as leader of
the party: when Blum threatened to retire from public life if his
policy was not accepted by the Congress of Montrouge, Faure
immediately withdrew his own resolution, and agreed to resubmit
it only after Blum had pledged to remain as leader whatever the

---

ated his belief that the risk of war must be accepted. He warned against a
"new Munich" over Spain, and urged Britain and France to insure the
independence of the Spanish Republic, although this was a step the Blumistes
were not prepared to take. *Le Populaire,* October 16, 24, 27, December 21,
1938. Consult also an article in a similar vein by Bracke in the same journal
on November 3, 1938.

[18] *La Vie du Parti,* supplement to *Le Populaire,* November 29, 1938. Blum's
resolution for the Congress of Montrouge contained the following major
provisions: (1) a pledge that the S.F.I.O. would participate in national
defense; (2) a demand that no concessions be made to Germany under the
threat of war; (3) a request that France's military forces be increased; (4) the
acceptance by the party of mutual assistance pacts; (5) a guarantee that all of
France's existing mutual assistance pacts would be supported by the party;
(6) a demand that the French government not tolerate the domination of
"strategic areas" by possible adversaries; and (7) a declaration that the party
was not opposed in principle to an international conference which would
discuss all outstanding problems.

result of the congress.[19] But worried as he was about a split in the party, Faure was even more anguished by what he believed to be Blum's double denial—of traditional Socialist beliefs and of himself. Faure could not comprehend, and was never able to comprehend, why Blum had "changed." Perhaps Faure allowed himself to be misled, over a period of years, by Blum's pacifist rhetoric, or perhaps, consciously or unconsciously, he ignored much else that Blum had said since 1933; more likely, Faure was imprisoned by his own beliefs. Just prior to the Congress of Montrouge, he lamented:

We want to understand. We have demonstrated our loyalty to Blum. . . .

We remained faithful throughout the "pause." . . . We recall our action in a certain National Council which approved the participation of our party in the Chautemps government. What of our attitude when Blum asked for approval of "national union"?

Léon Blum, the traditional arbiter of differences in the party, has taken sides in the struggle. His old friends are against him. His new allies? The militants of the *Bataille Socialiste*. . . .

Are we going to break with the tradition of Socialism? Are we going to break with its most recent decisions? Are we unfaithful to the ideas of our teachers when we condemn ideological blocs and preventive wars?

Our guide? Here he is: "Everything to avert the present and future risk of war. I refuse to consider war as possible today because it might be necessary or inevitable tomorrow. War is possible only when one admits it to be possible; inevitable only when one proclaims it to be inevitable."—Léon Blum at Luna Park, September, 1936.[20]

Faure's supporters, however, exhibited no enthusiasm for emulating the cautious behavior of their mentor. *Le Socialiste* did not merely praise Munich and preach the futility of war; it unleashed

[19] *Le Populaire*, December 17, 1938. Moch made Blum's intentions known, and the news spread quickly throughout the party. A letter from Faure and Sévérac compelled Blum to confirm the rumor. Although Blum agreed to remain as head of the parliamentary group, he added that a defeat at the congress would make his task "very difficult." While on the surface this appears to have been a bit of crude blackmail, Blum's decision was certainly genuine and quite realistic.

[20] *Ibid.*, December 18, 1938; *Le Socialiste*, December 1, 1938.

a systematic and highly vitriolic assault on the Communists, sparing no effort to demonstrate that the Communists wanted war. The Blumistes escaped being labeled warmongers, but it was openly stated that their policy would lead to war. Early in September *Le Socialiste* had carried a banner headline which expressed without equivocation the sentiments of the Fauristes: "Universal massacre to save the Czechs? NO, M. Thorez!" Shortly after the Munich conference, an editorial denounced what its author considered to be the "capitulation" of some Socialists to the "war party," that is the Communists, and in the same number a leading article characterized *La Bataille Socialiste* as a *"Stalino-belliciste"* journal.[21] Séverac, who described the Soviet Union as "no less totalitarian than Germany," openly advocated the abrogation of the Franco-Soviet Pact,[22] while one of his lesser known colleagues castigated those Socialists who had, he said, adopted the Communists' foreign policy as their own.[23] As the Congress of Montrouge drew near, the tempo of the Fauriste attack increased: "Peace is the supreme goal of our party. We will capitulate neither to Berlin nor to Moscow," declared a headline in *Le Socialiste*.[24] Thus for the Fauristes there was a single task facing socialism: the prevention of a war desired by the Communists, who were aided consciously by unscrupulous Socialists (the *Bataille Socialiste*) and unwittingly by errant Socialists (the Blumistes). War, the Fauristes believed, could result only in servitude either to "fascism" or to Communism.

While it was a simple matter to declare that war must be prevented, and easy to indulge in the popularization of such slogans as "Stalin is ready to fight . . . until the last French soldier!"[25] or "Youth is made to live, not to be cannon fodder"[26] or simply "War resolves nothing,"[27] the means by which war could

[21] *Ibid.,* September 15, October 15, December 15, 1938.

[22] *Le Populaire,* October 26, 1938. Séverac recommended "good relations with all, alliances with none." *Le Socialiste,* November 1, 1938; *La Vie du Parti,* supplement to *Le Populaire,* November 29, 1938.

[23] Jarjaille in *Le Socialiste,* November 15, 1938.

[24] *Le Socialiste,* November 15, 1938.

[25] Jean Le Bail in *Le Populaire du Centre* (Haute-Vienne), September 28, 1938.

[26] Chochoy in *Le Cri des Jeunes,* second number for October, 1938.

[27] Séverac in *Le Populaire,* October 26, 1938.

be prevented was a lively subject of discussion among the Faur-istes. The more extreme view was advanced by L'Hévéder, who considered a Franco-German entente to be the most satisfactory way to avoid war.[28] Others took refuge in vague and general suggestions: Arnol voiced his approval of "any gesture of appeasement,"[29] and Roucayrol asked for "any and all negotia-tions."[30] In late November, however, a statement of policy was drawn up by Allemane, Arnol, René Brunet (deputy from the Drôme and a friend of Georges Bonnet), Faure, L'Hévéder, Paz, Roucayrol, and Séverac.[31] Although couched in very general terms, it contained eight fundamental points. It declared: (1) that the Socialist party was *the* party of peace, for it had always been in the vanguard of the demand for Franco-German under-standing; (2) that Munich represented a temporary halt to the slide toward war, and that the respite must be used to ensure permanent peace; (3) that French socialism would defend the nation, its independence, and its liberties; (4) that "fascism" could not be fought by war; (5) that collective security would be achieved only by disarmament and through the League of Na-tions; (6) that France could not disarm unilaterally; (7) that France should seek negotiations on all subjects with all nations; (8) and finally, that France should take the initiative for the settlement of all international disputes.

This statement was submitted by the Fauristes for approval by the Congress of Montrouge as the party's international policy. But more significant than its declarations were its omissions and its vagueness: it made no mention of the proper scope of negotiations or of the extent of the concessions required to secure agreements, and it ignored the thorny problem of alliances. Thus, while the Fauristes based their formal appeal to the party on this very general resolution, the real basis of their appeal lay in their hostility to France's alliances and to the Soviet Union, and in

[28] *Le Rappel du Morbihan,* October 1, 8, 22, December 3, 1938; *Le Popu-laire,* October 31, December 22, 1938.

[29] *Le Droit du Peuple* (Isère), December 10, 1938.

[30] *Le Populaire,* December 13, 1938.

[31] *La Vie du Parti,* supplement to *Le Populaire,* November 29, 1938. The resolution received the immediate approval of sixty-five Socialist deputies.

their undisguised willingness to make further concessions to Germany.[32]

The newly born Workers and Peasants Socialist party also was disrupted by the Sudeten crisis. One minority group, led by Hélène Modiano, took refuge in a pacifism which refused to accept any kind of war, while another minority, led by Weil-Curiel, leaned toward Zyromski's position. The majority approved Pivert's injunction to fight against both "an imperialist war and a fascist peace"; Pivert assailed the "bellicose current" within the S.F.I.O., and Collinet described Czechoslovakia as an "imperalist bastion" of the French General Staff.[33] Like the Fauristes, the leaders of the P.S.O.P. became convinced that Stalin was determined to provoke a war between France and Germany.[34] Collinet argued that a war over Czechoslovakia would result in a situation from which only Stalin could benefit.[35] The sole means to avoid war and "fascism," the Pivertistes maintained, was revolution. But, weakened by internal dissension, the P.S.O.P. was in no

---

[32] The section of the *Syndicats* group within the C.G.T. closely paralleled that of the Fauristes within the S.F.I.O. At the height of the September crisis Delmas circulated a petition entitled "We do not want war," which received the signature of some Fauristes—Allemane, Paz, Caille, Prieur, Costedoat, Lazurick, and Desphelippon. *Le Peuple* refused to publish the petition, and it finally appeared in *L'Oeuvre*.

Syndicats published fiercely pacifist articles by Belin—e.g., on October 5 and 19, 1938—and a number of highly inflammable editorials by Froideval. The latter declared that "some members of the C.G.T. approve the war policy of one political party. They want war to permit the establishment of a European Soviet state. The French do not want to fight for Stalin" (October 12, 19, 1938). Delmas, who assured his readers that "most of the Sudeten residents went joyfully into the *Reich*" (*Le Peuple*, October 11, 1938), submitted a resolution to the Nantes Congress of the C.G.T.—which was signed by the Socialists Zoretti, Roy, and Legay—which urged further negotiations with Germany (*Le Peuple*, October 27, 1938). This resolution received 27 per cent of the total vote at the Congress (*Le Peuple*, November 16, 1938). Notable also is the fact that a banquet held by *Syndicats* in early October had as its honored guests the Socialists Allemane, Garchery (deputy from the Seine), and Costedoat, plus Marcel Déat! (*Syndicats,* October 19, 1938).

[33] *Juin 36,* September 30, November 11, 1938.

[34] Daniel Guérin, *Front Populaire, Revolution manquée,* 235.

[35] *Juin 36,* September 30, 1938.

position to exert any influence on the struggle that was taking place in the Socialist party.

More important was the motley assortment of individuals who created the new *tendance* known as *Redressement*. Essentially this group was composed of Pivertiste remnants and members of the almost forgotten *tendance* called *La Révolution Constructive*. The principal figure and moving force of *Redressement* was L. O. Zoretti, leader of the Calvados *fédération,* professor at the University of Caen, and a well-known figure in the Teachers Union, who exhibited unmistakable signs of antisemitism.[36] In cooperation with Deixonne, Berthe Fouchère, and Albertini (of the Aube *fédération*), Zoretti offered a resolution for consideration by the Montrouge Congress. It stated: (1) that Munich had saved peace, at least for the time being; (2) that French socialism should condemn the idea of a "democratic bloc" of powers, since none existed; (3) that arms and alliances constituted the principal threat to peace; (4) that collective security was impossible within the framework of capitalist society, but until the world was free of the capitalist yoke, hopes for peace resided in the attainment of international agreements; (5) that if war should erupt, socialism should make every effort to localize the conflict; (6) that the present conflict was between "democracy" and "despotism" (the U.S.S.R. was assigned to this category); (7) and that the peoples of the "despotic" nations must liberate themselves without outside assistance. Actually this resolution was much closer in spirit to that sponsored by the Fauristes than to the teachings of Marceau Pivert: it de-emphasized the prospects for revolution and concentrated on the prevention of war by an international conference and disarmament.[37]

Thus the Congress of Montrouge promised to be the most momentous congress since that held at Tours in 1920. It was to be compelled to choose between two contrary concepts of international policy—the Blumiste and the Fauriste. The resolutions offered by *Redressement* and by an ephemeral group known as

[36] Zoretti allegedly wrote in *Le Pays Normand* that Blum was willing to sacrifice millions of lives "in order to make things more comfortable for the Jews." See *La Lumière,* September 30, 1938.

[37] *La Vie du Parti,* supplement to *Le Populaire,* November 29, 1938; *Redressement,* December 1, 1938.

Integral Pacifists,[38] and two "synthesis" resolutions,[39] were of secondary importance. An accommodation between the major rivals appeared to be decidedly unlikely: the bitter public polemics and the acrimonious debates at a session of the National Council in November[40] had greatly widened the breach between them, and

---

[38] *La Vie du Parti,* supplement to *Le Populaire,* November 29, 1938. The unknown Nadia Gulkowski (sometimes spelled Gukowski) of the Loiret *fédération* offered this ultra-pacifist resolution which demanded that France disarm.

[39] One of these "synthesis" resolutions was offered by Etienne Weill-Raynal, who was supported by Albert Rivière and Thiolas (deputy from the Haute-Loire). Very close to the Fauriste position, it (1) accepted national defense; (2) stated that the S.F.I.O. was not bound by any treaties negotiated "outside of democratic forms and procedures"; (3) denounced the Czechs for violating the principle of self-determination, but conceded that a plebiscite should have taken place before the Sudeten areas were annexed by Germany; (4) stipulated that France's obligations under pacts of mutual assistance should be fulfilled only if the adversary of the power to which France was allied should refuse arbitration; and (5) envisaged the eventual renunciation of the Franco-Soviet Pact *(ibid)*.

The other synthesis resolution, introduced by the *fédération* of the Nord, was much closer to the Blum resolution. It (1) acknowledged that the threat to peace was due to the aggressive desires of the "fascist" powers; (2) stated that France must not permit herself to be isolated, and thus the party must support all pacts that had been democratically approved by parliament and had not been the object of a hostile vote by the party; and (3) declared that France must retain close relations with the Soviet Union and Great Britain *(La Bataille* [Nord], November 27, 1938).

[40] *Le Populaire,* November 6, 7, 8, 1938. No vote was taken on international policy, although a vigorous debate took place on this subject. As a sample of the character of the debate: Monnet praised the Communists for their attitude toward Munich, and denounced Séverac for recommending that France play the role of a third-rate power; Lévy said that no danger of war had existed in September, declaring that Hitler was ready to yield at the first sign of Anglo-French firmness. For the Fauristes, Paz asserted that during the crisis only Faure's articles in *Le Populaire* represented Socialist thinking, and noted that "war is stupid in general, and stupid for Czechoslovakia in particular"; Le Bail announced that all the deputies from the Haute-Vienne would vote against a declaration of war. Zyromski demanded a policy of "national union" and warned that a bilateral pact with Hitler would give Germany a free hand to act against the U.S.S.R.

The major issue in the area of domestic policy during this period was Daladier's move toward the Right, demonstrated by Reynaud's attempt, as Minister of Finance, to reintroduce strict financial orthodoxy and to secure

the work of the commission charged by the C.A.P. with reassessing the party's international policy simply had revealed the extent of their differences. The long germinating struggle, brutally ripened to maturity by the events of September, 1938, at last appeared to have reached its denouement.

THE CONGRESS OF MONTROUGE

The congress convened on the day before Christmas in the drab and drafty *mairie* of Montrouge. After a dull welcoming speech by the Socialist Mayor, the delegates were jolted by a proposition from the *fédération* of the Loir-et-Cher which recommended, "in order to avoid a difficult debate," that the question of international policy be referred to a special commission. The specter of the familiar "black-white" resolution had reared its head early in the proceedings, much to the distress of Zyromski, who asserted, quite justifiably, that the S.F.I.O. had no foreign policy, and warned that the party must make an unequivocal choice between the two principal motions.[41] Rumors were rife that Faure was behind the maneuver by the Loir-et-Cher *fédération* in the hope that he could isolate Zyromski and persuade Blum to settle for an innocuous resolution. Against the advice of Dormoy—who, as one observer noted, acted as if he were already General Secretary[42]— Blum agreed to the selection of a commission, but pledged that there would be no equivocation whatever on basic issues. The congress followed Blum's lead, and voted, by a wide margin, to place the question of international policy in the hands of a commission composed of thirty-three members.[43]

---

a modification of the forty-hour law. Blum and Faure united to denounce Daladier's actions, demonstrating their belief that the S.F.I.O. still counted as a powerful political force.

[41] *Le Populaire,* December 25, 1938. No official *Compte rendu sténographique* was ever published for this congress, and those responsible for the archives of the S.F.I.O. declare that the original stenographic account has disappeared.

[42] *Redressement,* February 1, 1939.

[43] *Le Populaire,* December 25, 1938. Places on the commission were assigned by proportional representation, i.e., according to the number of *mandats* pledged to each motion. Thus the Blum motion was represented by fifteen delegates; the Faure motion had nine delegates; the Nord "synthesis" resolution was assigned five places; the Weill-Raynal resolution was given two representatives; and the *Redressement* motion one.

The commission vanished behind closed doors for two days, while the rest of the delegates were abandoned to their own devices. At one point the exasperated presiding officer pleaded for speakers to address the congress, only to be rewarded by an anonymous voice which suggested that the congress be entertained by Tino Rossi recordings. Late in the afternoon of the second day, Séverac emerged furtively from the conference room to ask postponement of the commission's report until the next morning. His request was greeted by derisive shouts—"this is a comedy, not a congress"[44]—and several angry delegates demanded that the debate begin at once. Finally, however, with the aid of Dormoy, Séverac was able to secure acceptance of his request.

Obviously the only discussions of any consequence took place outside the public view. Fortunately one member of the commission, Georges Albertini, who sat as a representative of *Redressement,* kept a record of the proceedings and of his impressions, and Faure briefly described a key incident in the debates in his memoirs.[45] Evidently Lévy opened the first session with a belligerent demand that the Fauristes accept two preconditions, or else no agreement was possible. First, the party must state its commitment to the concept of collective security by mutual assistance pacts; second, it must reaffirm its fidelity to the Franco-Soviet Pact. A sharp exchange ensued, in which, according to Albertini, "the Franco-Soviet Pact preoccupied everyone."[46] Blum allegedly admonished the Fauristes for imitating the arguments of the "fascist" regimes, and, vocally seconded by Grumbach and Zyromski, he forcefully reaffirmed his complete acceptance of the Franco-Soviet Pact, declaring heatedly that he would not compromise on this question. Zyromski asserted that no international conference could take place until the Germans and Italians had been expelled from Spain, and Blum made no sign of disapproval. Late in the evening of the first day's session, news was leaked to the congress to the effect that Lebas fully accepted Lévy's two conditions and that the commission had voted, eighteen to eleven, with

---

[44] *L'Oeuvre,* December 26, 1938.

[45] *Le Pays Normand* (Calvados), February 5, 1939; Paul Faure, *De Munich à la Ve République,* 56.

[46] Albertini in *Le Pays Normand,* February 5, 1939. Unless otherwise noted, the account of the session is Albertini's.

four abstentions, to include them in the final draft resolution.[47] Shortly afterward the commission adjourned until the next morning.

When discussion resumed on Christmas morning, the Fauristes still clung to the lingering hope that a compromise might yet be attained. Blum buoyed this hope by offering a conciliatory text: the Socialist party, he said, should insist "on the need for France to maintain a close community of action with British democracy, and prepare the *rapprochement* of the British and American democracies with Soviet Russia for the preservation of peace." Faure argued in his memoirs that he proposed that the phrase "in order to realize the *rapprochement* of all peoples for the construction of peace" be inserted after the mention of Soviet Russia.[48] Albertini, however, noted that Faure asked that the phrase "with Soviet Russia for the preservation of peace" be stricken and that his phrase be placed after the word "democracies." No matter which version is closer to the truth, the difference between Blum's formula and that suggested by Faure was fundamental: Blum's would have committed socialism to support of an alliance resolved to resist "fascist" aggression; Faure's would have placed socialism on record as favoring negotiations with, and concessions to, the "fascist" powers. After a long discussion, Blum and his partisans retired to an adjoining room to consider Faure's proposal; forty minutes later Faure was told that Blum, despairing of compromise, had decided to present his motion to the congress. After thirty-six hours of squabbling, the effort to find a "synthesis" had failed.

The first working session of the congress opened on the morning of December 26 in an atmosphere of tension. Albertini announced that the *Redressement* motion was being withdrawn, and he instructed its supporters to cast their *mandats* for Paul Faure's resolution. Arnol angrily charged that Blum had made no effort to reach a compromise, and he cried that acceptance of Blum's

[47] *L'Oeuvre*, December 26, 1938; *Le Temps*, December 26, 1938. The majority consisted of the fifteen supporters of the Blum resolution plus three of the representatives of the Nord resolution: Lebas, Laurent, and Lagrange. The minority vote was cast by the Fauristes plus Deixonne and Albertini, and the abstentions were by Thiolas, Rivière, Chochoy, and Pantigny.

[48] Paul Faure, *op. cit.*

motion would encourage the development of a "war psychosis" in the nation, which could benefit only the Communists. Félix Gouin hailed the "immense role" played by Faure in the history of the party, and after reading Faure's resolution to the congress, concluded with a ringing appeal for its adoption.[49]

Shortly before noon Blum rose to read his resolution and to deliver his major speech. In an address that consumed well over two hours, Blum sought, with his habitual honesty and introspection, to soothe the disquiet that he knew to exist in the minds of many delegates. Consequently the speech was frankly defensive and highly emotional. Blum admitted that he had determined to retire from public life after the death of his wife, but acknowledged that he had been dissuaded by the thousands of encouraging messages that he had received from the rank and file. This outpouring of confidence, he said, had bolstered the great pride that he had always felt from knowing that he possessed the trust of the party. But, Blum declared, his conscience forbade him to remain silent on the grave problem of international policy, and recognizing that his own arguments were being used against him in the present debate, he asked, "Why have I changed?" Strenuously denying that he was influenced by the wave of virulent antisemitism in Germany, and repudiating the allegation that his thought had undergone a profound metamorphosis, Blum told the congress bluntly that socialism must recognize realities. France must commit herself to a policy of alliances or face the barren alternatives of capitulation or war. Turning to the Fauristes, he said sternly: "There is something that dominates everything. You are going to leave Germany free to act in central and eastern Europe. But are you certain that afterward a stronger Germany will not turn against you?"[50]

Blum had singled out the most sensitive and critical issue: the attitude of the Fauristes toward the Soviet Union. His euphemism "central and eastern Europe" could have deceived very few of his listeners: he was accusing his opponents of being willing to abandon not only Poland, Yugoslavia, Hungary, and the rump Czecho-Slovak state, but also the U.S.S.R. And for Blum, abandon-

---

[49] *Le Populaire,* December 27, 1938.
[50] Léon Blum, *L'Histoire jugera* (Paris and Montreal, 1945), 202.

ment was entirely unacceptable; no compromise was possible on this question. He concluded with an appeal to every Socialist to take stock of his conscience, to make himself aware of the frightening realities of contemporary Europe, and to realize that heavy sacrifices must be made for peace.

Late in the afternoon the General Secretary appeared at the rostrum and was greeted by prolonged shouts of *Vive la Paix!* Faure's speech was brief. Admitting that his resolution would fail to achieve a majority, he pledged that he would accept party discipline without any hesitation. Ignoring Blum's accusation concerning his attitude toward the Soviet Union, Faure asserted that there existed a close parallel between 1914 and 1938; instead of the Hohenzollerns and Hapsburgs, he said, there was Hitler. "Then why should socialism need different tactics?" he inquired with simplicity, and cried, "There is no merit in being a pacifist in untroubled times, but there is now, when war threatens us!" In conclusion he summarized his position, and added: "We preferred nonintervention to war; we also preferred Munich to war."[51]

After an abortive final effort to secure a synthesis resolution by Pantigny and Thiolas, the congress voted. The Blum resolution received 4,322 *mandats* or 52.9 per cent of the total, Faure's received 2,837 or 34.7 per cent, and there were 1,014 abstentions or 12.4 per cent.[52] The Blumiste–*Bataille Socialiste* coalition had emerged victorious; the congress had confirmed that a new majority had been created.[53]

Blum had stood firm and had won a narrow victory. But his triumph was deceptive: rather than a genuine acceptance of his international policy, the decision of the Congress of Montrouge

---

[51] *Le Populaire,* December 28, 1938.   [52] *Ibid.,* December 27, 1938.

[53] The concluding session of the congress was devoted to domestic policy, and in this instance the Fauristes were the victors. Blum, who either was afraid that his victory on international policy, if coupled with a reaffirmation of his policy of "national union," would alienate the Fauristes entirely, or believed that "national union" would not be endorsed by the congress because of Daladier's domestic policies, swung his support to a resolution offered by Roucayrol. This motion condemned the deflationary policy of the government and opposed the constitution of a "national union" government unless it was based upon "a clearly republican majority." This resolution was adopted, 7,076 to 910 for a motion offered by Deixonne, which called for the dissolution of the Chamber.

was essentially a striking personal success for the venerable party leader. Assuredly there were several ingredients in his victory formula: Blum had forged a majority coalition which included his former critics, the *Bataille Socialiste,* and in addition he had profited from the hesitancy of his opponents. But in substance Blum's success was due less to the combination of the appeal of his policy, the strength of supporters, and the timorousness of his adversaries, than to his immense prestige and his scarcely veiled threat to retire from public life. Blum's triumph, then, was not conquest: he had failed to alter the sentiments of most of the party's parliamentary group[54] and of the secretaries of the *fédéra-*

[54] Eighty-six Socialist deputies either signed the Faure resolution or publicly indicated their support of it; only twenty-nine signified their support of the Blum motion. The remainder either favored a "synthesis" or were silent. On the basis of my research, especially in local Socialist journals, the deputies favoring the Faure resolution or a synthesis barely distinguishable from it were: Albertin (Bouches-du-Rhône), Allemane (Seine), Andraud (Puy-de-Dôme), Arbeltier (Seine-et-Marne), Audeguil (Gironde), Arnol (Isère), Barthélemy (Seine), Beaugrand (Loir-et-Cher), Bèche (Deux-Sèvres), Bedin (Dordogne), Berlia (Haute-Garonne), Biondi (Oise), Blanchet (Creuse), Boulay (Saône-et-Loire), Brunet (Drôme), Buisset (Isère), Burtin (Saône-et-Loire), Cabannes (Gironde), Castagnez (Cher), Chasseigne (Indre), Chaussy (Seine-et-Marne), Chouffet (Rhône), Coulaudon (Puy-de-Dôme), Debrégeas (Haute-Vienne), Dubois (Oran), Dupont (Eure), Esparbès (Haute-Garonne), Pétrus Faure (Loire), Février (Rhône), Fié (Nièvre), Froment (Ardèche), Garchery (Seine), Gardiol (Basses-Alpes), Gouin (Bouches-du-Rhône), A. Gros (Jura), Guerret (Tarn-et-Garonne), Hussel (Isère), Jordery (Rhône), Larguier (Gard), Lazurick (Cher), Lefèvre (Charente-Inférieure), Lejeune (Somme), LeMaux (Côtes-du-Nord), L'Hévéder (Morbihan), Mabrut (Puy-de-Dôme), Maffray (Indre-et-Loire), Majurel (Hérault), Malroux (Tarn), H. Martin (Marne), Meunier (Indre-et-Loire), Morin (Indre-et-Loire), Naphle (Gironde), Nouelle (Saône-et-Loire), Noguères (Pyrénées-Orientales), Peschadour (Corrèze), Planche (Allier), Pringolliet (Savoie), Quinson (Ain), Rauzy (Ariège), Ravanat (Isère), Régis (Alger), Riffaterre (Creuse), Rivière (Creuse), Roche (Haute-Vienne), Roldes (Yonne), Rolland (Finistère), Roucayrol (Hérault), Hubert-Rouger (Gard), Roumajon (Corrèze), Roux (Saône-et-Loire), Saint-Martin (Gers), Saint-Venant (Nord), Salengro (Nord), Sibué (Savoie), Silvestre (Gard), Soula (Ariège), Spinasse (Corrèze), Tessier (Haute-Vienne), Thivrier (Allier), J.-M. Thomas (Saône-et-Loire), Vidal (Bouches-du-Rhône), Villedieu (Puy-de-Dôme), Vardelle (Haute-Vienne), Voirin (Ardennes), Vaillandet (Vaucluse), Vantielcke (Pas-de-Calais).

The deputies who supported the Blum motion or the Nord synthesis were:

tions,[55] and perhaps even of the majority of the rank and file. Instead he had capitalized upon a reservoir of prestige and widespread fear that his loss to the party would be irreparable. On this question, Blumistes and Fauristes have agreed.[56]

The essential task remaining is to ascertain the strength of the contending resolutions among the *fédérations.* Unfortunately no complete record exists of the vote taken at Montrouge, and it is necessary to rely on widely scattered bits of information, particularly on the reports of the congresses of the *fédérations* published in the local Socialist press. Of the 8,243 *mandats* cast, 6,393 can be accounted for: 3,372 of the 4,332 for the Blum resolution, 1,904 of the 2,837 for the Faure motion, 286 for *Redressement,* and 797 of the 1,014 abstentions. The disparity in the Faure totals can be rectified partially by adding the 286 *Redressement* votes to

---

Auriol (Haute-Garonne), Baron (Basses-Alpes), Basquin (Somme), Beauvillain (Nord), Blancho (Loire-Inférieure), Bloch (Aisne), Bloncourt (Aisne), Bouhey (Côte d'Or), Camel (Ariège), Collomp (Var), Dormoy (Allier), S. Grumbach (Tarn), Guy (Haute-Savoie), Lagrange (Nord), Lambin (Aisne), Laurent (Nord), Lebas (Nord), Mennecier (Aisne), Moch (Hérault), Monnet (Aisne), Moutet (Drôme), Paulin (Puy-de-Dôme), Philip (Rhône), Tanguy-Prigent (Finistère), Sérol (Loire), Tellier (Pas-de-Calais), E. Thomas (Nord), Vassal (Oise), Zunino (Var).

[55] Many of the secretaries attempted to preserve a scrupulous neutrality, but twenty-six favored the Faure resolution publicly, and six supported Blum. For Faure: Bleau (Gard), Roucayrol (Hérault), Noguères (Pyrénées-Orientales), Calvelli (Bouches-du-Rhône), Bouchier (Drôme), Toesca (Var), Bayol (Dordogne), Masquerre (Haute-Garonne), Souchier (Ardèche), Spinasse (Corrèze), Rivière (Creuse), Floyrac (Lot), Vardelle (Haute-Vienne), Chatagner (Ain), Arnol (Isère), Gendre (Rhône), Parpais (Indre), L'Hévéder (Morbihan), Bernard (Indre-et-Loire), Saint-Martin (Gers), Costedoat (Seine), LaCroix (Jura), Lamarque (Haute-Marne), Hohmann (Meuse), Pujol (Eure-et-Loir), LeCorre (Manche). For Blum: Montel (Aude), Monnet (Aisne), Lebas (Nord), Pantigny (Pas-de-Calais), Quessot (Ille-et-Vilaine), Muriene (Gironde).

[56] Interviews with Rosenfeld, Roucayrol, Laurat, and Rauzy. Rosenfeld declared: "The *militants* of the party were much closer to Paul Faure and his position than to Léon Blum and his position. The majority for Blum at Montrouge was due exclusively to his name and prestige, and to his threat to resign if his policy were to be defeated. I was sitting next to Séverac when the votes were counted, and I was very apprehensive that Faure would win. . . . The pacifist and anti-Soviet position taken by Faure was a reflection of the feelings of the bulk of the Socialist party."

Faure's column, resulting in a total of 2,190.[57] The pre-Montrouge vote of the *fédérations* is given in Table 12 (pp. 325–329) ; many of the *fédérations* which voted in favor of a synthesis resolution probably abstained at the National Congress.

The pattern of support for the resolutions should evoke no surprise whatever, for it closely followed the one that was established in 1936 and 1937 over the question of nonintervention in the Spanish Civil War and repeated in the period between the fall of the second Blum ministry and the Congress of Royan. As with the Spanish question, the interplay of several factors determined the attitude of each *fédération,* but the essential determinant was, once again, the role of key personalities, particularly the deputies and secretaries. Unquestionably the economic characteristics and the nature of the Socialist clientele of each department had an important bearing on the position of the *fédération,* but few meaningful generalizations in this regard can be made, owing to the multiplicity of exceptions. A third major factor was, as before, the political status of the S.F.I.O. in each department. These factors, plus the impact of Blum's personal appeal, offer the most plausible explanation for the behavior of the *fédérations.*

Léon Blum's position was strongest precisely within those *fédérations* where his nonintervention policy either had been opposed or passively tolerated—with some inevitable exceptions.[58] Zyromski's vigorous support paid handsome dividends in terms of votes for the Blum resolution: the powerful *Bataille Socialiste* organiza-

[57] The special commission which failed to reach a compromise on international policy was composed of thirty-three members, chosen according to the precongress strength of each resolution. *Redressement* received two delegates; thus its total must have been around 490 *mandats. Le Temps* reported on December 25 that *Redressement* held 451 *mandats;* if these are added to Faure's total, the result is 2,344, leaving 493 unaccounted for. Blum's precongress total, again according to *Le Temps,* was 3,566: It is known that the Nord *fédération* cast its 767 *mandats* for Blum, thus accounting for the final Blum total of 4,332. Nonetheless 847 of the Blum *mandats* are unaccounted for in Table 12 (pp. 325–329).

[58] The *fédération* of the Gironde was the most notable exception. In addition, some of the *fédérations* in departments situated in close proximity to the Spanish frontier—the Landes, Basses-Pyrénées, and the Pyrénées-Orientales—which had expressed grave misgivings over nonintervention, adopted a pacifist stance after Munich and their leaders appeared to support Faure.

tions in the Seine and Seine-et-Oise *fédérations* alone delivered 568 *mandats* to Blum while Zyromski's influential partisans in the Sarthe, Aube, and Deux-Sèvres gave the Blum motion a potent boost. In many departments where socialism was a relatively new political force and where the *fédérations* were dominated by vigorous new personalities—Tanguy-Prigent in the Finistère, for example—Blum's position was backed with enthusiasm; yet it was in many of these *fédérations* that indiscreet grumblings about Blum's international policy had been detected in 1936 and 1937.[59] The Blumistes themselves were able generally to swing their *fédérations* over to their side:[60] Lebas cast the Nord's 767 *mandats* for Blum; Dormoy was able to secure two-thirds of the Allier's *mandats* for his chief; and presumably Monnet firmly planted the 154 votes of the Aisne *fédération* in the Blum column. Finally, in many instances Blum's prestige undercut the hitherto unchallenged authority of the local leaders, and this resulted in many additional votes for his resolution.[61]

Particularly striking is the geographical distribution of Blum's support, for although it was widespread, it was concentrated rather heavily among the *fédérations* in departments with a sizable industrial proletariat. The *fédérations* of the Seine, Seine-et-Oise, Nord, Pas-de-Calais, Bouches-du-Rhône, Loire-Inférieure, Haut-Rhin, Var, and the Aisne all possessed a majority for Blum, and together—with the exception of the Pas-de-Calais—accounted for almost half the total vote for his resolution. Assuredly there were exceptions—the Loire and the Rhône *fédérations,* in departments with a large industrial working class, favored Faure's position—yet the fact that a majority of *fédérations* in industrial departments did back Blum is significant. Nonetheless, it does not follow that these *fédérations* favored the Blum resolution simply

[59] For example, the *fédérations* of the Var, Côte d'Or, Loire-Inférieure, and the Charente-Inférieure.

[60] Auriol failed to win a majority for Blum in the Haute-Garonne *fédération.*

[61] The Indre-et-Loire *fédération* is an excellent example: at its congress all its deputies supported Faure, yet the Blum resolution received 54 *mandats* to 44 for Faure. The situation in the Ariège *fédérations* was similar: despite the pleas of the Fauriste spokesmen Rauzy and Soula, the rank and file voted for Blum, 40–24.

because they may have believed that their working-class clientele was angered by the retreat before Hitler in September. It would seem more likely that their decision was an integral part of a straight line of development dating from 1934: forced to compete in their departments with the Communists, who had seized the antifascist banner in 1934 and who had been attacking alleged capitulations to "international fascism" since 1936, the leaders of these *fédérations* had long since adopted a tougher position toward "fascism" than had their counterparts in essentially rural departments where the S.F.I.O. far outdistanced its Communist rivals. This had been clearly demonstrated in the debate on the Spanish question; thus it would seem that the support of the Blum resolution by these *fédérations* was entirely logical and indicative of an attitude that predated Munich.

The Faure resolution had its greatest appeal in the *fédérations* that had demonstrated a strong sentiment in favor of nonintervention in the Spanish conflict—that is, those located in agricultural and semi-industrial departments where socialism was powerful electorally. Once again the decisive factor was the role of key personalities, usually the deputies, whose pacifist and anti-Soviet inclinations had been reinforced steadily since 1936—such men as Arnol in the Isère, L'Hévéder in the Morbihan, Silvestre in the Gard, Peschadour and Spinasse in the Corrèze, and Lejeune in the Somme. Despite the all too numerous exceptions, it would seem correct to conclude that Faure's principal strength resided in rural *fédérations*,[62] particularly in those which were strong politically. It has been widely assumed that the peasantry constituted the most pacifist element of the French population in this period,[63] and although there is no way to assess the extent of their pacifism, it is undeniable that most of the Socialist leaders in agricultural areas rallied to Paul Faure. The *fédérations* of the heavily agricultural Massif Central cast a pre-Montrouge vote of 192–33 in support of the Faure resolution, and if the *mandats* of the overwhelmingly Fauriste *fédérations* of the Corrèze and the Creuse are added to Faure's total, it becomes 312. Outside of the

[62] The notable exceptions were the Aude (Blum's personal fief), Finistère, Ariège, Indre, Aube, Haute-Saône, and the Sarthe.

[63] Gordon Wright, *Rural Revolution in France: The Peasantry in the Twentieth Century* (Stanford, 1964), 223.

Massif Central, the Fauristes won majorities in the rural *fédérations* of the Tarn—where the deputy Malroux emerged victorious over Grumbach—Ain, Saône-et-Loire, Drôme, Dordogne, Gers, Meuse, Pyrénées-Orientales, Lot, Cher, and the Manche.

In addition, Faure's resolution received a majority in the *fédérations* of the semi-industrial departments of the Isère, Haute-Garonne, Gard, and the Somme, and Faure nearly captured the *fédérations* of the Bouches-du-Rhône, Seine, and the Rhône, all in industrial departments. But in every instance this success was primarily attributable to the great influence of highly placed personalities.[64] Hence the general conclusion: although the rank and file in rural areas appear to have been extremely receptive to the Fauriste position, its strength derived principally from the attitudes of the leaders of the *fédérations*.[65] And since 1936 these men had clearly identified themselves with the international policy of Paul Faure.

Although the Socialist party had apparently abandoned its habitual tactic of clumsy subterfuge when confronted with an awkward problem, the Montrouge congress actually determined only one thing: the S.F.I.O. was no longer a viable political party. Both sides in the spectacular controversy shared the same illusion: both were so deluded as to believe that this splintered party, wracked and scarred by the struggle, could again play a prominent role in French political life. In this confrontation, itself the product of a

---

[64] Faure also profited from the sympathy of the *Redressement tendance* for his position. *Redressement* was, however, relatively limited in its appeal: it won a majority in the *fédérations* of the Cantal and the Calvados, owing to the dominance over these *fédérations* by Deixonne and Zoretti, respectively. In addition it scored some success in the Oise and the Seine-Inférieure.

Marceau Pivert, looking on from his splendid isolation, attacked the Blum resolution as "Stalinist" and criticized Faure for accepting a "policy of armaments" (*Juin 36,* January 6, 1939). As for *Redressement,* the P.S.O.P. had already dismissed it contemptuously as a "group of sentimentalists" (*Juin 36,* October 28, 1938).

[65] With respect to rural *fédérations* this conclusion is further substantiated by an examination of those which did not vote in favor of Faure. In the Aude and the Finistère, the Socialist leaders—Montel and Tanguy-Prigent—were Blumistes. In the *fédérations* of the Vienne, Haute-Saône, and Eure-et-Loir, which were weak politically, there were no leaders of sufficient stature to counter the influence of Blum's prestige.

long period of development, each group was resolved to commit socialism to its international policy, but, while each failed to annihilate the other, together they destroyed the S.F.I.O. as a workable political unit. Whatever the result of the narrowly divided Congress might have been, neither side would have accepted the decision as definitive—and the Fauristes most certainly did not. After Montrouge the Socialist party was led by a man whose policies were opposed by a majority of its parliamentarians, and it had a Secretariat which rejected the verdict of a theoretically sovereign congress. In the months preceding the outbreak of the Second World War, only the religion of Socialist unity prevented a formal break between the contending groups, and behind a transparent façade, the bitter struggle increased in intensity. After the Congress of Montrouge, the S.F.I.O. bore only slight resemblance to the buoyant party which had confidently embarked upon its first "exercise of power" just two and a half years before.

"FAURISTE" RESURGENCE

Interpreting his victory at the Congress of Montrouge as a vindication of his international policy rather than a personal success, Blum turned his attention to the Spanish problem. On the evening of January 18, 1939, Blum, Thorez, and Jouhaux addressed a boisterous throng at the Vélodrome d'Hiver. After a violent speech by Thorez, in which the Communist leader demanded that the Catalan frontier be opened immediately to the transit of arms and ammunition, Blum told the crowd that he was in complete agreement with Thorez. Rather apologetically Blum explained his reasons for adopting nonintervention, but he confessed candidly that his effort to secure observance of this policy by all the powers had lasted much too long. "History will say if I was wrong," he declared, "but I do not consider myself to be infallible. There comes a moment—and for me it did not come just yesterday—when reality demonstrates to you that your effort has been in vain."[66] And in an address to the Chamber on January 26, Blum asserted that France's vital interest was at stake in the situation in Spain; France, he argued passionately, could not

[66] *Le Populaire*, January 19, 1939; *L'Humanité*, January 19, 1939.

permit the Spanish Republic to collapse and must allow the shipment of arms to the beleaguered Republican forces. In a moving
conclusion, Blum appealed for a rebirth of national unity: every
party and every man had been divided over Munich, he said, but
"a reawakening of national energy" must replace division and
mistrust; the danger which confronted France demanded it.[67]

Blum's declarations in favor of aid to the crumbling Spanish
Republic threw the S.F.I.O. into a new crisis. At a stormy session
of the C.A.P. on February 2, the Fauristes were pitted squarely
against the new Blum-Zyromski majority over the Spanish issue. It
was decided, by a vote of seventeen to fifteen, that the party
should launch an appeal "to the people of France" in support of
the delivery of arms to Republican Spain. It is worth citing this
document because of its marked similarity to Zyromski's earlier
statements:

Hitler and Mussolini are still the masters of Franco. But Franco is not
yet the master of Spain. . . . It is absolutely true that they [the Spanish
Republicans] are fighting for the security of France. . . . The Spanish
Republicans, if they are furnished with arms and food, are still able to
drive the foreigners from their soil by themselves. . . . The Socialist
party makes an appeal to the country. It appeals in the name of French
security. In the name of justice. In the name of peace.[68]

At a second meeting of the C.A.P., held on February 15, Zyromski sought to put the S.F.I.O. on record as opposing any international conference on European problems until all "sovereign
rights" were restored to the Spanish Republic. The motion was
defeated by a vote of fifteen to fifteen.[69] While the Blumistes
Dormoy and S. Grumbach voted in favor, Blumel, who recalled
that Blum's Montrouge resolution included an appeal for an
international conference, voted against. But the affirmative votes
of Dormoy and Grumbach were symptomatic of an increasing
restiveness and discontent among the Blumistes, who were irritated by the open opposition of the Fauristes to the appeal in
favor of Republican Spain—and by the refusal of the Fauristes to
accept the Montrouge decision as the law of the party. As early as

---

[67] Léon Blum, *La Question d'Espagne*, (Paris, 1939), 1off.
[68] *Le Populaire*, February 3, 1939.   [69] *Ibid.*, February 17, 1939.

February 1, *AGIR,* an organ created by several Blumistes to combat *Le Socialiste,* rebuked the Fauristes for their alleged indiscipline and assailed the rival organ for describing Blum's international policy as "devoid of any pacifist spirit."[70] Intraparty strife was continuing unabated.

Actually the chagrin of the Blumistes was quite justifiable. Not only did the Fauristes reject the judgment of the Congress of Montrouge, but they attacked it relentlessly in public. Faure himself, stung by Blum's refusal to compromise, virtually severed all connection with *Le Populaire* and seized every opportunity to criticize the official policy of his party.[71] Early in January, Faure contributed a long article to the Paris daily *Paris-Soir* entitled "The Problems of War and Peace," in which he decried the "abandonment" of socialism's traditional opposition to superarmament and military alliances: "Socialism's pacifist doctrine truly would have no merit if it were to crumble under the strain of contact with the very first difficulties." Blum's position, Faure asserted, "does not lead to peace, but prepares the way for the most inevitable and most murderous of wars." In face of Germany's might, which, according to Faure, was vastly superior to France's demographic and economic potential, France would be doomed to "ruin and death" in the event of war. *"Up until now,"* Faure declared bluntly, "Socialists have proclaimed that security cannot be found in an arms race or in alliances." Socialism, he concluded, must return to its traditional pacifist posture, that is, to a policy of disarmament and approval of all efforts to secure peace by negotiation and conciliation.[72]

Faure's attack on Blum's international policy was once again mild in comparison to that undertaken by his partisans. *Le Soci-*

---

[70] *AGIR—Pour la Paix, Pour le Socialisme,* February 1, 1939. The journal was directed by Georges Monnet, and its editorial staff consisted of Bouhey, Pierre Brossolette, Camel, Daniel Mayer, E. Thomas, A. Guy, Georges Izard, Lagrange, Bloch, and Tanguy-Prigent. Occasional contributions were made by André Leroux (Tasca) and by Girard.

[71] In a speech at Lyons, Faure urged direct Franco-German negotiations (*Le Temps,* February 7, 1939), and in a speech in the Rhône, he demanded that the French government adopt what he called a "French policy" based upon Blum's speech at Lyons in January, 1937 (*L'Avenir Socialiste,* February 11, 1939). [72] *Paris-Soir,* January 10, 1939.

aliste led the assault: its editorials condemned the decision of the Congress of Montrouge as an outrageous error, and denounced Blum for interjecting his personality into the debate. This journal warned repeatedly that the S.F.I.O. was slipping steadily into *bellicisme,* and it argued that the party was being ostracized from political life because of its disastrous alliance with the Communists in support of a foreign policy which was, it said, "utterly discredited" in the eyes of the French people. *Le Socialiste* warmly welcomed contributions to its columns from the bitterly anti-Soviet personalities of the *Syndicats* group—Froideval, Dumoulin, and Roy—who pleaded for the unity of all "men of peace" in order to combat those individuals who, they said, were leading the working class and the nation into a "mad adventure."[73]

At the same time L'Hévéder declared his vigorous support of nonintervention, noting that "real Spaniards could want only peace."[74] Peschadour stepped up his savage criticism of the Soviet Union,[75] while Paz petulantly assailed the Blumistes for creating *AGIR,* inquiring sarcastically why they needed a journal in addition to *Le Populaire.*[76] And Séverac, taking full advantage of the opportunities offered by the Secretariat's control over *Le Bulletin Socialiste,* tirelessly propagated the idea that an international conference would settle all of Europe's problems.[77]

During the first two months of 1939 it became increasingly evident that the Fauristes, in open alliance with the Socialists of the *Syndicats* group, were pressing hard to reverse the verdict of the Congress of Montrouge. The first opportunity to put their case before an assemblage of the party came at the National Council, held in Paris on March 4 and 5. Although a National Council was not empowered by party statute to formulate policy, it provided an excellent forum for propaganda. As soon as the meeting con-

[73] *Le Socialiste,* January 1, February 1, 15, March 1, 1939.

[74] *Ibid.,* February 1, 1939; *Le Rappel du Morbihan,* January 21, February 11, 1939.

[75] *Le Socialiste,* February 15, 1939; *La Voix Corrèzienne,* February 1, 1939.   [76] *Le Socialiste,* February 15, 1939.

[77] *Le Bulletin Socialiste,* January 16, 30, February 6, 1939. The Socialist Youth Movement openly sided with Faure. The January, 1939 number of *Le Cri des Jeunes* declared that "the motion of our friend Paul Faure was defended especially by young people."

vened—in the absence of Léon Blum, who was ill and confined to his home—the Fauristes launched their offensive. The outspoken and pugnacious Le Bail—who was too violent even for some of his comrades—delivered an unrestrained tirade against Blum's international policy: it had, he said, no relationship with reality and it linked socialism with the policy of the Communist party. "Our party must be the party of peace," Le Bail cried, "we must avoid slipping into Stalinism." No Socialist gathering had ever heard a more blunt accusation: Le Bail was saying that the Communists were bent upon war.[78]

The remainder of the day's debate was tame in comparison to Le Bail's slashing attack on Blum's international policy. Lagrange professed shock and indignation at Le Bail's declaration; Roucayrol, in a mild rebuttal to the deputy from the Nord, criticized the Blumistes for desiring to "sabotage" an international conference by insisting upon the restoration of Republican sovereignty in Spain as a prerequisite. Roucayrol asserted that such a conference was vital to the cause of peace, and he declared that France had the most concessions to make at this conference. Zyromski retorted that acceptance of an international conference without first assuring the victory of the Spanish Republic would be an abysmal confession of weakness, and he stated flatly that Socialism must run the risk of war by supporting the formation of a "democratic bloc" against the Axis powers.

Lebas came to Zyromski's assistance by asserting that he would not accept an international conference until the Germans and Italians were expelled from Spain; presumably he was speaking in behalf of all the Blumistes. The session concluded with a counterattack from Arnol: he delivered a fervent plea for the maintenance of nonintervention and for an economic accord between France and Germany, and turning toward the Blumistes, he declared that opposition to the idea of an agreement with Germany was equivalent to favoring "ideological war."[79]

Discussion resumed the following afternoon and proceeded much in the same vein as before, with invective freely employed by all speakers. But the speech by Charles Spinasse, who had hitherto played an inconspicuous role among the Fauristes,

[78] *Le Populaire,* March 5, 1939.   [79] *Ibid.,* March 6, 1939.

caused a sensation. Carefully choosing his words, the former Minister of the National Economy opened his speech by declaring that
the policy adopted at Montrouge was basically negative, not only
because it could not preserve peace and probably would lead to
war, but also because it permitted Hitler to choose the time and
place of his next aggressive act. To intervene in Spain, Spinasse
continued, unquestionably would precipitate a war, and to make
the restoration of the Spanish Republic the prerequisite to any
negotiations with Germany would insure that there would be no
negotiations. Spinasse asserted that the way to peace lay in economic and financial accords between France and Great Britain on
the one hand, and Germany on the other. The essence of his
argument was this: Germany was in the throes of an economic
crisis; her industry had attained its full productive capacity, and,
owing to her lack of an adequate supply of raw materials, she
could not hope to increase her output appreciably. With the
recent addition of ten million people to her population, Germany
would be compelled to import foodstuffs or to restrict domestic
consumption drastically. Since industrial production had reached
its peak, and since Germany's industries were geared to the manu-
facture of armaments, she was unable to import a sufficient supply
of foodstuffs because her lack of exportable products prevented
her from engaging in extensive foreign trade. In substance, according to Spinasse, Germany's autarkical system was in a deep
crisis, and thus she was unable to purchase abroad the agricultural products and raw materials necessary to alleviate her distress. Hence, Spinasse believed, Hitler soon would be compelled
to embark upon aggression, not to secure "living space," but to
satisfy economic needs.

According to Spinasse, however, Germany's economic crisis afforded a splendid opportunity for France and Great Britain; to
prevent aggression and to have peace, one course was open: Britain and France should be willing to conclude an economic and
financial accord with Germany. Such an accord would provide for
the free exchange of goods among the three powers, and Britain
and France would grant credits to Germany. In return, Germany
would be required to agree to a disarmament convention.

Spinasse concluded on a polemical note—and created an uproar. He declared that rejection of this opportunity would sen-

tence France to war, and he asserted that there were some members of the Socialist party who did, in fact, want war. Monnet shouted angrily, "We are not aggressors!" and Auriol protested inaudibly above the din. Calmly, Spinasse retorted:

Tell me, do you still hope that the Hitlerian regime will collapse without war? . . . If you do not, you are accepting the idea of war. And although Socialists can never accept the idea of war, I have heard it said that war . . . would be a form of the class struggle! As if the class struggle can be led on the battlefields! As if Socialism can be born in charnel houses![80]

The speech by Spinasse contributed a great deal to the cause of Fauristes, who up to this point had been adamant in demanding negotiations with Germany, but had never been able to specify exactly what should be negotiated. Faure had spoken often of raw materials, Arnol had mentioned colonies, but Spinasse gave the Fauristes what they lacked: a specific program.

After the anticipated failure of a special commission to agree upon a synthesis resolution, two motions were placed before the National Council. One, submitted by Lebas, reaffirmed the policy adopted at Montrouge and insisted upon the "liberation" of Spain as a prerequisite to any international conference. The other, offered by Spinasse, embodied the essentials of Faure's Montrouge resolution and suggested that France undertake negotiations with Germany in order to reach an economic and financial accord. The Lebas resolution received 4,018 *mandats,* or 53.3 per cent of the total, the Spinasse resolution received 3,140, or 41.6 per cent, and there were 200 abstentions and 183 absent, which, taken together, represented 5.1 per cent of the total.[81] Although the total number of outstanding *mandats* was less than the number at Montrouge (owing to the decline in party membership in 1938), the Fauristes gained 303 more votes than at Montrouge, while the Blumistes lost 304. The clear Fauriste progression is better demonstrated by a comparison of the percentages:

[80] *Le Pays Socialiste,* March 18, 1939.
[81] *Le Populaire,* March 6, 1939. The vote cast by the individual *fédérations* was not published.

the Blumistes gained only a fraction, while the Fauristes increased their percentage by seven points. This 7 per cent came from the ranks of the uncommitted—that is, from those *fédérations* that had abstained at Montrouge. Nonetheless, the Fauristes had narrowed considerably the gap between themselves and their opponents.

The formidable strength of the Fauristes was demonstrated vividly by their performance on the question of the party's relationship with the Communists. Arnol sponsored a resolution which, in effect, demanded a suspension of "unity of action" with the Communist party. He was opposed by Zyromski, who offered a resolution which stipulated that the S.F.I.O. should encourage a "regrouping" of "proletarian organizations" in order to fight fascism. The Blumistes were placed in an awkward position: fearing defections from their camp, and sensing defeat, Dormoy, in their name, urged that no vote be taken. His appeal was soundly rejected by a vote of 4,135 to 2,792. In the vote on the resolution, Arnol's motion received 3,330, or 45 per cent of the total, Zyromski's received 1,387, or 19 per cent, and there were 2,642 abstentions, or 36 per cent.[82]

Thus in both of the votes taken at the National Council, the Fauristes gave evidence of their very real strength. The vote on the question of the party's relationship with the Communists indicated that the Blumistes commanded a smaller share of the party's allegiance than did the Fauristes, and that the former were entirely dependent upon the *Bataille Socialiste* for their majority on international policy.[83]

[82] *Ibid.*

[83] It may be argued that there was a shift by some of the *fédérations* from a Blumiste position on international policy to a Fauriste position on relations with the Communists. In all probability the increase in the Fauriste percentage from 41.6 on the first vote to 45.0 on the second was due to such a shift. On the other hand some of the *fédérations* which abstained on international policy may also have abstained on the second question; thus all of the abstentions on the second question may not have represented Blumistes. Thus the latter may not have held 36 per cent of the *mandats* as the percentage of abstentions on the question of relations with the Communists would seem to indicate. However, since the vote of the *fédérations* is not available, no definitive conclusions can be reached.

The period of uneasy calm within the Socialist party following the hectic meeting of the National Council was abruptly shattered by the disintegration of the rump Czecho-Slovak state and the establishment of German protectorates over Bohemia and Moravia. While this blatant example of Hitler's perfidy shocked the British and French governments into adopting a firmer policy toward Germany, it simply exacerbated the tensions and antagonisms within the S.F.I.O. Léon Blum and his supporters abandoned entirely the slim hope that Germany could be satiated by whatever settlement an international conference could propose to her, and they were convinced that France—and the S.F.I.O.— must speak the language of force. To the contrary, Faure and his partisans refused to despair of a peacefully negotiated solution of the European crisis and tenaciously clung to their pacifist and anti-Soviet policy.

Blum's position during the months of March, April, and May needs little explanation. Almost daily in *Le Populaire* he insisted that *only* the alliance of Great Britain, France, and the U.S.S.R. could prevent further German aggression and that France's essential task was to effect a *rapprochement* between London and Moscow as quickly as possible. Blum believed the disappearance of the remnant of Czechoslovakia to have been the inevitable consequence of the Munich settlement and the persistence of the spirit of appeasement in the policies of Britain and France. He demanded that Daladier and Bonnet resign and make way for a government that would build "an ideological bloc of peace" consisting of France, Britain, and the Soviet Union, which, he said, would present an insurmountable barrier to Axis aggression. Blum moderated his attack against Daladier when the latter announced that France would adopt a firm policy toward Germany,[84] and the Socialist leader hailed Chamberlain's resolve to reject all German territorial demands, arguing that the "new policy" of Britain and France was basically the policy adopted by the Congress of Montrouge. Blum's many articles were directed squarely to his fellow Socialists:

[84] *Le Populaire,* March 16, 18, 25, 30, April 2, 3, 16, 1939.

Our [Montrouge] resolution and the speech by Mr. Chamberlain are inspired by the same principles. The single ambition of free peoples is peace. . . . But they must not close their eyes to reality, to the evidence. . . . War will be imposed on all peoples who are still free if they fail to organize a resistance powerful enough to make the aggressors hesitate. . . . This means . . . the constitution of an ideological bloc of peace, and the conclusion of powerful and loyal pacts. . . .

At the present moment there is no other way to save peace without being enslaved. . . . For Socialists, for pacifists, *the appeal to force today is the appeal to peace.*[85]

Blum's rational appeal to the Fauristes, urging them to recognize the brutal realities of the situation in Europe, was not wholly emulated by many of his supporters. Lebas savagely assailed the "silly illusions" of the pacifists,[86] and Monnet alleged that he was "stupefied" by the attitude of Spinasse.[87] Leroux described the raw materials question as a "fascist slogan," and declared that peace could not be considered as one of socialism's supreme values.[88] Moreover, the militant *AGIR* group began to develop a pronounced aggressive spirit. Arguing that pacifism was an outdated doctrine, these men were prepared intellectually to accept war if it should be imposed upon them by "fascism": "socialism," Monnet declared, "must be a doctrine of combat," and Lagrange summarized the sentiments of his comrades when he asserted that "socialism must have the soul of a conqueror."[89] The influence of this group is impossible to determine, but it was symptomatic of the spirit that was to be the motivating force of the clandestine Socialist party under the German occupation.[90]

The Blum resolution for the Congress of Nantes, signed by Zyromski and twenty-eight deputies, did not, however, reflect the militancy of the *AGIR* group, but closely followed the position spelled out by Blum in *Le Populaire*. Essentially this resolution was a complete affirmation of the policy adopted at Montrouge: it declared that the primary task facing socialism was to combat

[85] *Ibid.*, April 2, 16, May 4, 23, 24, 1939. (Italics mine.)
[86] *Le Peuple Libre* (Nord) , April 28, 1939.   [87] *AGIR*, March 15, 1939.
[88] *Ibid.*, April 15, 1939.   [89] *Ibid.*, April 1, May 1, 1939.
[90] Daniel Mayer, who was the leader of the clandestine Socialist party, was a prominent member of the *AGIR* group. Consult his articles in the March 1 and August 1 numbers of *AGIR*.

"international fascism." France, it stated, should rally all the pacific nations to her side in a system of collective security; assured of meeting the collective resistance of these nations, the "fascist aggressor" would be compelled to desist from attacking any nation.[91]

The subjugation of all of Czechoslovakia did not dim the hopes of the Fauristes about the prospects for successful negotiations with Germany, and, in fact, the events of mid-March served to intensify their pacifism. Paul Faure assumed the direction of a newly created weekly, *Le Pays Socialiste*, which, he said, would publicize "our will to maintain peace."[92] Under Faure's guidance the organ indulged in an orgy of pacifist propaganda; in its first number, Roucayrol spoke for all of his comrades when he denounced "the inanity of a war for a truncated Czechoslovakia."[93] The entire roster of Fauristes contributed liberally to this journal: Peschadour advanced the suggestion that France should make a peace treaty with Germany before war could occur; presumably this implied that France should play the part of the defeated power.[94] Similarly, Arnol wrote exuberantly that socialism's duty was to save peace, not to win a war,[95] and the indefatigable Maurice Paz attributed socialism's "erroneous posture" on

[91] *Le Populaire,* May 5, 1939.

[92] *Le Pays Socialiste—par la liberté—par la paix,* March 18, 1939. It replaced *Le Socialiste* as the Fauriste organ. Faure contributed regularly to this journal: in the March 31 number he wrote that France had had no means with which to save Czechoslovakia even if she had desired to do so. Faure wrote a series of fervently pacifist articles; see, e.g., the numbers for April 7 and 21, and May 5 and 20, 1939. *Le Pays Socialiste* ordinarily ran about sixteen pages, and it published articles by virtually all the prominent Fauristes, including many by members of the *Syndicats* group.

[93] *Ibid; L'Aube Sociale* (Hérault), March 25, 1939. Roucayrol attacked the Blum motion for the Nantes Congress as the epitome of "neo-nationalism." See *L'Aube Sociale,* May 13, 1939.

L'Hévéder dismissed the end of Czechoslovakia neatly by stating that it never should have been created. See *Le Rappel du Morbihan,* March 25, 1939.

[94] *Le Pays Socialiste,* April 14, 1939; *La Voix Corrèzienne,* March 12 and 29, 1939. See a similar article by Spinasse in *La Voix Corrèzienne,* March 22, 1939.

[95] *Le Pays Socialiste,* April 14, 1939; *Le Droit du Peuple* (Isère) April 1, 1939.

the problem of war to its unholy alliance with the Communists, whose orders, he said, came from a totalitarian country.[96] Chochoy and his henchman Max Norel, the new leader of the *Jeunesses Socialistes,* boasted that this organization was fully committed to the Fauriste position.[97] In addition, members of the *Syndicats* group collaborated openly with *Le Pays Socialiste:* Dumoulin hinted broadly that an accord between Hitler and Stalin was under discussion in Berlin and Moscow, and he insisted that a European war would be profitable only to Bolshevism or fascism. Froideval predicted any European war would be fought exclusively on French soil, and Marcel Roy argued that war would be suicidal for France.[98] Clearly the Fauristes were not embarrassed by Hitler's most recent act of aggression; to them it demonstrated conclusively that France must come to terms with Germany.

In addition to this pacifist frenzy—the repeated declarations that war must be prevented at all costs and that socialism's highest value was peace—the Fauristes began to define what they meant by "any and all negotiations." Faure himself was very willing to satisfy German and Italian colonial demands, declaring, in fine Bismarckian style, that "the skin of a vineyard worker of Mâcon is worth more than the port of Djibouti."[99] L'Hévéder encountered no dissent from his Fauriste friends when he stated that the Poles could not be protected from invasion, thus interpreting a French guarantee to Poland as an invitation to suicide.[100] More specifically, the Fauristes believed that Germany would not commit aggression if her economic needs were satisfied; hence they adopted the position set forth by Spinasse at the National Council as the formula for peace. This idea emerged as the core of all their

[96] *Le Pays Socialiste,* April 28, 1939.

[97] *Ibid.,* April 14, 28, 1939. See also an article by Norel in *Le Cri des Jeunes,* second number for May 1939. The resolution adopted by the *Jeunesses Socialistes* at its National Conference declared that it "puts confidence in the great Socialist party to save the young lives of the French proletariat. They appeal, with all their voices, for an international conference."

[98] *Le Pays Socialiste,* March 24, 31, April 28, May 20, 1939. André Delmas also contributed to this journal.

[99] Speech by Faure at Mâcon (Saône-et-Loire), reported in *Le Temps,* April 4, 1939. [100] *Le Rappel du Morbihan,* April 1, 1939.

propaganda[101] and of the motion drawn up by Faure for presentation to the Congress of Nantes:

The party proclaims the necessity and the urgency of measures for a new division of raw materials, a solution to the problem of surplus population, the development of commercial exchange, the association of peoples in a community of labor and economic organization. Once again, it emphasizes that such measures are contingent upon the achievement of a limitation of armaments.

The Faure resolution also proclaimed the party's determination to defend the independence of France, but it stated that the arms race was leading the nation to economic ruin: thus France must take the initiative for an international conference. Finally, it warned that unless international economic agreements were achieved soon the "dictators" would be driven to take more aggressive actions.[102]

Three other resolutions were submitted to the party. The first, offered by the *Redressement* group—if only to preserve the illusion of their independence from the Fauristes—was very similar to the Faure resolution. It decried the "policy of force" of the British and French governments, and urged that both make peace desirable to Hitler. Even if the democratic powers were victorious in a war, the resolution declared, the underlying tensions would persist and eventually carry another Hitler to power. *Redressement* went further than Faure, however, in its vision of the future:

---

[101] Paul Faure in *Le Droit du Peuple* (Isère), April 22, 1939; *La Volonté Socialiste* (Drôme), April 15, 1939; *La Dépêche Socialiste* (Saône-et-Loire), March 1, April 1, 1939; *Le Pays Socialiste*, April 29, 1939. See L'Hévéder in *Le Rappel du Morbihan*, May 6, 1939; Spinasse in *La Voix Corrèzienne*, March 22, 1939; Séverac in *Le Bulletin Socialiste*, April 17, May 1, 8, 15, 1939; Roucayrol in *L'Aube Sociale* (Hérault) May 6, 13, 1939; Rivière in *La Justice* (a Parisian daily founded by L.-O. Frossard in January, 1939), February 2, 23, 1939; Le Bail in *Le Populaire du Centre*, May 10, 22, 1939.

[102] *Le Populaire*, May 5, 1939. The resolution also included a stinging condemnation of the Communist party. In addition the Fauristes sponsored a special resolution, offered by the *fédération* of the Loire, which would forbid party members to participate in activities organized by any other political party; in other words, this was a thinly disguised attempt to repeal "unity of action" with the Communists.

denouncing "Anglo-Saxon capitalism," the resolution envisaged the creation of a "United States of Europe," and postulated that the first step, the economic cooperation of all European nations, should be taken immediately. Finally, it stated that Hitler's occupation of all of Czechoslovakia should present no barrier to fruitful negotiations on economic problems, and it observed that it would be "perfectly useless and vain" to oppose German expansion in eastern and southeastern Europe.[103]

The second of these other resolutions was offered by the irrepressible Nadia Gulkowski. It was simply a reaffirmation of utopian pacifism, denouncing rearmament and any mobilization of France's armed forces.[104]

The third, a vague "synthesis" resolution offered by Albert Rivière, called for party unity around certain basic points: approval of national defense, support for an international conference, and a recognition of the necessity for controlled disarmament. The majority of the signatories to this resolution were Fauristes.[105]

The contest between the major contending groups took place within the *fédérations* rather than at the Congress of Nantes, which adopted a synthesis resolution on international policy. The Fauristes, profiting from their cohesiveness and determination— as well as from a serious blunder committed by the Blumistes, who had attacked Faure personally and engineered a public censure of the General Secretary by the C.A.P[106]—clearly were on the

---

[103] *Ibid.*, May 6, 1939. Looking at the struggle within the Socialist party, Marceau Pivert attacked both Blum and Faure for their policies of "class collaboration," and he singled out Faure for special condemnation: Faure was, according to Pivert, "playing the game of the pro-Hitlerians" (*Juin 36*, May 12, 1939). Pivert, however, still had no taste for war; on May 5, *Juin 36* ran this headline: "Down with Hitler, down with Poland, down with war!"

[104] *Le Populaire*, May 6, 1939. [105] *Ibid.*, May 14, 1939.

[106] At a meeting of the C.A.P. on April 12, it was decided, by a vote of 15–13, to eliminate the customary presentation of the "Moral Report" by the General Secretary to the National Congress. This was done by the Blumistes to prevent Faure from employing the report, which ordinarily was distributed to the *fédérations* about a month before a congress, in support of his own resolution. Faure stalked out of the meeting, declaring that he would no longer participate in the deliberations of the C.A.P., and sent out his "Moral Report" to the *fédérations* anyway. It declared that the Congress of Montrouge "had resolved nothing at all." The Blumistes, enraged at Faure's

ascendant within the S.F.I.O. On the basis of information gleaned from *Le Populaire* and the local Socialist press, it is possible to account for 5,993 of the 7,578 outstanding *mandats*. Prior to the Congress of Nantes, 2,861 of these were committed to the Blum resolution, 1,946 to Faure's, 276 to the *Redressement* resolution— or a total of 2,222 for the substance of the Faure resolution—and 807 were in favor of a synthesis, which ordinarily was closer to Faure's position than to Blum's. With 1,608 *mandats* unaccounted for, the overall totals have less meaning than do the votes of the *fédérations* themselves; these demonstrate the progression of the Fauristes in certain key areas. The vote of each *fédération* is shown in Table 13 (pp. 330–333).

Comparison of these figures with those for the Congress of Montrouge (Table 12, pp. 325–329) reveals that the Fauristes either were maintaining their strength or making steady advances in all regions. The distribution of *mandats* remained stable in the Languedoc and the Rhone Valley–Provence regions, although the Fauristes increased their majorities in the *fédérations* of the Gard[107] and Haute-Garonne, and even won a larger share of the *mandats* in Blum's own *fédération* of the Aude! Faure made spectacular gains in the North: in the *fédération* of the Nord, Lebas' iron-fisted rule broke down as the Fauriste deputies Salengro and Saint-Venant swung the powerful section of Lille into Faure's column;[108] in the *fédération* as a whole, Faure's resolution received 223 *mandats* to Blum's 396, and 117 went to Rivière's

---

action, joined with the representatives of the *Bataille Socialiste* at a meeting of the C.A.P. on May 10 to obtain the passage of a motion which stated, as it said, "with infinite sadness . . . that the General Secretary is in a state of insurrection against the C.A.P." Faure refused to accept the condemnation, and announced that he would expose the "lies" of the majority at the Congress of Nantes. See *Le Populaire,* May 12, 1939; *Le Petit Parisien,* May 8, 1939.

[107] The *fédération* of the Gard unanimously adopted a resolution paying homage to Paul Faure. Such resolutions were quite common and demonstrate Faure's popularity in the party. The Gard resolution read: "All the Socialists in the Gard express their confidence in Paul Faure, who symbolizes socialism in our country and whose untiring efforts for over twenty years have permitted our party . . . to become the most important French political party" (*Le Populaire,* May 23, 1939).

[108] *Le Peuple Libre* (Nord), May 5, 19, 26, 1939.

synthesis resolution. Similarly, in the Pas-de-Calais *fédération,* Faure's resolution received 110 votes, owing to the influence of Chochoy and Vantielcke. Although figures for only half the region are available, the Fauristes undeniably were gaining strength in the Garonne Basin, and in the Massif Central Faure's seventy-six *mandats* would have been augmented at the congress by the addition of the votes of the Fauriste *fédérations* of the Haute-Vienne and Creuse—and by most of the votes of the Puy-de-Dôme *fédération.*

Faure retained his two to one majority in the Lyonnais, but the *fédérations* in the Northeast remained heavily in favor of Blum's position. The *fédérations* in Brittany cast a total vote roughly equivalent to that which they cast at Montrouge—if it is assumed that there occurred no drastic shift in the *fédération* of the Loire-Inférieure. Among the *fédérations* of the West Central region Blum's Montrouge majority was cut drastically by a slide toward a synthesis, and although the statistics for the Southwest region are insufficient, it should be noted that three prominent figures of the Gironde *fédération* maintained their allegiance to Faure—Vielle, Luquot, and Naphle. Most spectacular was the capture of the Seine *fédération* by the Fauristes, although the value of the prize was diminished by 270 *mandats,* owing to the decline in the membership of the *fédération* during 1938. The totals for the regions of Eastern France, the Orleanais, and Western France are much too incomplete to justify any conclusions, but the *fédérations* in Normandy certainly contained a solid majority for the Faure-*Redressement* combination.

Thus despite mounting evidence of Hitler's bad faith and aggressive intentions, the Socialist party failed to rally overwhelmingly to Blum's international policy, but remained closely and bitterly divided. Paul Faure's pacifist policy did not lose, but gained strength during the months between the congresses of Montrouge and Nantes. Not only did the Fauristes retain their grip on many politically powerful *fédérations* in essentially rural areas, but, with the vital assistance of key personalities, they made inroads into the large *fédérations* in industrial departments. In addition, the sizable vote for Rivière's synthesis resolution, itself weighted toward Faure's position, hardly constituted a mark of confidence in Léon Blum. Had a synthesis not been achieved at

Nantes, Blum's resolution probably would have been adopted, but by a very slender margin.[109] Blum had long since lost the support of the majority of his party's parliamentary group on the question of international policy: now it appeared that he was in danger of losing the support of the majority of his party's membership as well.

The last prewar congress of the Socialist party—and the last congress of this Socialist party[110]—convened at Nantes on May 27, 1939. The debates need not be examined extensively, for they followed a familiar pattern of repetitive speeches highlighted by exchanges of vituperation. Before the inevitable "special commission" was created, however, the Fauristes scored two handsome victories: Faure read his "Moral Report" to the congress, and the resolution of the Loire *fédération* was adopted.

The entire first session was devoted to the touchy problem of the "Moral Report," which had been handled so clumsily by the Blumistes on the C.A.P. Several speakers exchanged insults until Blum, pale and obviously ill from a respiratory ailment that was to confine him to his hotel during most of the congress, attempted to settle the quarrel by offering to ask a special commission to compose a resolution of "sympathy and gratitude to Paul Faure." Faure retorted heatedly that he desired neither sympathy nor gratitude, but only "cold justice," and he demanded that the issue be brought to a vote. The congress voted to hear the "Moral Report,"[111] and Faure proceeded to read it. It was, of course, largely an apologia for his actions and an exposition of his posi-

---

[109] In my interviews with Rosenfeld, Roucayrol, and Laurat, I asked what the result of a vote at Nantes might have been. All agreed that Blum's resolution would have won, but by a narrow majority. Rosenfeld estimated the division as 51 per cent Blum, 49 per cent Faure (including the *Redressement mandats*) ; Roucayrol and Laurat believe that it was 52 per cent Blum, 48 per cent Faure. The correspondent for *L'Oeuvre* (May 27, 1939) thought that the congress would split evenly between the Blum and Faure resolutions, while the respected correspondent for *Le Temps*, Raymond Millet, wrote that Blum possessed 51 per cent of the *mandats*, Faure 32 per cent, *Redressement* 13 per cent, and Gulkowski 4 per cent. See *Le Temps*, May 30, 1939.

[110] The postwar Socialist party, the product of the wartime clandestine Socialist party, excluded the Fauristes.

[111] *Le Populaire*, May 28, 1939. 3,302 votes were cast in favor of hearing the report, 1,116 were opposed, and there were 2,747 abstentions.

tion. It recommended that the Socialist party preserve its complete independence from all other political parties, denounced unity with the Communists as dangerous and worthless, and declared that the Congress of Montrouge had resolved "nothing at all." Blum, exercising his great charm, remarked gently that "some less attentive readers" might construe the section on the Montrouge congress as a condemnation of the party's international policy, and he offered to accept the "Moral Report" if Faure would delete the offending passage. Faure, mollified by Blum's graciousness, agreed to withdraw that section, but only after delivering a slashing attack against Blum's supporters.[112] Finally, the report was accepted by the congress.

The Fauristes, demonstrating determination and a remarkable organization of their forces—both of which they had lacked at Montrouge—pressed their attack with precision. At issue was the motion officially submitted by the *fédération* of the Loire which would forbid members of the party to participate in activities sponsored by any other political party; if adopted, Socialists could belong no longer to such organizations as the Friends of the U.S.S.R. In essence, the resolution implied that virtually all cooperation with the Communists must cease. In support of the resolution, Paz revealed that one Communist-led organization described Faure as an agent of Hitler, and he hinted darkly that there were many pro-Communists in the S.F.I.O.[113] Auriol attempted to inject a bit of rationality into the debate, but, nettled by insults from the floor, he demanded that the question be referred to a special commission. Faure jumped from his seat to protest vehemently, crying that the congress should not allow debate to be snuffed out by such a tactic. And when Dormoy formally moved that the matter be handed to a special commission, his motion was trounced soundly, by a vote of 4,054 to 3,299, with 197 absten-

[112] *Ibid.* Faure declared that "what is grave is that at each meeting they [the Blumistes and the *Bataille Socialiste*] looked for an international incident in order to use it to put the General Secretary in the minority."

[113] S. Grumbach shouted at Paz that "we were never members of the Communist party"—referring to Paz' membership in the Communist party in the 1920's—and Paz retorted, "At least when I was there, everyone knew it publicly." See *L'Oeuvre*, May 30, 1939.

tions. The Loire resolution was adopted immediately thereafter; the Fauristes had won another victory.[114]

Upon learning of the outcome of the vote, Dormoy sputtered that the Blumistes would not participate in the deliberations of the commission charged with the task of formulating a synthesis resolution on international policy. But Blum decided otherwise: recognizing that his majority would be slim if a vote were taken, he was willing to settle for a synthesis. Likewise, Faure, who had rejected the synthesis approach on the Loire resolution, was not adverse to a compromise solution, despite the strenuous objections of many of his supporters.[115] Faure, of course, was calculating for the future: by working out a settlement with Blum he could retain his firm grip on the Secretariat, without which his chances of capturing a solid majority of the party would be negligible. Thus, on the afternoon of May 30, Faure had a long private discussion with the ailing Blum at the latter's hotel: the two leaders agreed that a synthesis resolution would be drawn up by a commission composed of themselves, plus Zyromski, Dormoy, Spinasse, Arnol, Rivière, Salomon Grumbach, and Deixonne. They also decided that Faure would retain his post as General Secretary and that the composition of the C.A.P.—which had been elected at the Congress of Royan—would remain unchanged.[116]

Meanwhile the ritual of debate was not eliminated. A great number of speakers repeated, usually in intransigent and exaggerated language, the well-known positions of their *tendances*. Moch assailed those who, he said, would accept servitude rather than death—to whom he was referring, however, was not altogether clear, inasmuch as the Fauristes had vowed to defend France's soil and independence. Le Bail pointed an accusing finger at those

[114] *Le Populaire,* May 28, 1939. It was adopted by a vote of 5,490 to 1,761, and 268 abstentions.

[115] Interview with Roucayrol. Roucayrol declared that most of the Fauriste leaders—he mentioned Arnol, L'Hévéder, and himself—advised Faure not to accept a "synthesis," arguing that a formal schism of the party would be preferable. Roucayrol said that Faure was determined to avoid a schism.

[116] Interviews with Roucayrol, Rauzy, Castagnez, and Rosenfeld. Consult also *L'Oeuvre,* May 31, 1939; *Le Temps,* May 31, 1939; *Le Petit Parisien,* May 30, 1939; *Redressement,* June–July, 1939.

Socialists who supported the policies of "the totalitarian Soviet state," and Grumbach replied, quite logically, that a Chamberlain-Stalin bloc could hardly qualify as an "ideological" bloc. Roucayrol, designated by the Fauristes as their spokesman, declared bluntly:

We prefer Munich to war. We prefer compromise to war. . . . When we gratefully accepted the Munich accord, *we were faithful, Léon Blum,* to your Luna Park speech. . . . Your policy [today] leads to the encirclement of Germany. . . . In following your formula, we will become the docile instrument of international capitalism.[117]

Finally the moment arrived for Blum's address. Bundled tightly in an overcoat, the feeble and visibly tired leader was assisted to the speaker's platform by Faure and Séverac. His exceptionally brief speech, delivered in low tones, was solemn and not without a touch of sadness. Painfully Blum confessed that, despite his efforts since Munich, the party remained deeply divided, and he announced that he was prepared to accept a compromise solution. But, he declared, socialism would forfeit its very existence if it failed to recognize that the hour dictated a policy of resistance. On the international level this meant the union of all peaceful nations in the struggle to prevent "fascist" aggression; in France it implied the active collaboration of the Socialist and Communist parties, so that their joint action might be the catalyst of the union of all democrats. His voice cracking with emotion, Blum concluded with a pathetic appeal to the party:

I have the feeling that, by my attitude at the end of last year, I rendered a service to the party. I have the feeling that it can arrive at a common resolution. But this resolution will be efficacious only if it is frank and clear, and accepted by all with an open heart, with a complete resolve to apply it in its letter and spirit.[118]

For the loyal Socialist to have applied, "in its letter and spirit," the resolution which was the product of a tortured night of wran-

[117] *Le Populaire,* May 31, 1939. Faure's speech was much more conciliatory. He declared that differences should exist in a democratic party, and he emphasized, in a general fashion, the necessity to rejuvenate the party with pacifist sentiment. Italics mine.   [118] *Ibid.*

gling by the special commission, he would have to have been schizophrenic. The resolution that was submitted to the congress at 4:20 A.M. on the morning of May 31 by Rivière was simply an amalgamation of the Blum and Faure resolutions into a single text, although its emphasis was more Blumiste than Fauriste. It declared that the Socialist party recognized the necessity of opposing the threat of aggression "by an unbreakable will of resistance and a coalition of pacific nations powerful enough to make the Axis governments prefer free discussion to a costly and uncertain victory." "Free discussion," however, occupied a key place in the second paragraph of the resolution: the Socialist party, it read, also recognized that the organization of military resistance could not safeguard peace indefinitely; thus the party maintained its confidence in the value of "peaceful negotiations." The final paragraph juxtaposed the ideas of both Blum and Faure: it stated that the S.F.I.O. was prepared to support all efforts for

the establishment of economic cooperation [among all nations] which would assure to every nation its just share of the division of riches and its just place in a tranquil world. But it thinks that such efforts would be in vain unless they were undertaken by governments resolved to respect their word.[119]

When Rivière completed his reading of the resolution Zyromski bellowed that it was "an inferior work . . . unworthy of a Socialist congress," and, declaring that it bore little resemblance to Blum's ideas, he announced that he was placing the Blum resolution before the congress in his own name. Deixonne rebuked Zyromski for rejecting the synthesis text and declared that *Redressement* would submit its resolution to the congress because of Zyromski's obstinacy. But the weary delegates were in no mood for further argument, and they gratefully accepted the synthesis by a

[119] *Ibid.,* June 1, 1939. The resolution also stipulated that economic accords should be part of "an organization of peace," requiring progressive and controlled disarmament.

In domestic policy, the resolution declared that the party was "resolved to maintain its total independence." It added that the party was always ready to cooperate with all parties that were willing to defend republican institutions. This was far removed from the endorsement of Socialist-Communist collaboration desired by Blum.

vote of 6,395 to 565 for Zyromski, 401 for *Redressement,* and 45 for Gulkowski.[120]

The Congress of Nantes must have been a keen disappointment to Léon Blum. Rather than receiving an impressive vote of confidence, he was compelled to accept a stalemate and to recognize that his international policy commanded the support of only slightly more than half of the S.F.I.O., and that his opponents had increased their strength substantially since the Congress of Montrouge.[121] But what Blum failed to comprehend was that the degree of support that he wanted was impossible to attain: in fact, both Blum and Faure—and most of their supporters—were unable to understand that the Socialist party as they had known it since 1920 no longer existed. The S.F.I.O. was crumbling under the weight of its internal dissensions: events between the congresses of Montrouge and Nantes had accelerated the pace of the party's decomposition, and, in reality, the Nantes synthesis was merely a belated effort to shore up an already collapsing edifice. Acknowledgment of the stalemate by the leaders of the major groups averted a total collapse of the party—but only temporarily.

A LINGERING EXISTENCE

The respite from intraparty strife afforded by the adoption of the synthesis resolution was woefully brief. Blum hailed the work of the Congress of Nantes as a harsh blow to the reactionary prognosticators who had predicted freely that a formal schism would take place at Nantes, and he asserted most unconvincingly that the synthesis resolution represented "a perfectly positive,

[120] *Ibid.* There were 153 abstentions and 21 *mandats* were not cast at all. No account of the vote of the individual *fédérations* is available since the stenographic account of the congress was never published. A single typewritten stenographic account of the proceedings is available at the headquarters of the S.F.I.O. in Paris, but it does not contain a record of the votes taken at the congress.

[121] This estimate of Fauriste strength is at considerable variance from the opinion of Daniel Ligou, who argues that the final collapse of Czechoslovakia strengthened Blum's position within the party. Ligou concludes that "the debate on general policy [at Nantes] was marked by a veritable collapse of the 'Munichites'" (*Histoire du Socialisme en France, 1870–1960* [Paris, 1962], 453).

coherent, and clear doctrine, neither contradictory nor equivocal."[122] Faure's assessment, however, was a bit more perceptive: he chortled that his adversaries in the party were furious over the result of the congress.[123] Beneath the superficial atmosphere of normality in the party—Faure began to write in *Le Populaire* again—the conflict was quickly resumed.

During these months Blum frantically demanded that France take more vigorous action for the construction of a "peace front" against the menace of aggression: peaceful peoples, he said, "must signify that they are not afraid of war." Blum frequently displayed his irritation at the fact that no concrete Franco-British-Soviet accord was concluded, and he was indignant that anyone could deny the good faith of the U.S.S.R. "No one," he said, "can doubt reasonably what the position of Soviet Russia would be if an armed conflict were to erupt in Europe. . . . We are impatiently waiting for her integration into the defensive front of peaceful peoples." At the same time, worried as he was about the delay in building a "peace front," Blum was no longer frightened by the prospect of war. He even began to speak as if war was likely to occur: "If a universal war should once again desolate the world, we must determine, this time, to build a truly stable and durable peace." After such a war, he wrote, the "other Germany," the "democratic" Germany, would be reborn, and she would be the bulwark of a European democratic system. For Blum, security in the present rested upon armaments and a powerful coalition of powers willing to resist German aggression, but in the future— and in the summer of 1939 Blum was clearly looking to the future —security must be the collective endeavor of democratic and disarmed nations. Thus real peace required the existence of a democratic Germany, and if, by Blum's own admission, the present armed peace could not last indefinitely, then war was likely to be the vehicle for the achievement of a real peace. If war should come, Blum was prepared to accept it with a heavy heart, but also with hope and confidence.[124]

[122] *Le Populaire,* June 2, 1939.   [123] *Le Pays Socialiste,* June 9, 1939.

[124] *Le Populaire,* June 18, 25, July 2, 23, 25, 27, 29, 1939. Faith in the Soviet Union's determination to stand with Great Britain and France was shared by Blum's supporters, e.g., Daniel Mayer: "The Communists have come over to our concepts of national defense and democracy" (*AGIR,* August 1, 1939).

Faure and his many comrades also believed war to be danger-ously near, but, unlike Blum, they were determined to keep France out of the conflict. Faure himself, driven by a sense of urgency, delivered innumerable speeches and wrote dozens of articles, tirelessly exalting the pacifist creed. "Why not negotia-tions?" he asked feverishly. "With whom does one negotiate if not with the masters of Germany and Italy?" For the General Secre-tary of the S.F.I.O., war offered only the certainty of the devasta-tion of civilization. France's salvation, he cried, lay in renouncing war: "We must understand the needs of the German people," he declared; "we must avoid war even at the risk of sacrifices." Steadfastly maintaining that none of Europe's problems were insoluble, Faure noted suspiciously that the Soviet Union was negotiating for a commercial accord with Germany, and he in-quired, "Why cannot we negotiate to save the lives of millions?"[125]

Some Fauristes, however, were certain that Stalin was seeking more than a commercial accord with Hitler. L'Hévéder declared that Germany and the Soviet Union were conspiring together,[126] and Roucayrol voiced his suspicions about a possible German-So-viet Pact;[127] Rauzy openly predicted that Hitler would be assured of Soviet neutrality in the event of European conflict.[128] Thus, after Nantes, the Fauristes renewed their pacifist and anti-Soviet offensive.[129] Like Blum, they were concerned with negotiations, but unlike Blum, they desired negotiations with Germany, not the Soviet Union; they were prepared to make further concessions to Hitler; and, above all, they were determined to spare France from what was to them the ultimate tragedy—war.

Blum was staggered by the news of the Nazi-Soviet Pact. Con-

Zyromski added his powerful voice in support of Blum's plea, and he added: "Let us be frank. Do not certain of our comrades consider 'Bolshevism' as the principal enemy and do they not believe the elimination of the Communist party to be an essential objective?" (*ibid.*, July 12, 1939. Of course, Zyromski was absolutely correct).

[125] *Le Pays Socialiste*, June 16, 30, July 7, 21, 1939; *Le Travailleur des Alpes* (Basses-Alpes) August 19, 1939; *L'Auvergne Socialiste* (Puy-de-Dôme), July 1, 1939; *La Volonté Socialiste* (Drôme), July 15, 1939; *Le Populaire*, June 5, July 17, 25, 1939. [126] *Le Rappel du Morbihan*, June 10, 1939.

[127] *Le Pays Socialiste*, July 7, 1939.

[128] *Le Midi Socialiste* (Haute-Garonne), August 7, 1939.

[129] *Le Pays Socialiste*, August 25, 1939.

fessing his "stupor," he lamented that this event was "almost unbelievable," and a "rude blow to the cause of peace."[130] It was also a "rude blow" to his international policy and consequently to his position as leader of the Socialist party. Blum's international policy since March, 1938, had been predicated on the achievement of a Franco-British-Soviet entente; now his hopes were devastated. Nonetheless, Blum appealed weakly for unity and determination on the part of Britain and France: "Our guarantee of Poland," he declared, "must not be abandoned."

For the Fauristes, however, this was a moment of jubilant triumph: the Nazi-Soviet Pact, they believed, represented a total vindication of their long-standing suspicion of the Soviet Union. Paul Faure declared:

Some among us can boast of having anticipated this event and of having denounced for a long time—since 1920 to be exact—Russian Bolshevism and its agents, and of never placing any faith in Moscow's policy.

It was senseless to play the Russian card, for peace as for war.

Naturally it was difficult to cry this from the rooftops, under the threat of being accused of sacrificing French interests and being classed among the traitors of the Fifth Column.

But no one was ignorant of our attitude, not even the members of the government.[131]

Moreover, Faure considered that the pact fully demonstrated the correctness of his international policy:

[130] *Le Populaire,* August 23, 24, 1939.

[131] *Ibid.* Jean Le Bail summarized the Fauriste indictment of Blum's international policy in *Le Populaire,* September 2, 1939. He wrote, in part: "We were right when we attacked communism for monopolizing and sabotaging the struggle of the Spanish Republicans at the risk of creating a general war. We were right when we refused, in the Czechoslovakian affair, to become the soldiers of Stalin, who was pushing France to engage in a disastrous adventure. . . . We were right at Montrouge in our struggle to prevent the party from forgetting Jaurès and from making the Russian alliance the pivot of a 'policy of firmness.' We were right when, very recently, we declared that a 'peace front' with Russia to be impossible. With what sarcasm and with what patriotic indignation were we greeted for this warning! . . . Those who had not foreseen this eventuality have sinned by ignorance or by an inexplicable blindness. The truth is that for a year the partisans of 'firmness' have built their policy upon myths."

Now, let us have the courage—yes, the courage—to face reality.

Even without official signatures, those who demanded an attitude of firmness had always counted on the effective military assistance of Russia. . . .

Franco-British diplomacy can and should appeal publicly to Warsaw, Berlin, Rome, Tokyo, and Washington.

It can and should offer peace to the world.[132]

The celebration of the Fauristes was brutally terminated by the outbreak of war, responsibility for which they assigned to the Soviet Union as well as to Hitler.[133] Faure himself believed the war to be a great and unnecessary tragedy, and although he was disheartened by his failure to secure an appeal for peace by the Socialist International, he vowed not to abandon his efforts for

[132] *Le Pays Socialiste,* October 6, 13, 1939. In the earlier number, Fernand Roucayrol wrote: "One thing is certain. They [the Soviets] very deliberately wanted and provoked the war. . . .

"It was not without reason that they [the Communists] brusquely abandoned revolutionary defeatism to pass over to the highest form of chauvinism. Under the cover of antifascism and unstinting opposition to Hitler, it was their duty to prepare the 'Communist masses,' and as many others as possible, for the idea of a war against Germany, and to suppress every desire and every attempt to prevent war. . . .

"At the time of the Spanish war, no effort was spared to throw France into an adventure on a terrain admirably chosen to oppose her squarely against Germany and Italy. . . .

"There was a single task [for Stalin]. To make Hitler fight in the west.

"What is necessary now for Stalin is the mutual exhaustion of the combatants that he has set against each other; then after a long and hard struggle, Russian forces, as meager as they may be, will be the only forces intact and capable of serving the interests of Russian nationalism and of sovietizing those states weakened by war."

In the number of October 13, Faure wrote: "It [the Communist party] is a party which did everything possible—on the command of its masters in Moscow—to push France into war over Spain, then over Czechoslovakia, and now over Poland."

[133] André Delmas, *A Gauche de la barricade* (Paris, 1950), 202–203. Faure and Delmas, on the afternoon of August 27, agreed upon the text of an "international pacifist manifesto" which declared their unalterable opposition to a war. Faure appointed Paz and Roucayrol to accompany Delmas to Brussels in order to persuade the bureau of the I.O.S. and F.S.I. to adopt this "manifesto" as its own, but the emissaries met with an unenthusiastic response.

peace: "In any event, our opinions and our sentiments are known. They have been neither modified nor attenuated by the outbreak of war, but have been bolstered and reinforced."[134]

Blum, recovering from his shock over the Nazi-Soviet Pact, accepted war with resignation, but not without strong hope for the future. His declaration to the party was clearly an expression of the sentiments that he had felt in July and August:

Thus the most pacific people in the world finds itself carried into war. It will fight for its liberty, for its existence, for its honor. . . . It will fight in war for peace, for a real peace based upon justice and reason, a peace which will rest on the freedom and fraternal cooperation of all peoples.[135]

[134] *Le Pays Socialiste,* September 15, 1939.
[135] *Le Populaire,* September 4, 1939.

Conclusion

During his wartime incarceration, Blum sought to account for the failure of the Socialist party, after Munich, to offer leadership to the working class and to the nation. This failure, he lamented, was attributable to the party's ambiguous and equivocal attitude, and to the fact that

after Munich, French socialism was split into two factions, in conflict with each other over the fundamental problem of the day. . . .

It was this internal division which condemned the party to impotence and almost to silence. It was anxious to preserve its formal unity at all costs, and any clear action, or even any categoric statement, would have revealed the division and doubtless would have provoked a schism. The opposing forces within the party were balanced to the point of mutual cancellation. . . . And so, for nearly two years, the party dragged out its existence, humiliated and suspected, until finally no one seemed to be aware of its presence.[1]

As Blum admits, even after the outbreak of war, the leaders of the S.F.I.O. were unable to speak with a single voice or to demonstrate a united will. Léon Blum and Paul Faure were as profoundly divided on the responsibilities for the war as they had been on the means to prevent it. Although an epilogue to this sorry chapter in the history of French socialism was to come at Vichy in July, 1940, where Blum sat mute and humiliated as the overwhelming majority of the Socialist parliamentary group voted in favor of full powers for Marshal Pétain,[2] the S.F.I.O.

[1] Léon Blum, *L'Oeuvre, 1940–1945, A l'Echelle humaine* (Paris, 1955), 455–456. I have consulted the translation of this passage by W. Pickles (Léon Blum, *For All Mankind* [New York, 1946], 110).

[2] Daniel Ligou, *Histoire du Socialisme en France, 1870–1960* (Paris, 1962), 469; *Journal Officiel*, July 11, 1940, 6–7. Only twenty-eight Socialist deputies

278

already was shattered by September, 1939. Paralyzed by its deep internal crisis since Munich, the Socialist party had offered to the working class and to the nation only an ignominious spectacle of dissension and conflict.

Yet Munich was not solely, or even primarily, responsible for the intraparty strife, but was the catalyst of a clash that had been developing steadily since Hitler's accession to power. The S.F.I.O. had attained maturity within a stable political system, when it was suddenly vaulted into preeminence as a consequence of the French Left's reaction to "fascism," a phenomenon of which Socialists had little understanding. By 1936 the Socialist party had become a truly mass party, but many of its established leaders held firm to the ideas, beliefs, and ways of the past, and were successful in carrying much of the party with them. And as the question of a decisive response to the aspirations of Nazi Germany became ever more acute, Socialists discovered that they could renounce ambiguity only at the cost of ruin for their party. After Munich the S.F.I.O. could no longer afford the luxury of indecision, and it was compelled to choose between the views associated with Léon Blum on the one hand and Paul Faure on the other. The international policies of Blum and Faure had moved in quite dissimilar directions after 1933, although the evolution of Blum's position was tortuous and less steady, and not without several oscillations. Faure's reaction to each increase in international tension—the Ethiopian affair, the German reoccupation of the Rhineland, the Spanish Civil War, the *Anschluss,* and the Sudeten crisis—was to reinforce his pacifist and anti-Soviet position, while Blum reluctantly and laboriously turned away from his ideals and adopted what to him was the only conceivable response to harsh realities. Their differences over Soviet Russia

voted with Blum against the grant of special powers. They were: Auriol, Audeguil, Bedin, Biondi, Buisset, Cabannes, Camel, Chaussy, Collomp, Froment, Gouin, Guy, Hussel, Jordery, Lucquot, Malroux, Martin, Mauger, Moch, Moutet, Noguères, Philip, Tanguy-Prigent, Roche, Rolland, Rous, Thivrier, and Zunino. Faure was not present, but the great majority of the deputies that had supported his position at the congresses of Montrouge and Nantes voted in favor. The exceptions were: Biondi, Audeguil, Chaussy, Cabannes, Froment, Gouin, Hussel, Lucquot, Malroux, Noguères, Roche, Rolland, and Thivrier.

were a major source of their discord. Faure never abandoned his
suspicion that Stalin was seeking to provoke a general war; Blum
relied increasingly on the U.S.S.R. as the keystone of his international policy. After Munich, opinion in the S.F.I.O. polarized
around these two leaders: behind each stood approximately one-
half of the party. Blum was supported by his close associates,
many of the larger *fédérations,* and by his former critics, the
members of the *Bataille Socialiste.* Faure held the allegiance of a
majority of the party's parliamentarians and of numerous *fédérations,* plus the remnants of the *Gauche Révolutionnaire.* The
road to the political collapse of socialism that occurred after
Munich had been well illuminated, but few Socialists had taken
the care to see where it was leading. Although the polarization of
opinion had begun in earnest over the problem of nonintervention in the Spanish Civil War, the post-Munich conflict caught
most of the Socialist party unprepared.

Much of the responsibility for the debacle of French socialism
lies with Léon Blum. Despite the magnificence of his personality
and the rigid integrity of his intellect, a severe indictment of his
leadership is unavoidable. In his domestic actions, his performance was highly creditable: he reacted with alacrity to what he
believed to be the threat of "fascism" within France and secured
his party's acceptance of cooperation with the Communists and
the Radicals, and although he was imprisoned by his scrupulous
fidelity to his conception of the "exercise of power," his government was undermined from the very beginning by unforeseen
difficulties and by the formidable obstacles placed before it by
both his opponents and his nominal allies. Blum's real failure was
in the area of international policy. It was not until after the shock
of the *Anschluss* that his international policy shed its dualism and
much of its ambiguity; only then did Blum recognize that his
dreams of a peaceful and disarmed Europe must be held in abeyance, and he forced himself first to acknowledge that only the
willingness to use force could prevent Nazi aggression and later to
accept war in order to secure a genuine peace. But prior to March,
1938, his policy suffered from the conflict between his aspirations
and his growing awareness of reality; still he consistently explained his actions in the vocabulary of pacifism. Blum never
tired of pledging his devotion to peace and of vowing to do

everything to prevent war, and while it is unquestionable that his position underwent a perceptible evolution during the years from 1933 to 1938, the path to his post-*Anschluss* international policy was effectively camouflaged by his persistent exaltation of pacifist idealism. This left an indelible stamp on the Socialist party and was a very real contribution to its decline and ultimate collapse.

Blum's pacifist rhetoric might not have damaged the S.F.I.O. so severely had he been the sole and unquestioned leader of the party. But Blum's public declarations, over a long period, appeared to be fully consonant with those of a man who was held in high esteem by the great majority of the party and who was considered to be the personification of socialism by many. Unlike Blum, Paul Faure experienced no harrowing intellectual crisis over the problem of international policy, but instead was motivated by certain basic and immutable beliefs. To the General Secretary of the S.F.I.O. and to a majority of the party's notables, peace was socialism's supreme value, and to them Blum's position after the *Anschluss* constituted a betrayal of traditional Socialist ideals. Faure's international policy from 1933 through 1939 was marked by a rigorous consistency: imprisoned by his beliefs and suspicions, Faure's policy embodied a nationalist pacifism which had at its core an unbending hostility to the Soviet Union. More afraid of Stalin than of Hitler, Faure refused to admit of any fundamental difference between the aspirations of Imperial Germany and the Third *Reich,* and was willing to make lavish concessions to Hitler's Germany in order to save France from a war in which, he believed, she would meet with certain defeat. Faure's share of the responsibility for the collapse of the Socialist party is commensurate with Blum's: Faure tenaciously refused to question his fixed beliefs, even after the dismemberment of Czechoslovakia, or for that matter, after the outbreak of war. But the attitude of Faure and his many supporters in 1938 and 1939 should have evoked no surprise, for it was the logical product of a policy that they had followed since 1933.

And so the years of crisis were also years of decline for the S.F.I.O. It is only too clear that, during the three and a half years preceding the outbreak of the Second World War, the French Socialist party was unable to sustain the antifascist reflex which had brought it to power. Our investigation has demonstrated the utter futility of attempting to define a specifically "Socialist" position on any of the major international problems during these years. Each increase in international tension, from the Spanish Civil War to the Sudeten crisis, sharpened the division within the S.F.I.O., until, after Munich, the party became so divided that, in the words of Léon Blum, it "dragged on its existence, humiliated and suspected, until finally no one seemed to be aware of its presence."

Tables

Table 1. Socialist vote in the elections of 1936, by department

Department	Party position	% of votes	No. of deputies	S.F.I.O. total vote 1936	S.F.I.O. total vote 1932
Region 1. LANGUEDOC					
Ariège	7	36.0	3	15,620	13,395
Aude	6	37.2	1	26,804	25,336
Gard	12	32.1	3	29,239	29,210
Hérault	23	27.0	3	28,276	48,395
Py.-Or.	37	20.8	1	15,421	19,285
Tarn	15	30.6	3	24,742	33,389
Region		30.0	14 (9.5% of Soc. dep.)	140,102 (7% of Soc. tot.)	169,010 (8.1% of Soc. tot.)
Region 2. RHONE VALLEY–PROVENCE					
Alp.-Mar.	80	8.4	0	5,506	1,749
B.-du-Rhône	11	33.1	5	62,499	74,367
Drôme	8	34.6	2	22,969	31,745
Var	31	22.9	2	15,740	25,995
Vaucluse	17	29.9	2	16,576	14,482
Region		27.6	11 (7.5% of Soc. dep.)	123,290 (6% of Soc. tot.)	148,338 (7% of Soc. tot.)

Note. "Party position" indicates the rank of the department according to the percentage of the vote received by the S.F.I.O. on the first ballot as determined by the party's Secretariat. The third column, "per cent of votes," indicates the percentage of the vote received by Socialist candidates on the first ballot. The composite regional percentage at the bottom of the column is computed according to the total number of votes cast for the S.F.I.O. in the entire region. The percentages at the bottom of columns five and six are the percentages of the nation-wide Socialist vote cast by each region in 1932 and 1936.

Sources. Georges Lachapelle, *Elections législatives, 1er et 8 mai 1932, Résultats officiels* (Paris, 1932), 348–351; *Le Populaire*, April 27 and 28, 1936.

Department	Party position	% of votes	No. of deputies	S.F.I.O. total vote	
				1936	1932
Region 3. NORTH					
Nord	13	31.8	13	161,903	162,062
Oise	48	17.5	2	16,924	19,627
P.-de-Cal.	26	25.6	6	71,331	76,578
Somme	41	20.3	2	24,533	29,885
Region		26.3	23 (15.7% of Soc. dep.)	274,691 (13.8% of Soc. tot.)	288,152 (14.6% of Soc. tot.)
Region 4. GARONNE BASIN					
Dordogne	53	16.3	1	17,324	13,553
H.-Gar.	1	48.8	5	53,460	44,795
L.-et-Gar.	83	6.1	0	4,967	8,916
T.-et-Gar.	27	25.2	1	10,784	7,246
Region		25.8	7 (4.8% of Soc. dep.)	86,535 (4.3% of Soc. tot.)	74,510 (3.8% of Soc. tot.)
Region 5. MASSIF CENTRAL					
Ardèche	25	26.1	1	19,225	17,539
Aveyron	87	3.6	0	3,027	11,627
Cantal	32	21.6	0	18,370	4,824
Corrèze	10	33.9	3	23,201	12,989
Creuse	2	47.4	3	25,301	27,734
Haute-Loire	52	17.1	1	10,861	538
Lot	74	9.5	0	4,652	5,397
Lozère	92	0.6	0	106	2,172
Puy-de-Dôme	21	27.7	5	33,611	52,309
Haute-Vienne	3	45.8	5	43,303	39,925
Region		25.7	18 (12.3% of Soc. dep.)	181,657 (9% of Soc. tot.)	175,054 (8.9% of Soc. tot.)
Region 6. LYONNAIS					
Ain	54	15.9	1	12,054	4,384
Isère	14	30.8	5	50,113	38,216
Loire	57	14.5	1	22,319	23,331
Rhône	39	20.5	4	40,374	38,518
S.-et-Loire	5	40.9	6	56,860	55,860
Region		24.9	17 (11.6% of Soc. dep.)	181,720 (9% of Soc. tot.)	160,309 (8.1% of Soc. tot.)

Department	Party position	% of votes	No. of deputies	S.F.I.O. total vote	
				1936	1932
Region 7. CENTRAL FRANCE					
Allier	4	44.8	6	44,138	47,254
Cher	30	23.2	2	19,384	17,673
Côte d'Or	19	29.5	2	21,161	24,440
Indre	75	9.2	0	6,293	17,588
Nièvre	20	29.0	2	19,746	19,751
Yonne	33	21.5	2	15,354	14,521
Region		24.6	14	126,076	141,227
			(9.5% of	(6% of	(7.2% of
			Soc. dep.)	Soc. tot.)	Soc. tot.)
Region 8. NORTHEAST					
Aisne	18	29.6	6	34,557	29,040
Ardennes	35	21.0	1	14,109	17,893
Aube	55	15.9	0	9,549	6,354
Marne	28	23.9	1	22,399	19,195
Region		24.2	8	80,614	72,482
			(5.5% of	(4% of	(3.1% of
			Soc. dep.)	Soc. tot.)	Soc. tot.)
Region 9. BRITTANY					
C.-du-Nord	70	10.8	1	13,067	9,799
Finistère	63	13.6	2	22,635	19,672
Ille-et-V.	56	15.2	0	20,137	15,013
Loire-Inf.	24	26.4	4	42,494	33,090
Morbihan	46	18.0	1	20,221	16,071
Region		17.1	8	118,554	93,645
			(5.5% of	(5.5% of	(4.8% of
			Soc. dep.)	Soc. tot.)	Soc. tot.)
Region 10. WEST CENTRAL FRANCE					
Char.-Inf.	44	19.3	1	20,718	8,003
I.-et-Loire	22	27.5	3	24,517	20,228
M.-et-Loire	85	3.9	0	4,375	3,508
Sarthe	29	23.3	0	22,039	12,690
Deux-Sèvres	60	14.2	1	12,165	4,495
Vienne	58	14.4	0	12,009	7,437
Region		16.6	5	95,823	56,361
			(3.4% of	(4.8% of	(2.4% of
			Soc. dep.)	Soc. tot.)	Soc. tot.)

Department	Party position	% of votes	No. of deputies	S.F.I.O. total vote 1936	S.F.I.O. total vote 1932
Region 11. ALGERIA					
Alger	34	24.1	1	14,155	3,212
Constantine	79	8.5	0	6,106	2,419
Oran	51	17.3	1	10,626	7,789
Region		15.5	2 (1.4% of Soc. dep.)	30,887 (1.6% of Soc. tot.)	13,420 (0.7% of Soc. tot.)
Region 12. SOUTHWEST					
Charente	68	11.1	0	9,294	17,203
Gers	16	30.1	2	14,454	9,614
Gironde	50	17.4	3	35,262	67,809
Landes	45	18.8	0	13,025	2,032
Basses-Pyr.	82	6.4	0	6,707	5,551
Hautes-Pyr.	65	12.7	0	6,230	614
Region		15.3	5 (3.4% of Soc. dep.)	84,972 (4.3% of Soc. tot.)	102,823 (5.2% of Soc. tot.)
Region 13. ALPS REGION					
Basses-Alpes	9	34.2	2	7,776	10,948
Hautes-Alpes	47	17.5	1	3,829	4,827
Savoie	81	7.4	1	4,238	8,746
Haute-Savoie	62	13.7	1	9,170	11,508
Region		14.8	5 (3.4% of Soc. dep.)	25,013 (1.3% of Soc. tot.)	36,029 (1.8% of Soc. tot.)
Region 14. PARIS REGION					
Seine	61	14.0	3	139,740	158,398
Seine-et-Marne	40	20.3	2	20,284	16,442
Seine-et-Oise	59	14.1	1	46,168	40,043
Region		14.4	6 (4.1% of Soc. dep.)	206,192 (10.1% of Soc. tot.)	214,883 (10.9% of Soc. tot.)
Region 15. EASTERN FRANCE					
Doubs	43	19.6	0	13,800	10,855
Jura	36	20.9	1	11,078	9,682
Haute-Marne	78	8.7	0	4,212	1,997
Meuse	64	12.9	0	6,560	3,059

Department	Party position	% of votes	No. of deputies	S.F.I.O. total vote 1936	S.F.I.O. total vote 1932
Region 15. EASTERN FRANCE (*continued*)					
Meurthe-et-M.	77	9.0	0	10,875	20,932
Moselle	90	1.0	0	1,380	4,817
Belfort	49	17.4	0	3,678	1,872
Bas-Rhin	69	11.0	0	16,345	20,250
Haut-Rhin	38	20.6	0	26,100	29,132
Haute-Saône	72	9.9	0	5,757	6,732
Vosges	84	5.1	0	4,847	8,639
Region		10.8	1 (0.7% of Soc. dep.)	104,632 (5% of Soc. tot.)	117,967 (6% of Soc. tot.)
Region 16. THE ORLÉANAIS					
Loiret	89	1.6	0	1,420	14,332
Loir-et-Cher	42	19.8	2	13,553	22,237
Region		9.5	2 (1.4% of Soc. dep.)	14,973 (0.8% of Soc. tot.)	36,569 (1.8% of Soc. tot.)
Region 17. WESTERN FRANCE					
Eure	71	10.6	1	7,992	7,343
Eure-et-Loir	76	9.1	0	5,594	8,813
Mayenne	93	0.2	0	105	—
Orne	88	2.7	0	1,741	1,710
Vendée	66	12.3	0	12,451	5,859
Region		7.9	1 (0.7% of Soc. dep.)	27,883 (1.4% of Soc. tot.)	23,725 (1.2% of Soc. tot.)
Region 18. NORMANDY					
Calvados	67	11.2	0	9,369	8,199
Manche	73	9.5	0	9,315	4,535
Seine-Inf.	86	3.8	0	6,654	17,985
Region		7.0	0	25,338 (1.3% of Soc. tot.)	30,719 (1.6% of Soc. tot.)

Table 2. Active male population in 1936, by department

Department	Active male population (in thousands)	% engaged in agriculture	% of industrial workers
Region 1. LANGUEDOC			
Ariège	51.1	60.0–67.5	15.0–22.5
Aude	92.0	52.5–60.0	7.5–15.0
Gard	120.7	37.5–45.0	30.0–37.5
Hérault	159.0	45.0–52.5	15.0–22.5
Pyrénées-Orientales	74.5	45.0–52.5	15.0–22.5
Tarn	94.5	45.0–52.5	15.0–22.5
Total	591.8		
Region 2. RHONE VALLEY–PROVENCE			
Alpes-Maritimes	152.1	15.0–22.5	22.5–30.0
Bouches-du-Rhône	353.0	1.0– 7.5	30.0–37.5
Drôme	86.5	45.0–52.5	15.0–22.5
Var	138.7	22.5–30.0	22.5–30.0
Vaucluse	79.4	45.0–52.5	15.0–22.5
Total	809.7		
Region 3. NORTH			
Nord	604.1	7.5–15.0	52.5–60.0
Oise	120.4	30.0–37.5	30.0–37.5
Pas-de-Calais	352.9	15.0–22.5	52.5–60.0
Somme	138.4	30.0–37.5	30.0–37.5
Total	1,215.8		
Region 4. GARONNE BASIN			
Dordogne	127.3	60.0–67.5	15.0–22.5
Haute-Garonne	143.6	37.5–45.0	30.0–37.5
Lot-et-Garonne	80.6	60.0–67.5	7.5–15.0
Tarn-et-Garonne	53.8	60.0–67.5	7.5–15.0
Total	405.3		
Region 5. MASSIF CENTRAL			
Ardèche	84.1	60.0–67.5	15.0–22.5
Aveyron	95.3	60.0–67.5	15.0–22.5
Cantal	53.8	60.0–67.5	7.5–15.0

Sources. Etat Français, Ministère de l'Economie Nationale et des Finances, *Annuaire Statistique abrégé*, I (Paris, 1943), 79–80. The percentage of the active male population engaged in agriculture and industry is taken from Georges Dupeux, *op. cit.*, 164–165.

Department	Active male population (in thousands)	% engaged in agriculture	% of industrial workers
Region 5. MASSIF CENTRAL (*Continued*)			
Corrèze	82.6	60.0–67.5	7.5–15.0
Creuse	66.3	60.0–67.5	1.0– 7.5
Haute-Loire	72.8	60.0–67.5	7.5–15.0
Lot	52.9	67.5–74.0	7.5–15.0
Lozère	27.1	60.0–67.5	15.0–22.5
Puy-de-Dôme	154.4	60.0–67.5	15.0–22.5
Haute-Vienne	107.9	45.0–52.5	15.0–22.5
Total	797.2		
Region 6. LYONNAIS			
Ain	101.6	52.5–60.0	15.0–22.5
Isère	182.0	30.0–37.5	30.0–37.5
Loire	203.8	22.5–30.0	45.0–52.5
Rhône	285.3	7.5–15.0	37.5–45.0
Saône-et-Loire	168.6	45.0–52.5	22.5–30.0
Total	941.3		
Region 7. CENTRAL FRANCE			
Allier	119.9	45.0–52.5	22.5–30.0
Cher	94.2	45.0–52.5	22.5–30.0
Côte d'Or	105.0	37.5–45.0	22.5–30.0
Indre	80.3	60.0–67.5	7.5–15.0
Nièvre	79.5	45.0–52.5	22.5–30.0
Yonne	84.5	45.0–52.5	15.0–22.5
Total	563.4		
Region 8. NORTHEAST			
Aisne	141.8	30.0–37.5	30.0–37.5
Ardennes	88.6	22.5–30.0	37.5–45.0
Aube	77.0	30.0–37.5	30.0–37.5
Marne	131.4	30.0–37.5	22.5–30.0
Total	438.8		
Region 9. BRITTANY			
Finistère	214.9	45.0–52.5	15.0–22.5
Ille-et-Vilaine	164.8	52.5–60.0	15.0–22.5
Loire-Inférieure	198.6	37.5–45.0	30.0–37.5
Morbihan	161.9	60.0–67.5	7.5–15.0
Côtes-du-Nord	149.2	60.0–67.5	7.5–15.0
Total	889.4		

Department	Active male population (in thousands)	% engaged in agriculture	% of industrial workers
Region 10. WEST CENTRAL FRANCE			
Charente-Inf.	137.5	52.5–60.0	15.0–22.5
Indre-et-Loire	109.1	45.0–52.5	15.0–22.5
Maine-et-Loire	144.4	45.0–52.5	15.0–22.5
Sarthe	113.5	45.0–52.5	15.0–22.5
Deux-Sèvres	96.9	60.0–67.5	7.5–15.0
Vienne	98.0	52.5–60.0	7.5–15.0
Total	699.4		
Region 11. ALGERIA—No information			
Region 12. SOUTHWEST			
Charente	100.3	52.5–60.0	15.0–22.5
Gers	67.1	67.5–74.0	1.0– 7.5
Gironde	265.4	30.0–37.5	30.0–37.5
Landes	85.3	60.0–67.5	15.0–22.5
Basses-Pyrénées	127.8	60.0–67.5	15.0–22.5
Hautes-Pyrénées	60.3	60.0–67.5	15.0–22.5
Total	706.2		
Region 13. ALPS REGION			
Basses-Alpes	29.1	52.5–60.0	7.5–15.0
Hautes-Alpes	30.1	60.0–67.5	7.5–15.0
Savoie	79.2	45.0–52.5	15.0–22.5
Haute-Savoie	84.3	45.0–52.5	15.0–22.5
Total	222.7		
Region 14. PARIS REGION			
Seine	1,696.4	1.0– 7.5	52.5–60.0
Seine-et-Marne	118.4	30.0–37.5	30.0–37.5
Seine-et-Oise	313.9	15.0–22.5	37.5–45.0
Total	2,128.7		
Region 15. EASTERN FRANCE			
Doubs	96.9	30.0–37.5	37.5–45.0
Jura	68.4	45.0–52.5	22.5–30.0
Haute-Marne	58.9	30.0–37.5	30.0–37.5
Meuse	69.5	30.0–37.5	22.5–30.0
Meurthe-et-M.	182.8	7.5–15.0	45.0–52.5
Moselle	235.1	15.0–22.5	37.5–45.0

Department	Active male population (in thousands)	% engaged in agriculture	% of industrial workers
Region 15. EASTERN FRANCE (*Continued*)			
Belfort	33.1	15.0–22.5	30.0–37.5
Bas-Rhin	232.7	22.5–30.0	30.0–37.5
Haut-Rhin	158.3	15.0–22.5	37.5–45.0
Haute-Saône	63.2	45.0–52.5	22.5–45.0
Vosges	117.0	22.5–30.0	37.5–45.0
Total	1,315.9		
Region 16. THE ORLÉANAIS			
Loiret	108.4	45.0–52.5	22.5–30.0
Loir-et-Cher	74.8	52.5–60.0	15.0–22.5
Total	183.2		
Region 17. WESTERN FRANCE			
Eure	92.3	37.5–45.0	22.5–30.0
Eure-et-Loir	77.5	45.0–52.5	15.0–22.5
Mayenne	75.6	60.0–67.5	7.5–15.0
Orne	81.3	52.5–60.0	15.0–22.5
Vendée	118.6	60.0–67.5	7.5–15.0
Total	445.3		
Region 18. NORMANDY			
Calvados	119.4	37.5–45.0	22.5–30.0
Manche	128.6	52.5–60.0	15.0–22.5
Seine-Inférieure	276.5	15.0–22.5	37.5–45.0
Total	524.5		

Table 3. Socialist deputies elected, 1924–1936, by department

Department	1924	1928	1932	1936
LANGUEDOC				
Ariège		1	1	3
Aude	1	1	1	1

Sources. Georges Lachapelle, *Elections législatives, le 11 mai 1924* (Paris, 1924); *Elections législatives, 22 et 29 avril 1928* (Paris, 1928); *Elections législatives, 1er et 8 mai 1932* (Paris, 1932); *Elections législatives, 26 avril et 3 mai 1936* (Paris, 1936).

Department	1924	1928	1932	1936
LANGUEDOC (*Continued*)				
Gard	2	3	4	3
Hérault	2	1	4	3
Pyrénées-Or.	1	1	3	1
Tarn	2	4	2	3
Totals	8	11	15	14
RHONE VALLEY–PROVENCE				
Alpes-Maritimes				
Bouches-du-Rhône	5	6	7	5
Drôme	1	3	3	2
Var	3	5	4	2
Vaucluse	1	1	1	2
Totals	10	15	15	11
NORTH				
Nord	11	5	9	13
Oise	1	2	1	2
Pas-de-Calais	6	5	4	6
Somme			3	2
Totals	18	12	17	23
GARONNE BASIN				
Dordogne			1	1
Haute-Garonne	4	2	2	5
Lot-et-Garonne				
Tarn-et-Garonne	1	1		1
Totals	5	3	3	7
MASSIF CENTRAL				
Ardèche	1		2	1
Aveyron		1	1	
Cantal	1		1	
Corrèze	1	1	1	3
Creuse	1	1	3	3
Haute-Loire				1
Lot	1			
Lozère				
Puy-de-Dôme	3	4	3	5
Haute-Vienne	5		3	5
Totals	13	7	14	18

Department	1924	1928	1932	1936
LYONNAIS				
Ain	1	1		1
Isère	3	4	4	5
Loire	1	1	1	1
Rhône	5	5	3	4
Saône-et-Loire	5	5	4	6
Totals	15	16	12	17
CENTRAL FRANCE				
Allier	3	3	5	6
Cher			2	2
Côte d'Or	1		1	2
Indre	1	1	2	
Nièvre	2	4	1	2
Yonne		1	1	2
Totals	7	9	12	14
NORTHEAST				
Aisne		3	3	6
Ardennes		1	2	1
Aube				
Marne	1			1
Totals	1	4	5	8
BRITTANY				
Côtes-du-Nord				1
Finistère	2	2	1	2
Ille-et-Vilaine				
Loire-Inf.		1	2	4
Morbihan			1	1
Totals	2	3	4	8
WEST CENTRAL FRANCE				
Charente-Inf.	1			1
Indre-et-Loire	2	1	1	3
Maine-et-Loire				
Sarthe	2			
Deux-Sèvres	1			1
Vienne				
Totals	6	1	1	5

Department	1924	1928	1932	1936
ALGERIA				
Alger				1
Constantine				
Oran				1
Totals				2
SOUTHWEST				
Charente		1	1	
Gers				2
Gironde	2	2	7	3
Landes				
Basses-Pyrénées				
Hautes-Pyrénées				
Totals	2	3	8	5
ALPS				
Basses-Alpes	2	2	2	2
Hautes-Alpes	1	1	1	1
Savoie			1	1
Haute-Savoie	1	1		1
Totals	4	4	4	5
PARIS REGION				
Seine	4	4	9	3
Seine-et-Marne	1		1	2
Seine-et-Oise				1
Totals	5	4	10	6
EASTERN FRANCE				
Doubs		1	1	
Jura	1	1	1	1
Haute-Marne				
Meuse				
Meurthe-et-Moselle				
Moselle				
Terr. de Belfort				
Bas-Rhin	2	1	1	
Haut-Rhin		1		
Haute-Saône		1	1	
Vosges				
Totals	3	5	4	1

Department	1924	1928	1932	1936
THE ORLÉANAIS				
Loiret	1	1	1	
Loir-et-Cher	1	2	2	2
Totals	2	3	3	2
WESTERN FRANCE				
Eure				1
Eure-et-Loir			1	
Mayenne				
Orne				
Vendée				
Totals			1	1
NORMANDY				
Calvados				
Manche				
Seine-Inf.	1	1	1	
Totals	1	1	1	
Total deputies elected	102	101	130*	147

* Includes one deputy from Martinique.

Table 4. Socialist, Communist, Radical, and splinter Left[a] votes, first round of legislative elections of 1928 (Socialist only), 1932, and 1936, by department, in thousands

Department	Socialists S.F.I.O.			Communists		Radicals		Splinter Left	
	1928	1932	1936	1932	1936	1932	1936	1932	1936
LANGUEDOC									
Ariège	7.6	13.3	15.6	3.0	4.7	13.0	15.6	13.7	5.9
Aude	20.5	25.3	26.8	1.9	4.2	36.8	28.0		2.7
Gard	26.7	29.2	29.2	12.1	24.6	14.6	9.1	3.5	9.3
Hérault	38.0	48.3	28.2	5.5	13.2	32.8	23.6		20.5
Pyrénées-Or.	12.4	19.2	15.4	2.9	9.7	6.3	10.7	2.0	0.3
Tarn	28.4	33.3	24.7	3.2	5.8	33.3	19.1	0.4	4.9
Totals	131.4	169.0	140.1	28.9	62.5	137.0	106.3	19.6	43.7
RHONE VALLEY–PROVENCE									
Alp.-Mar.	3.9	1.7	5.5	3.4	19.7		1.8	0.2	7.7
B.-du-Rhône	72.2	74.3	62.4	15.1	55.2	11.0	6.1	10.4	22.1
Drôme	20.4	31.7	22.9	3.2	12.4	30.1	15.9		1.0
Var	21.5	25.9	15.7	5.5	20.2	0.7		31.5	25.8
Vaucluse	11.0	14.4	16.5	4.7	13.4	24.2	8.4	4.8	1.7
Totals	130.9	148.3	123.2	32.1	121.0	66.1	34.4	47.0	58.6
NORTH									
Nord	143.7	162.3	161.9	77.9	111.9	21.8	31.1	10.5	10.1
Oise	22.0	19.6	16.9	5.8	15.0	32.8	23.8	3.2	
Pas-de-Calais	98.4	76.5	71.3	37.5	49.7	14.2	28.6	20.2	8.0
Somme	19.5	29.9	24.5	8.3	20.0	18.3	16.9	9.4	17.2
Totals	268.9	288.4	274.6	129.6	196.8	87.3	100.9	43.3	35.4

Note. Complete vote totals for each department were used in compiling the totals for each region, which then were rounded off to indicate the vote in thousands.

[a] In 1932, the "splinter Left" was composed of the *Républicains socialistes*, in 1936 of the *Union Socialiste et républicaine*, the *Gauche Indépendante*, the *Parti Camille Pelletan*, the *Parti Frontiste*, the *Jeune République*, and the *Unité Prolétarienne*.

Sources. La Vie Socialiste, May 26, 1928; Georges Lachapelle, *Elections législatives, 1er et 8 mai 1932: Résultats officiels* (Paris, 1932); Georges Lachapelle, *Elections législatives, 26 avril et 3 mai 1936* (Paris, 1936); and *Le Populaire*, April 27 and 28 1936.

Department	Socialists S.F.I.O.			Communists		Radicals		Splinter Left	
	1928	1932	1936	1932	1936	1932	1936	1932	1936
GARONNE BASIN									
Dordogne	10.5	13.5	17.3	9.1	22.8	40.4	24.5	16.5	19.0
H.-Gar.	40.7	44.8	53.4	3.3	7.6	25.8	30.1	9.7	0.8
Lot-et-Garonne	5.8	8.9	4.9	11.4	20.6	8.9	12.3	0.3	
T.-et-Gar.	7.7	7.2	10.7	0.7	2.2	13.6	12.9	0.1	
Totals	64.7	74.4	86.5	24.7	53.3	88.7	79.8	26.7	19.8
MASSIF CENTRAL									
Ardèche	12.8	17.5	19.2	2.5	3.9	13.9	11.7		11.5
Aveyron	9.4	11.6	3.0	2.9	7.5	15.8	14.0	8.3	7.4
Cantal	6.7	4.8	18.3	0.6	2.5	18.6	5.9		7.4
Corrèze	7.7	12.9	23.2	10.1	15.0	27.7	12.9	5.4	4.6
Creuse	16.6	27.4	25.3	3.1	6.0	10.4	11.5	11.9	1.1
Haute-Loire		0.5	10.8	0.3	3.2	12.5	5.3	6.9	2.7
Lot	8.2	5.4	4.6	1.0	10.5	12.5	6.9	8.0	7.0
Lozère	4.7	2.1	0.1	0.2	2.4	0.5	4.1	4.4	3.4
Puy-de-Dôme	35.9	49.5	33.6	3.4	11.7	28.1	25.0	14.7	22.0
Haute-Vienne	29.8	39.9	43.3	9.8	15.7		1.6	39.7	7.2
Totals	121.2	172.1	181.6	34.4	78.7	140.4	99.5	99.7	74.8
LYONNAIS									
Ain	10.4	4.3	12.0	3.7	11.5	17.7	8.9	23.9	13.5
Isère	40.6	38.2	50.1	6.1	10.2	31.8	20.4	7.8	9.7
Loire	23.2	23.3	22.3	6.4	23.6	39.8	21.2		17.6
Rhône	43.3	38.5	40.3	13.8	44.4	63.6	39.4	2.8	0.6
Saône-et-Loire	48.8	55.7	56.8	8.8	16.9	32.1	18.5	0.2	10.8
Totals	169.1	160.2	181.7	38.9	106.9	185.3	108.6	34.9	52.4
CENTRAL FRANCE									
Allier	31.4	47.2	44.1	15.1	25.3	19.1	10.7	6.2	7.3
Cher	9.3	17.6	19.3	15.3	20.7	10.4	3.8	11.1	8.9
Côte d'Or	19.3	24.4	21.1	2.7	5.2	7.7	5.1	3.0	7.7
Indre	9.0	19.0	6.2	3.2	6.3	8.8	11.7	0.8	17.2
Nièvre	19.7	19.7	19.7	7.1	8.8	6.8	13.0	6.1	5.4
Yonne	12.0	14.5	15.3	2.6	6.3	4.9	6.0	14.8	12.5
Totals	95.0	142.8	126.0	46.2	70.8	58.0	60.0	42.1	58.3

Department	Socialists S.F.I.O.			Communists		Radicals		Splinter Left	
	1928	1932	1936	1932	1936	1932	1936	1932	1936
NORTHEAST									
Aisne	20.1	29.0	34.5	6.7	14.2	29.9	21.6	1.5	8.7
Ardennes	14.8	17.8	14.1	8.4	13.0	12.4	21.0	3.2	5.2
Aube	6.5	6.3	9.5	4.6	5.1	19.3	12.9		9.1
Marne	15.8	19.1	22.3	4.7	8.0	33.1	29.5	7.8	
Totals	56.8	72.5	90.6	24.6	40.4	94.8	85.1	12.6	23.1
BRITTANY									
Côtes-du-Nord	10.8	9.8	13.6	1.6	7.1	28.0	34.9	0.5	
Finistère	27.4	19.6	22.6	8.1	13.2	43.9	25.6	15.4	2.1
Ille-et-Vilaine	15.2	15.1	20.1	1.8	5.0	10.6	7.8	4.0	1.8
Loire-Inf.	24.2	34.2	42.4	2.5	3.3	9.2	6.2		
Morbihan	7.9	16.0	20.2	1.7	2.6	20.5	2.6		2.7
Totals	84.9	94.9	119.0	16.0	31.5	112.3	77.2	19.8	6.7
WEST CENTRAL FRANCE									
Charente-Inf.	8.2	8.0	20.7	3.1	8.7	52.1	35.6	8.6	13.2
Indre-et-Loire	17.2	20.2	24.5	4.0	7.7	25.6	16.1	4.2	4.6
Maine-et-Loire	6.7	3.6	4.7	1.6	3.5	31.7	24.3		1.9
Sarthe	13.8	12.6	22.0	1.6	2.2	5.0	11.3	5.3	
Deux-Sèvres	13.6	4.4	12.1	1.4	4.6	41.7	24.7		7.8
Vienne	4.4	7.4	12.0	1.7	6.5	22.3	12.3		2.2
Totals	63.9	56.5	96.2	13.7	33.4	178.7	124.7	18.2	29.9
ALGERIA									
Alger	4.7	3.2	14.1		4.9	12.9	1.4	11.4	7.2
Constantine	4.0	3.0	6.1	0.3	0.3	4.9			6.6
Oran	2.0	7.7	10.6	1.4	7.3	2.0	3.5		5.3
Totals	10.7	14.1	30.8	1.7	12.5	19.9	4.9	11.4	19.1
SOUTHWEST									
Charente	9.1	17.2	9.2	2.2	8.1	25.1	24.1	6.2	11.1
Gers	7.3	9.6	14.4	1.2	2.5	20.4	14.2	6.0	
Gironde	50.1	71.6	35.2	5.2	15.7	32.1	18.5	1.8	38.0
Landes		2.0	13.0	6.8	5.1	43.0	28.2	4.3	5.8
Basses-Pyrénées	6.6	6.0	6.7	2.1	5.0	26.4	17.9	0.3	10.8
H.-Pyr.	2.6	0.6	6.2	1.5	2.2	19.1	16.0		
Totals	74.7	107.2	84.9	19.3	38.8	166.2	119.2	18.7	65.0

Department	Socialists S.F.I.O.			Communists		Radicals		Splinter Left	
	1928	1932	1936	1932	1936	1932	1936	1932	1936
ALPS									
Basses-Alpes	8.1	10.9	7.7	0.7	2.3		2.6	0.9	
Hautes-Alpes	3.1	4.8	7.2	1.2	2.9	4.8	0.1		1.9
Savoie	2.5	8.7	4.2	1.2	4.2	21.8	20.6	1.4	4.0
Haute-Savoie	5.7	11.5	9.1	1.8	6.0	18.5	16.6		
Totals	19.3	36.0	28.2	5.1	15.5	45.2	40.0	2.3	5.9
PARIS REGION									
Seine	150.5	157.9	139.7	214.8	360.8	88.5	50.4	62.2	131.9
S.-et-Marne	14.2	16.4	20.2	10.9	19.9	22.2	15.7		0.5
Seine-et-Oise	27.9	40.0	46.1	51.1	96.6	54.2	30.2	4.3	14.9
Totals	192.7	214.4	206.1	276.9	477.3	165.0	96.4	66.6	147.5
EASTERN FRANCE									
Doubs	5.9	10.8	13.8	2.9	2.6	22.0	13.1		
Jura	10.3	9.8	11.0	2.1	5.4	19.6	12.3		1.5
Haute-Marne	1.2	1.9	4.2	0.9	1.7	24.5	20.6		
Meuse	6.7	3.0	6.5		1.4	3.8	6.3		
M.-et-Mos.	5.9	20.9	10.8	7.8	11.9	3.8	8.2	7.4	18.0
Moselle	2.8	4.9	1.3	18.7	21.9	2.3	0.2		7.3
Terr. de Belfort	2.9	1.8	3.6	1.0	1.1	8.4	6.1		
Bas-Rhin	29.5	19.9	16.3	24.5	27.6	2.5	2.4		0.5
Haut-Rhin	25.7	29.1	26.1	9.4	12.4	3.5	1.1		
Haute-Saône	6.9	7.2	5.7	0.6	2.0	18.6	15.5		11.4
Vosges	4.3	8.6	4.8	5.7	8.8	30.1	27.1		5.5
Totals	102.6	118.4	104.6	74.0	97.3	139.5	113.4	7.4	44.4
THE ORLÉANAIS									
Loiret	14.5	13.9	1.4	4.5	9.7	33.3	27.2		13.8
Loir-et-Cher	26.7	22.2	13.5	1.3	4.5	14.6	10.5		6.2
Totals	41.2	36.1	14.9	5.9	14.2	48.0	37.8		20.0
WESTERN FRANCE									
Eure	5.9	7.3	7.9	1.6	3.5	16.2	22.7	5.7	5.3
Eure-et-Loir	3.8	8.8	5.6	1.4	4.0	18.9	13.9	9.0	13.6
Mayenne			0.1	0.9	0.9		17.5	15.1	
Orne	1.9	1.7	1.7	0.5	4.0	15.6	2.2		3.1
Vendée	3.2	5.8	12.4	0.5	6.5	6.2	7.0	6.9	
Totals	14.9	23.7	27.8	5.1	19.0	57.1	63.5	36.8	22.1

Department	Socialists S.F.I.O.			Communists		Radicals		Spliter Left	
	1928	1932	1936	1932	1936	1932	1936	1932	1936
			NORMANDY						
Calvados	13.0	8.2	9.2	1.5	5.0	2.5	1.4		3.1
Manche	4.7	4.5	9.3	1.2	1.6		7.6	10.1	5.0
Seine-Inf.	16.0	18.8	6.6	15.6	27.0	60.6	65.0		6.9
Totals	33.7	31.6	25.3	18.4	33.6	63.1	74.2	10.1	15.1

Table 5. Socialist deputies returned in 1936 compared with 1932, by department

S.F.I.O. deputies elected	Department	Re-elected	Retained	Seats gained from	Seats lost to	+ or −
			LANGUEDOC			
3	Ariège	1		2 (1 R, 1 USR)		+2
1	Aude	1				
3	Gard	2	1		1 (1 C)	−1
3	Hérault	1	1	1 (1 R)	2 (1 R, 1 N)	−1
1	Pyrénées-Or.	1			2 (1 R, 1 N)	−2
3	Tarn	1	1	1 (1 R)		+1
14	Totals	7	3	4 (3 R, 1 USR)	5 (1 C, 2 R, 2 N)	−1
			RHONE VALLEY–PROVENCE			
	Alpes-Maritimes					
5	Bouches-du-Rhône	4		1 (1 Rt)	3 (2 C, 1 I)	−2
2	Drôme	2			1 (1 R)	−1
2	Var		2		2 (1 C, 1 N)	−2
2	Vaucluse		1	1 (1 Rt)		+1
11	Totals	6	3	2 (1 R, 1 Rt)	6 (3 C, 1 N, 1 R, 1 I)	−4
			NORTH			
13	Nord	4	2	7 (5 Rt, 1 R, 1 USR)	3 (2 C, 1 Rt)	+4
2	Oise	1		1 (1 USR)		+1
6	Pas-de-Calais	2	1	3 (2 Rt, 1 USR)	1 (1 C)	+2
2	Somme	1		1 (1 Rt)	2 (2 Rt)	−1
23	Totals	8	3	12 (8 Rt, 3 USR, 1R)	6 (3 C, 3 Rt)	+6
			GARONNE BASIN			
1	Dordogne			1 (1 Rt)	1 (1 C)	
5	Haute-Garonne	2		3 (1 R, 1 Rt, 1 USR)		+3
	Lot-et-Garonne					
1	Tarn-et-Garonne			1 (1 R)		+1
7	Totals	2		5 (2 Rt, 2 R, 1 USR)	1 (1 C)	+4

Note. C = Communist; I = Independent; N = Neo-Socialist; R = Radical; Rt = Right; USR = Union Socialiste et Républicaine.

Sources. See Table 4, p. 296.

S.F.I.O. deputies elected	Department	Re-elected	Retained	Seats gained (from)	Seats lost (to)	+ or −
			MASSIF CENTRAL			
1	Ardèche	1			1 (1 R)	−1
	Aveyron				1 (1 N)	−1
	Cantal				1 (1 Rt)	−1
3	Corrèze	1		2 (2 R)		+2
3	Creuse	2		1 (1 R)	1 (1 R)	
1	Haute-Loire			1 (1 R)		+1
	Lot					
	Lozère					
5	Puy-de-Dôme	2		3 (2 R, 1 USR)	1 (1 Rt)	+2
5	Haute-Vienne	3		2 (1 Rt, 1 USR)		+2
18	Totals	9		9 (6 R, 1 Rt, 2 USR)	5 (1 N, 2 R, 2 Rt)	+4
			LYONNAIS			
1	Ain			1 (1 USR)		+1
5	Isère	3	1	1 (1 R)		+1
1	Loire	1				
4	Rhône	2		2 (1 R, 1 Rt)	1 (1 C)	+1
6	Saône-et-Loire	4		2 (2 R)		+2
17	Totals	10	1	6 (4 R, 1 Rt, 1 USR)	1 (1 C)	+5
			CENTRAL FRANCE			
6	Allier	5		1 (1 R)		+1
2	Cher	1		1 (1 R)	1 (1 Rt)	
2	Côte d'Or	1		1 (1 Rt)		+1
	Indre				2 (2 N)	−2
2	Nièvre	1		1 (1 Rt)		+1
2	Yonne	1		1 (1 Rt)		+1
14	Totals	9		5 (2 R, 3 Rt)	3 (1 Rt, 2 N)	+2
			NORTHEAST			
6	Aisne	1	2	3 (1 R, 2 Rt)		+3
1	Ardennes	1			1 (1 C)	−1
	Aube					
1	Marne			1 (1 USR)		+1
8	Totals	2	2	4 (1 R, 2 Rt, 1 USR)	1 (1 C)	+3
			BRITANNY			
1	Côtes-du-Nord			1 (1 R)		+1
2	Finistère			2 (1 USR, 1 R)	1 (1 Rt)	+1
	Ille-et-Vilaine					
4	Loire-Inf.	2		2 (2 Rt)		+2
1	Morbihan	1				
8	Totals	3		5 (2 R, 2 Rt, 1 USR)	1 (1 Rt)	+4
			WEST CENTRAL FRANCE			
1	Charente-Inf.			1 (1 USR)		+1
3	Indre-et-Loire	1		2 (1 R, 1 USR)		+2
	Maine-et-Loire					
	Sarthe					
1	Deux-Sèvres			1 (1 R)		+1
	Vienne					
5	Totals	1		4 (2 USR, 2 R)		+4

S.F.I.O. deputies elected	Department	Re-elected	Retained	Seats gained from	Seats lost to	+ or −
			ALGERIA			
1	Alger			1 (1 Rt)		+1
	Constantine					
1	Oran			1 (1 Rt)		+1
2	Totals			2 (2 Rt)		+2
			SOUTHWEST			
	Charente				1 (1 N)	−1
2	Gers			2 (2 R)		+2
3	Gironde	1	2		4 (4 N)	−4
	Landes					
	Basses-Pyrénées					
	Hautes-Pyrénées					
5	Totals	1	2	2 (2 R)	5 (5 N)	−3
			ALPS			
2	Basses-Alpes	2				
1	Hautes-Alpes		1			
1	Savoie			1 (1 Rt)	1 (1 USR)	
1	Haute-Savoie			1 (1 Rt)		+1
5	Totals	2	1	2 (2 Rt)	1 (1 USR)	+1
			PARIS REGION			
3	Seine	1		2 (2 Rt)	8 (8 C)	−5
2	Seine-et-Marne	1		1 (1 R)		+1
1	Seine-et-Oise			1 (1 R)		+1
6	Totals	2		4 (2 R, 2 Rt)	8 (8 C)	−4
			EASTERN FRANCE			
	Doubs				1 (1 Rt)	−1
1	Jura	1				
	Haute-Marne					
	Meuse					
	M.-et-Mos.					
	Moselle					
	Terr. de Belfort					
	Bas-Rhin				1 (1 I)	−1
	Haut-Rhin					
	Haute-Saône				1 (1 I)	−1
	Vosges					
1	Totals	1			3 (1 Rt, 2 I)	−3
			THE ORLÉANAIS			
	Loiret				1 (1 I)	−1
2	Loir-et-Cher	1		1 (1 Rt)	1 (1 I)	
2	Totals	1		1 (1 Rt)	2 (2 I)	
			WESTERN FRANCE			
1	Eure			1 (1 R)		+1
	Eure-et-Loir				1 (1 N)	−1
	Mayenne					
	Orne					
	Vendée					
1	Totals			1 (1 R)	1 (1 N)	

S.F.I.O. deputies elected	Department	Re-elected	Retained	Seats gained from	Seats lost to	+ or −
			NORMANDY			
	Calvados					
	Manche					
	Seine-Inf.				1 (1 N)	−1
	Totals				1 (1 N)	−1
	Martinique				1 (1 I)	−1
147	Totals	64	15	68	51	+17

SUMMARY Gained from	Party	Lost to	Balance
0	Independent	6	−6
28	Radical	5	+23
0	Communist	18	−18
28	Right	8	+20
12	U.S.R.	1	+11
0	Neo-Socialist	13	−13
68	Totals	51	+17

Table 6. Socialist deputies elected in 1936:
the mechanics of election, by department

Department	No. el.	F	W	R	C	N
		LANGUEDOC				
Ariège	3		2	1		
Aude	1	1				
Gard	3		1	1	1	
Hérault	3		1		1	1
Pyrénées-Orientales	1				1	
Tarn	3	1		1	1	
Totals	14	2	4	3	4	1

Note:

F = won on first ballot.

W = won on second ballot, Radical or Communist abstention unnecessary for victory.

R = won on second ballot owing to Radical abstention.

C = might not have won without Communist abstention.

N = none of the above.

Sources. See Table 4, p. 296.

Department	No. el.	F	W	R	C	N
RHONE VALLEY–PROVENCE						
Alpes-Maritimes						
Bouches-du-Rhône	5	2	2		1	
Drôme	2		1		1	
Var	2		1		1	
Vaucluse	2		1	1		
Totals	11	2	5	1	3	
NORTH						
Nord	13		6		7	
Oise	2		1		1	
Pas-de-Calais	6		3		3	
Somme	2				2	
Totals	23		10		13	
GARONNE BASIN						
Dordogne	1			1		
Haute-Garonne	5	3		1		1
Lot-et-Garonne						
Tarn-et-Garonne	1		1			
Totals	7	3	1	2		1
MASSIF CENTRAL						
Ardèche	1		1			
Aveyron						
Cantal						
Corrèze	3		1	1	1	
Creuse	3	2	1			
Haute-Loire	1	1				
Lot						
Lozère						
Puy-de-Dôme	5	2	2	1		
Haute-Vienne	5	1	3		1	
Totals	18	6	8	2	2	
LYONNAIS						
Ain	1					1
Isère	5	1	2	2		
Loire	1		1			
Rhône	4		2		2	
Saône-et-Loire	6	2	2	1	1	
Totals	17	3	7	3	3	1

Department	No. el.	F	W	R	C	N
CENTRAL FRANCE						
Allier	6	2	3		1	
Cher	2				2	
Côte d'Or	2				2	
Indre						
Nièvre	2			1	1	
Yonne	2		1	1		
Totals	14	2	4	2	6	
NORTHEAST						
Aisne	6	1		3	2	
Ardennes	1			1		
Aube						
Marne	1			1		
Totals	8	1		5	2	
BRITTANY						
Côtes-du-Nord	1				1	
Finistère	2		2			
Ille-et-Vilaine						
Loire-Inférieure	4	2	1		1	
Morbihan	1	1				
Totals	8	3	3		2	
WEST CENTRAL FRANCE						
Charente-Inférieure	1			1		
Indre-et-Loire	3	1		1	1	
Maine-et-Loire						
Sarthe						
Deux-Sèvres	1				1	
Vienne						
Totals	5	1		2	2	
ALGERIA						
Alger	1			1		
Constantine						
Oran	1					1
Totals	2			1		1
SOUTHWEST						
Charente						
Gers	2			2		
Gironde	3				3	

Department	No. el.	F	W	R	C	N
SOUTHWEST (*Continued*)						
Landes						
Basses-Pyrénées						
Hautes-Pyrénées						
Totals	5			2	3	
ALPS						
Basses-Alpes	2				2	
Hautes-Alpes	1		1			
Savoie	1			1		
Haute-Savoie	1				1	
Totals	5		1	1	3	
PARIS REGION						
Seine	3		1		2	
Seine-et-Marne	2			1	1	
Seine-et-Oise	1				1	
Totals	6		1	1	4	
EASTERN FRANCE						
Doubs						
Jura	1					1
Haute-Marne						
Meuse						
Meurthe-et-Moselle						
Moselle						
Territoire de Belfort						
Bas-Rhin						
Haut-Rhin						
Haute-Saône						
Vosges						
Totals	1					1
THE ORLÉANAIS						
Loiret						
Loir-et-Cher	2	1		1		
Totals	2	1		1		
WESTERN FRANCE						
Eure	1			1		
Eure-et-Loir						
Mayenne						
Orne						
Vendée						
Totals	1			1		

Department	No. el.	F	W	R	C	N
		NORMANDY				
Calvados						
Manche						
Seine-Inférieure						
Totals	0					
Grand totals	147	24	44	27	47	5
			95			

Table 7. Socialist party membership, 1935–1938, by *fédération*]

Fédération	1935	1936	1937	1938
	LANGUEDOC			
Ariège	828	1,396	1,900	1,509
Aude	1,852	2,400	2,850	2,905
Gard	1,357	1,948	2,400	2,472
Hérault	1,556	2,135	2,780	2,800
Pyrénées-Orientales	2,372	2,495	2,650	2,240
Tarn	1,215	1,440	2,050	1,870
Totals	9,180	11,814	14,630	13,796
	RHONE VALLEY–PROVENCE			
Alpes-Maritimes	438	1,500	2,470	1,506
Bouches-du-Rhône	5,678	6,300	9,441	7,766
Drôme	807	1,200	1,800	1,900
Var	1,500	2,483	3,455	3,455
Vaucluse	990	1,420	1,500	1,100
Totals	9,413	12,903	18,666	15,727
	NORTH			
Nord	12,500	17,000	23,000	23,000
Oise	1,100	2,090	3,100	2,490
Pas-de-Calais	3,400	4,730	10,500	11,500
Somme	705	1,600	3,550	3,525
Totals	17,705	25,420	40,150	40,515

Fédération	1935	1936	1937	1938
	GARONNE BASIN			
Dordogne	969	1,145	1,760	1,450
Haute-Garonne	3,000	4,050	4,138	4,650
Lot-et-Garonne	260	577	911	965
Tarn-et-Garonne	470	702	790	700
Totals	4,699	6,474	7,599	7,765
	MASSIF CENTRAL			
Ardèche	693	902	1,329	1,187
Aveyron	297	903	1,382	1,520
Cantal	200	480	930	715
Corrèze	728	1,415	2,350	2,500
Creuse	517	883	1,200	1,100
Haute-Loire	355	719	1,315	1,335
Lot	232	537	892	610
Lozère	188	265	436	400
Puy-de-Dôme	1,400	2,155	4,100	3,868
Haute-Vienne	3,100	4,045	5,000	3,500
Totals	7,710	12,304	18,934	16,735
	LYONNAIS			
Ain	595	956	1,690	1,635
Isère	2,096	2,908	4,500	4,750
Loire	647	880	1,660	1,656
Rhône	1,360	2,030	2,445	2,600
Saône-et-Loire	1,804	2,070	3,200	2,950
Totals	6,502	8,844	13,495	13,591
	CENTRAL FRANCE			
Allier	1,700	2,281	3,930	3,880
Cher	520	805	1,672	1,585
Côte d'Or	1,292	2,510	3,590	3,190
Indre	375	630	1,148	1,310
Nièvre	805	1,122	1,420	1,490
Yonne	400	830	1,595	1,593
Totals	5,092	8,178	13,355	13,048
	NORTHEAST			
Aisne	1,095	3,054	4,600	3,653
Ardennes	780	916	1,900	1,725

Sources. Parti Socialiste S.F.I.O., *XXXIVe Congrès National, Marseille, Rapports* (Paris, 1937), 178–189; *XXXVe Congrès National, Royan, Rapports* (Paris, 1938), 192–207; *XXXVIe Congrès National, Nantes, Rapports* (Paris, 1939), 148–157.

Fédération	1935	1936	1937	1938
Aube	340	625	1,051	980
Marne	720	1,380	2,440	2,250
Totals	2,935	5,975	9,991	8,608
BRITTANY				
Côtes-du-Nord	508	1,020	1,380	1,450
Finistère	819	1,255	1,802	1,723
Ille-et-Vilaine	360	540	778	700
Loire-Inférieure	1,345	1,825	3,210	3,000
Morbihan	690	1,200	1,850	1,700
Totals	3,722	5,840	9,020	8,573
WEST CENTRAL FRANCE				
Charente-Inférieure	865	2,305	3,540	3,210
Indre-et-Loire	1,320	2,000	3,230	3,200
Maine-et-Loire	268	480	580	650
Sarthe	670	1,330	2,343	1,840
Deux-Sèvres	950	1,335	1,600	1,430
Vienne	290	660	1,270	1,160
Totals	4,363	8,110	12,563	11,490
ALGERIA				
Alger	370	980	1,470	1,120
Constantine	282	912	1,450	1,569
Oran	508	880	1,335	1,480
Totals	1,160	2,772	4,255	4,169
SOUTHWEST				
Charente	400	830	1,345	990
Gers	524	1,229	1,700	1,375
Gironde	1,950	3,500	5,550	5,500
Landes	268	743	1,871	2,100
Basses-Pyrénées	360	960	1,800	1,710
Hautes-Pyrénées	278	963	1,089	850
Totals	3,780	8,225	13,355	12,525
ALPS				
Basses-Alpes	120	324	660	595
Hautes-Alpes	200	282	348	260
Savoie	120	600	1,310	1,015
Haute-Savoie	424	900	1,131	1,292
Totals	864	2,106	3,449	3,162

Fédération	1935	1936	1937	1938
PARIS REGION				
Seine	7,450	12,725	18,940	10,850
Seine-et-Marne	850	2,100	2,900	2,050
Seine-et-Oise	4,100	6,600	10,500	8,500
Totals	12,400	21,425	32,340	21,400
EASTERN FRANCE				
Doubs	515	813	2,630	2,200
Jura	600	1,000	1,330	1,200
Haute-Marne	220	308	817	771
Meuse	213	332	620	640
Meurthe-et-Moselle	355	1,230	4,600	3,800
Moselle	124	283	1,126	1,400
Territoire de Belfort	260	441	380	600
Bas-Rhin	1,500	2,150	2,150	2,150
Haut-Rhin	2,600	2,400	2,800	2,600
Haute-Saône	440	518	560	620
Vosges	180	391	1,159	1,228
Totals	7,007	9,866	18,172	17,209
THE ORLÉANAIS				
Loiret	440	683	895	862
Loir-et-Cher	1,031	1,225	1,350	1,500
Totals	1,471	1,908	2,245	2,362
WESTERN FRANCE				
Eure	400	834	1,490	1,330
Eure-et-Loir	516	1,180	1,810	1,550
Mayenne	120	219	420	528
Orne	136	238	405	441
Vendée	394	585	846	880
Totals	1,566	3,056	4,971	4,729
NORMANDY				
Calvados	155	570	960	894
Manche	396	552	1,010	1,020
Seine-Inférieure	580	1,115	2,469	2,256
Totals	1,131	2,237	4,439	4,170
Grand totals	100,700	157,457	241,629	219,574

Table 8. Increases and decreases in Socialist party membership, 1936–1938, by *fédération*, in percentage

Fédération	1936	1937	1938
LANGUEDOC			
Ariège	40	26	−21
Aude	23	15	
Gard	30	19	
Hérault	27	23	
Pyrénées-Or.	5	6	−15
Tarn	15	30	− 9
All region	22	19	− 5
RHONE VALLEY–PROVENCE			
Alpes-Maritimes	68	39	−39
Bouches-du-Rhone	10	33	−17
Drôme	33	33	6
Var	40	28	
Vaucluse	30	5	−27
All region	27	31	−16
NORTH			
Nord	26	26	
Oise	48	33	−20
Pas-de-Calais	28	55	9
Somme	55	60	
All region	30	37	1
GARONNE BASIN			
Dordogne	15	35	−18
Haute-Garonne	37		11
Lot-et-Garonne	56	36	5
Tarn-et-Garonne	33	11	−11
All region	27	14	
MASSIF CENTRAL			
Ardèche	22	32	−11
Aveyron	67	35	9
Cantal	58	48	−23
Corrèze	48	40	6
Creuse	40	26	− 8
Haute-Loire	50	45	
Lot	57	40	−31
Lozère	30	38	− 8
Puy-de-Dôme	35	46	− 6
Haute-Vienne	23	19	−30
All region	37	35	−13

Fédération	1936	1937	1938
LYONNAIS			
Ain	38	43	
Isère	28	35	5
Loire	26	47	
Rhône	33	17	6
Saône-et-Loire	26	35	− 8
All region	26	34	
CENTRAL FRANCE			
Allier	25	42	
Cher	25	52	− 5
Côte d'Or	48	30	−11
Indre	40	45	12
Nièvre	28	20	5
Yonne	52	47	
All region	36	39	
NORTHEAST			
Aisne	64	34	−21
Ardennes	15	52	− 9
Aube	45	40	− 7
Marne	50	43	− 8
All region	51	40	−14
BRITTANY			
Côtcs-du-Nord	50	26	5
Finistère	35	30	− 4
Ille-et-Vilaine	33	30	−10
Loire-Inf.	26	43	− 6
Morbihan	43	35	− 8
All region	36	36	− 4
WEST CENTRAL FRANCE			
Charente-Inf.	63	35	− 9
Indre-et-Loire	34	38	− 1
Maine-et-Loire	44	17	11
Sarthe	50	43	−21
Deux-Sèvres	29	17	−11
Vienne	56	48	− 9
All region	46	35	− 9
ALGERIA			
Alger	62	33	−24
Constantine	69	37	8
Oran	22		10
All region	60	36	− 2

Fédération	1936	1937	1938
	SOUTHWEST		
Charente	52	38	−26
Gers	57	41	−19
Gironde	44	36	
Landes	64	60	11
Basses-Pyrénées	63	47	− 5
Hautes-Pyrénées	71	11	−22
All region	54	38	− 6
	ALPS		
Basses-Alpes	63	51	−10
Hautes-Alpes	29	19	−25
Savoie	80	54	−22
Haute-Savoie	53	20	12
All region	57	37	− 9
	PARIS REGION		
Seine	42	33	−43
Seine-et-Marne	60	27	−29
Seine-et-Oise	38	37	−19
All region	42	34	−34
	EASTERN FRANCE		
Doubs	57	69	−16
Jura	40	25	−10
Haute-Marne	30	62	− 6
Meuse	36	46	3
Meurthe-et-Moselle	70	73	−17
Moselle	56	74	20
Terr. de Belfort	40	−14	37
Bas-Rhin	30		
Haut-Rhin	− 8	14	− 7
Haute-Saône	15	7	10
Vosges	54	66	5
All region	29	46	− 5
	THE ORLÉANAIS		
Loiret	36	24	− 3
Loir-et-Cher	16	9	10
All region	21	15	
	WESTERN FRANCE		
Eure	52	44	−11
Eure-et-Loir	56	35	−15
Mayenne	45	52	20
Orne	43	40	8

Fédération	1936	1937	1938
WESTERN FRANCE (*Continued*)			
Vendée	33	31	4
All region	48	39	− 5
NORMANDY			
Calvados	73	40	− 6
Manche	30	45	1
Seine-Inf.	50	54	− 9
All region	50	50	− 6
All party	36	35	− 9

Table 9. Comparison of votes cast by the *fédérations* at the Congress of Marseilles and at the National Council, November 7, 1937

Fédération	Mandats	"Center" CM	"Center" NC	Zyromski CM	Zyromski NC	Pivert CM	Pivert NC
LANGUEDOC							
Ariège	47	16		30	47	1	
Aude	81	38	81	38		5	
Gard	66	42	66	24			
Hérault	70	43	57	14		15	13
Pyrénées-Orientales	84	52	52	23	23	9	9
Tarn	49	22	23	26	25	1	1
Totals	397	213	279	155	95	31	23
RHONE VALLEY–PROVENCE							
Alpes-Maritimes	51	6	2	18	17	27	32
Bouches-du-Rhône	210	210	210				
Drôme	41	11	11	20	20	10	10
Var	83	63	63	12	12	8	8
Vaucluse	48	35	48	3		10	
Totals	433	325	334	53	49	55	50

		Resolutions					
		"Center"		Zyromski		Pivert	
Fédération	*Mandats*	CM	NC	CM	NC	CM	NC
		NORTH					
Nord	567	560	554	7	11		2
Oise	70	23	42	24		23	28
Pas-de-Calais	158	134	158	22		2	
Somme	54	32	22	14	12	8	20
Totals	849	749	776	67	23	33	50
		GARONNE BASIN					
Dordogne	39	10	16	24	13	5	10
Haute-Garonne	136	136	136				
Lot-et-Garonne	20	16	10	1	6	3	4
Tarn-et-Garonne	24	8	18	14		2	6
Totals	219	170	180	39	19	10	20
		MASSIF CENTRAL					
Ardèche	31	12	12	14	14	5	5
Aveyron	31	28	28	3			3
Cantal	17	11	8	2		4	9
Corrèze	48	25	48	22		1	
Creuse	30	30	30				
Haute-Loire	25	20	20	1	2	4	3
Lot	19	5	11	6		8	8
Lozère	10	10	10				
Puy-de-Dôme	73	51	51	15	15	7	7
Haute-Vienne	136	68	68	68	68		
Totals	420	260	286	131	99	29	35
		LYONNAIS					
Ain	33	21	20	8	5	4	8
Isère	98	79	75	16	15	3	8
Loire	37	25	27	8		4	
Rhône	68	53	26	5	3	10	39
Saône-et-Loire	70	66	70	3		1	
Totals	306	244	218	40	23	22	55

Sources. Parti Socialiste S.F.I.O., *XXXIVe Congrès National, Compte rendu sténographique* (Paris, 1938), 606–607; *La Vie du Parti*, supplement to *Le Populaire*, November 25, 1937.

Fédération	Mandats	"Center" CM	NC	Zyromski CM	NC	Pivert CM	NC
CENTRAL FRANCE							
Allier	77	47	57	20	10	10	10
Cher	28	14	15	10	5	4	8
Côte d'Or	84	27	27	20	10	37	17
Indre	22	15	20	2		5	2
Nièvre	38	13	23	23	12	2	3
Yonne	28	5	6	14	13	9	9
Totals	277	121	148	89	50	67	49
NORTHEAST							
Aisne	102	7	72	47		48	30
Ardennes	31	25	31	5		1	
Aube	22	7	22	13		2	
Marne	47	16	20	11	27	20	
Totals	202	55	145	76	27	71	30
BRITTANY							
Côtes-du-Nord	35	11	15	13	12	11	8
Finistère	43	42	43			1	
Ille-et-Vilaine	19	6	19	12		1	
Loire-Inférieure	62	40	20	20	40	2	2
Morbihan	41	33	33		2	8	6
Totals	200	132	130	45	54	23	16
WEST CENTRAL FRANCE							
Charente-Inférieure	78	36	53	29	12	13	13
Indre-et-Loire	67	47	67	14		6	
Maine-et-Loire	17	6			14	7	3
Sarthe	45			41	45	4	
Deux-Sèvres	46	2	40	31		12	6
Vienne	23	12	12	5	3	6	8
Totals	276	103	172	120	74	48	30
ALGERIA							
Alger	33		33				
Constantine	31	25	20	5	7	1	4
Oran	27	19	27	4		4	
Totals	91	44	80	9	7	5	4

		Resolutions					
		"Center"		Zyromski		Pivert	
Fédération	*Mandats*	CM	NC	CM	NC	CM	NC
SOUTHWEST							
Charente	28	3	16	15		10	12
Gers	42	11	38	19		12	4
Gironde	117			110	102	7	15
Landes	25	15		4	15	6	10
Basses-Pyrénées	33	22	33	10		1	
Hautes-Pyrénées	33	10	10	15	13	8	10
Totals	278	61	97	173	130	44	51
ALPS REGION							
Basses-Alpes	12	11	10			1	2
Hautes-Alpes	10	5	8	3		2	2
Savoie	21	9	16	11	5	1	
Haute-Savoie	31	8		10	29	13	2
Totals	74	33	34	24	34	17	6
PARIS REGION							
Seine	425	73	95	178	136	174	194
Seine-et-Marne	71	19	15	31	44	21	12
Seine-et-Oise	221	44	44	96	97	80	80
Totals	717	136	154	305	277	275	286
EASTERN FRANCE							
Doubs	28	11	20	8		9	8
Jura	34	24	34	4		5	
Haute-Marne	11	11	5		5		1
Meuse	12	2	12	7		3	
Meurthe-et-Moselle	42	3		9		30	42
Moselle	10	4	1		1	6	7
Belfort	15	13	15			2	
Bas-Rhin	72	67	72	5			
Haut-Rhin	81	60	81	20		1	
Haute-Saône	18	5	16	10		3	2
Vosges	14		2			14	12
Totals	337	200	258	63	6	73	72
THE ORLÉANAIS							
Loiret	23	8	1	8	1	7	21
Loir-et-Cher	42	14	30	25	10	3	2
Totals	65	22	31	33	11	10	23

Fédération	Mandats	"Center" CM	"Center" NC	Zyromski CM	Zyromski NC	Pivert CM	Pivert NC
		Resolutions					

Fédération	Mandats	"Center"		Zyromski		Pivert	
		CM	NC	CM	NC	CM	NC
WESTERN FRANCE							
Eure	28	9	1	10	11	9	16
Eure-et-Loir	40	11	35	25		4	5
Mayenne	8	3	8	4		1	
Orne	9	2	1	3	2	4	6
Vendée	20	8	14	6		6	6
Totals	105	33	59	48	13	24	33
NORMANDY							
Calvados	20	1		7		12	
Manche	19	13	1		1	6	7
Seine-Inférieure	38	5	9	25	21	8	8
Totals	77	19	10	32	22	26	15

Table 10. Response of the *fédérations* to the Spanish Civil War

Fédération	"Fauriste"	"Blumiste"	B.S.	G.R.	No Inf.
LANGUEDOC					
Ariège	xx	x	x		
Aude		xx			
Gard	xx				
Hérault	xx				
Pyrénées-Or.	x	x	x	x	
Tarn		xx			
RHONE VALLEY–PROVENCE					
Alpes-Maritimes			x	xx	
Bouches-du-Rhône	xx	x			
Drôme	x	x	x	x	
Var	x	x			
Vaucluse	xx	x			x

Note. The symbol "xx" signifies that the dominant attitude on the Spanish war and nonintervention was expressed by the leadership and/or the *fédération*, while "x" means that another attitude was expressed by a significant personality or by elements of the *fédération*. When none of the four positions—"Fauriste," "Blumiste," *Bataille Socialiste* (B.S.), or *Gauche Révolutionnaire* (G.R.)—appears to have been predominant, only an estimate of the currents of opinion is indicated.

Fédération	"Fauriste"	"Blumiste"	B.S.	G.R.	No Inf.
	NORTH				
Nord	x	xx			
Oise	x		x	x	
Pas-de-Calais	x	x			
Somme	x	x			
	GARONNE BASIN				
Dordogne	xx		x	x	
Haute-Garonne	xx	x			
Lot-et-Garonne			x	x	
Tarn-et-Garonne					x
	MASSIF CENTRAL				
Ardèche	x	x	x		
Aveyron	x	xx	x		
Cantal	xx			x	
Corrèze	xx				
Creuse	xx				
Haute-Loire					x
Lot			x	xx	
Lozère					x
Puy-de-Dôme	xx	x			
Haute-Vienne	xx				
	LYONNAIS				
Ain	xx			x	
Isère	xx				
Loire	xx			x	
Rhône	x	xx	x	x	
Saône-et-Loire	xx				
	CENTRAL FRANCE				
Allier	x	x	x	x	
Cher	xx				
Côte d'Or	x	x	x	x	
Indre	xx				
Nièvre					x
Yonne					x
	NORTHEAST				
Aisne		x	xx	x	
Ardennes	x	x	x		
Aube					x
Marne	x		x	x	

Fédération	"Fauriste"	"Blumiste"	B.S.	G.R.	No Inf.
BRITTANY					
Côtes-du-Nord		x	x	x	
Finistère	x	xx			
Ille-et-Vilaine		x	xx	x	
Loire-Inf.	x	x			
Morbihan	xx		x	x	
WEST CENTRAL FRANCE					
Charente-Inf.		x			
Indre-et-Loire	xx				
Maine-et-Loire					x
Sarthe		x			
Deux-Sèvres	x	x	x	x	
Vienne					x
ALGERIA					
Alger			xx		
Constantine					x
Oran					x
SOUTHWEST					
Charente					x
Gers	x	xx	x	x	
Gironde		xx	x		
Landes			xx		
Basses-Pyrénées	x	xx	x		
Hautes-Pyrénées			xx	x	
ALPS					
Basses-Alpes	xx				
Hautes-Alpes					x
Savoie	xx				
Haute-Savoie			xx		
PARIS REGION					
Seine			x	x	
Seine-et-Marne		x	x	x	
Seine-et-Oise		x	x	x	
EASTERN FRANCE					
Doubs					x
Jura	xx			x	
Haute-Marne	x	x			
Meuse			xx		
Meurthe-et-Moselle			x	xx	

Fédération	"Fauriste"	"Blumiste"	B.S.	G.R.	No Inf.
Moselle				xx	
Terr. de Belfort	x			x	
Bas-Rhin		x			
Haut-Rhin		x			
Haute-Saône		x		x	
Vosges				xx	
THE ORLÉANAIS					
Loiret					x
Loir-et-Cher			xx		
WESTERN FRANCE					
Eure					x
Eure-et-Loir	x	x	x	x	
Mayenne					x
Orne				xx	
Vendée					x
NORMANDY					
Calvados				xx	
Manche					x
Seine-Inf.			x	x	

Table 11. Vote on general policy at the Congress of Royan in 1938, by *fédération*

Fédération	Mandats	Synthesis	B.S.	G.R.	Abstentions
LANGUEDOC					
Ariège	64	54	10		
Aude	96	96			
Gard	81	81			
Hérault	93	76		15	2
Pyrénées-Orientales	89	55	22	12	
Tarn	69	20	5	2	42
Totals	492	382	37	29	44

Source. Parti Socialiste S.F.I.O., *XXXVe Congrès National, compte rendu sténographique* (Paris, 1939), 612–614.

Fédération	*Mandats*	Synthesis	B.S.	G.R.	Abstentions
	RHONE VALLEY–PROVENCE				
Alpes-Maritimes	83	14	34	35	
Bouches-du-Rhône	315	265	21	29	
Drôme	61	18	30	13	
Var	116	91	8	17	
Vaucluse	51	45		6	
Totals	626	433	93	100	
	NORTH				
Nord	767	713	43	11	
Oise	104	32	32	40	
Pas-de-Calais	351	319		20	12
Somme	119	58	17	43	1
Totals	1,341	1,122	92	114	13
	GARONNE BASIN				
Dordogne	59	16	29	14	
Haute-Garonne	139	139			
Lot-et-Garonne	31	13	3	5	10
Tarn-et-Garonne	27	19			8
Totals	256	187	32	19	18
	MASSIF CENTRAL				
Ardèche	45	34	8	3	
Aveyron	47	47			
Cantal	32	11		21	
Corrèze	79	73	5	1	
Creuse	41	35		6	
Haute-Loire	45	8	8	28	1
Lot	30	4	17	9	
Lozère	15	14		1	
Puy-de-Dôme	133	87	25	21	
Haute-Vienne	167	167			
Totals	634	480	63	90	1
	LYONNAIS				
Ain	57	23		34	
Isère	151	143	8		
Loire	56	34	6	16	
Rhône	82	22	34	7	19
Saône-et-Loire	107	107			
Totals	453	329	48	57	19

Fédération	Mandats	Synthesis	B.S.	G.R.	Abstentions
CENTRAL FRANCE					
Allier	132	88	16	28	
Cher	66	43	7	16	
Côte d'Or	120	65		55	
Indre	39	20	10	9	
Nièvre	48	28	15	5	
Yonne	54	22	18	14	
Totals	459	266	66	127	
NORTHEAST					
Aisne	154		63	63	28
Ardennes	64	47	17		
Aube	36	10	19	7	
Marne	82	38	7	37	
Totals	336	95	106	107	28
BRITTANY					
Côtes-du-Nord	47	9	26	12	
Finistère	61	11	50		
Ille-et-Vilaine	27	4	10	3	10
Loire-Inférieure	108	65	35	8	
Morbihan	62	42	7	13	
Totals	305	131	128	36	10
WEST CENTRAL FRANCE					
Charente-Inférieure	119	82		29	
Indre-et-Loire	108	88	19	1	
Maine-et-Loire	20		7	13	
Sarthe	79	3		3	73
Deux-Sèvres	54	6	26	22	
Vienne	43	34		9	
Totals	423	213	52	77	73
ALGERIA					
Alger	50	2	18	22	8
Constantine	49	35	7	7	
Oran	45	33	3	9	
Totals	144	70	28	38	8
SOUTHWEST					
Charente	46	32	3	10	1
Gers	57	26	14	14	3
Gironde	186	2	154	30	

Fédération	*Mandats*	Synthesis	B.S.	G.R.	Absentions
Southwest (*Continued*)					
Landes	63	10	42	11	
Basses-Pyrénées	61	21	31	2	7
Hautes-Pyrénées	37	3	23	11	
Totals	450	94	267	78	11
Alps Region					
Basses-Alpes	23	20	2	1	
Hautes-Alpes	12	8	2	2	
Savoie	44	44			
Haute-Savoie	38	4	12	22	
Totals	117	76	16	25	
Paris Region					
Seine	632	390[a]	222		20
Seine-et-Marne	97	1	79	17	
Seine-et-Oise	351	56	127	168	
Totals	1,080	447	428	185	20
Eastern France					
Doubs	88	6	76	6	
Jura	45	25		20	
Haute-Marne	28	16	9	3	
Meuse	21	14	3	4	
Meurthe-et-Moselle	154	29	16	106	3
Moselle	38	11	14	13	
Belfort	13	10		3	
Bas-Rhin	72	58	14		
Haut-Rhin	94	94			
Haute-Saône	19	19			
Vosges	39	23	3	13	
Totals	611	305	135	168	3
The Orléanais					
Loiret	31	6	4	21	
Loir-et-Cher	46	34	10	2	
Totals	77	40	14	23	

[a] This was the vote cast by the *fédération* as reorganized by Allemane and Costedoat.

Fédération	Mandats	Synthesis	B.S.	G.R.	Absentions
		WESTERN FRANCE			
Eure	50	4	25	21	
Eure-et-Loir	61	20	31	10	
Mayenne	15	8	5	2	
Orne	14	1	3	9	
Vendée	29	8	6	15	
Totals	169	41	70	57	
		NORMANDY			
Calvados	31	1		27	3
Manche	34	25	4	5	
Seine-Inférieure	83	38	14	31	
Totals	148	64	18	63	3

Table 12. Reconstruction of the vote on international policy for the Congress of Montrouge in 1938, by *fédération*

Fédération	Blum	Faure	Redress.	Gulkowski	Synthesis
		LANGUEDOC			
Ariège	40	24			
Aude	89	7			
Gard	26	46		9	
Hérault					
Pyrénées-Orient.	38	47	4		
Tarn	24	45			
Totals	217	169	4	9	
	RHONE VALLEY–PROVENCE				
Alpes-Maritimes					
B.-du-Rhône	178	138			
Drôme	26	35			
Var	93	23			
Vaucluse					51
Totals	297	196			51

Sources. Le Populaire and journals of the *fédérations.*

Fédération	Blum	Faure	Redress.	Gulkowski	Synthesis
NORTH					
Nord	767				
Oise	13	5	18		68
Pas-de-Calais					351[a]
Somme	52	57			10
Totals	832	62	18		429
GARONNE BASIN					
Dordogne	21	38			
Haute-Garonne	62	77			
Lot-et-Garonne	18	13			
Tarn-et-Garonne					
Totals	101	128			
MASSIF CENTRAL					
Ardèche					
Aveyron					
Cantal	7	3	22		
Corrèze					79[b]
Creuse					41
Haute-Loire	17	11			11
Lot	9	11	10		
Lozère					
Puy-de-Dôme					133[c]
Haute-Vienne		167			
Totals	33	192	32		264
LYONNAIS					
Ain	19	26		12	
Isère	60	91			
Loire	22	34			
Rhône	34	28	20		
Saône-et-Loire	10	96			
Totals	145	275	20	12	

[a] The congress of the *fédération* voted in favor of the Blum resolution by a margin of 70% to 30%, but Pantigny, desirous of synthesis, abstained in behalf of the entire *fédération*. See *Le Petit Parisien*, December 27, 1938.

[b] Although the congress of the *fédération* of the Corrèze expressed a desire for a "synthesis," the three Socialist deputies from the department spoke out in support of Faure. See *La Voix Corrèzienne*, November 19, December 25, 1938.

[c] Four of the Socialist deputies from the department favored Faure. See *L'Auvergne Socialiste*, December 17, 1938.

Fédération	Blum	Faure	Redress.	Gulkowski	Synthesis
		CENTRAL FRANCE			
Allier	85	44	3		
Cher	22	44			
Côte d'Or	108	9	3		
Indre	27	10	2		
Nièvre	26	19	3		
Yonne					
Totals	268	126	11		
		NORTHEAST			
Aisne[d]					
Ardennes					
Aube	24	5	7		
Marne					
Totals	24	5	7		
		BRITTANY			
Côtes-du-Nord					
Finistère	46	15			
Ille-et-Vilaine					
Loire-Inférieure	91	8			
Morbihan	24	38			9
Totals	161	61			9
		WEST CENTRAL FRANCE			
Charente-Inf.	93	26			
Indre-et-Loire[e]	54	44	1		9
Maine-et-Loire					
Sarthe	74	5			
Deux-Sèvres	42	6	5	1	
Vienne	27	12	2	2	
Totals	290	93	8	3	9
		ALGERIA			
Algiers					
Constantine					
Oran	16	11			
Totals	16	11			

[d] Under the leadership of Monnet and Bloch, the Aisne probably cast all of its *mandats* for Blum.

[e] At the congress of this *fédération* every speaker spoke in support of the Faure motion. *Le Réveil*, December 24, 1938.

Fédération	Blum	Faure	Redress	Gulkowski	Synthesis
		SOUTHWEST			
Charente					
Gers	24	23	7		
Gironde*f*					
Landes					
Basses-Pyrénées					
Hautes-Pyrénées	25	4	8		
Totals	49	27	15		
		ALPS REGION			
Basses-Alpes	12	10		1	
Hautes-Alpes					
Savoie	31	12		1	
Haute-Savoie	14	2	8		
Totals	57	24	8	2	
		PARIS REGION			
Seine	329	291	12		
Seine-et-Marne					
Seine-et-Oise	239	68	44		
Totals	568	359	56		
		EASTERN FRANCE			
Doubs					
Jura					
Haute-Marne					
Meuse		21			
Meurthe-et-Moselle	67	59	28		
Moselle					
Belfort	7	6			
Bas-Rhin					
Haut-Rhin	60	4			30
Haut-Saône	15	3			1
Vosges	18	17			4
Totals	167	110	28		35

f The Gironde *fédération* continued to be marked by paradox, making the un-availability of its journal all the more lamentable. Vigorously opposed to non-intervention, nonetheless many of its leaders rallied to the Faure resolution—Naphle, Vielle, Luquet, Cabannes, and Audeguil. The secretary, Muriene supported the Blum resolution. See *Le Socialiste*, December 1, 1938.

Fédération	Blum	Faure	Redress	Gulkowski	Synthesis
THE ORLÉANAIS					
Loiret	11	12		8	
Loir-et-Cher	40	5	1		
Totals	51	17	1	8	
WESTERN FRANCE					
Eure					
Eure-et-Loir	39	22			
Mayenne					
Orne	7		7		
Vendée					
Totals	46	22	7		
NORMANDY					
Calvados	6		25		
Manche	16	17	1		
Seine-Inférieure	28	10	45		
Totals	50	27	71		
Totals (6,393)	3,372	1,904 / 286 ⟵ 286		34	797
Missing (1,850)	960	2,190 647		26	217
Grand totals (8,243)	4,332	2,837		60	1,014

Table 13. Reconstruction of the preliminary vote on international policy for the Congress of Nantes in 1939, by *fédération*

Fédération	Mandats	Blum	Faure	Redress.	Gulkow-ski	Rivière synthesis
LANGUEDOC						
Ariège	51	29	8			14
Aude	98	76	17			5
Gard	83	22	61			
Hérault	94	43	34			17
Pyrénées-Orientales	75	20	21	4		30
Tarn	63	24	26			13
Totals	464	214	167	4		79
RHONE VALLEY–PROVENCE						
Alpes-Maritimes	51					
Bouches-du-Rhône	260	136	101			23
Drôme	64	27	34			3
Var	116	70	16	7		23
Vaucluse	37	18	18			
Totals	528	251	169	7		49
NORTH						
Nord	767	396	223			117
Oise	81	30	30	13	8	
Pas-de-Calais	384	269	110	5		
Somme	118	51	51	6	10	
Totals	1,350	746	414	24	18	117
GARONNE BASIN						
Dordogne	49					
Haute-Garonne	156	56	94	4		
Lot-et-Garonne	33	7	26			
Tarn-et-Garonne	24					24
Totals	262	63	120	4		24
MASSIF CENTRAL						
Ardèche	40					
Aveyron	51	35	11			
Cantal	25	2	2	17		4
Corrèze	84	19	65			
Creuse	37	7	2			27
Haute-Loire	45	3	6			36
Lot	21					
Lozère	14					

Sources. Le Populaire and journals of the *fédérations.*

Fédération	*Mandats*	Blum	Faure	Redress.	Gulkow-ski	Rivière synthesis
MASSIF CENTRAL (*Continued*)						
Puy-de-Dôme	130					
Haute-Vienne	117					117
Totals	564	66	86	17		184
LYONNAIS						
Ain	55	21	22	7		
Isère	159	56	103			
Loire	56	21	35			
Rhône	87	29	40		12	6
Saône-et-Loire	99	25	73			1
Totals	456	152	273	7	12	7
CENTRAL FRANCE						
Allier	132	75	35	20		
Cher	54					54
Côte d'Or	107	98	8	1		
Indre	44	19	19	4	2	
Nièvre	50	33	17	1	3	
Yonne	54					
Totals	441	225	79	26	5	54
NORTHEAST						
Aisne	122	99	2	7	1	12
Ardennes	58	46	10			
Aube	33	24	4	5		
Marne	76	63	3	4	2	
Totals	289	232	19	16	3	12
BRITTANY						
Côtes-du-Nord	49	28	15	6		
Finistère	58	35	11	5		
Ille-et-Vilaine	24	11	3	5		5
Loire-Inférieure	101					
Morbihan	57	19	21	2	1	14
Totals	289	93	50	18	1	19
WEST CENTRAL FRANCE						
Charente-Inférieure	108	50	16	5		37
Indre-et-Loire	107	24	37	3	1	42
Maine-et-Loire	22					
Sarthe	62	53	7			2

Fédération	Mandats	Blum	Faure	Redress.	Gulkow-ski	Rivière synthesis
WEST CENTRAL FRANCE (*Continued*)						
Deux-Sèvres	48	8				40
Vienne	39	25	10	4		
Totals	386	160	70	12	1	121
ALGERIA (AND MOROCCO)						
Alger	38					
Constantine	53					
Oran	50	18	26		6	
Morocco	35	24	9	2		
Totals	176	42	35	2	6	
SOUTHWEST						
Charente	34	7	6	1		20
Gers	47	9	5	2	9	20
Gironde	184					
Landes	71					
Basses-Pyrénées	58					
Hautes-Pyrénées	29	15	3	11		
Totals	423	31	14	14	9	40
ALPS REGION						
Basses-Alpes	21	6	12			3
Hautes-Alpes	9					
Savoie	35	8	11			16
Haute-Savoie	44	23	10	11		
Totals	109	37	33	11		19
PARIS REGION						
Seine	362	159	189	14		
Seine-et-Marne	69					
Seine-et-Oise	284	147	54	29		54
Totals	715	306	243	43		54
EASTERN FRANCE						
Doubs	74					
Jura	41	9	23			
Haute-Marne	26	8	18			
Meuse	22					
Meurthe-et-Moselle	127	43	37	27	7	13
Moselle	47	45	2			
Belfort	21	12	9			
Bas-Rhin	72					

Fédération	Mandats	Blum	Faure	Redress	Gulkow-ski	Rivière synthesis
EASTERN FRANCE (*Continued*)						
Haut-Rhin	87					
Haute-Saône	21					
Vosges	42	9	27	3		3
Totals	580	126	116	30	7	16
THE ORLÉANAIS						
Loiret	29	11	10	2	5	
Loir-et-Cher	51	37	2	2	10	
Totals	80	48	12	4	15	
WESTERN FRANCE						
Eure	45					
Eure-et-Loir	52					
Mayenne	18					
Orne	15					
Vendée	30	21		7		
Totals	160	21		7		
NORMANDY						
Calvados	30	6	4	19	1	
Manche	35	20	12	3		
Seine-Inférieure	76	22	30	8	3	12
Totals	141	48	46	30	4	12
Totals	7,413	2,861	1,946	276	80	807
(Missing)	1,443		276			
Known	5,970	2,861	2,222		80	807

Bibliography

MATERIALS PERTAINING TO THE SOCIALIST PARTY

Socialist Periodicals

AGIR—Pour la Paix, Pour le Socialisme, February-August, 1939. Bimonthly journal under the direction of Georges Monnet.

La Bataille Socialiste, 1933. Left-wing organ directed by Jean Zyromski and Marceau Pivert.

Le Bulletin Socialiste, January 6, 1936–August 14, 1939. Weekly information sheet sent to the Socialist *fédérations* by the party's Secretariat.

Les Cahiers Rouges, August-September, 1937. Only one number available. A journal published by the *Gauche Révolutionnaire*.

Le Cri des Jeunes, January, 1936–June, 1939. Bimonthly organ of the *Jeunesses Socialistes*, under the control of Bernard Chochoy.

L'Espagne Socialiste, Organe franco-espagnol illustré du Comité d'Action Socialiste pour l'Espagne (C.A.S.P.E.), April 16–November 1, 1937. Bimonthly journal directed by Zyromski and supported by Pivert in the interest of obtaining support within Socialist ranks for the Spanish Republic.

Jeune Garde, Organe des Jeunesses Socialistes (S.F.I.O.) de la Seine, July, 1936–November, 1937. Appeared irregularly.

Juin 36, February 15, 1938–August 25, 1939. Weekly journal of the Seine *fédération* under the control of Marceau Pivert, and, following his departure from the S.F.I.O., it became the central organ of the *Parti Socialiste Ouvrier et Paysan* (P.S.O.P.).

La Paix Socialiste, December, 1938. Only one number available. A journal created by Auriol, Monnet, and Dormoy to publicize Blum's position on international policy prior to the Congress of Montrouge.

Le Pays Socialiste—Par la Liberté, par la Paix, March 18, 1939–June 7, 1940. Weekly journal under the direction of Paul Faure and a major source for the opinion of the "Fauristes" in 1939 and 1940.

335

Le Populaire de Paris, 1931–1940. Daily organ of the Socialist party and the major source for this study.

Redressement, December, 1938–June, 1939. Monthly organ of the *tendance* of the same name led by Zoretti and Deixonne.

La République Libre, January 7, 1949–December 9, 1960. Weekly journal directed by Paul Faure in the postwar period. Occasional contributors were Roucayrol, Castagnez, and Rauzy.

La Revue Socialiste, Nouvelle Série, 1946–1963.

Le Rouge et Le Bleu, Revue de la pensée socialiste française, November 1, 1941–August 22, 1942. Weekly journal directed by Charles Spinasse. Published in occupied Paris.

Le Socialiste, April 15, 1938–March 1, 1939. "Fauriste" weekly published in Paris.

La Vague, Organe de Rassemblement Révolutionnaire, November 15, 1936–November 15, 1937. A bimonthly publication nominally open to all shades of Socialist opinion, but its contributors were drawn from the ranks of the *Gauche Révolutionnaire.*

La Vie du Parti, 1931–1940. Irregular supplement to *Le Populaire.* It contained the texts of resolutions offered at party congresses and councils and details of votes taken at these meetings and those of the C.A.P.

Journals of the Socialist Fédérations

Ain: *Le Travailleur de l'Ain,* August 8, 1936–June 10, 1939. Weekly.
Aisne: *Le Réveil Populaire,* January 25, 1936–June 4, 1938. Weekly.
Algiers: *Alger Socialiste,* January 24, 1936–January 4, 1939. Weekly.
Allier: *Le Combat Social,* February 2, 1936–June 4, 1939. Weekly.
Alpes-Maritimes: *L'Alerte,* July 25, 1936–April 10, 1938. Weekly.
Ardèche: *Le Réveil Populaire,* February 1, 1936–October 8, 1937. Weekly.
Ardennes: *Le Socialiste Ardennais,* March 1, 1936–July 31, 1938. Bi-weekly.
Ariège: *La Montagne Socialiste,* July 30, 1936–May 29, 1938. Weekly.
Aude: *La République Sociale,* July 30, 1936–December 22, 1938. Weekly.
Aveyron: *Le Socialiste Aveyronnais,* January 9, 1937–May 27, 1939. Weekly.
Bas-Rhin: *La Presse Libre,* 1936–1938. Daily.
Basses-Alpes: *Le Travailleur des Alpes,* January 25, 1936–August 26, 1939. Weekly journal of the *fédérations* of the Basses-Alpes and the Hautes-Alpes.

Basses-Pyrénées: *Le Travail*, January 7, 1936–May 28, 1939. Weekly.

Belfort: *Germinal*, January 11, 1936–June 10, 1939. Weekly.

Bouches-du-Rhône: *Marseille Socialiste*, July 25, 1936–November 28, 1936. Weekly.

——: *La Provence Socialiste*, December 5, 1936–June 16, 1939. Weekly.

Calvados: *Le Pays Normand*, November 22, 1936–May, 1939. Irregular.

Cantal: *Le Socialiste du Cantal*, May 24, 1936–March 18, 1939. Weekly.

Charente-Inférieure: *La Voix Socialiste*, August 15, 1936–May 6, 1939. Bimonthly.

Cher: *Le Réveil Socialiste du Cher*, November 14, 1936–July 24, 1937. Bimonthly.

——: *Le Populaire du Cher*, February 20, 1938–May 27, 1939. Weekly.

Corrèze: *La Voix Corrèzienne*, July 26, 1936–August 27, 1939. Biweekly.

Côte d'Or: *Le Socialiste Côte d'Orien*, May 30, 1936–July 30, 1938. Weekly.

——: *La Bourgogne Républicaine*, December 19, 1938–January 29, 1939. Daily.

Côtes-du-Nord: *Le Combat Social*, August 8, 1936–January 28, 1939. Weekly.

Creuse: *Le Mémorial de la Creuse*, August 1, 1936–May 28, 1938. Weekly.

Deux-Sèvres: *Le Travail*, March 1, 1936–March 11, 1939. Weekly.

Dordogne: *La Voix Socialiste*, August 1, 1936–July 31, 1938. Weekly.

Drôme: *La Volonté Socialiste*, July 25, 1936–July 15, 1939. Weekly.

Eure-et-Loir: *Le Populaire de l'Eure-et-Loir et de l'Eure*, July 24, 1936–May 26, 1939. Weekly.

Finistère: *Le Breton Socialiste*, July 25, 1936–May 27, 1939. Weekly.

Gard: *Le Combat Social*, August 1, 1936–January 23, 1937. Weekly.

Gers: *Le Gers Socialiste*, July 25, 1936–June 24, 1939. Weekly.

Gironde: *L'Unité Socialiste*, July 25, 1936–June 12, 1937. Weekly.

Haute-Garonne: *Le Midi Socialiste*, 1936–1939. Daily.

——: *L'Emancipation*, May 17, 1936–March 11, 1939. Weekly journal of the Saint-Gaudens section.

Haute-Marne: *Le Réveil Ouvrier et Paysan*, December 12, 1936–April 10, 1938. Bimonthly.

Haute-Saône: *Le Socialiste*, September 5, 1936–June 3, 1939. Bimonthly.

Haute-Savoie: *Le Socialiste Savoyard*, August 1, 1936–January 21, 1939. Weekly.

Hautes-Pyrénées: *La Bigorre Socialiste,* January 1, 1937–December 31, 1938. Bimonthly.

Haute-Vienne: *Le Populaire du Centre,* 1936–1939. Daily.

——: *Le Petit Limousin,* March 11, 1936–August 26, 1939. Biweekly directed to the rural population.

——: *Bulletin d'Informations Socialistes,* December, 1936–June, 1937. Monthly.

Haut-Rhin: *Der Republikaner,* 1936–1939. Daily.

Hérault: *L'Aube Sociale,* February 1, 1936–August 20, 1939. Weekly.

Ille-et-Vilaine: *L'Aurore,* July 26, 1936–February 18, 1939. Weekly.

Indre: *Le Berry Républicain,* July 26, 1936–April 28, 1939. Weekly under the personal control of François Chasseigne, a deputy who rejoined the S.F.I.O. in March, 1937.

Indre-et-Loire: *Le Réveil,* August 1, 1936–July 1, 1939. Weekly.

Isère: *Le Droit du Peuple,* January 4, 1936–July 8, 1939. Weekly.

Jura: *Le Jura Socialiste,* July 25, 1936–May 27, 1939. Weekly.

Landes: *Le Travailleur Landais,* January 2, 1937–February 18, 1939. Weekly.

Loire: *Le Courrier de l'Ondaine,* July 4, 1936–December 30, 1938. Weekly under the personal control of the deputy Pétrus Faure.

Loire-Inférieure: *Le Travailleur de l'Ouest,* August 1, 1936–June 10, 1939. Weekly.

Loir-et-Cher: *Le Populaire de Loir-et-Cher,* August 8, 1936–June 3, 1939. Weekly.

Lot: *Le Travail du Lot,* July 25, 1936–June 3, 1939. Weekly.

Lot-et-Garonne: *Le Réveil Socialiste,* February 1, 1936–May 13, 1939. Weekly.

Manche: *L'Avenir de la Manche,* April 2, 1938–September 17, 1938. Weekly.

Marne: *Le Travail de la Marne,* January 9, 1937–May 20, 1939. Weekly.

Meurthe-et-Moselle: *Le Populaire de l'Est,* August 2, 1936–June 3, 1939. Bimonthly in 1936; weekly after January, 1937.

Meuse: *L'Eveil de la Meuse,* September 10, 1936–April 19, 1939. Weekly.

Morbihan: *Le Rappel du Morbihan,* April 4, 1936–June 24, 1939. Weekly.

Nord: *La Bataille,* July 19, 1936–January 22, 1939. Weekly official organ of the *fédération.*

——: *La Bataille Ouvrière,* July 19, 1936–March 26, 1939. Weekly journal of the Roubaix section.

——: *L'Avenir du Nord,* January 9, 1938–May 14, 1939. Weekly under the control of the deputies Laurent, Beauvillain, and E. Thomas.

——: *Le Peuple Libre,* January 3, 1936–May 26, 1939. Weekly organ of the Lille section.

Oise: *Le Cri Populaire de l'Oise,* March 1, 1936–March 19, 1939. Weekly.

Pas-de-Calais: *L'Éclaireur,* March 14, 1936–March 5, 1938. Official weekly journal of the *fédération.*

——: *L'Eglantine,* August, 1936–July, 1939. Monthly under the control of the deputy Vantielcke.

Puy-de-Dôme: *L'Auvergne Socialiste,* February 1, 1936–July 22, 1939. Weekly.

Pyrénées-Orientales: *Le Socialiste,* October 9, 1936–June 30, 1939. Weekly.

Rhône: *L'Avenir Socialiste,* January 1, 1936–April 8, 1939. Weekly.

Saône-et-Loire: *La Dépêche Socialiste,* March 28, 1936–August 19, 1939. Weekly.

Sarthe: *La République Sociale de l'Ouest,* August 23, 1936–May 26, 1939. Bimonthly.

Seine-et-Marne: *L'Aurore,* July 30, 1936–August 28, 1937. Weekly.

Seine-et-Oise: *L'Egalité,* August 1, 1936–January 28, 1939. Weekly journal of the Corbeil section.

Seine-Inférieure: *Le Progrès Social,* July 25, 1936–December 9, 1938. Weekly.

Somme: *Le Cri du Peuple,* May 21, 1936–July 8, 1939. Weekly.

Var: *Le Populaire du Var,* January 1, 1936–March 25, 1939. Weekly.

Vaucluse: *Le Réveil Socialiste,* May 28, 1936–June 22, 1939. Weekly.

Vosges: *Le Travailleur Vosgien,* August 1, 1936–June 10, 1939. Bimonthly.

Official Publications of the S.F.I.O.

Parti Socialiste S.F.I.O., *L'Action des Socialistes en 1936.* Arras, 1953.

——, *Almanach Socialiste 1937.* Paris, 1937.

——, *XVIII° Congrès National, Tours, Compte rendu sténographique.* Paris, 1921.

——, *XXXI° Congrès National, Toulouse, Compte rendu sténographique.* Paris, 1934.

——, *XXXII° Congrès National, Mulhouse, Compte rendu sténographique.* Paris, 1935.

——, *XXXIII° Congrès National, Paris, Compte rendu sténographique.* Paris, 1937.

——, *XXXIV° Congrès National, Marseille, Compte rendu sténographique.* Paris, 1938.

——, *XXXIV° Congrès National, Marseille, Rapports.* Paris, 1937.

——, *XXXV° Congrès National, Royan, Compte rendu sténogra-phique.* Paris, 1939.
——, *XXXV° Congrès National, Royan, Rapports.* Paris, 1938.
——, *XXXVI° Congrès National, Nantes Rapports.* Paris, 1939.
——, *Elections législatives de 1936. Questions diverses.* Paris, 1936.

Léon Blum

Works by Léon Blum

Blum, Léon. *Bolchevisme et Socialisme.* 2nd ed. Paris, 1927.
——. *Commentaires sur le programme d'action du Parti Socialiste.* Paris, 1919.
——. *Les Devoirs et les tâches du Socialisme.* Paris, 1945.
——. *Discours de Romans, 24 juillet 1932.* Valence, 1932.
——. *L'Exercice du pouvoir.* Paris, 1937. Speeches delivered from May, 1936, to January, 1937.
——. "Exercice et conquête du pouvoir," *La Revue Socialiste, Nou-velle Série,* 12–16 (1947), 385–395.
——. *Jean Jaurès: Conférence donné le 16 février 1933 au Théâtre des Ambassadeurs.* Paris, 1933.
——. *La Jeunesse et le Socialisme.* Paris, 1934.
——. *Léon Blum en "action" pour la paix.* Paris, 1936. Text of Blum's speech to the Chamber of Deputies on the Spanish problem, December 5, 1936.
——. *La Méthode Socialiste.* Paris, 1945.
——. "Notes sur la doctrine," *La Revue Socialiste, Nouvelle Série,* 3 (1946), 257–261.
——. *L'Oeuvre, 1934–1937. Du 6 février 1934 au Front Populaire. Les Lois sociales de 1936. La Guerre d'Espagne.* Paris, 1964.
——. *L'Oeuvre, 1937–1940. La Fin du Rassemblement Populaire. De Munich à la guerre. Souvenirs sur "l'Affaire."* Paris, 1965.
——. *L'Oeuvre, 1940–1945. Mémoires. La prison et le procès. A l'échelle humaine.* Paris, 1955.
——. *L'Oeuvre, 1945–1947. Naissance de la Quatrième République. La Vie du parti et la doctrine socialiste.* Paris, 1958.
——. *L'Oeuvre, 1947–1950. La Fin des alliances. La Troisième force. Politique européenne. Pour la justice.* Paris, 1963.
——. *Pour être Socialiste.* Paris, 1919.
——. *Pour la vieille maison.* Paris, 1921.
——. *Les Problèmes de la paix.* Paris, 1931.
——. *La Question d'Espagne.* Paris, 1939. Text of Blum's speech to the Chamber of Deputies, January 26, 1939.

——. *Radicalisme et Socialisme.* 5th ed. Paris, 1938.

——. *Les Radicaux et nous* (1932–1934) . Paris, 1934.

——. *Le Socialisme a vu clair.* Paris, 1936.

——. *Le Socialisme devant la crise.* Paris, 1933.

Works Relating to Léon Blum

Audry, Colette. *Léon Blum, ou la politique du juste.* Paris, 1955. An analysis of Blum's career by a follower of Marceau Pivert.

Bibliothèque Nationale. *Léon Blum.* Paris, 1962. Catalog of Blum's works on display at the Bibliothèque Nationale in 1962.

Blumel, André. *Léon Blum, juif et sioniste.* Paris, 1952.

Bourgin, Hubert. *De Jaurès à Léon Blum: L'École Normale et la politique.* Paris, 1938.

Colton, Joel. *Léon Blum, Humanist in Politics.* New York, 1966. Clearly the best single work on Blum's political career. We disagree on several counts, especially on Blum's international policy: where Colton sees coherence, I am prone to emphasize Blum's indecision and ambivalence. We are also in disagreement on Blum's role in the decline of the Socialist party.

Dalby, Louise E. *Léon Blum: Evolution of a Socialist.* New York, 1963.

Drachkovitch, Milorad. *De Karl Marx à Léon Blum: La crise de la sociale-démocratie.* Geneva, 1954.

Dupeux, Georges. "L'échec du premier gouvernement Léon Blum," in *Revue d'histoire moderne et contemporaine,* X (1963) , January-March, 35–44.

——. "Léon Blum et la majorité parlementaire," *Colloque des 26 et 27 mars 1965: Léon Blum, chef de gouvernement, 1936–1937.* Paris, Fondation Nationale des Sciences Politiques, 1965.

Fraser, Geoffrey, and Natanson, Thadée. *Léon Blum, Man and Statesman.* London, 1937.

Harmel, Claude. *Lettre à Léon Blum sur le Socialisme et la paix.* Paris, 1947.

Izard, Georges. *Le Testament Socialiste de Léon Blum* (*Le Socialisme français, victime du marxisme?*) . Paris, n.d.

Joll, James. *Intellectuals in Politics.* London, 1960. Essays devoted to Blum, Rathenau, and Marinetti.

Mayer, Daniel. "Léon Blum face à Franco," *L'Express,* VI (1958) , 392.

Mirkine-Guetzévitch, Boris. "La République parlementaire dans la pensée politique de Léon Blum," *La Revue Socialiste, Nouvelle Série,* 43 (1951) , 10–24.

Naegelen, Marcel-Edmon. "Quelques images de Léon Blum," *La Revue Socialiste, Nouvelle Série,* 37 (1950) , 407–411.

Ramadier, Paul. *Le Socialisme de Léon Blum.* Paris, 1951.

Rémond, René, and Bourdin, Janine. "Les Forces adverses," *Colloque des 26 et 27 mars 1965, Léon Blum, chef de gouvernement, 1936–1937.* Paris, Fondation Nationale des Sciences Politiques, 1965.

Renouvin, Pierre. "La Politique extérieure du premier ministère Leon Blum," in Edouard Bonnefous, *Histoire Politique de la Troisième République.* Vol. VI. *Vers la guerre (1936–1938)*. Paris, 1965, 393–409.

Rogers, Lindsay. "M. Blum and the French Senate," *Political Science Quarterly*, LII (1937), 321–327.

Stokes, Richard L. *Léon Blum: Poet to Premier.* New York, 1937.

Vichniac, Marc. *Léon Blum.* Paris, 1937.

Windell, George C. "Léon Blum and the Crisis over Spain, 1936," *The Historian*, XXXV (1962), 423–449.

Ziebura, Gilbert. *Léon Blum: Theorie und Praxis einer sozialistischen Politik.* Vol. I, 1872–1934. Berlin, 1963.

Paul Faure

Faure, Paul. *Le Bolchevisme en France: Farce et Imposture.* Paris, 1921.

——. *La Crise agricole.* Paris, 1932.

——. *Discours. Banquet des "mille" du 14 mars 1948.* Paris, 1948.

——. *Histoire d'un faux et de ses conséquences.* Paris, 1958. An attack against the ineligibility for election to the National Assembly of those parliamentarians who had voted full powers to Marshal Pétain in July, 1940.

——. *Les Intrus du capitole.* Unpublished manuscript. Contains an attack on Blum for allegedly wanting war in 1939 and a brief account of his own role at the Congresses of Montrouge and Nantes in 1938 and 1939 respectively.

——. *Les Marchands de canons contre la paix.* Paris, 1936.

——. *De Munich à la Cinquième République.* Paris, 1948. A defense of the author's activities in the post-Munich period.

——. *Ou va le Socialisme français?* Paris, 1946.

——. *Pacifisme et défaitisme.* Paris, 1945.

——. *Un Patron du droit divin: Schneider.* Paris, 1933.

——. *Le Problème du désarmement.* Paris, 1932.

——. *La Scission socialiste en France et dans l'Internationale.* Paris, 1928.

——. *Au seuil d'une révolution.* Limoges, 1934.

——. *Si tu veux la paix.* Paris, 1934.

——. *Le Socialisme dans la bataille électorale.* Paris, 1936.

——. *Le Socialisme en action: arguments et ripostes.* Paris, 1928.

——. *Le Socialisme et la petite propriété.* Paris, 1936.

——, and Jean-Baptiste Séverac. *Le Parti Socialiste, ses principes, son organisation, son action.* Paris, 1936.

Jean Zyromski

Zyromski, Jean. *Comment lutter contre le fascisme international.* Paris, 1938.

——. "Une enquête sur le problème de l'unité," *Idée et Action,* 6 (January, 1937), 34–46.

——. *Pour sauver la démocratie et la paix, ouvrez la frontière!* Paris, 1938.

——. *Sur le chemin de l'unité.* Paris, 1936.

——. "Union des démocraties et unité ouvrier," *Clarté,* 16 (December, 1937), 502–504.

——, Otto Bauer, Théodor Dan, and Amédée Dunois. *L'Internationale et la guerre: pour la discussion internationale.* Paris, 1935.

La Gauche Révolutionnaire

Marceau Pivert

Pivert, Marceau. *Action directe contre la guerre et le guerre et le fascisme.* Paris, 1938.

——. "Juin 36 et les défaillances du mouvement ouvrier," *La Revue Socialiste, Nouvelle Série,* 98 (1956), 2–33.

——. *Révolution d'abord!* Paris, 1935. A slashing polemic against Zyromski's international policy.

——. *Tendre la main aux catholiques?* Paris, 1938.

——, Lucien Hérard, and René Modiano. *Quatre discours et un programme.* Paris, 1937.

——, Madeline Hérard, and Lucien Hérard. *Rupture nécessaire.* Paris, 1938. An explanation of Pivert's departure from the Socialist party.

——, and Victor Picard. *L'Armée prétorienne des trusts.* Paris, 1936.

Works by Other Members of the *Gauche Révolutionnaire*

Collinet, Michel. "La structure sociale et la guerre des classes en Espagne," *Idée et Action,* 5 (December, 1936), 56–61.

Guérin, Daniel. *Front Populaire, Révolution manquée.* Paris, 1963. The only account of the activities and aspirations of the *Gauche Révolutionnaire.*

Modiano, Hélène. *Les Militaires contre la nation.* Paris, 1936.

——. *Les Munitionnaires contre la nation.* Paris, 1936.

Prader, Jean. *Au secours de l'Espagne Socialiste!* Paris, 1936.

——. "La politique de non-intervention et les principes du Socialisme," *Idée et Action,* 5 (December, 1936) , 36–46.

Weill-Curiel, Andre. *Le Temps de la honte.* Vol. II. *Eclipse en France.* Paris, 1946.

Secondary Source

Weill-Raynal, Etienne. *Marceau Pivert.* Arras, 1958. A summary of Pivert's career.

Publications of Other Members of the S.F.I.O.

Auriol, Vincent. *Hier . . . Demain.* Tunis, 1944.

Blumel, André, "La Non-intervention en Espagne," in Georges Lefranc, *Histoire du Front Populaire.* Paris, 1965, 460–466.

Cabannes, René. *De Jules Guesde à Staline, ou le problème du pouvoir.* Paris, 1932.

Castagnez, Jean. *Précisions oubliées . . . ! Vichy: 9 et 10 juillet 1940.* N.p., n.d.

Déat, Marcel. *Perspectives Socialistes.* Paris, 1930.

Dumoulin, Georges. *Carnets de route: souvenirs.* Lille, 1938.

——. *Le Parti Socialiste et la C.G.T.* Paris, 1935. A member of both the S.F.I.O. and the C.G.T., Dumoulin was General Secretary of the *Union des Syndicts du Nord.*

Fauchère, Germaine. *L'Action parlementaire 1932–1936.* Paris, 1936.

Frossard, Ludovic-Oscar. *Sous le signe de Jaurès: De Jaurès à Léon Blum, souvenirs d'un militant.* Paris, 1943. Frossard left the S.F.I.O. in 1935.

Gros, Louis. *République toujours.* Avignon, 1945.

Laurat, Lucien. *La Liquidation Socialiste du crise.* Paris, 1934.

——. *Le Socialisme à l'ordre du jour, problèmes et tâches du marxisme contemporaine.* Paris, 1933.

Lebas, Jean. *Critique Socialiste du Parti Communiste.* N.p., n.d.

——. *Le Socialisme, but et moyen.* Lille, 1935.

Lévy, Louis. *Comment ils devenus Socialistes.* Paris, 1932.

——. *The Truth About France.* London, 1941. A useful study of the Popular Front and the fall of France in 1940 by a member of the staff of *Le Populaire.*

Moch, Jules. *Pour marcher au pouvoir.* Paris, 1935.

——. *Le Socialisme, la crise, les nationalisations.* Paris, 1932.

——, and Germaine Picard-Moch. *L'Espagne républicaine.* Paris, 1933.

Montagnon, B., A. Marquet, and M. Déat. *Néo-Socialisme.* Paris, 1933.

Paz, Maurice. *Le six février.* Paris, 1934.

Pivert, Charles. *Le Parti Socialiste et ses hommes*. Paris, n.d.
Séverac, Jean-Baptiste. *Lettres à Brigitte: Le Parti Socialiste, ses principes, ses tâches*. Paris, 1933.
Spinasse, Charles. *La Crise économique*. N.p., n.d.

Interviews and Correspondence

Blum, Robert. Interview. June 17, 1962.
Blumel, André. Interview. November 22, 1961.
Castagnez, Jean. Interviews. June 8 and 29, 1962.
Cusin, Gaston. Interview. December 1, 1961.
Laurat, Lucien. Interview. July 26, 1962.
Mayer, Daniel. Interview. June 17, 1962.
Moch, Jules. Interview. November 24, 1961.
Pivert, Madame Marceau. Letter. November 17, 1961.
Rauzy, Alexandre. Interview. June 8, 1962.
Rosenfeld, Oreste. Interview. June 19, 1962.
Roucayrol, Fernand. Interview. July 28, 1962.
Weill-Raynal, Etienne. Interview. November 8, 1961.
Zyromski, Jean. Letter. June 22, 1962.

Secondary Works

Colton, Joel. "Léon Blum and the French Socialists as a Government Party," *Journal of Politics*, XV (1953), 517–543.
Combes, Annie. *Monographie de la fédération Socialiste de la Sarthe*. Thesis, Institut d'Etudes Politiques, Université de Paris, 1953.
Fourchy, P. *Les Doctrines du Parti Socialiste Français (S.F.I.O.)*. Thesis, Université de Nancy, 1929.
Gaucher, François. *Contribution à l'histoire du socialisme français, 1905–1933*. Paris, 1934.
Hymans, Daniel. *La S.F.I.O. devant l'Allemagne hitlérienne*. Mémoire, Institut d'Etudes Politiques, Université de Paris, 1960. A very general and frequently inaccurate treatment.
Kriegel, Annie. *Le Congrès de Tours*. Paris, 1964. Excerpts from the congress.
Lefranc, Georges. *Le Mouvement socialiste sous la Troisième République*. Paris, 1963. Informative and very helpful.
Lenoble, Jean. *L'Evolution politique du socialisme en Haute-Vienne sous la Troisième République*. Thesis, Institut d'Etudes Politiques, Université de Paris, 1950.
Ligou, Daniel. *Histoire du socialisme en France, 1871–1961*. Paris, 1962. Contains little more than accounts of party congresses and excerpts from the pertinent writings of the Socialist leaders.

Louis, Paul. *Histoire du socialisme en France, 1789–1945.* 5th ed., Paris, 1945. A general survey, not at all helpful for the interwar period.

Marcus, John T. *French Socialism in the Crisis Years, 1933–1936: Fascism and the French Left.* New York, 1958. Valuable for its analysis of Zyromski and Pivert. Useful bibliography.

Mead, Robert C. *The Struggle for Power: Reformism in the French Socialist Party (S.F.I.O.), 1919–1939.* Doctoral dissertation, Columbia University, 1953. Very general treatment.

Prélot, Marcel. *L'Évolution politique du socialisme français.* Paris, 1939. Valuable as an introductory survey.

Spire, Alfred. *Le Déclin du marxisme dans les tendances socialistes de la France contemporaine.* Paris, 1937. Excellent analysis of the Neo-Socialists.

——. *Inventaire des socialismes français contemporains.* Paris, 1946.

Vidal, Pierre. "Le Congrès extraordinaire du Parti Socialiste Français," *International Communiste,* February, 1939.

Zéaves, Alexandre B. *Histoire du socialisme et communisme en France de 1871 à 1947.* Paris, 1947.

——. *Le Socialisme en France depuis 1904.* Paris, 1934.

MATERIALS PERTAINING TO FRANCE IN THE 1930's

Documents

Assemblée National, Première Législature, Session de 1947, Annexe au Procès-verbal de la Deuxième Séance du 8 août 1947, No. 2234, *Rapport fait au nom de la commission chargée d'enquêter sur les événements survenus en France de 1933 à 1945, témoignages et documents.* Paris, n.d. Nine volumes of testimony and two devoted to the commission's report. Unquestionably the most important single source of information concerning Blum's attitude toward the Spanish Civil War.

Confédération Générale du Travail, *Renseignements administratifs sur la C.G.T.* Versailles, 1936.

Etat Français, Ministère de l'Economie Nationale et des Finances, *Annuaire Statistique Abrégé.* Vol. I. Paris, 1943.

Journal Officiel de la République Française, Chambre des Députés, Débats Parlementaires. Paris, 1936–1939.

Lachapelle, Georges. *Elections legislatives, le 11 mai 1924. Résultats officiels.* Paris, 1924.

——. *Elections législatives, 22 et 29 avril 1928. Résultats officiels.* Paris, 1928.

——. *Elections législatives, 1ᵉʳ et 8 mai 1932. Résultats officiels.* Paris, 1932.

——. *Elections législatives, 26 avril et 3 mai 1936.* Résultats officiels. Paris, 1936.

Ministère de l'Economie Nationale, *Résultats statistiques du recensement general de la population effectué le 8 mars 1936.* Paris, 1938.

Ministère des Affaires Etrangères, *Le Livre jaune français. Documents diplomatiques, 1938–1939.* Paris, 1939.

Ministère des Affaires Etrangères, Commission de Publication des Documents Relatifs aux Origines de la Guerre 1939–1945, *Documents diplomatiques français, 1932–1939, 2ᵉ série (1936–1939)*, Vol. III *(19 juillet-19 novembre 1936)*. Paris, 1966. This volume deals primarily with the French response to the Spanish Civil War. My work was finished when this volume appeared, but I have found nothing among these documents which would alter either my narrative or my conclusions.

Periodical Sources

Les Cahiers des Droits de l'Homme, January 10, 1936–November 1, 1938. Bimonthly.

Clarté, Revue mensuelle du Comité contre la Guerre et le Fascisme, August, 1936–December, 1937.

La Commune, October 23, 1936–December 1, 1938. Irregular organ of the *Parti Communiste International.* Trotskyite.

La Dépêche de Toulouse, 1936–1939. The famous Radical daily.

L'Echo de Paris, July 24–September 10, 1936. Parisian daily directed by Henri de Kérillis. It was the first to publish reports that the Blum government was preparing to send arms to the Spanish Republic.

L'Europe Nouvelle, August 8, 1936–December 31, 1938. Weekly. Contained articles by the Socialist Pierre Brossolette, as well as by Bertrand de Jouvenel.

La Flèche de Paris, March 11, 1938–August 29, 1939. Weekly organ of Gaston Bergery's *Frontiste* movement.

L'Humanité, January 1, 1936–August 22, 1939. Daily organ of the Communist party.

Idée et Action, June 6, 1936–April-May, 1937. Monthly journal of Socialist and trade-union opinion.

Le Journal des Débats, July 20–December 31, 1936. Conservative daily published in Paris.

La Justice, January 10–June 2, 1939. Parisian daily directed by L.-O. Frossard.

La Lumière, January 21, 1938–June 2, 1939. Weekly directed by Georges Boris. It featured articles by Salomon Grumbach.

L'Œuvre, July 19, 1936–August 25, 1939. Left-leaning Radical daily, published in Paris.

Paris-Soir, January 10, 1939. An article by Paul Faure appeared in this number.

Le Petit Parisien, 1936–1939. This daily contained excellent accounts of the activities of the Socialist *fédération* of the Seine.

Le Peuple, April 1, 1936–August 23, 1939. Daily organ of the C.G.T. published in Paris.

La République, July 20–September 12, 1936. Daily organ of the right wing of the Radical party.

Le Socialiste Girondin, Organe officiel de la fédération du Parti Socialiste de France, August-December, 1936. Weekly journal of the Neo-Socialists in the Department of the Gironde. Directed by Adrien Marquet.

Syndicats, October 17, 1936–July 26, 1939. Weekly journal of the anti-Communist group of the C.G.T., led by René Belin, André Delmas, and Raymond Froideval.

Le Temps, 1936–1939. Conservative daily published in Paris. Well-informed on diplomatic matters. One of its journalists, Raymond Millet, was an astute observer of developments among the French Left.

Works by personalities prominent in the 1930's

Bonnet, Georges. *Défense de la paix: De Washington au Quai d'Orsay.* Geneva, 1946.

———. *Fin d'une Europe: De Munich à la guerre.* Geneva, 1948.

Chautemps, Camille. *Cahiers secrets de l'armistice (1939–1940).* Paris, 1963.

Cot, Pierre. *L'Armée de l'air, 1936–1938.* Paris, 1938.

———. *Le Procès de la République.* 2 vols. New York, 1942. Extremely valuable for its account of the deliberations of the Council of Ministers on the Spanish problem in July and August, 1936.

Coulondre, Robert. *De Staline à Hitler: Souvenirs de deux Ambassades, 1936–1939.* Paris, 1950.

Daladier, Edouard. *Défense du Pays.* Paris, 1939. A collection of speeches.

de Gaulle, Charles. *The Call to Honour.* New York, 1955.

de Monzie, Anatole. *Ci-devant.* Paris, 1941.

Delmas, André. *A gauche de la barricade, chronique syndicale de l'avant-guerre.* Paris, 1950.

Duclos, Jacques. *En avant pour le front unique d'action anti-fasciste.* Paris, 1934.

———. *L'Unité pour la victoire.* Bourges, 1936.

Flandin, Pierre-Etienne. *Politique française, 1919–1940.* Paris, 1947.

François-Poncet, André. *Souvenirs d'une ambassade à Berlin, Septembre 1931–Octobre 1938.* Paris, 1946.

Gamelin, Maurice Gustave. *Servir.* Vol. II. *Le Prologue du drame.* Paris, 1946.

Herriot, Édouard. *Jadis.* Vol. II. *D'une guerre à l'autre, 1914–1936.* Paris, 1952.

Kayser, Jacques. "Le Parti Radical-Socialiste en le Rassemblement Populaire, 1935–1938," *Bulletin de la Société d'Histoire de la Troisième République,* 14 (1955), 271–284.

Lamoureux, Lucien. "Mussolini et la France en 1936: Une mission officieuse de M. J.-L. Malvy (député, ancien ministre)," in Edouard Bonnefous, *Histoire Politique de la Troisième Republique.* Vol. VI. Paris, 1965, 410–411.

Marty, Andre. *Avec l'Espagne pour nos libertés et la paix!* Paris, 1936.

Paul-Boncour, Joseph. *Entre deux guerres. Souvenirs sur la Troisième République.* 3 vols. Paris, 1945–1946.

Reynaud, Paul. *Memoires.* Vol. II. *Envers et contre tous.* Paris, 1963.

Thorez, Maurice. *France To-Day and the Peoples' Front.* New York, n.d.

———. *Notre lutte pour la paix.* Paris, 1938.

———. *Oeuvres.* Book III, Vol. II. Paris, 1953.

———. *Oeuvres.* Book III, Vol. XII. Paris, 1954.

———. *La Sécurité française et l'Espagne.* Paris, 1939.

Zay, Jean. *Souvenirs et solitude.* Paris, 1946.

Important Secondary Sources

Bell, J. Bowyer. "French Reaction to the Spanish Civil War, July–September 1936," in Wallace and Askew, eds., *Power, Public Opinion, and Diplomacy.* Durham, North Carolina, 1959, 267–296.

Bodin, L., and J. Touchard. *Front Populaire 1936.* Paris, 1961. One of a series of volumes under the general title *Kiosque: Les faits, la presse, l'opinion.*

Bonnefous, Edouard. *Histoire politique de la Troisième République.* Vol. III. *L'Après-guerre (1919–1924).* Paris, 1959.

———. *Histoire politique de la Troisième République.* Vol. IV. *Cartel des gauches et union nationale (1924–1929).* Paris, 1960.

———. *Histoire politique de la Troisième République.* Vol. V. *La*

République en danger: des ligues au Front Populaire (1930–1936). Paris, 1962.

——. *Histoire politique de la Troisième République.* Vol. VI. *Vers la guerre (1936–1938)*. Paris, 1965.

——. *Histoire politique de la Troisième République.* Vol. VII. *La course vers l'abime (1938–1940)*. Paris, 1967.

Cameron, Elizabeth R. "Alexis Saint-Léger Léger," in Craig and Gilbert, eds., *The Diplomats.* Princeton,, New Jersey, 1953, 378–405.

Caute, David. *Communism and the French Intellectuals, 1914–1960.* London, 1964.

Chambaz, Jacques. *Le Front Populaire pour de pain, la liberté, et la paix.* Paris, 1961. A Communist interpretation.

Chastenet, Jacques. *Histoire de la Troisième République.* Vol. VI. *Le Déclin de la Troisième, 1931–1938*. Paris, 1962. Chatty and highly opinionated, this is unquestionably the least valuable volume of the series. Chastenet was editor of *Le Temps* during this period.

Cotta, Michèle. *Le Frontisme et "La Flèche" de 1934 à 1939.* Mémoire, Institut d'Etudes Politiques, Université de Paris, 1959.

Cristiani, Leon. *La Fin d'une régime: tableau de la vie politique française de 1919–1939.* Lyons, 1946.

Danos, J., and M. Gibelin, *Juin 1936.* Paris, 1952.

Debu-Bridel, Jacques. *L'Agonie de la Troisième République, 1929–1939.* Paris, 1948. Lavish in its praise for Tardieu.

Demangeon, A. *La France économique et humaine,* in P. V. de la Blanche, and L. Gallois, eds., *La Géographie universelle.* Vol. VI, Book II. Paris, 1946.

deWilde, John C. "The New Deal in France," *Foreign Policy Reports,* XIII (1937), no. 12.

Dolléans, Édouard. *Histoire du mouvement ouvrier.* Vol. III. *De 1921 à nos jours.* 2nd ed. Paris, 1960.

Dupeux, Georges. *Le Front Populaire et les élections de 1936.* Paris, 1959.

Duverger, Maurice, ed. *Partis politiques et classes sociales en France.* Paris, 1955.

Ehrmann, Henry W. *French Labor from Popular Front to Liberation.* New York, 1947.

Fauvet, Jacques. *Histoire du Parti Communiste Français.* Vol. I. *De la guerre à la guerre.* Paris, 1964.

Ferlé, T. *Le Communisme en France.* Paris, 1937.

Gautier, Georges. *La Politique extérieure du Front Populaire de mai 1936 à avril 1938.* Paris, 1938. Hostile to Blum; a defense of Laval.

Georges, Bernard, and Denise Tintant. *Léon Jouhaux: Cinquante ans de syndicalisme.* Vol. I. *Des origines à 1921.* Paris, 1962.

Germain-Martin, Louis. *Le Problème financier 1930–1936.* Paris, 1936.

Goguel, François. *Geographie des élections françaises de 1870 à 1951.* Paris, 1951.

——. *La Politique des partis sous la Troisième République.* Paris, 1946.

——, and Georges Dupeux. *Sociologie électorale.* Paris, 1951.

Herbette, François. *L'Expérience marxiste en France.* Paris, 1960.

Joll, James, ed. *The Decline of the Third Republic. St. Antony's Papers, Number 5.* London, 1959.

Larmour, Peter J. *The French Radical Party in the 1930's.* Stanford, 1964. The only significant work on the Radical party.

Lazareff, Pierre. *De Munich à Vichy.* New York, 1944.

Lefranc, Georges. *Histoire du Front Populaire.* Paris, 1965. Helpful insights from point of view of a Socialist. History of the Popular Front, however, is still to be written.

Léger, B. *Les Opinions politiques des provinces françaises.* Paris, 1936. Useful analysis of the electoral districts.

Lorwin, Val R. *The French Labor Movement.* Cambridge, Massachusetts, 1954.

Maizy, H. *Les Groups antiparlementaires républicaines de droite en France de 1933 à 1939.* Thesis, Institut d'Etudes Politiques, Université de Paris, 1951.

Micaud, Charles A. *Communism and the French Left.* London, 1963.

——. *The French Right and Nazi Germany.* Durham, North Carolina, 1943.

Millet, Raymond. *Jouhaux et la C.G.T.* Paris, 1937.

Montreuil, Jean (pseud. of Georges Lefranc). *Histoire du mouvement ouvrier en France des origines à nos jours.* Paris, 1946.

Perrot, Marguerite. *Le Problème monnaie et l'opinion publique en France et en Angleterre, 1924–1936.* Paris, 1955

Prost, Antoine. *La C.G.T. à l'epoque du Front Populaire.* Paris, 1964. Excellent statistical study.

——. *L'Opinion catholique française et la guerre d'Espagne.* Mémoire, Université de Paris, n.d.

Prouteau, Henri. *Les Occupations d'usines en Italie et en France, 1920–1936.* Paris, 1938.

Rémond, René. *Les Catholiques, le communisme, et les crises, 1929–1939.* Paris, 1960. Another volume of the "Kiosque" series.

Siegfried, André, *De la Troisième à la Quatrième République.* Paris, 1957.

Sturmthal, Adolf. *The Tragedy of European Labor.* New York, 1951.

Walter, Gérard. *Histoire du Parti Communiste Français.* Paris, 1948.

Weill-Raynal, Etienne. "Les obstacles économiques à l'expérience Léon Blum," *La Revue Socialiste, Nouvelle Série,* 98 (1956), 49–56.

Werth, Alexander. *France and Munich.* New York, 1942.

———. *The Twilight of France, 1933–1940.* New York, 1942.

Wolfe, Martin. *The French Franc Between the Wars, 1919–1939.* New York, 1951.

Wright, Gordon. *Rural Revolution in France: The Peasantry in the Twentieth Century.* Stanford, California, 1964.

OTHER IMPORTANT SOURCES

Documents

Documents on German Foreign Policy, 1918–1945. Series D: Volume I, *From Neurath to Ribbentrop, September, 1937–September, 1938,* Washington, 1949; Vol. III, *Germany and the Spanish Civil War.* Washington, 1950.

The Foreign Relations of the United States. Diplomatic Papers 1936. Vol. II. *Europe.* Washington, 1954.

Periodical Source

The New York Times, May 2–December 31, 1936.

Memoirs

Bowers, Claude G. *My Mission to Spain.* New York, 1954.

Dalton, Hugh. *The Fateful Years: Memoirs, 1931–1945.* London, 1957.

Eden, Anthony, Earl of Avon. *Memoirs: Facing the Dictators, 1923–1938.* Cambridge, Massachusetts, 1962.

Hull, Cordell. *Memoirs.* 2 vols. New York, 1948.

SECONDARY SOURCES

A complete listing of the many works consulted from the vast literature on the 1930's would not serve a useful purpose. The following are those works that are cited in the notes.

Beloff, Max, *The Foreign Policy of Soviet Russia.* Vol. I, *1929-1936.* London, 1947. Vol. II, *1936-1941.* London, 1949.

Einzig, Paul, *World Finance, 1935–1937.* New York, 1937.

Feiling, Keith, *The Life of Neville Chamberlain.* London, 1946.

Foss, William, and C. Cecil Gerahty, *The Spanish Arena*. London, 1938.

George, Margaret, *The Warped Vision: British Foreign Policy, 1933–1939*. Pittsburgh, 1965.

Nenni, Pietro. *La Guerre d'Espagne*. Paris, 1959.

Puzzo, Dante A., *Spain and the Great Powers, 1936–1941*. New York, 1962.

Thomas, Hugh P.. *The Spanish Civil War*. New York, 1961.

Index